Knowledge Is Power

KNOWLEDGE IS POWER

The Diffusion of Information
in Early America, 1700–1865

RICHARD D. BROWN

New York   Oxford
OXFORD UNIVERSITY PRESS
1989

Oxford University Press

Oxford   New York   Toronto
Delhi   Bombay   Calcutta   Madras   Karachi
Petaling Jaya   Singapore   Hong Kong   Tokyo
Nairobi   Dar es Salaam   Cape Town
Melbourne   Auckland
and associated companies in
Berlin   Ibadan

Copyright © 1989 by Richard D. Brown

Published by Oxford University Press, Inc.,
200 Madison Avenue, New York, New York 10016
Oxford is a registered trademark of Oxford University Press

Library of Congress Cataloging-in-Publication Data
Brown, Richard D.
Knowledge is power : the diffusion of information
in early America, 1700–1865 / Richard D. Brown
p.   cm.   Includes index.   ISBN 0-19-504417-7
1. Communication—United States—History.
2. United States—Civilization—18th century.
3. United States—Civilization—1783–1865.
I. Title.   , P92.U5B7   1989   302.2′0973—dc20
89-9335   CIP

AGYP

2 4 6 8 9 7 5 3 1
Printed in the United States of America

For
Irene,
Josiah,
Nicholas

Acknowledgments

Over the years, many people and institutions have contributed to this project, and I am eager to express my gratitude. Assistance has come in many forms, both abstract and concrete, and because the book could never have been completed without help from many sources, it is truly the result of an extensive collaboration. In the paragraphs that follow I have tried to remember everyone.

Years ago, in 1971 I think, after listening to me speak on communication activities, John P. Demos pointed out that by concentrating as I did on the agencies that engaged in the diffusion of information—political parties, churches, schools, and other voluntary associations—I was missing a crucial part of the process, namely, actual personal experience. When, after several years, I sought to respond to this suggestion by exploring diaries and letters, Richard Buel, Jr., and David Hackett Fischer provided valuable suggestions as to how and where I might begin. Later on, when I was especially confused on the direction of the study, Bernard Bailyn and Harry S. Stout helped to sort out the alternatives. When I finally completed a first chapter in 1978, Bernard Bailyn, Nancy F. Cott, Robert A. Gross, Alan Macfarlane, Donald M. Scott, and Michael Zuckerman were kind enough to read it and criticize constructively. As more chapters took shape, Timothy H. Breen, Irene Quenzler Brown, Richard L. Bushman, Louise Chipley, Jere R. Daniell, Nathan O. Hatch, Linda K. Kerber, Sheldon Meyer, Edmund S. Morgan, R. Kent Newmyer, Mary Beth Norton, Kathryn L.C. Preyer, Harry S. Stout, and Laurel Thatcher Ulrich each provided suggestions for improvement. Finally, when I finished the first draft of the entire manuscript, David Courtwright, John P. Demos, Eric Foner, David D. Hall, Robert Jervis, Sheldon Meyer, and Harry S. Stout read it and supplied more help. If I have not always followed the advice offered, I trust that all of those who so kindly shared their thoughts will understand. Alas, the book still has its flaws, but it is certainly better thanks to their comments.

Appreciation is also owed to several scholars who shared work-in-progress: Andrew H. Baker, Francis J. Bremer, Irene Quenzler Brown, Richard L. Bushman, Daniel R. Coquillette, Anne Farnam, Elizabeth Fox-

Genovese, William J. Gilmore, Robert A. Gross, Nathan O. Hatch, Holly V. Izard, Richard R. John, Jr., Barbara Karsky, Richard B. Kielbowicz, Jack Larkin, Catherine Menand, John E. Miller, George Selement, Laurel Thatcher Ulrich, Maris Vinovskis, and Robert M. Weir. As with the published scholarship on which I have so often relied, I trust that their particular contributions are identified in the notes. It is also a special pleasure to acknowledge the contributions that several University of Connecticut graduate students have made both to research and the editorial process: David W. Conroy, James Fenimore Cooper, David J. Kiracofe, Paul Lasewicz, Alden M. B. Morse, and Doris D. Sherrow. Though some of their tasks were so boring as to require great patience, they worked cheerfully, as diligent professionals.

At historical societies, libraries, and archives, many specialists have favored me with knowledgeable and perceptive guidance. At the American Antiquarian Society, where I studied with the support of an AAS–National Endowment for the Humanities fellowship in 1977–78 and have since been a frequent visitor, the whole staff has always been friendly and helpful. However, I especially want to thank Georgia G. Barnhill, Nancy H. Burkett, Mary E. Brown, John B. Hench, William L. Joyce, Joyce A. Tracy, and the director, Marcus A. McCorison, for their many suggestions concerning how I could best take advantage of the Antiquarian Society's vast and diverse collections. At the Massachusetts Historical Society I was also the beneficiary of the kind of assistance all scholars treasure. The late John D. Cushing, Peter Drummey, Malcolm Freiberg, who edited an earlier version of Chapter three for the Society's *Proceedings,** and the director, Louis Leonard Tucker, all helped substantially, as did Stephen T. Riley, director emeritus, who guided me through the Robert Treat Paine papers and generously shared transcripts he has prepared of part of the collection. Other institutions whose staffs provided assistance include: Chicago Historical Society, Connecticut Historical Society, Connecticut State Library and Archives, the Essex Institute, Historical Society of Cheshire County (New Hampshire), Historical Society of Pennsylvania, Houghton Library at Harvard University, Maryland Historical Society, New-York Historical Society, Ohio Historical Society, Old Sturbridge Village Research Library, Rhode Island Historical Society, Virginia Historical Society, and Yale University Library's manuscript division and the Beinecke Library. Finally, at the University of Connecticut the library staff deserves accolades for being immensely helpful year after year. While it is hard to single out individuals among so many, I particularly want to thank Richard H. Schimmelpfeng, director of Special Collections, and Robert W. Vrecenak, who heads the inter-library loan department.

*Volume 94 (1982), 1–14. Another version of this chapter appeared in *Autre Temps Autre Espace/Another Time Another Space: Etudes sur l'Amérique pré-industrielle,* ed. by Elise Marienstras and Barbara Karsky (Presses Universitaires de Nancy: Nancy, 1986), pp. 53–65.

There are also several University of Connecticut administrators and colleagues who deserve thanks for helping in key ways: Anthony T. DiBenedetto, Julius A. Elias, Thomas G. Giolas, Bruce M. Stave, and Edmund S. Wehrle. Their encouragement and commitment to the support of research during years of austerity were crucial to the completion of this project. For financial assistance I am grateful to: The University of Connecticut for sabbatic leaves in 1977–78 and 1984, and for grants-in-aid from its Research Foundation; the American Philosophical Society for a grant-in-aid; and the National Endowment for the Humanities, which supported the fellowship granted by the American Antiquarian Society and later supplied a Fellowship for Independent Study and Research. For the typing of the manuscript, I am especially indebted to Debra L. Crary of the University of Connecticut Research Foundation.

Storrs, Connecticut   R. D. B.
February 1989

Contents

8

William Bentley and the Ideal of Universal
Information in the Enlightened Republic, 197

9

Choosing One's Fare:
Northern Men in the 1840s, 218

10

The Dynamics of Contagious Diffusion:
The Battles of Lexington and Concord,
George Washington's Death, and the Assassination
of President Lincoln, 1775–1865, 245

Knowledge Is Power

Introduction

"A wise man is strong; yea, a man of knowledge increaseth strength," according to the Biblical proverb, a perception that Renaissance Englishmen found appealing. "Ignorance is the curse of God," Shakespeare wrote, "Knowledge the wing wherewith we fly to heaven." And Francis Bacon, the philosopher and courtier, reduced the essentials to "knowledge itself is power," an epigram which became in time the common saying "knowledge is power."[1] Whether knowledge has concerned techniques of farming or fighting, or the knowledge of events great or small, or the possession of holy information, we have generally recognized that people "in the know" command powers that the ignorant lack. For centuries history has demonstrated the wisdom expressed in Bacon's aphorism. Perhaps this is why over the last few centuries, certainly from the printing press onward, Western society has been caught up in an information and communication revolution that now, at the end of the 20th century, appears to have entered a more dynamic, accelerating phase than ever before.[2] Bouncing words and images off satellites in space, storing and manipulating undreamed of quantities of information in the twinkling of an eye, we have been creating an awesome communications technology that is leading society into many dimensions of unknown territory. Since we cannot peer into the future, the meaning and significance of this movement are clouded and uncertain. To find our bearings we can only search the past.

The present study, which explores the history of what was to become the United States during the century-and-a-half from 1700 to 1865, is one small effort to probe that past. Incomplete, uneven, and subjective as the following chapters are, they seek to delineate some of the ways in which information moved through society, in an attempt to discern who commanded what sort of knowledge, and with what kinds of social consequences. For if it is true that "knowledge is power," it is also true that there are as many kinds of power as there are of knowledge; and the possession of different kinds of information can serve different social functions. Knowledge of crops and livestock empowered farmers to pursue their calling no less than knowledge of classical learning and cosmopolitan affairs enabled colonial American gentlemen to command high social rank and to wield political power. The first objective of the pages that follow is to identify how several kinds of information moved through society, and how such information fit into the lives of people in different walks of life and at different stages of the life cycle.

A second, closely related purpose of this investigation is to grasp the social significance of the possession of various types of information. This work seeks to comprehend, for example, what it meant if 18th-century country clergymen and country lawyers combined both the technical knowledge of their professions with a broad familiarity with local affairs. It explores the eagerness with which young women at the turn of the 19th century sought to master the repertoires of sentimental perspectives available in contemporary novels; and it examines a comparable enthusiasm among young men in succeeding decades to become, or at least to appear, broadly knowledgeable. By analyzing what kinds of information various sorts of people have craved, and by tracing the ways in which they acquired that knowledge and fitted it into their lives, this study can clarify several dimensions of the information and communication revolution as it was sweeping through the Anglo-American world.

In addition, though the study spans less than two centuries, it can provide insights into changes that were taking place across time. Powers associated with the possession of certain kinds of knowledge changed as innovations in social and political ideology and organization transformed American society. Economic and technological development rearranged familiar expectations by opening new possibilities for information distribution, and by creating a new and fluid geography of spatial relationships. The rise of republican notions of an informed citizenry after the American Revolution combined with electoral politics and the broad dissemination of printed matter to make a modicum of extra-local political knowledge and power broadly accessible. The transportation revolution that started with turnpikes and canals and culminated in railroad trains began to shrink physical distances even before telegraphy made the nearly instantaneous transmission of messages across thousands of miles a reality. This study cannot, of course, comprehend the multitude of consequences these historical developments generated. But by taking a close look at the experiences of a variety of people who lived at various times during the decades from 1700 to 1865, we can perhaps extract insights that can be helpful in beginning to grasp this vast, complicated historical process.

Fortunately, however elementary this inquiry must be in some respects, there are solid, thoroughly researched, sometimes brilliant historical studies that have already provided a clear picture of many aspects of the history of the diffusion of information. The history of printing and of journalism[3] and, more recently, studies in the history of the book and of literacy[4] have revealed not only that there was an information revolution, but also its basic chronology and dimensions in Europe and the United States. New research into the history of the post office has revealed it to be a key institution for the dissemination of printed goods locally and nationally, while a wealth of studies of electoral politics and party systems has enabled us to see how republican forms of government and the voluntary associations that flourished under them not only promoted the dissemination of political information but information touching every cause, secular and religious, from abolitionism through salvation and from temperance to xenophobia.[5] The history of education and of schools and colleges, which, not coincidentally, multiplied during precisely the decades when communications were expanding rapidly, has permitted us to understand the broad institutional commitment Americans made to the propagation of knowledge. Investigations of libraries, lyceums, and the lecture movement have shown how this drive to command information became a popular pastime; while studies of popular literature and recreation have supplied an awareness of the kinds of experience people were seeking.[6] As a result of all this scholarship, many aspects of the history of information diffusion are becoming well-known.

Yet our perspective has often been fragmented because our analyses have been arranged according to the issues and chronologies suitable to each topic, whether printing and journalism, politics and voluntary associations, or education and recreation. Consequently the relationships among all these phenomena have not been closely examined or fully understood, and so the nature of their collective impact and significance eludes us. Alas, this study cannot conquer this problem nor will it supply the comprehensive synthesis that would enable us to grasp fully the communication revolution of recent centuries.

The present inquiry, however, does explore some familiar topics from a new angle—the perspective of individual experience, a vantage point that is new only because until recently social historians, aware of the hazards of idiosyncrasy and subjectivity, have rejected it.[7] These dangers are real, of course, and in spite of conscientious efforts to contain them they have, no doubt, distorted some part of what follows. Yet because tracing personal experience offers such rich possibilities for grasping the ways in which major social trends and events affected behavior and consciousness, I have selected this approach, knowing, too, that every other alternative also has limitations. Indeed what follows is distinct less because of its content than its perspective. Rather than exploring general social phenomena directly, this study probes the particular. This is due less to an Emersonian faith in the idea that a whole world is reflected in a raindrop, than to the belief that specific, individual experiences are actual and comprehensible in a way that is different from the general and abstract. Some realities of a subject that may be concealed when it is viewed whole, from afar, can be distinguished only through close inspection. As instructive as it is to fly over the American historical landscape and to view its overall topography, it is also revealing to investigate it on foot, as a pedestrian who can view in context the small details and episodes of ordinary experience and witness their connections. There is, it is true, always the danger in such an excursion that one will not see the forest for the trees; yet in order to understand the forest one must also come to know individual trees.

It is for this reason that this study is based chiefly on personal documents, especially diaries, journals, and letters. No other kind of source permits us to view the movement, by written and oral means, of a wide range of types of information. Personal documents contain reports on conversations as well as reading, and on solitary as well as family and group activities. Here we can see men and women at work and at leisure, engaged in their public and private roles. Here, uniquely, we can see connections between what people heard in face-to-face encounters and what they read in print. At this level we can grasp what kinds of information mattered most to specific people, and how they acquired that knowledge and passed it on to others. In diaries, especially, where entries are full and systematic one can sometimes grasp fundamental patterns of information acquisition and exchange week-by-week, month-by-month, year after year. Through such personal experiences we can witness the actual, particular, quotidian workings of the large phenomenon called the communication revolution—in printing and journalism, in republican politics and associational activity, in educational agencies, and in transportation and commerce. At the personal level the interactions of great, general phenomena can be scrutinized.

Of course not all personal documents lend themselves to such a study. In fact my own research leads to the conclusion that the great majority of surviving diaries, journals, and letters do not supply an adequate foundation for this kind of description or analysis.[8] For every diary or journal that provides the kind of full, systematic record of daily experience needed to assess patterns of information moving through society, there are perhaps one hundred extant that are either so irregular—five entries in one year, fifteen in the next—or that record such a limited range of experience—such as weather conditions, expenditures and receipts, or devotional reflections—as to be of little use for the purposes outlined here. As a result, the diaries and letters on which this study rests have been selected according to an evaluation of their usefulness for illuminating the subject, and not by any objective, scientific process. That other scholars would make different choices and so reach different conclusions is certain. Moreover the remarkably unique character of some of the diaries and diarists considered here—such as the Puritan Samuel Sewall, the Virginia magnate William Byrd II, the revolutionary John Adams, and the Unitarian pastor William Bentley—makes any claim of typicality absurd. Indeed the nearly two dozen mostly obscure men and women upon whom this study also rests were in many respects equally unique, and so where I have offered generalizations in the pages that follow, it has been with some diffidence. After all, subjectively chosen sources that treat personal experiences seldom furnish the surest basis for generalization.

Yet, these limitations notwithstanding, possibilities remain. The fact that Samuel Sewall, and the diary he created, was exceptional does not mean that in all of his activities he was different from others who dwelled alongside him in early 18th-century Boston. The family and community business that engaged him could no more transcend his time and place than could Sewall's food, dress, and shelter, or the social ceremonies in which he routinely participated. A pillar of the Puritan establishment, Sewall spoke its language, shared its vocabulary of assumptions, and sought to live according to its values. So if the behavior he recorded was unique at one level, sometimes it could also be representative. Prudence, I trust, has guided me in making such judgments.

To guard against forming eccentric interpretations from singular evidence I have, where possible, considered the experiences of several people whose lives were in some sense comparable. In certain cases, as with the chapters treating the clergymen or the farmers of rural New England, the people have shared occupation, ethnicity, and region. But there has been no attempt to sample rigorously the experience of any one group, and in other cases perhaps all that the people have had in common is race, gender, and time period. By multiplying personal experiences and expanding their range, sometimes overlapping, sometimes drawn from different periods, regions, occupations and walks of life, I have tried to achieve a perspective broad enough to permit balanced assessments of many varied kinds of incidents.

Most of the time a biographical approach has served to illuminate what was happening, because the same item of information—such as news of the Battles of Lexington and Concord in 1775 or word of a yellow fever epidemic in Philadelphia in the 1790s—could have a whole different significance depending on where you lived and who you were. Even readers of the same authors invested the experience with distinct meanings according to such personal and social considerations as gender, stage of life, and career. When people actually took in information, of whatever sort, they had to receive it within some cognitive framework that made it pertinent and gave it meaning. Because such frameworks were formed through the influence of time, place, and personal history, a biographical perspective seems imperative in order to understand the realities of how information moved among people.

But if personal history is one necessary part of the story, another is a consideration of the varieties of information and the ways in which information was arranged—sometimes wrapped together and packaged—for distribution. As printed goods and public oratory became more and more widespread, their several formats, each appealing to distinct audiences and markets, exercised major influences on the diffusion of information. At the time of Abraham Lincoln's death, for example, newspapers were presenting very different kinds of information than they had in Samuel Sewall's

day; newspaper functions were as different as their audiences. Popular
novels, an 18th-century innovation, came to reach a vast public in the
following century, and the information they imparted also changed. Public
oratory, which was almost unknown outside the pulpit before the Revolution, was subsequently employed in new ways to convey not only religious
messages, but a wide range of political and cultural information as well.
Indeed, as the decades unfolded, every agent of information—print, oratory, and face-to-face exchanges—came to reflect the continuing interaction between personal and social experience.

At the broadest level this study seeks to explore just such intersections
between personal and social experience, so as to reveal relationships between information diffusion and the workings of the social order. For if, as
we imagine, knowledge was power, we need to understand what kinds of
knowledge meant what kinds of power, and how such knowledge and power
were distributed in different historical settings. We need to explain the connection between classical learning, personal identity, and political power in
18th-century Tidewater society and the relationship between the same kind
of learning and the emergence of lawyers as public officials in the substantially different social circumstances of Revolutionary Massachusetts. We
need to understand how the 19th-century expansion of print and public
speech—the emergence of mass communications—affected the political and
social order.

This study cannot supply a comprehensive explanation of the myriad
relationships having to do with the diffusion of information, knowledge, and
power. Nor can it furnish answers for all of the questions raised by such an
investigation. Yet there are certain themes that can be discussed fruitfully.
Until now, for example, though scholars have been aware that printing,
conversational exchanges, and public oratory all played key roles in the
spread of information, we have had little sense of the relative importance of
each, their interactions, or how they function individually and together.
Although scholars of literacy have illuminated some of the uses of reading in
certain times and places—starting to answer the question of who reads what
and why—the role of reading in relation to speaking and letter-writing has
remained obscure. In the chapters that follow, the relationships between
reading, the exchange of letters, and face-to-face communications are explored in a variety of historical situations among people whose occupations,
social standing, ages, and genders vary. And while no capsule generalization
can be formulated to describe their experience, it will be evident that each
form of communication could possess particular advantages and liabilities
that led to their specialized uses, uses that might change over time. Letter-
writing, for example, once a quasi-public form of transmitting information,
became essentially a private form; while printing, once so expensive and
scarce that it was used selectively for information that should be preserved,

became a medium so cheap and widely distributed that it could be used casually for the most ephemeral sorts of information.

Such historical changes point to other themes that emerge in the experiences treated in this study. Whether in reading, conversation, or public speech, I have looked for the interplay of the high cultures of elites with the common vernacular cultures of ordinary people.[9] Magistrates like Sewall and Byrd, the clergy of rural New England, and country lawyers such as Adams and Robert Treat Paine, all were exposed to both kinds of influence. Place and period were crucial here, for the connections between vernacular and high cultures were shifting and complex. Moreover the emergence of the mass cultural marketplace in the 19th century demands a redefinition of terms as well as a recognition of the influences that ran up and down the social hierarchy.

This study also bears on some of the great public developments of the 18th and 19th centuries, manifest events like the Anglo-American imperial conflict, the rise of republicanism, and the revolutions in commerce, transportation, and industry.[10] For all of these influenced and were affected by the movement of information. The political mobilization during the American Revolution, for example, depended on the circulation of printed matter as well as on public oratory and extensive networks of face-to-face exchanges. The Revolution, in turn, reshaped public consciousness concerning the diffusion of political information while simultaneously calling into being a new political and social order that exercised dynamic influences on both the substance of the information and the ways that it was distributed. Expectations, assumptions, and realities in regard to the diffusion of information were all transformed as post-independence republicanism took hold.

At a macroscopic level all of this is so obvious as to be virtually self-evident. What is not so clear, however, as one descends from the grand level of generality to the plane of actual behavior, is precisely how such dynamic forces were expressed. The chapters that follow explore these subjects at the level of individual consciousness, examining themes of public concern in the context of everyday personal priorities. Here, as will be evident, such private, personal considerations as family relationships, gender, and stage of life might be crucial. Republicanism, for example, offered different prescriptions to young men and young women as to what books and periodicals they should read in order to fulfill their quite separate duties as citizens. Nor were such self-conscious concerns with the character of information diffusion among youth and according to gender the only personal matters that changed across the decades of the 18th and 19th centuries. Circumstances of occupation and rank, like social and geographic considerations, carried different meanings respecting access to information before and after the Revolution. Indeed there were so many variables and their interactions were so complex, that it is only by examining individual experience that we can begin to grasp the human realities that collectively become great macroscopic events.

Yet in spite of all these important and genuine advantages, the approach employed here still has limitations and offers insights more often than conclusions. For although the study spans over a century-and-a-half, I have made no attempt to achieve comprehensiveness. Instead, the extended chronological scope is intended to permit recognition of changes across time. But much has been omitted. I have not tried to reconstruct interpersonal connections with the precision that anthropologists and communications specialists employ for network analysis. Only a handful of extant 17th- and 18th-century diaries are sufficiently full and systematic to make such an endeavor rewarding, and even these sources are so scattered in time and place as to exist in isolation from each other.[11] And although the use of content analysis might have altered some of my conclusions, for the most part the questions explored here go beyond the limits of that method.

Nor will there be found in the pages that follow any systematic assessment of the impact of organizations and institutions—schools, political parties, churches, or other voluntary associations. School curricula, political platforms, religious movements, and reformers' messages all affected information diffusion in vital ways, but for the most part they, too, are outside the scope of this study. Where necessary, I have relied on scholarly monographs that treat these subjects; however, because the concentration here has been on personal experience and the intersections between private forms of communication such as conversation and letters, and public forms like printed matter and oratory, institutional agencies of information diffusion have been considered only in passing. The focus here is on consumers of information rather than publicists; and the study explores the diffusion of information at the retail rather than the wholesale level.

The book also concentrates particularly on the experiences of northern white people, mostly men. The foremost reason for this emphasis is the fact that it was northern white men who were the most active and visible participants in the communication revolution of the early republican era. Culturally as well as politically enfranchised by the American Revolution, northern white men were key targets of the vast outpouring of newspapers, periodicals, and books, as well as of political parties and other voluntary associations. They were also affected earliest and most immediately by the commercial and industrial developments of the 18th and 19th centuries. As a result, it seems probable that changes in information diffusion would be recognized in their experiences most readily. Another important reason for focusing on northern white men is that the social, economic, and occupational differences among them were greater than those among women, whose primary occupation at every social level was most often domestic.

There are also practical, technical reasons for concentrating on this population, since the incidence of surviving diaries that touch on information questions is greatest for property-owning northern white men of the 18th and 19th centuries. Women's diaries of any description from the 18th century are scarce, and though they survive in greater abundance from the first half of the 19th century, their range is still relatively limited. The chapter "Daughters, Wives, Mothers" is based on a selection of diaries drawn from the generations spanning the years from the 1780s to the 1860s. The omission of blacks and industrial workers from this study results from the even greater severity of this technical problem for those populations. Because of such limitations of substance and method this work makes no claims to being comprehensive or definitive.

Indeed because what follows must be tentative and exploratory, revision based on further evidence and different perspectives will be necessary. No one, at this time, can pretend to a comprehensive understanding of information diffusion and its social implications during the communication revolution; we still have much to discover. What this study can contribute, I hope, is some appreciation of the complex patterns of personal experience, as well as the interdependence of different communication forms, and the ways in which alterations in politics, economy, and technology disturbed existing balances, sending surges of change coursing through society that led, in turn, to adjustments in outlook and behavior.

Bacon's aphorism that "knowledge itself is power" is true; but it so simplifies the realities of individual and social experience as to conceal more than it reveals. Moreover Bacon's insight implies stasis in human affairs and suggests that we should pay more attention to continuity than to change. The chapters that follow, while longer and more elaborate than Bacon's pithy epigram, use it as a point of departure for exploring both continuities and changes among a variety of Anglo-Americans who in various ways experienced firsthand the great communication revolution of the modern era. By exploring their day-to-day encounters we can further grasp the meanings of that great, many-sided event.

Before launching this inquiry with a consideration of some very specific relationships between information and authority at the beginning of the 18th century, it may be helpful first to look ahead briefly and to sketch the history of some of the mechanics of information diffusion. In particular, literacy and the availability of print, the incidence of public oratory, the development of the postal system, and changes in transportation all affected the movement of information across space and through society. Because the chapters that follow assume some familiarity with these elements in the history of communication, a few words here will provide some background for what follows.

Literacy, it is agreed, was widely diffused among the white population of the Anglo-American colonies.[12] Indeed no European population, with the possible exception of the Scots, was more generally capable of signing names and reading. While there were regional differences, with residents of the colonies north of Chesapeake Bay being more literate than those in the South, it appears that over half of the white male population was literate. In New England, with its Puritan heritage, more than 80 percent of the men could sign their names in the early 18th century; and by the beginning of the next century the proportion that was literate exceeded 90 percent. In the South a similar pattern of increasing literary was also evident among whites, though a regional gap remained. In both regions literacy was more frequent among propertied than unpropertied men, but even the poor were often literate.

More important than differences of region or property was the gap between male and female literacy, which in 1700 was considerable throughout the colonies. This gender gap, manifest in writing skills, all but vanished during the course of the 18th century, and by the early 19th century the difference between male and female literacy rates became negligible, mostly reflecting the continued presence of elderly women who could not write. Young women, in a general population where the median age was about sixteen years, were just as literate as men.

Actual estimates regarding literacy are a little vague because they are derived from counting written signatures and marks in sets of documents that are not fully representative of the entire population. Moreover the meaning of "literacy" involves some uncertainties, since the relationship between writing one's name and being able to read is not entirely clear. Reading, after all, requires different skills than writing and fulfills different functions; and the two activities were not necessarily so closely linked in the colonial period as they became in the late 19th century.[13] Scholars agree, however, that the capacity to read and to write was always present among a broad range of Anglo-Americans, and that by the early decades of the 19th century virtually all of the nothern white population was literate.

The profusion of printed matter and the multiplication of presses in the generations following American independence reinforces the perception of general literacy as a matter of common sense. It is my contention that this explosion of printed goods was not a reaction to a newly achieved literacy, but a response to cultural demands, some of which had long been present, while others were new and associated with the American Revolution. Reading as such was certainly not a new experience in the early national era; but reading tastes and objectives changed dramatically.[14]

The rapid emergence of secular oratory in the new republic also represented a major departure from the past. Prior to the Revolutionary era virtually the only secular oratory presented before the public had been the narrow, technical, legal arguments offered to judges and juries at court. The opposition to British rule, however, was a catalyst that led to the construction of public galleries in several colonial legislatures and transformed debates in the assemblies into public events. The conflict with Britain also led to the creation of public memorial speeches, such as the Boston Massacre orations from 1771 onward. By the war's end, the Independence Day address was widely established, and in the succeeding generation partisan speeches associated with political parties became a feature of public life. Later still, in the 1820s and 1830s, public oratory entered a "golden age," becoming a vehicle for all sorts of reformers and educators, politicians and salesmen. Combining information and entertainment, oratory become almost as ubiquitous as print.[15]

The history of postal service was parallel to that of public speech in that it, too, expanded sharply in the early national era so that in the decades after 1820 post offices became generally available and widely used. Before independence there were perhaps sixty-five post offices in operation, about one for every 22,000 people.[16] However, as with printing shops, they were concentrated chiefly in port towns and commercial centers because their principal functions were to service merchants and to raise revenue through fees for the English government. Postal rates were so high that ordinary people seldom used the post office, preferring instead to call on friends and acquaintances to carry letters whenever possible. In the new republic, however, ideology and political exigency dictated an expansive, publicly oriented policy for the dissemination of information. Newspapers were seen as critical to the survival of the republic, so Congress encouraged their nationwide distribution through the mails to virtually every town and county in the United States. Starting with a network of seventy-five post offices in 1790, the United States post office came to comprehend some 28,000 offices in 1860– one for every 1100 people, free and slave, adult and juvenile.[17] As a result, ordinary people used the mails routinely, especially for newspaper subscriptions and to reship their old papers to friends and relatives. After a major revision of postage rates in the 1840s, they also turned first to the post office for letters. By the 1860s, cast-iron post boxes to receive individual letters had been set up on the streets of great cities like New York, and postmen working for both the United States post office and its private competitors were delivering mail door-to-door.[18]

Advances in postal service were partially a result of improved transportation, for the advent of turnpike roads and canals in the early 19th century permitted people and the mails, as well as merchandise, to move more rapidly than ever before. Moreover steam-powered boats and then railroad trains in the 1830s literally accelerated the passage of information across space. By 1860 Americans were operating some 4500 miles of canals connected to far more extensive river systems, together with a network of over 30,000 miles of railroads.[19] Even before the advent of the telegraph, the time it took for information to move across space had diminished radically. By 1841 news from Philadelphia covered the entire eastern seaboard, from Raleigh, North Carolina, to Pittsburgh, Pennsylvania, to Albany, New York, and north to Portland, Maine, within five days. Information from

"The Postman," by Charles F. Blauvelt, was painted in New York City sometime before 1861. Note that he wears ordinary clothes, not a uniform. His small mail sack was for letters only, and the capacious pockets of his overcoat also carried letters. Since most door-to-door delivery in America's cities prior to the Civil War was done by independent delivery companies, this somewhat disreputable-looking postman was probably a private rather than a government employee.
Courtesy of The New-York Historical Society, New York City

New York City was now arriving in nearly every city east of the Mississippi River within two weeks.[20] From the standpoint of the mechanics of information diffusion, a climax occurred in the decades from 1845 to 1865, when the construction of a national telegraph network made possible the nearly instantaneous transmission of information across thousands of miles, from the Atlantic seaboard to the Pacific coast in 1861. It was in this setting that news of the assassination of President Lincoln became a national media event, illustrating that the history of the diffusion of information had entered an era that touches with our own time.

Yet in order to appreciate the implications of such dramatic developments we need to consider the longer historical context. This study begins with a consideration of the circumstances of information diffusion in early 18th-century Boston and in Tidewater Virginia. Then readers will move on to consider the roles of clergymen and lawyers—learned professionals—in the information networks of rural New England. Next, the influence of commerce and a comparison of the experiences of some port dwellers—merchants, lawyers, and an artisan—will be explored. Experiences among the two largest classes of Americans, farmers and women, supply further comparisons of people whose primary interests were domestic and for whom public affairs were only intermittent concerns.

The study then turns to people who were actively caught up in the enormous changes in 19th-century information diffusion: one, an urban clergyman, the others, town and city dwellers—a lawyer's clerk, an engraver, a cabinetmaker's apprentice, and a lawyer-farmer. Before offering a concluding interpretation, the book presents a comparison of the diffusion of major news events at the end of the colonial era, in the early republic, and at the beginning of the electronic era. Overall, it is a story of complexity and richness, of many people at many different times and places, that aims to reward readers seeking to journey through the formative era of the present day information and communication revolution.

Chapter 1

Information and Authority
in Samuel Sewall's Boston,
1676–1729

When the newly married Samuel Sewall moved into his in-laws' Boston home in 1676 he was entering a small but densely settled port town of some 1000 households, a community of about 6000 people.[1] To Sewall, who had been born in England, raised in Newbury, Massachusetts, and educated at Harvard College, Boston was a cosmopolitan commercial center. No matter if the hogs that scavenged in the streets and the cows that grazed the common gave the town a farmyard flavor; Boston was the political and economic capital of the Massachusetts-Bay Colony, seat of the governor, legislature, and courts, as well as the principal entrepôt of New England commerce. Boston's shipping, which spanned the Atlantic and the Caribbean, together with its political role, made it the most highly developed information center in New England. According to Cotton Mather, Boston was the "Capital of North America."[2]

It was also in 1676, as it had been from its founding in 1630, a bastion of Puritanism which, together with its political and economic functions, influenced both the circulation and the substance of public and private information in Boston. In contrast to other major ports, Boston authorities routinely monitored social behavior. On the Sabbath people could not practice their trades, and traveling was sharply curtailed. "Frivolous" amusements like bowling, dancing, and horseracing, were absolutely prohibited. Churches were thronged on Sabbath mornings and afternoons, and on Thursday mornings serious Christians attended religious lectures. Boston recognized none of the old-fashioned religious holidays, no festivals for merrymaking, not even Christmas. The chief irregularities in the calendar were occasional days set aside for thanksgiving, fasting, and prayer—all reinforcing the sobriety that overlay Boston's diversity and cosmopolitanism. The only time that public boisterousness was tolerated, and then but barely, was on militia training days.

Such ideals and customs were not necessarily popular among all of the inhabitants; these standards were prescribed by Puritan political and religious officials whose hegemony was accepted. Even though economic and political realities had forced many compromises since 1630—Baptists, for example, had been permitted to organize a church in 1665–Boston retained some of the character of its utopian Puritan origins. Insofar as the diffusion of information was concerned, Puritanism influenced the places and occasions for public assembly as well as the boundaries of what was and was not permissible. Sewall's Boston was not at the outset the land of John Milton and John Locke, not yet a haven for free speech and full religious tolerance.

By the time of Sewall's death on the first day of 1730, Boston remained more insular and sober than other seaports in the British empire, but in many respects the town had been moved in a secular, more freewheeling direction—from Puritan to Georgian. Now possessing a population of some 16,000 people—over 2500 households—both the scale and character of Boston society had changed so as to make it more open and cosmopolitan.[3] Among Boston's eleven churches there were seven Congregational societies of various shadings, some traditional Calvinists like the Mathers' Old North Church, and others leaning toward the liberalism and Protestant ecumenicism of Benjamin Colman's Brattle Street Church. Where no Anglican church had existed in 1676, by 1730 there were two, in addition to the Huguenot and Baptist societies. Quakers and Catholics, who had once been anathema to Bay Colony rulers, now conducted their services openly without the least interference. Religious toleration was a condition of participation in the British Empire.

Bringing its complement of royal officials and government patronage, the Empire also made Boston society more Anglophile and conventional than in Puritan days. Clubs and coffeehouses flourished among Boston merchants and officials who looked less and less to the sermons and lectures of the clergy for guidance, and more and more to each other and to England. The newspapers they patronized—there were now three, the most of any provincial town in the British Empire—testified to and reinforced the transatlantic, secular orientation of Boston's elite.[4] Though old-timers like Sewall might scorn the introduction of festivities on April Fools' Day, Easter, province election day, Pope's day, and Christmas, the current ruling establishment accepted and even encouraged popular cultural expression.[5] There had been no room for superstition, tippling, and nonsense in the New Jerusalem, but there was room for all of them in Georgian Boston, and it made the community of Samuel Sewall's old age very different from that of his youth.

Emblematic of the transformation of Boston society was the shift in public policy toward drinking houses. Where beverage licenses had long been issued only in limited numbers to accommodate public necessities, and then solely to substantial citizens who could regulate behavior in their establishments, by the 1720s the authorities had thrown open access to licenses, so that the per capita incidence of drinking houses soared. Indeed they even used licenses as a form of public assistance for impoverished widows—people with no political or economic standing who could not possibly serve as deputies of the government in preventing abuses of alcohol.[6] Since taverns and ordinary drinking establishments had always been centers of face-to-face communication and hence agencies for the diffusion of information, the new attitude toward licensing signaled a fundamental shift in the use of authority. Withdrawing from its positive, didactic role in monitoring drinking and social centers, the government now accepted Bostonians as they were, allowing them to pursue their pastimes as they wished, virtuous or not. Government would step in to prohibit flagrant disorders, but virtuous behavior was up to the clergy and the churches, not the civil authorities. Much like truth and falsehood grappling in Milton's free market of ideas, virtue and vice could struggle for supremacy without prior governmental restraints.

To Samuel Sewall's deep regret such attitudes and policies, so alien to the Puritan city on a hill, became dominant in Georgian Boston. Though Boston's town-meeting politics gave it a democratic character that was exceptional, by the time of Sewall's death the town was more English and enlightened than it was Puritan and pious. Its clergy were numerous and articulate, and they influenced public discourse substantially in private conversation, with sermons from their pulpits, and in print; but they no longer commanded center stage. Now the merchants and royal officials who organized the town's economy and social hierarchy determined the public agenda. Their information requirements and preferences had assumed preeminence in Boston, shaping diffusion in ways that were generally consistent with the town's more secular, open, commercial orientation.

Although Samuel Sewall held high public office and was one of Boston's richest merchants from the 1690s through the 1720s—all the while an active participant in the highest circles of leadership—the record of his actions suggests that he did not so much shape events as bear witness to Boston's transformation. Although he became a learned and cosmopolitan gentleman, his values had been fixed in Puritan Cambridge and Boston so, more backward- than forward-looking, Sewall was often fighting in the rear guard—as in the witchcraft trials in 1692 and in the struggle over the presidency of Harvard in 1718–against the more liberal and secular forces that were overtaking his generation. During these decades no one individual or group dominated Boston. Rather, a disparate array of notables—clerics like Increase and Cotton Mather, Harvard College's president John Leverett, crown officials and merchants such as Joseph Dudley, Andrew Belcher, and the Elisha Cookes, father and son—vied for power and privilege, seeking to shape Boston according to their own and their associates' preference. Sewall, who dealt with all these people both officially and informally, lived at the core of town and province affairs and for years on end knew what was going on in current affairs, as well as the context of past relationships that so often shaped perceptions and alignments.

Sewall had been born in England in 1652 to a family that was already connected to Massachusetts Bay and owned land in the colony. Following the restoration of the Stuarts to the English throne, in 1661 the nine-year-old Sewall moved with his family to Newbury, north of Boston, where he was prepared for Harvard College by the local pastor. Following his graduation in 1671 he first considered a clerical career and did some preaching before returning to Harvard in 1673 for a season as a tutor. His plans changed, however, upon his marriage in 1676 to Hannah Hull, a daughter of the rich Boston merchant and colony mint-master John Hull. With his wife's dowry and his father-in-law's patronage, a mercantile career immediately seemed more promising, and Sewall moved into the Hull homestead, where he would reside until his death.

Sewall's business was characteristic of Boston overseas trade at this time. He exported fish, farm products, and beaver pelts, and imported sugar, rum, textiles, and various luxury goods including books.[7] Corresponding with merchants in London and Bristol in England, Bilbao in Spain, and with others in Bermuda and the Caribbean, Sewall was connected directly to the flow of commercial and political information of the Atlantic world. His relationship to John Hull, a central figure in Boston and colony affairs, also made Sewall an insider to much of the information that passed in elite Boston circles. His entry into Boston's select Ancient and Honorable Artillery Company in 1679 and his appointment to manage the colony's press two years later, were only preliminaries to the responsibilities he would assume after his father-in-law's death in 1683. Now made a captain in the colony militia and elected to the Governor's Council, the legislature's upper house, Sewall became part of Massachusetts best informed circle on public affairs as well as commerce.

Sewall's precise role in the turmoil surrounding the crown takeover of Massachusetts Bay when Charles II created the Dominion of New England is obscure. But before the successful uprising against Governor Edmund Andros, Sewall had journeyed to London with the Reverend Increase Mather, partly to lobby at court on behalf of the colony's interests and also to attend to family affairs and property in England. Sewall was a central participant in the network between English and New England Puritans of the late 17th century.[8] When he returned to Boston in November 1689, just a year after he had left, his friends who championed the old Massachusetts-Bay Colony charter controlled the government, so he remained in close touch with public affairs. When the new charter was brought from England in 1692, Sewall was immediately elected to the Superior Court of Judicature, the highest court, where he would remain until he resigned in 1728; and he was once more elected to the Governor's Council (legislative upper house), an office to which he was to be annually re-elected thirty-two consecutive times until 1725, when he declined further service. By conviction Sewall was a traditional Puritan, but being of a moderate and flexible temperament and modest about his own opinions, he usually played a conciliatory role. The confidence Sewall came to command grew out of widespread recognition of his personal probity and his readiness to make accommodations so as to secure community peace.

It is therefore ironic that the most dramatic episode in Sewall's long magisterial career, and the event for which he has often been known, was as a judge in the witchcraft disaster of 1692, when he was as yet an inexperienced jurist. Appointed to the special Commission of Oyer and Terminer that was set up to deal with the accusations, Sewall was one of the judges who sent nineteen men and women to the gallows. Four years later, after the death of his two-year-old daughter Sarah—the eighth child he and his wife had lost prematurely—Sewall concluded that God was punishing him for the part he had taken in "the Salem tragedie," because he believed he had "condemned the guiltless."[9] Conscious of the terrible wrong he had committed, and eager to escape further divine retribution, Sewall made a public confession in January 1697 on the fast day that the province had set aside to repent the wrongs it had visited on some of its subjects. Standing erect in the midst of his meetinghouse, Sewall listened silently as his minister read publicly his confession "that as to the Guilt contracted . . . he is, upon many accounts, more concerned than any that he knows of, [and so] Desires to take the Blame and Shame of it, Asking pardon of Men, And especially desiring prayers that God, . . . would pardon that Sin and all his other Sins."[10] This act of personal contrition and courage set Sewall apart from his colleagues and testifies to the authenticity of his humility and the depth of his piety.

The reason we know all this about Sewall is because most of the detailed diaries that he kept for over fifty years have survived. These, plus a substantial number of his letters, enable us to follow Sewall's activities and to observe the society in which he dwelled more closely than that of any other colonial American of his generation. The Sewall record is of special importance for the study of information diffusion in early America because it spans Boston's transition from a modest Puritan enclave to a busy Georgian port. Samuel Sewall was on hand and making his private notes when the first American newspaper was issued on September 15, 1690, as he was when this paper was suppressed by order of the government four days later. He was also present when the *Boston News-Letter* appeared on April 24, 1704, the first long-lived newspaper in Anglo-America. Living in Boston during a dynamic era, Sewall was an eyewitness during a seminal period in the history of information diffusion in America.

The Sewall record is also valuable because of the extraordinary length of time that it covers in one person's life. It permits a view of private conversations and public activities during most of Sewall's long life, from his bachelor days through his marriage, parenthood, and grandparenthood. Similarly, we can see concretely the kinds of information that absorbed his interest, and the ways information came to him as he moved from being a neophyte college graduate to a notable merchant and magistrate moving in the highest circles of government, to, in the end, a retired relic of an earlier time. Sewall's diary and letters are remarkable documents that offer rich possibilities for understanding some of the ways in which information moved through society at the beginning of the 18th century.

The centrality of family news to all of Sewall's experience throughout his life was of fundamental importance and exerted a crucial influence on Sewall's record of his comings and goings, his visitors, their messages and conversations. For Sewall, who moved into his father-in-law's home and subsequently succeeded him as master of the household, family relationships combined the deep emotional bonds of his own nuclear family with attention to the personal, spiritual, and material well-being of a wider circle of siblings, nieces, nephews, cousins, and in-laws who dwelled in and around Boston, Salem, Newbury, and elsewhere in eastern Massachusetts. After Sewall's marriage especially, news of these people—their health, travels, and business and family affairs—entered into Sewall's life virtually every day either through direct observation, messages carried by visitors, or news gleaned from third parties as Sewall went about his business. Sometimes such news came by a messenger sent specifically for the purpose: it was thus that Sewall, attending court at Ipswich, learned of the stillbirth of a son and, a few years later, received word of the birth of a healthy grandson.[11] Only rarely did news of his Massachusetts family come by letter, and then usually to announce a death or as an aside in a business note.[12] Regarding Sewall's English relatives, whose connections were necessarily more attenuated, letters were virtually the only form of communication and, rare at best, this correspondence came to an end as Sewall grew older.[13]

Much of the family news that moved in and out of Sewall's household, while personal in nature, could scarcely be called private. Births, marriages, and deaths were also public news, as were any contagious illnesses. Besides, whatever the content, face-to-face transmission in crowded homes, in taverns, or on the street, did not provide much in the way of privacy. Usually this was not seen as a problem; but where one's innermost thoughts and feelings were concerned, privacy might be essential. Sewall was used to dealing with property and business affairs in public and semi-public settings, but for emotional and spiritual matters he sought opportunities for private conversation. "Being alone . . . by the fire I speak earnestly to Sister to make sure of an Interest in Christ," Sewall noted.[14] Public preaching was all very well, but he also saw the need for intimate conversation to impart certain kinds of information as well as to fulfill emotional needs. When his fourteen-year-old daughter Betty was troubled about her spiritual state and came to him anxiously seeking comfort, they prayed privately together, as Sewall also did when his son Samuel was uncertain about his future at age seventeen.[15] Characteristically for the era, the interior design of Sewall's dwelling permitted scarcely any privacy; but on questions that touched the soul and in a few other cases, there was a recognition that privacy was not merely legitimate but necessary.[16]

Where the extended family was concerned, Sewall, who became its most highly placed and centrally located member, made his home an information hub. Indeed so central was family to information exchange that in Sewall's case one can speak of an extended family information network using messengers and letters to keep other households within the family network informed, not only of family events, but of pertinent public news. When, for example, an account was brought to Boston "of the danger they [residents] were in at Casco of an Assault from the Enemy, 30 Indian Canoes being seen, and Several Fires in the Land," Sewall dispatched a letter with the news to his father and brother.[17] Sewall assumed not only that he was better informed than his kinsmen scattered around Massachusetts Bay, but that he also had a responsibility to keep them apprised of events. The responsibility, indeed, was reciprocal, and when news came to relatives that might be pertinent to Sewall, they would send word either orally or in writing. The commitment to a family information network endured for life, although as key members of the network in his own and the previous generation died, the size and shape of the network changed and the avidity of Sewall's participation waned. This erosion was partly the consequence of a generational cycle as well as a more general ebbing of what has been called "Puritan tribalism"; but it also resulted from the development of alternative, non-family networks of information and the increasing availability of print.[18] Certainly all of these phenomena were at work before the 1720s. For Sewall, however, the extended family information network remained primary in the 1720s as in the 1670s.

Second to Sewall's family in information transactions was a circle of clergymen, mostly in Boston, with whom Sewall spoke frequently throughout his life. His own pious inclinations coupled with his offices in the Old South (Third Congregational) Church and in government, gave him many occasions to speak to his pastors: Samuel Willard, who held the pulpit from 1678 to 1707, Ebenezer Pemberton; who assisted Willard for seven years and then followed him from 1707 to 1717; and Sewall's own son Joseph, who assisted Pemberton for four years before succeeding him as head minister. In addition Sewall was in close touch with Increase Mather and his son Cotton, pastors of the Old North (Second Congregational) Church between 1664 and 1728, as well as Benjamin Colman of Brattle Street from 1699 onward, and Benjamin Wadsworth, pastor of the First Church from 1695 to 1725. All told, and setting aside his son Joseph, among the ten people with whom Sewall most frequently noted a conversation, four were Boston clergymen.[19]

The information they discussed varied widely. Often they were concerned with the physical or spiritual health of family and parishioners and would include some prayer or scriptural comment in the exchange. Church and community business and politics were also common topics as they sought each other's judgment and measured their own knowledge of events in relation to each other. Since each moved in a slightly different circle and possessed a distinct persona, the information they disclosed could include a new dimension or at least reinforce existing knowledge. In a community as small as Boston was in the 1680s and 1690s, and much later in key religious and political circles, great attention was paid to who-said-what-to-whom, the precise words, the tone of voice and inflection. For Sewall, frequent conversation with the handful of clergymen who numbered the colony's leading men among their parishioners was certainly informative with respect to Boston and Massachusetts affairs.

Yet although Sewall's clerical circle served to enlarge his understanding of community business and personalities, there is no reason to suppose that this was Sewall's objective. He was, after all, a pious man who regularly attended and seriously reflected on Thursday morning lectures as well as meetings twice on Sunday, and a host of occasional sermons. In talking with Willard, Pemberton, or one of the Mathers, the conversation often focused on an interpretive point raised in a sermon, in Sewall's private devotions, or in some text he was reading. Abstract discussions were no less central to these conversations than personal concerns. With Willard and Pemberton and his son Joseph—but not with the Mathers—he could divulge his own intimate apprehensions regarding himself and his family.

The relationship with the Mathers, and hence the character of their communication, could not be characterized as wholly trusting and candid, though it was certainly frequent. It is true that Sewall was close to both Increase and his son Cotton Mather—Increase came to pray when Sewall's children were sick, Cotton prayed "excellently" with Hannah Hull Sewall on her deathbed,[20] and Sewall himself was one of Increase's pallbearers—but both Mathers were so political, so manipulative, and so ready to take offense that Sewall could scarcely be unmindful of what he disclosed in their presence. When Increase Mather was ousted from the Harvard presidency in 1701, he and Cotton blamed Sewall, who had to explain that he had not spoken against Increase in the Governor's Council.[21] What Sewall's relationship with the Mathers underscores is the overlapping, interconnected character of secular and religious politics in Sewall's Massachusetts, and the fact that for a secular leader like him, possessing an information circle of clergymen that ranked second only to his family in importance was not only compatible with his public role but probably reinforced it.

With Sewall, as with a substantial number of leading families, the boundary between family and clergy was likely to be breached through marriage or the entry of a son or a nephew into the pastorate. For high-ranking people it was common at some stage of life to have a relative by blood or marriage who was a practicing clergyman. Even more common, and along a broader social spectrum, were kinship ties that bound family into business and political circles, since kinship was a traditional instrument for advancing and securing individual and family interests. For Sewall, whose eldest son and namesake married Governor Joseph Dudley's daughter in 1702, this interweaving of family and political communication was evident from the day of the marriage ceremony itself. There, following the exchange of vows and a prayer, the families sang a psalm and then, because Governor Dudley's son Paul, the attorney general of the province, had just been called away on business, the governor read aloud his absent son's letter which described the business—the seizure of a pirate—to the wedding party.[22] Thereafter for many years whenever Sewall attended a Council meeting—often at the governor's house—in the intervals before and after the formal proceedings, conversation between them regarding family business was almost inevitable. Sewall and Dudley came to have six grandchildren in common and, when the marriage of their son and daughter foundered and came apart, they also had to discuss terms of separation and reconciliation.[23] Though this particular example is extreme, the interpenetration and overlap between family, business, and political information relationships and networks were characteristic of Sewall's Massachusetts.

Sewall's third circle of information connections comprised the men with whom he worked in ruling the province and the town of Boston—justices, councilors, selectmen, and a variety of other officials. Like Sewall, many of these men were also engaged in commercial and real estate enterprises, and there was no real boundary between business and politics in their conversations. Whether they met formally or encountered each other by chance, the information they conveyed to one another ran the gamut from war and peace in Europe to the enforcement of Boston's chimney ordinances, as well as news of the well-being of their associates and their families. In Sewall's case this circle of associates included not only major crown officials, but also the leading opposition figures in the General Court and in Boston. Sewall's own commercial affairs and the business of ruling society forbade insularity in his associations, which crossed boundaries of faction, parish, denomination, and family as a matter of course.

Sewall's circles of conversation and information exchange did not, however, transcend Boston's hierarchic social structure or its class boundaries. Magistrates, clerics, and merchants—the ruling class—were the people with whom he did business and socialized, the people whom he joined in attending ceremonial occasions and in taking a cup of tea, a glass of wine, and sitting down for dinner. Sewall seldom exchanged words with tradesmen, mariners, farmers, and servants except to transact business, to seek assistance in finding a road or a person, or when they carried a message to him from another gentleman. Common people did bring local and personal news to Sewall, like the illness of a relative, in exchange for which he often gave a coin as a tip. And occasionally in his capacity as a magistrate Sewall admonished a commoner for excessive drinking or some other disorderly conduct. But casual cross-class information sharing was not part of Sewall's Boston. Common people seldom seemed to possess information of more than very particular interest that was not also easily accessible to gentlemen. For their part, the information the ruling class chose to share with common inhabitants was mostly formal, intended to guide and instruct them in religious and civil affairs, and they provided this instruction at suitable ceremonial occasions in the meetinghouses, the town house, and the public square. Only toward the end of Sewall's life, when town-meeting politics became competitive and a caucus is said to have been formed around the younger Elisha Cooke did this comparatively formal, hierarchic pattern of information diffusion begin to change.[24]

Nevertheless what stands out in the range of Sewall's communication experiences over more than fifty years is continuity rather than change. As a young Harvard graduate Sewall ranked as a gentleman and when he became John Hull's son-in-law and moved into his house he entered the highest circle of provincial affairs. Hull was a member of the Governor's Council and a militia captain, so news from the Indian frontier and from England in addition to provincial political matters and commercial events all entered the household with Hull himself or with men who called on him. Still, since Sewall held no office he was at the periphery, and his own conversational contacts were more often with recent graduates of the college and clergymen than with the shapers of town and colony policy. His "father" Hull was not especially secretive, but as there was no need for Sewall to be well-informed on public matters the quality of his information was more bookish than it would later be and also more dependent on the common talk of the town.

Sewall's special stature as Hull's son-in-law is illustrated by his frequent inclusion in his "father's" information circle. When, for example, several men came to see Hull to discuss means for the suppression of the Quakers and the Baptists, Sewall witnessed the whole conversation and so became informed not only on the direction of policy toward disorderly dissent, but also on the Reverend Samuel Willard's "Animosity" towards Increase Mather.[25] When a couple of weeks later the rich merchant Thomas Dean visited Hull and "spent a considerable time in discoursing" with him, Dean went on to invite Sewall to join in the merchants' "Caballs" so that he too might become a knowledgeable commercial insider.[26] Yet unlike his "father" Hull, and in contrast to his own life after he became one of the province's leading men, the young Sewall devoted much more time to spiritual than secular discourse and joined in informal prayer meetings once or twice each week.

More and more, however, Sewall was drawn into the ruling circle as responsibilities ranging from service on town committees to chores for the General Court were thrust on him. Perhaps most significant, in October 1681 the General Court placed him in charge of running the printing press in Boston, from which issued all official printing as well as a number of sermons and other religious publications. Because printing was a slow and a very limited source of information, this appointment did not mean that Sewall was suddenly one of the colony's most informed or influential leaders, but it did mark his emergence as a trusted insider. By the time of "father" Hull's death in October 1683, Sewall was already incorporated into the information networks of Boston's political and commercial elite, a position he would retain for the rest of his life, nearly fifty years. In the following year, at the age of thirty-two, he was elected by the deputies in the General Court to serve in the Governor's Council which was, next to the governorship, the colony's highest office and which carried with it membership on the board of overseers of Harvard College. Twice Sewall would be reelected to these posts until 1686, when, following the Crown's revocation of the Bay Colony's 1629 charter, the King installed Sir Edmund Andros as the military governor of the Dominion of New England.

For staunch Puritans like Sewall the advent of Governor Andros was a political horror that put them outside the governor's inner circle, even though only temporarily. For the Dominion did not destroy the Puritan elite's information networks or their influence. When they seized control of the government in 1689 and arrested Andros, Sewall, though away on a visit to England, was so highly esteemed and so well-connected that on his return he was elected to the Governor's Council and the Superior Court of Judicature when the new government was organized under the charter of 1692.[27] Henceforward, from the age of forty until the age of seventy-three when he retired from the Governor's Council, Sewall would be one of the best informed people on public affairs in Massachusetts.

His public role made Sewall both participant and eyewitness to much of what happened in provincial government, and as a concomitant of his offices, he saw the dispatches and heard the reports on which government actions were based. Whether these were letters from England or reports of pirates off the coast or of Indians on land, as a matter of course Sewall obtained the news as early and in as much detail as was available. As a councilor and judge he enjoyed comparable access to public and private controversies over property and privileges and violations of law. Simultaneously Sewall's overlapping family and clerical connections, and his commercial correspondence, enhanced the extent of his information at additional levels. From the perspective of information diffusion, Sewall in the prime of his public career became an information magnet and, to a lesser degree, something of an information monitor as well.

Traveling, which was always informative because it extended the range of direct observation and personal contact, and also allowed gentlemen like Sewall to impart information, was a small part of Sewall's offices, but trips to Plymouth, or Salem, or Ipswich were required from time to time, and as he grew older such travel and even routine attendance at Council meetings became burdensome. Consequently in June 1725, after once more being elected to the Governor's Council, Sewall resigned, explaining that "my enfeebled state" and his other public and private responsibilities required this step.[28] Thereafter Sewall's information networks contracted perceptibly, and information of the sort that he had recently acquired as a firsthand observer or in conversation—the contents of a speech by the lieutenant governor, the adjournment of the General Court, the sale of the Reverend Thomas Prince's library—came to him from the newspaper.[29] It was not that Sewall became an isolated shut-in. He remained engaged and active, and in Boston, where news came from frequent visitors as well as proximity to the sources, anyone of Sewall's disposition and stature who was in reasonable health would always be better informed on public affairs than the best informed resident of Salem or Springfield.

But as he slowed down in old age and reduced the sphere of his activities he was bound to become more dependent on second-hand information, both by word of mouth and newspapers. When word reached Boston of King George's death in 1717, Sewall would have been among the first to know, had he been a Council member; but having been off the Council for two years, he was dependent on a visitor who brought "the great News" which had come from London after "7 weeks passage."[30] Indeed for information that would once have been brought to him immediately by one of his peers or an official messenger, Sewall was now dependent even on younger female relatives, as when his "cousin Mrs. Jane Green told me of Govr. Burnet's Commission being come, which I heard not of before; though twas known in Town the evening before."[31] Sewall still knew something of what Harvard's governors were doing because his son Joseph, now one of them, "comes and gives me an account"; but Sewall's increasing dependence was clear, and his ability to pass information along to others declined, because he was less often capable of speaking with certainty.[32] There were also fewer occasions for exchange since he saw fewer people and circulated less. Still, even in the final months of his life Sewall was giving out printed sermons as he had for decades and writing letters to clarify Scriptural doctrines.[33]

The cycle that is evident in Sewall's lifetime, a cycle that saw his level of public information rise from his early manhood through his full maturity and then diminish in his brief semiretirement, did not correspond to the unfolding of any general information diffusion pattern in Boston or Massachusetts during these decades. For in both the town and the province the character of information diffusion remained remarkably stable. Even though some notable changes occurred, such as the advent of newspapers, in 1730—as in 1676—the central feature of the transmission of public information remained hierarchic—that is, public news traveled from the highest circle of the ruling elite downward through the ranks. Since the Bay Colony's elite was still concentrated in Boston in 1730, it reinforced the pattern of spatial diffusion whereby information spread outward from Boston, the center of colony politics and commerce. As there was a hierarchy in the social order, so there was a hierarchy among Massachusetts towns for the flow of information.

One of the primary attributes of this hierarchic diffusion pattern was its closed, privileged character. Information concerning the public, having to do with war, peace, law, and government officials, was only disclosed to the public on a case-by-case basis at the discretion of the authorities. Such information usually announced a decision or a new law, or confirmed news that had hitherto circulated in the doubtful guise of rumor. The ruling assumption was that the population at large need not and could not be generally informed on public matters. In its broad outlines the information system resembled modern military arrangements where information is dispensed on a "need-to-know" basis. In contrast to modern military security, however, Sewall's generation operated without the use of misleading "cover" stories, under the serene conviction that public information was not so much secret as it was simply useless and irrelevant to most people. Being informed was only important to the ruling class.[34]

Within that class, as we have seen in Sewall's case, there were intricate networks that carried information orally and by letter to those for whom being informed mattered. For Sewall personally, formal meetings may have been most important since they were often occasions where information from beyond Boston was first disclosed or confirmed, and in official proceedings news was often generated through consultations or decisions. Moreover, a meeting of the Governor's Council or the adjournment of the General Court was itself news, and on the rare occasions when Sewall missed a meeting, he felt a gap in his knowledge keenly because he was sometimes at a loss to make it up.[35] Indeed even when the meeting led to no newsworthy outcome, being absent made a difference since just bringing notables together led to exchanges of information about public and private business.

This spontaneous aspect of information diffusion within elite circles warrants particular emphasis because any chance meeting might offer information opportunities. After one Council meeting, Sewall went home with his distant cousin and fellow Councilor William Dummer, who handed him a letter from Dummer's brother in New York that reported the installation of a new governor.[36] Several weeks later, while on a family visit to Governor Dudley to discuss a piece of real estate, first one of Sewall's daughters stopped in with two of his grandchildren, and then, without warning, two gentlemen came to see the governor with news from Albany which he then passed on to Sewall.[37] Such chance transmissions of information were not everyday occurrences, but they were common enough, especially in connection with local and provincial people and events. Being in circulation—proximity—was a crucial part of the elite information system.

Sewall's stature as a public official also meant that people visited him expressly to bring news. Where personal matters were concerned, advice and assistance were commonly sought; but on public matters Sewall's own immediate action might be required. It was thus at six o'clock on the morning of June 9, 1704, when Sewall was still "a-bed" that a messenger came and reported to the fifty-two-year-old "Commissioner for Seizing the Pirates," that "9 or 11 Pirats, double arm'd," had just been seen on Cape Ann, about fifteen miles northeast of Boston. Immediately Sewall assumed command, sending oral and written messages to officials in Boston and Essex County, before setting out for Cape Ann so that he and his colleagues could "give necessary orders upon the place." The maneuvers that Sewall and the others directed succeeded, though it was his brother Stephen who was the hero of the seaborne expedition that captured the pirates the next day some seventy miles off at Casco Bay. Sewall, who believed the victory was "all order'd and Tim'd and effected by the singular all-powerfull gracious Providence of God," knew firsthand the whole sequence of events in detail.[38]

Sewall's public role and his personal effort to live as an exemplary Christian also meant that in the course of his life he attended several thousand community ceremonies. At one level all of these were newsworthy local events; that is the ceremonies were the subject of conversation that circulated among at least some Bostonians. Who said what publicly, even weekly sermons and lectures, might be local news. Moreover some of these occasions—the installation of a clergyman, the Harvard commencement, the annual sermons of the Ancient and Honorable Artillery Company, and the sermons delivered at the election of the Governor's Council—provided platforms for political statements that might be far-reaching and controversial. Attendance at the ceremony by elite figures like Sewall made one an eye- and ear-witness to events.

There were also other information advantages that were by-products of these ceremonial and ritual activities. Not only was news of unrelated events publicly announced from the pulpit—such as news of a peace treaty, the killing of a lion at Andover, or an earthquake in Lima, Peru—but casual conversations also yielded significant fruits.[39]

The same kinds of information as passed elsewhere—from England, the world beyond, and from within the community—moved among acquaintances inside the meetinghouse as well as outside it. The magnificent reception of Governor Bellomont at New York, for example, was told to Sewall inside the building.[40] Similarly, after a service ended, the gentleman seated next to Sewall turned and asked whether he had "heard the sad News from England, and then told me the Queen was dead, which was the first I heard of it."[41] On another occasion, when Sewall was about to leave "as Mr. Lewis went by me, he told me twas reported the President [John Leverett of Harvard College] was found dead in his Bed this morning."[42] And, again, when services ended Sewall was told that Edward Randolph had actually arrested Increase Mather, and that a notorious pirate had been captured.[43] All of this was public news; yet it passed privately, haphazardly, from gentleman to gentleman by word of mouth.

At funerals, which Sewall attended every week or so, the same kinds of information were exchanged. But the procession to the grave, which paired gentlemen in twos, also furnished opportunities for extended conversations.[44] Because the mourners were connected to each other through the deceased, and were grouped by family and rank for the procession, it was all but inevitable that Sewall walked or rode with an official colleague or a clergyman at each funeral; and when it was over, one gentleman was likely to accompany the other home or to his next appointment. Conversation on mortality was common, of course; however, it is also evident that in Sewall's Boston business which in another society might have been transacted in a home or a tavern was being conducted in transit between meetinghouse, burying ground, and residence. And, as with information diffusion at church, the system remained as exclusive as its participants wished.

From the perspective of insiders like Sewall this manner of diffusion was usually satisfactory, but occasionally there were hazards. Talking about individuals and their particular affairs, and passing news of the province and the town in public places like the street or in the semi-public environs of meetinghouses and taverns, virtually invited others to overhear. The problem was less often secrecy as such than it was discretion and decorum. When, for example, Sewall was disputing with Harvard tutor Henry Flynt the use of "Saint" in connection with the apostles "Luke" and "Matthew," Flynt, Sewall reported, approached him "in the way from Lecture . . . and would have discoursed about it in the street: [but] I prevail'd with him to come and dine with me, and after that I and he discours'd alone."[45] What was at issue here was not the secrecy of information, but the decorum of two learned gentlemen having a religious dispute in front of ordinary people who might misunderstand the significance of the division of opinion between the two orthodox gentlemen.

Decorum was not a mere nicety from the perspective of Sewall and his associates; it was vital to the maintenance of order in society and government. As Sewall put it: "Such discourses and arguings before the People do but make us grow weaker and weaker."[46] The significance of this aspect of information diffusion and of communication generally is illustrated in a rare episode of conflict between Sewall and his pastor, Ebenezer Pemberton, who was visiting him. The latter, who was jealous of Sewall's connection with Increase and Cotton Mather, and who for the moment believed that he, Pemberton, was being excluded from Sewall's inner circle, flew into a rage:

> Mr. Pemberton with extraordinary Vehemency said, (capering with his feet) If the
> Mathers order'd it, I would shoot him thorow. I told him he was in a passion. He

said he was not in a Passion. I said, it was so much the worse. . . . [He] Upbraid-
ing me, very plainly, as I understood it, with Partiality. . . . I said his carriage was
neither becoming a Scholar nor a Minister. The Truth is I was supris'd to see
myself insulted with such extraordinary Fierceness, by my Pastor. . . . [Later,
outside] In the way Mr. Pemberton charg'd me again, I was griev'd and said, what
in the Street! he answer'd, No body hears. But Mr. Sergeant heard so much that
he turn'd back to still us. Mr. Pemberton told me that Capt. Martin, the
Commadore [of the fleet that had just captured Port Royal from the French] . . .
call'd him Rascal in the Street, and said had it not been for his coat, he would have
cân'd him.[47]

The source of the conflict was Pemberton's misunderstanding of his not
being invited to a certain dinner and his suspicion that Sewall was siding with
his enemies, the Mathers and Captain Martin. In fact Sewall remained Pemberton's friend and the explanation of events lay in a tangle of affairs beyond
Sewall's control. As Sewall summed it up: "Reasons of State require the
overlooking many grievous Things."[48] However, what was crucial in the
subsidiary outburst with Pemberton was that their argument remain a private, indoor matter. To display it in the street was to announce the conflict
to all of Boston and to invite inquiries that would reflect poorly on the two
principals, on the South Church, and the entire Boston leadership. No wonder their fellow parishioner Peter Sergeant "turn'd back to still" his two
associates.

Yet another dimension of this closed, corporate approach to information
diffusion is evident in the ways that letters and messengers were employed.
While it was perfectly acceptable and common to send a child or a servant
with a private message dealing with family or health, for example, where
information concerning public matters was concerned, gentlemen normally
made an effort to resort to messengers whose status was commensurate with
the message and its intended recipient. When the Council sent a written
message to the governor, for example, it was not carried by a servant but by
one or two councilors themselves. When packets of letters came to Sewall
from Sir William Ashurst in London addressed to Province Secretary Isaac
Addington, Speaker of the House Nathaniel Byfield, and to the Reverend
Increase Mather, Sewall delivered them by hand, but not before reading
them himself.[49] By opening the letters—which had not been marked as
private—Sewall violated none of the contemporary canons because he, like
the addressees, was a fellow ruler equally interested in public news. Indeed
his reading them in advance might enable him better to discuss their contents, which in this case pertained to the province's agent in England. Within
the corporate circle of the elite, public information might be used for personal advantage but it was also properly shared.[50]

Where official dissemination of public information was concerned, the
connection between letters and messengers was close and coupled with the
expectation that the bearer would know the contents of the letter or letters,

and would be equipped to expand on them in response to the recipient's questions. So when a letter arrived in March 1691 from Governor Henry Sloughter of New York which told of his conflict with would-be Governor Jacob Leisler, the letter-bearer was plied with questions and in response furnished the most detailed account of Leisler's suppression available.[51] Evidently the messenger—whether a councilor calling on the governor, or Sewall going to his colleagues, or Sloughter's representative coming into the Bay Colony—was supposed to transmit more than an isolated text and to supply a commentary that would enable recipients to better understand and interpret the message. In light of contemporary technical impediments to swift, accurate information diffusion, such expectations were practical, since a messenger could revise the thrust of a letter to accommodate additional information and changed circumstances and could provide other assurances in an era when face-to-face encounters provided the normal context for information exchange. The presence of an appropriate message bearer reinforced and explicated the test itself.

The principle of exclusivity and the joining of message and messenger even applied in some measure to the dissemination of printed texts—proclamations, laws, and sermons. For even though anything that was printed was intended for a large audience and was in that sense an instrument of general (though not mass) communication, oftentimes the bearer was still connected to the substance of the print in some positive way and for some of the same reasons that applied to letters. The bearer of a proclamation, a law, or a newspaper from afar might be able to enlarge on its circumstances and significance, answering the questions that surrounded it. Indeed it appears that in some cases just as a printed text passed through several hands in a chain across many miles, so might its accompanying oral gloss pass from person to person. The most common instance of this connection between print and people in diffusion was the distribution of laws and proclamations by members of the House of Representatives as they returned to their home towns. Where towns sent no representative, diffusion of text and gloss depended on serendipity and the private networks of traders, clergymen, and families that haphazardly bound the leaders in one town to those of others.

The assumption that ruled the operation of this diffusion system regardless of whether the information was printed or not, was that the leading people would have the news first and that they would then, as needed, make it generally known. In the case of a smallpox epidemic, as in matters of war and defense where anxieties, rumor, and misinformation were rife, this approach provided safeguards against ill-advised actions and panic. Not only were the sober, experienced men who led each community better equipped by their travel and extra-local connections to transmit the information and to certify its accuracy, but in this way they could assimilate it, decide individually and collectively on a response, and then inform the townspeople at

large. This approach, which relied on networks of gentlemen, was not especially intended to keep secrets from the common people—such practices
would await a more democratic age—it was simply part of a political outlook
that recognized the elite as the active, initiating element in the body politic—
that is, as leaders—and the general population as followers. The dissemination of printed election sermons, which was an annual event where no rumors, no panic, no dangers were at issue, reveals this customary, everyday
attitude: for the sermons were printed so that each town received three
copies to supply the representative(s), the clergy, and the leading gentlemen. The substance of the sermons, which usually contained some topical
remarks together with conventional admonitions to both rulers and ruled to
conduct their civic duties in a harmonious, responsible way, was in no sense
secret. In another age a tract society might have printed election sermons by
the thousand and pressed them into the hands of the multitude. But in
Sewall's era if the message was to reach the general public at all, it was only
through the medium of town leaders who might, if they chose, read the
sermon aloud in a private prayer meeting, a tavern, or in a meetinghouse.

To a considerable extent this meant that the gentlemen of Massachusetts,
especially public officials and the clergy, were not only key transmitters of
information, they were also gatekeepers who were broadly responsible for
screening the passage of information and its diffusion to the public at large.
This arrangement operated less by design than as a natural consequence of
the deferential expectations that surrounded the social and political structure. Even where information that might have had practical use for farmers
was concerned, like agricultural commodity prices, it was generally limited
to merchants and public officials who traded the commodities or whose
responsibility it was to assure adequate supplies of food in war and in peacetime.[52] Common farmers, it was assumed, would always produce as much of
whatever products they could and sell them at harvesttime regardless of
market fluctuations. Matters of state, like the raising and supplying of
troops, taxation, regulating courts, provisions for dealing with property and
publicly owned real estate, did, to be sure, concern the general population,
but that was why they elected representatives to consult and to act on their
behalf. Even so, many of the smaller, more remotely located farming communities did not even exercise this right to participate in extra-local affairs
by proxy; by the 1720s more than a quarter of the representatives' seats in
the General Court were empty, and the number of vacancies sometimes
approached one-half as more towns were settled and incorporated.[53] That
the people at large were not generally informed was largely by default—a
default in which acquiescence seemed universal.

The information that the ruling elite chose to disseminate was relatively
limited and may be divided into two categories: public instruction and formal public notices. The first consisted of sermons that supplied moral and
religious instruction and might, depending on the occasion and the preach-

er's inclinations, be based on non-Scriptural information like a notable
death, a natural disaster, military affairs, or the passing of a monarch. The
nature of the information that was disseminated was wholly up to the
preacher, except for ordination sermons (which always dealt with the mutual
obligations of clergy and parishioners), sermons preached on publicly proclaimed fast days, and those delivered to militia companies about to depart
for the front. The sermon was the sole form of legitimate public address.[54]

Public announcements, which were far less frequent, especially outside of
Boston, were short, straightforward, and either highly functional or ceremonial in nature. Seldom printed, they often carried a note of urgency or
immediacy as with fire and military alarms and when the arrival of a new
governor or the death of a monarch was announced. Information of more
limited interest included the arrival of ships carrying notable passengers,
such as the governor of another colony, or the safe return of a ship from the
scene of battle in Canada. There were also announcements regarding the
actions of the General Court. Boston also had a town crier charged with
notifying the public of lost and found goods.

The ways in which this information was communicated reveals the limited
nature of mass communication in this society where face-to-face diffusion
was the dominant mode. Drums were beaten, cannons fired, flags flown,
bells rung, and trumpets sounded as authorities tried to assemble some
fraction of the populace in the central place where the information could be
loudly spoken. To reinforce the message a visual statement might accompany the announcement, as when a proclamation was "Publish'd . . . by
Beat of Drum" and read out from "the Council-Chamber Gallery" with an
array of officials including a clergyman who led a prayer in public view.[55]
When word arrived from London telling of crown actions regarding Massachusetts laws, first the bells were tolled to assemble the members of the
Governor's Council, and after they were shown the papers from the ministry, the "Drum is beat, and Allowance and Dissallowance of the Acts is
published, Lt. Govr. and Council standing in the Gallery. Great many Auditors below."[56] The spoken words reinforced by the visual display provided
spectators with a double set of impressions. With a "chorus" of notables on
display, the information was instantly authenticated as it rippled outward
from its source across the town and the province. Indeed even after Boston
possessed a weekly newspaper the old practice continued as when, Sewall
reported, "after Lecture, the Act of Parliament regulating Coin, is published
by Beat of Drum and Sound of Trumpet."[57] Not everyone would be informed of course, but some people would, and the drums and trumpet
invited those who were interested to make inquiries, as indeed Sewall did
when he was unable to go in person to witness an announcement. This
approach to "mass" communication, in which information moved out from
the elite into the general public through face-to-face encounters and personal information networks seldom relied much on printing.

There were, of course, occasions where information moved in other ways, contagiously, at it were, independent of the status hierarchy. News of epidemics like that in Charleston, South Carolina, in 1699 was interesting to persons of all ranks and was likely to spread in this manner.[58] Sensational and lurid events aroused comparable interest and tended to move in much the same way. On September 22, 1685, Sewall's "Neighbour Fifield," a commoner who was not someone he conversed with frequently, brought "the News . . . that runs throw the Town, viz. that James late D[uke] of Monmouth was beheaded on Tower-Hill on the 15th July last. [And that] Argyle [was] drawn, hanged and quartered." Fifield had this "from the Cryer of Fish," though its original source was said to be a specific shipmaster who had come in the night before.[59] The next day, however, Sewall heard a corrected story from Captain William Clutterbuck who arrived from Newcastle with "Ocular Testimony" that "he saw Argile's head cut off June the last; and the certain Newes of the Death of Monmouth about the middle of July."[60] A week later Captain Samson Stoddard arrived, having left London on July 25, bringing with him "the particulars of the Taking and Executing of the Late Duke of Monmouth whoes Head he saw struck off."[61] Here, as often happened with sensational news, contagious diffusion had moved more swiftly but somewhat less accurately than when diffusion occurred first within the elite.

At the same time it is important to recognize that misinformation could enter the system at any level and that everyone was liable to be misled on occasion. One September morning in 1703, for example, as Sewall was on his way to artillery training, Thomas Oakes, a physician and Harvard graduate, "ask'd if I had not heard the News? He said French King; he had his Neck broken by a fall from his Horse, as he was viewing an Army." Oakes, as was usual, supplied the story's genealogy: "Bodwin brings the Report, who comes from New Castle, and had it at Sea from Commodore Taylor."[62] But Sewall reserved judgment as to its veracity and then finally dismissed it when, two weeks later, a ship arrived from Dublin carrying no such momentous news.[63] Certain news of the death of Louis XIV, whose demise was often rumored wishfully in the Anglo-American world, finally came to Sewall from a shipmaster twelve years later.[64] The fact is that false and erroneous information circulated often among merchants and gentlemen, and it was their particular responsibility to use their superior information networks to verify reports before disseminating them to the public at large.

Public ceremonies were yet another, albeit indirect way that information was passed within the town and colony elite and outward to common people. To the initiated, the order and sequence of participants in a public procession or a funeral—who was placed where, who walked together, who was present, who absent—could supply the most up-to-date information about political and family interrelationships within local hierarchies. Like today's Kremlinologists, Sewall carefully noted the size and composition of the crowd and, in the case of funerals, the identities of pallbearers and those who received mourning rings, scarves, and gloves. In Boston's intensely personal social and political order such observations could be valuable and anyone, elite or not, could read such public ceremonies freely. What people gleaned from their observations might of course vary, from a naive sense of ruling class solidarity, to a keen appreciation of the dynamic intricacies of relationships within that class. Such ceremonies—as when Sewall and about fifty other whites walked with 150 blacks at the funeral of Boston, an exemplary free black man—always imparted messages.[65]

Although the dominant mode for the diffusion of public information was hierarchical—within the elite first and, after verification and screening, outward to a broader spectrum of society—it is vital to recognize that much information moved in more spontaneous and irregular pathways through the social order. If sensational news could move through the population like a contagion, with other matters that aroused general curiosity—life and death, exceptional weather, reports of pirates and of Indians, of victory and defeat, of disease and disaster—sociability and proximity combined to create an omnipresent conversational imperative that made interesting information spread rapidly. A youth whom Sewall met casually along a road near Boston volunteered the news that the Reverend Nehemiah Hobart had died that morning at sunrise, the youth not knowing that Hobart was part of Sewall's particular circle.[66] In Boston, when Harvard's president the Reverend Urian Oaks died in 1681, the news "was sadly told up and down the street," which was how Sewall learned if it.[67] At Rehoboth, forty miles southwest of the capital and close to Rhode Island, Sewall and his fellow justices were "stun'd in hearing the Defeat of the Canada Expedition."[68] Returning home from Providence, Rhode Island, Sewall stopped to have his hair "Trim'd at Roxbury; [where] my Barber told me the awful News of the Murder of Mr. Simeon Stoddard, in England."[69] Because of such casual information transmission, even though Sewall was away from home and the ordinary routines where his information networks centered and hence his access to information was reduced, he was by no means cut off. In eastern Massachusetts, at least, there was a significant general circulation of news by word of mouth, not only within the elite, but among the many common people whom gentlemen encountered every day.

Under these circumstances the introduction of the newspaper, which began continuous publication in Anglo-America at Boston on Monday, April 24, 1704, was not the momentous event that it may seem in retrospect. Instead it embodied only a marginal improvement in convenience for merchants and officials like Sewall, who were its chief patrons and audience. Appearing weekly, and including information culled from an English newspaper or two, together with a summary of the past week's news, the *Boston News-Letter* and its later counterparts were modest, two-column broadsides that were closely printed on both sides of a single sheet that at 6½ by 11½ inches, was smaller than a modern sheet of typing paper. Indeed in view of the well-developed networks that already existed for transmitting information face-to-face and by letter, it is surprising perhaps that one newspaper, and before Sewall's death two more, could actually find a niche to survive at all. Though in time they would become institutions exercising major political, economic, and cultural impact, newspapers began as non-essential, minor commercial ventures.

During Sewall's lifetime, the niches occupied by the newspapers were small indeed. John Campbell, the Scots immigrant who founded the *News-Letter* and who simultaneously held the strategic office of postmaster for Massachusetts, rarely sold more than 300 copies per issue even fifteen years after he had started, and more often, especially in the early years, the figure was closer to 200—this in a growing, prosperous, commercial town of 2000 to 3000 households that was located in the center of a hinterland that was several times more populous.[70] Such newspapers were not mass media, and they possessed only a somewhat narrow, fragile appeal even among the top tenth of the inhabitants of Boston and the surrounding towns. In order to understand why the appetite for locally produced newspapers was so limited it is instructive to consider the use Sewall made of them. For Sewall and the town and province officials and merchants with whom he worked were certainly conscious of the *News-Letter*—Sewall himself was proud to be the first person to carry one across the Charles River into Cambridge to give to the Harvard president and fellows—and officials and merchants may be said to have promoted the *News-Letter* by their patronage and by supplying Campbell with information.[71] But the contents of the newspaper were necessarily derivative, so for Sewall and the others who had been getting news for years from the London papers, the *News-Letter* could provide very little, very late. During the fall and winter months there was a hiatus in shipping from England, so fresh London papers were unavailable, but that did not make the *News-Letter* any more attractive because its publisher was not getting any news from overseas either.

The pattern of use that Sewall practiced reveals how the early newspaper functioned among the elite in the contemporary setting. It was, in the first instance, a reference source that recorded political texts such as royal and gubernatorial speeches and proclamations, and facts such as the arrivals of persons and ships, the deaths of leading men and women, and extraordinary events. Sewall himself retained his issues of the paper fairly systematically, binding them in volumes. For some years at least he made a calendar of the paper's most interesting contents, as well as marginal notes. Except in old age he rarely if ever learned of an event by means of a Boston newspaper, but in his diary and letters he cited them as references. For information Sewall looked to ship captains and to the newspapers they brought from London, Amsterdam, and even New York—papers imported so routinely that it was worthy of remark when a ship arrived from overseas without

them. Consequently before Campbell or his successors could get anything
into print in Boston, Sewall already knew about it, and usually in greater
depth and detail than the newspaper could present.[72]

But if Sewall's own reading of the newspaper was chiefly for reference,
Boston papers had additional uses for people who were not residents of
Boston or who, if they did reside there, were not so tightly enmeshed in elite
information networks. From time to time Sewall sent issues that carried some
pertinent information to family members residing outside of Boston, since for
them a Boston paper might be as informative as a London paper was for him.
Sewall also routinely enclosed newspapers with letters to distant friends like
his college roommate the Reverend Edward Taylor, who resided 100 miles
distant in the village of Westfield in the Connecticut Valley.[73] What is perhaps
most unexpected, however, is that Sewall also brought newspapers as gifts to
the widows he courted in the 1720s—mature women who, when their husbands had been alive, had been substantially included in the elite information
network but who now, in widowhood, entered into it only sporadically.[74] For
them a newspaper was an interesting diversion that broadened the range of
their conversation, either when Sewall visited or in mixed company generally.

Boston papers were also useful for distributing copies of scarce, interesting public texts such as the King's speech at the opening of Parliament.
Cases like this collapsed the distinction between the newspaper and broadside. Yet even where a text was duplicated by Boston printers, outside of
Boston the text might remain so scarce and the demand for it limited to such
a few people, that a handwritten copy might be made from a newspaper, as
indeed happened at the minor port of Plymouth in 1717.[75] The economics of
publishing and distribution made printing presses slow and costly mechanisms for simply multiplying texts.

In 1719 Boston got a second weekly paper, the *Gazette,* which survived by
following the same format as the *News-Letter*—reprints from English papers
and a few local items in two columns on both sides of a single sheet. Because
it appeared on Thursday, Boston now had semiweekly news coverage. In
Boston the impact was negligible, but for the province at large adding a
second paper was a significant event. Addressing the public in the opening
issue the publisher, William Brooker, referred to the urgent demand from
"People that live remote from hence," and he promised to print a weekly
"Account of the Prices of all Merchandize" in Boston so as to accommodate
outlying merchants and traders.[76] Two weeks later Brooker cut this feature
out, however, when Boston merchants complained; and he hastened to assure them and everyone that "the chief Design of this Undertaking [is] to
endeavour to advance, but not prejudice Trade."[77] Evidently Brooker had
failed to recognize that being informed on Boston prices was one of the
advantages local merchants enjoyed in their trade and competition with
counterparts stretching from Portsmouth, New Hampshire, to Newport,
Rhode Island, to New London, Connecticut. His Boston *Gazette* might aim

to serve New England commerce as a whole, but not at the expense of the Boston mercantile community that was its principal patron.

Boston added a third paper of a different sort during the smallpox epidemic in August 1721, when James Franklin, the son of an immigrant tallow chandler, set up the *New-England Courant,* which he modeled on the London *Spectator* and *Guardian.*[78] Literary diversion rather than hard news was the object of this sheet, which catered to the cultural preferences of an increasingly prosperous community of would-be British gentlemen in Boston. Lively, humorous, satiric, and contentious, it was intended to tweak rather than amuse Sewall's generation of Puritan gentlemen and the orthodox clergy. In contrast to both the *News-Letter* and the *Gazette,* which announced on their mastheads that they were printed by authority—that is, their texts were read over and approved by the governor or province secretary before publication—Franklin's *Courant* was the product of a free and uncensored press, which was itself a significant new and, for some, unsettling departure.

Consequently even though the immediate impact of a newspaper had been marginal in 1704, by the 1720s newspapers were helping to change the communication environment of Sewall's Boston. One, two, then three newspapers had gained a foothold in the town and province, and gradually they came to have important effects on the character of the information system. It was not that they signaled the sudden advent of mass communication— nothing of that sort happened. But they did expand the pattern of diffusion within the elite, opening it up so that, in some measure, anyone with access to a newspaper—whether a wealthy Boston merchant and magistrate like Sewall, or a petty trader sitting in a tavern in Marblehead and reading the proprietor's *Gazette*—could follow province, imperial, and international affairs in a rudimentary way. Information that in 1700 had been, as a practical matter, limited to men who lived in Boston and who were of a rank to enjoy access to English papers and the conversation of officials and merchants, was now available to a larger (though still elite) audience. Within and beyond Boston, more men and women, young and old gained a greater measure of access than ever before.

These were the circumstances when the policy of prior censorship came under challenge. Censorship was bound to become controversial when the Massachusetts elite become more diverse culturally, but it was the changes in the information system that heightened awareness of the issues. Because Boston's very first newspaper, *Public Occurrences,* published September 25, 1690, had not been authorized, it was immediately suppressed by the Massachusetts ruling council. Its aims were respectable—to record memorable events, to enlarge understanding of public affairs, and to stop "False Reports, maliciously made, and spread among us"—but the newspaper was dangerous nevertheless. Its comments on Louis XIV's immorality and the criticism it printed pointing out the barbarity of England's Indian allies were indiscreet, and suggested how dangerous a newspaper could be in encouraging ill-advised public discussion among inappropriate persons.[79] No outcry greeted the suppression of this first newspaper, and before the next one was launched fourteen years later, prior government censorship was arranged.

The dimensions of the problem from the perspective of the ruling elite are suggested by the anxieties raised by the publication of a seemingly innocuous almanac in 1708. It did not matter that its text came from the respectable hands of Edward Holyoke, a recent Harvard graduate and future president of the college. It still had to be submitted to the governor, who passed it along to Sewall for perusal. The judge's deletions included mention of Saint Valentine's Day, Annunciation, Easter, Michaelmas, and Christmas—Governor Dudley had already striken out the anniversary of King Charles I's "martyrdom"—so as to preserve Massachusetts' Puritan heritage.[80] What was at stake here, and in the variety of political and cultural censorship cases that cropped up with increasing frequency, was the maintenance by the traditional elite of a unified, hierarchical social, cultural, and political system.

During Sewall's lifetime England had required the colony to tolerate religious dissent and to accept a royal governor. Now, in the early decades of the 18th century, England's popular and political culture were making inroads, especially in the growing, cosmopolitan port of Boston, capital of the once Puritan colony. Controling public speech and printing, preserving the communication system as it had been, keeping it closed and confined to the right sort of people was increasingly difficult because the cultural and political orientation of elite people was no longer homogeneous. The union of class and culture was dissolving.

Sewall and his kinsman Governor Dudley, with their political and clerical friends, struggled to hold the line, but society and the communication system were slipping beyond their control. The infamous mock sermon episode of February 19, 1712 (Shrove Tuesday), is instructive. On that night at Ephraim Savage's tavern, one of the company donned a clerical gown and delivered a "Mock-Sermon full of Monstrous profaneness and obscenity," which was so well received by the spectators that it was then printed and distributed. It was not until four days later that Sewall and responsible authorities learned of the affair, and then they immediately rounded up and destroyed as many copies of the offending publication as they could, while starting proceedings against the perpetrator. But nothing they could do could erase the event or the fact that it had been the product of men whose discretion and rank ought to have forbidden such a performance. That the outrage occurred at a tavern operated by Sewall's cousin and Harvard classmate, a man who was a member of Sewall's church and a captain in the militia, suggests how far the old standards had eroded.[81] The battle to maintain a society where censorship was effective had become a losing, rear guard action. By the 1720s, virtually anyone could get a license to keep a public house and in such establishments a mock sermon, or worse, could occur with impunity. Prior restraints on printing went the same way, and from September 1725 onward, both the *News-Letter* and the *Gazette* dropped "Printed by Authority" from their mastheads.[82] In this the Bay Colony was coming into line with contemporary Britain.

These were momentous changes which encouraged the gloomy sense of general moral and spiritual declension that flourished in the minds of pious members of Sewall's generation. From their perspective, any changes in the communication system itself were of secondary importance, and were in any case scarcely perceptible because such changes had come about gradually, without much design, and with none of the intense self-consciousness that marked their religious lives. Moreover from the perspective of a single individual whose information networks were quite stable over his adult lifetime, and who was also surrounded by others who dwelled in a communication environment dominated by face-to-face encounters, the advent of American newspapers, the multiplication of taverns and clubs, the gradual opening and loosening of information networks, were all perceived as small changes in degree, not in kind. Only with a perspective that allows all of these changes to be considered cumulatively over two generations is it possible to recognize that printing was escaping from the control of authority and playing a more significant role in facilitating the diversity that was growing within the elite and beyond it.

What Sewall and his associates did see, though from a different angle than our own, was a generalized challenge to authority as they were used to exercising it. Intra-elite conflict and the communication networks that sustained such divisions were expanding the diffusion of public information to a broader range of people in the Massachusetts of 1730 than would have been possible in 1675. When Sewall died on the first day of 1730 the mournful news would still travel up and down the streets of Boston by word of mouth. In addition, however, a short, simple announcement would appear that week in both Boston papers, making a public record of Sewall's passing that for days, weeks, even months, spread the news indiscriminately way beyond Boston and even to some readers who had no interest at all in Sewall dead or alive. Such a phenomenon of information moving freely, without the exercise of personal discretion and out of context, was a new phenomenon with important ramifications for the redistribution of cultural and political power.

Chapter 2

William Byrd II
and the Challenge of Rusticity
Among the Tidewater Gentry

Isolation, Perry Miller asserted, "is not a matter of distance or the slowness of communication: it is a question of what a dispatch from distant quarters means to the recipient."[1] Isolation is both a relative condition and a state of mind. Dwelling in the heart of New York City, Melville's Bartleby was far more isolated than was Henry Thoreau alone in his cabin at Walden Pond. For British colonists residing at the margin of the American continent, three thousand miles beyond Land's End in England, the threat of isolation could be especially keen. It all depended on the location of one's cultural and psychological center. Because new England Puritans believed the center moved with them to the American shore, they only slowly and incompletely came to recognize themselves as provincial. But for English settlers elsewhere, and especially in Tidewater Virginia, the sense of isolation was so much a part of the colonizing experience from Roanoke and Jamestown onward, that it became prominently embedded in the region's common culture.

So pervasive was this consciousness that, paradoxically, the growth of transatlantic communication that accompanied the expansion of imperial trade and government in the 18th century actually reinforced the perception of physical and cultural distance. Among the great Tidewater gentry this sense was especially marked, and it shaped their participation in local and long-distance information networks. In time, the communication patterns they fashioned supplied them with a way of reconciling the conflict posed by the reality of their Virginia residence with their sense of themselves as Englishmen. For without the assiduous cultivation of appropriate communication networks, they believed, not only would access to power and prestige vanish but that as "creoles" and "hermits" they would degenerate into boorish materialism.[2]

The origins of their particular dilemma lay in the post-Restoration immigration of scores of fortune-seeking English gentry. These men, among them William Byrd I and William Fitzhugh, came to America seeking to improve their economic and social stature as Englishmen. Like the gentry who had first come to Jamestown, the Virginia adventure implied no rejection of English society and culture; it was at first only a means to an end, to perfect their lives as English gentlemen. But neither tobacco growing nor real estate speculation, the key routes to wealth, were armchair enterprises. Both demanded close supervision of one's interests in and on the ground. To succeed, one had to live in Virginia and become entangled in its politics and social relationships. Though some men did make their fortunes and return to England after a sojourn in the Tidewater, it was difficult to extricate oneself and one's assets. William Fitzhugh, a 1670 immigrant lawyer, was homesick for years, and he repeatedly offered his Virginia plantation for sale in order to purchase an equivalent estate in England.[3] But with tobacco prices in a long-term decline, he could never get his price; so he stayed and accumulated a larger and larger stake. When he died in 1701 he owned 54,000 acres—84 square miles—of Tidewater Virginia.

One must not suppose that successful immigrants like Fitzhugh or Byrd regretted their decision to settle outside of England; but there were misgivings. Although all manner of luxuries could be and were imported—Fitzhugh bought a coach to ride on muddy, winding forest tracks, and a brilliant array of table silver to reflect his polished self-image—one could not import English society. "Society that is good & ingenious is very scarce," Fitzhugh lamented, "and seldom to be come upon except in books."[4] Worst of all, Fitzhugh complained, "is the want of spirituall help & comforts, of which this fertile Country in everything else, is barren and unfruitful."[5] From a gentleman's perspective, Virginia was raw frontier, as uncouth as the remotest corners of Wales, Scotland, or Ireland.

It was for this reason that the "best people" often sent their children back to England to be educated. "Better be never born than ill bred," Fitzhugh avowed; and because he was convinced that "Good education of Children is almost impossible" in Virginia, he sent his sons to England at the age of eleven.[6] William Byrd thought so too, and to make certain his namesake and heir was properly educated, he enrolled his seven-year-old son in an English school. William Byrd II did not return to his native land until the age of twenty-two, and departed again for England within months, not coming home again until after his father's death, when, at the age of thirty-one, he assumed a leading position as a lawyer and landowner in the Tidewater.[7] Since he hoped to retain or augment his wealth without sacrificing the amenities of his own and his heirs' social stature, he had no choice but to return to Virginia. He could not sell his American holdings for their "true" value, and even if he could, in England the life of a great landholder would be beyond his means. So it was back to the Tidewater for Byrd, where he joined a circle of several dozen great families whose aspirations were English, but whose economic well-being and social status were rooted in Virginia.

The great gentry's cultural dilemma did not trouble humbler, less self-conscious settlers who would have gladly stepped up into the ruling circle had the Burwells, Byrds, Carters, Fitzhughs, Harrisons and their like chosen to sell their Virginia estates and return to England. That they did not sell, in spite of their misgivings about the rough texture of Virginia society, testifies to the recognition by those who enjoyed positions of great power and prestige that returning to England would mean retreating into the comfortable mediocrity of reduced status and aspirations. Much better, they thought, to stay in Virginia and find ways to cope with the problem of being English gentlemen overseas.

Among the most alluring but most expensive individual responses for the overseas Englishman was the visit to England. One might travel and visit for a few years, enter fully into London literary, political, and ecclesiastical circles, and then return to Virginia au courant, confident of one's English identity. But absence from the Tidewater meant not only large out-of-pocket expenses, it also led to deterioration of plantations and plantation income. For the well-connected, one partial remedy was to travel to England on colony business so that the Virginia treasury would pick up many of the costs. The lawyer-planter William Byrd and a handful of others availed themselves of these opportunities, but such trips were necessarily limited to only several dozen people during the entire colonial era. Usually, visiting England was a once-in-a-lifetime experience, most often connected to a youth's education. As a rule, Tidewater gentlemen had to find indirect ways of being English in Virginia, and the communication systems they established were crucial for shaping their own and the colony's identities.[8]

Trading networks determined shipping patterns and so created the underlying structure for transatlantic as well as inter- and intra-colonial communications. Outside well-travelled commercial routes, communication was ordinarily impossible, except where particular, private arrangements could be made. When, in 1736, William Byrd II wanted to correspond with his old law school friend Benjamin Lynde of Massachusetts, his letter traveled by way of London.[9] Even as late as the 1770s, Tidewater communication with Philadelphia was irregular and often relied on individual travelers rather than routine commerce or the post office.[10] Since the Tidewater in the 18th century was generally self-sufficient in provisions and other American goods, coastal traders seldom put into the Chesapeake until the decades after 1750.[11] The bulk of Virginia shipping was transatlantic, touching England, Scotland, and Ireland.

The cultural cargoes these ships carried, though dwarfed in bulk by tobacco, decisively shaped the character of Tidewater culture, provided the means whereby the great gentry established their standards.[12] Clothing, porcelain, glassware, silver, wallpaper, and fabrics, typically in the latest style, were unpacked from the barrels that rolled down planks onto plantation wharves. Even more important were the barrels of books and gentleman's magazines, and the packets of letters that ship captains delivered. Though shipmasters themselves were not much respected—Byrd scornfully remarked that "their understanding rises little higher than instinct. . . . One may as soon tutor a monkey to speak, . . . as to bring a skipper to higher flights of reason"—they were valuable conduits, so magnates like Byrd entertained them readily.[13] No captain need dine alone once he reached Virginia.[14]

Most of the letters these captains carried, like most of their table conversation with planters, was the mundane stuff of commerce: commodity prices, markets, business affairs. But they were no less eagerly greeted on that account; commercial news was interesting in the most literal way, and amongst the invoices and agents' balance sheets they carried were occasional nuggets of urgent or exciting information. Indeed, when the tobacco fleet sailed into Chesapeake Bay, the ships fired their guns to signal publicly their arrival.

"Our lives are uniform without any great variety, til the seasons bring in the ships," Byrd explained in June 1736—"then we tear open the letters they bring us from our freinds [sic], as eagerly as a greedy heir tears open a rich fathers will."[15] When batches of letters arrived, everything else could wait, whether one was at home or visiting.[16] Even the scheduled sitting of a county court came to nothing compared to letters; for when packets were brought into the courtroom the justices called a halt to the proceedings and "much time was taken up in reading our letters."[17] Letters sustained the transatlantic communication that was vital to Tidewater commerce and culture.

Great planters like Byrd wrote and received at least a hundred letters annually.[18] Most of these traveled overseas and dealt with commercial affairs; but since business could also include politics and international questions, it is hard to classify correspondence precisely. Some letters, it is true, might seem to be devoid of any cultural significance beyond being business artifacts in which details of a contract, an account, or a shipment were laid out. Yet a letter requesting credit reflected a concrete bond, just as one ordering fashionable porcelain and flatware or giving instructions on the packing of books, also conveyed its author's English cultural aspirations.[19] Likewise a letter seeking preferment for office was a manifestation of the integration of planters like Byrd into the English political system.[20] Moreover every letter that was carried across the ocean, no matter how dry or mechanical, embodied an actual physical connection between correspondents that linked Virginia with England.

Apart from the rare business or political letter that brought news of some great gain or loss, the most stimulating, absorbing letters were those that came from family and friends.[21] When Byrd's wife, the English-born Maria

Taylor Byrd, heard from any of her relatives, Byrd reported "she sleeps no more that live-long-night. . . . Therefore I find it necessary, when any English letters come to hand late in the day, to pocket 'em up till next morning."[22] Letters from family and friends restored and refreshed Virginians' confidence that their English connections endured even though they resided in a "lonely part of the world."[23] Letters furnished this reassurance and sense of connectedness concretely; and in contrast to oral messages, they could be renewed by rereading. They were treasures, to be read and reread, alone or in company, sometimes many years later.[24] "The next pleasure to being in the fine world." Byrd declared, "is to receive an elegant account of it," enabling one to be there vicariously. "I have almost worn out the paper with often reading it," Byrd wrote of such a letter in 1728.[25] Even allowing for some rhetorical inflation, it is evident that Byrd's morale depended on the renewal that letters from English friends and family supplied.

Years before, a planter's paean to the letter form explained just why letters possessed such profound significance:

> the first Inventer of letters deserves eternal Commendations, by whose means I have not only the opportunity, of the first acquaintance with so worthy & judicious a friend, but a continued Communication & Society, which I as really enjoy, whilst I am reading your most endearing letters, or answering them, as if happily present with you.[26]

Because letters collapsed the distance between the Tidewater and England, they nourished the Tidewater gentry's sense—part illusion and part reality—that they themselves remained Englishmen who happened to be residing in Virginia.[27]

If visits and letters provided the most direct personal connection to England, the importation of English printed goods was also essential. London newspapers and gentlemen's magazines, especially *Tatler* and *Spectator,* joined a wide range of books in Tidewater mansions. Whereas the lesser gentry read little and owned only a few practical books on religion, law, and medicine, the great gentry collected and read polite literature and politics, in addition to the classics, history, theology, and philosophy. Why, one might wonder, did a great Virginia planter who had no connection to English ecclesiastical politics, need to import and then wade through the polemics surrounding Dr. Sacheverell's sermons?[28] In London being so informed was necessary for anyone who would participate actively in the conversations that flourished in taverns and coffeehouses, in drawing rooms and clubs. In Virginia only a select few knew or cared about the Sacheverell case or the hundreds of other controversies that waxed and waned in print across England in the first half of the 18th century. Yet for William Byrd, being informed about Sacheverell's case and scores of other subjects was crucial, both for giving his correspondence with England a knowing quality, and for reassuring himself that he remained up-to-date. Newspapers and magazines might arrive in the Tidewater as little as two months or as much as two years after publication, but whenever they came to hand, the great gentry read them in an effort to inhabit the same mental world as cultivated Englishmen at home. Moreover, as Byrd repeatedly complained in the early decades of the century, he could find scarcely any other polite diversions in Virginia.

One way of coping with Virginia's isolation was to make a virtue of necessity so that country retirement could be viewed favorably. English belles-lettres already furnished models that were rooted in the writings of the Latin poet Horace, who had contrasted the decadent over-sophistication of urban high society with the moral and natural beauties or rural content-ment. For Byrd and other Tidewater magnates this classical vision, so useful to country gentry all over rural England, Wales, Scotland, and Ireland, offered an attractive way of reconciling their ideals with the mundane reali-ties of their situation. Themes of Virginia's rustic virtue and contentment run through many of Byrd's surviving letters to high-born English friends.[29] Byrd elaborated these thoughts most fully in a 1726 letter to Charles Boyle, the Earl of Orrery, when, after praising the beauty and healthfulness of the tidewater's climate, he boasted:

> I have a large family of my own, and my doors are open to every body, yet I have no bills to pay, and half-a-crown will rest undisturbed in my pocket for many moons together.

> Like one of the patriarchs, I have my flocks and my herds, my bond-men and bond-women, and every soart of trade amongst my own servants, so that I live in a kind of independance on every one, but Providence. . . .

> Another thing my Lord, that recommends this country very much, we sit securely under our vines, and our fig-trees without any danger to our property. . . . we have no such trades carried on amongst us, as that of housebreakers, highway-men, or beggers. We can rest securely in our beds with all our doors and windows open, and yet find every thing exactly in place the next morning. We can travel all over the country, by night and by day, unguarded and unarmed, and never meet with any person so rude as to bid us stand. We have no vagrant mendicants to seize and deaften [?] us wherever we go, as in your island of beggers.

> Thus my Lord we are very happy in our Canaan, if we could but forget the onions, and flesh-pots of Egypt. There are so many temptations in England to inflame the appetite, and charm the senses, that. . . . they could keep me so long from the more solid pleasures of innocence, and retirement.[30]

As long as Byrd lived in Virginia, he never forgot that he was far from English society or lost his desire to enjoy it; yet Horace's formula enabled him to view his own circumstances to advantage; "We that are banish't from these polite pleasures," Byrd wrote, "are forct to take up with rural enter-tainments. A library, a garden, a grove and a purling stream are the innocent scenes that divert our leizure."[31]

At Westover, Byrd carefully tailored the grounds surrounding his elegant Georgian mansion so that gardens and groves extended the refinement of his dwelling into the landscape. But in his life as a self-styled "poor hermit" residing in "this lonely part of the world," nothing was more important to his cultural identity than the library of 3500 volumes that he painstakingly im-ported from England.[32] This collection, a balanced assortment of titles in-cluding the most highly regarded scholarship and literature of Byrd's era, reflected his desire to remain in the same intellectual milieu he had known in England. This "poor hermit" had at his disposal shelves filled with the history, philosophy, and literature of classical antiquity, religious texts and commentaries in Hebrew, Greek, and Latin, as well as English, and a full collection of modern English and European works on philosophy, history and travel, natural sciences and technology, religion, law, and literature. With such an array of resources, Byrd's daily retreats to his library—where he also kept a collection of English newspapers and periodicals—enabled him to ward off the encroachment of his rustic environment. Though the lesser gentry may have viewed such a library as primarily a symbol of author-ity and high status, for Byrd it was a necessary retreat, a bastion of high culture in the wilderness. The library enabled him to realize the Horatian ideal and thereby justify his Virginia existence.

Byrd's library was greater than those of his Tidewater peers, but though he was more broadly learned than any of them, lay or clerical, the outlook he expressed was by no means unique.[33] The same presentation of self—the cultivated man deliberately choosing a life of rural virtue—is evident in the writings and behavior of other great planters, and even a Virginia governor such as Alexander Spotswood employed the Horatian ideal as a way to reconcile the desire to enjoy Virginia's bounties with the conflicting urge to reside as a great gentleman in England.[34] Though this internal conflict was strongest in the early decades of the century, it persisted. Indeed in the last quarter of the 18th century the polymath Thomas Jefferson would embody a new and attractive variant of the Horatian motif; no longer Byrd's English gentleman, the natural American aristocrat Jefferson became instead a gen-tleman of the world in his splendid isolation on a Blue Ridge hilltop.

Throughout the century great planters sought to make a virtue of their isolation, but they also worked to make Tidewater society fulfill their polite ideals. Though some like Landon Carter of Sabine Hall and Thomas Jeffer-son of Monticello truly found it congenial to live apart, in general great planters earnestly cultivated social connections in a society that they self-consciously modeled on Augustan English prescriptions for courtesy and polish. The Horatian pose, overseas travel and correspondence, and their consumption of high culture through print could enable individual gentlemen to sense themselves part of England's beau monde. But however satisfying solitary cultivation such as Byrd pursued in his library might be for an individual, it did not create polite society. The problem that Fitzhugh identified in the 1680s—"Society that is good and ingenious is very scarce"—could not be solved by one hundred civilized but secluded gentlemen dwelling in Horatian isolation.[35] As with gentlemen living in remote counties within the British Isles, the Tidewater magnates aspired to create an urbane society of their own that would overcome the boorish localism of not only their servants and slaves, but of the lesser gentry and ordinary planters who enjoyed political rights and who outnumbered them.

The starting place was private, at home, with a plantation manor house that could serve as the great English country houses did, as islands of refinement in a rural land. Like their English counterparts, Tidewater manors were named, as if to suggest a life and significance of their own that was broader than mere private residences, and more durable than a generation or two of a single family. Brick masonry, as at Westover or the Lees' Stratford Hall, was the preferred building material. Within mansion walls quasi-public spaces for entertaining visitors and "holding court" dominated. Though imitated by the lesser gentry, the great Tidewater houses were distinctive, not only for their physical size and grandeur, but for the patterns of sociability and communication they sheltered. The great houses and the carefully planned gardens that extended their ambiance outdoors were conceived as colonies of polite society.

Within the society of the great houses dining was a central activity. Scheduled by the clock, the whole ceremony followed customary forms, from the seating of the family and guests to the order of the dishes. Decorous dining was a centerpiece of polite sociability. At Major Nicholas Merriweather's house, Byrd noted disapprovingly that his host, one of the lesser gentry, "sat at the upper end of the table and helped himself first. His wife did not appear."[36] At his own estate Byrd never tolerated such breaches of etiquette even when, after a quarrel, it took "much persuasion" to bring his wife to join the company at dinner.[37] If standards lapsed in his own small private environment of gentlemen and gentlewomen at Westover, then the struggle to surround oneself with English courtesy in the Tidewater was lost. The dining tables of the great gentry, where sharing the host's food and drink served to bond a social circle, were among the key institutions for the creation of polite Virginia society.

The imported porcelain, silver, and crystal, the japanned, walnut-veneered, and mahogany sideboards and chairs, even the food, were props that furnished a suitably genteel setting for the key activity of the dinner table: sociability, and especially talk.[38] For if all one wanted was food, one could eat simply and alone. Companionship came first because it shattered the boredom of repetitive days and the tedium of solitary leisure on isolated estates. The purpose of conversation was entertainment, improvement, and usefulness, though not necessarily in that order. The exchange of personal sentiments, rather than a single person holding forth, was expected, and information on virtually any topic imaginable—from astronomy, to matrimony, to zoology—was freely shared around the table.

The common topics of conversation, whether in Byrd's era or the later 18th century, were not esoteric and were more or less accessible to all members of the group seated together, young people as well as ladies and gentlemen. Personal news of neighbors and kin, their health, travels, marriages, and births were always present, as was news of crops, the weather, prices, the arrival of ships, the doings of Virginia courts, the legislature, and the governor. In wartime, military news was common, coming from the Indian frontier, Williamsburg, or London. In times of drought or epidemic, news touching these scourges was readily exchanged. Subjects demanding erudition such as literature, theology, and natural philosophy, were seldom discussed over dinner where a mixed company participated.

At the table of Robert Carter of Nomini Hall in the 1770s, illness and health were probably the most frequently discussed subjects as neighbors and visitors exchanged information on which diseases were circulating in the colony and how best to treat them. Such talk provided more than just a psychological catharsis for anxieties, it furnished practical guidance respecting travel plans, plantation management, and medical treatment. Since the great planters, from Byrd to Washington, all functioned as medical practitioners (and some actually read the latest scientific treatises), these conversations could include discussion of the most advanced medicine of the day. At the same time it is significant that Byrd, a learned medical amateur, listened carefully to the views of an unread but experienced midwife on a childbearing question, and later recorded her advice.[39]

When politics, another common topic, was discussed, women and youth generally kept silent. In the company of mature men, often trained in law and serving as councilors, burgesses, justices of the peace, and vestrymen, their opinions were not sought. But there is no reason to suppose they could not grasp what was said. On one occasion in 1774 after her husband had left the table, Frances Anne Tasker Carter of Nomini Hall continued the conversation with the children's tutor, Philip Fithian, and to his surprise revealed "her perfect acquaintance with the American Constitution."[40] Mrs. Carter may have been a reader of law and politics, since she was unusually well-read and such texts were available in her husband's library, but it is more likely that her knowledge of American constitutional ideas—"the American Constitution"—resulted from her attention to dinner table and drawing room conversation.[41] For the talk that flourished on social occasions—whether it was on the seasons or on horses, on slavery or on fashions—was cultivated for improvement and instruction as well as amusement. Among the books at Nomini Hall were the posthumously published letters of Philip Dormer Stanhope, Lord Chesterfield, whose advice to his son was first published in 1774 and was reprinted and imitated in scores of British and American courtesy books for over a century thereafter. Repeating themes that were rooted in Renaissance prescriptions, Chesterfield asserted that there were three paths to cultivation, refinement, and wisdom: reading, which supplied knowledge of times past; travel, which provided a comparative perspective and information about the world beyond one's own precincts; and conversation, through which one could be enriched by listening to others and could gain an understanding of people and their motives.[42] Chesterfield's prescriptions confirmed the importance of dinner-table society in the minds of Tidewater magnates. Fifty years earlier, Byrd himself was guided by the genteel homily "by Reading he's acquainted with ages past, and with the present by voyageing & conversation."[43]

The significance and functions of dinner-table society, or more broadly the whole phenomenon of great house sociability, extended beyond the conscious intentions of the magnates who supported it for the sake of their own morale. At their houses social standards for the Tidewater were effectively promulgated. Ideals were affirmed, taboos and sanctions established, social codes and boundaries were enforced. In conversation and in deportment, by the timely expression of gravity or humor, by conveying censure or approval, the great gentry expressed their collective identity and elaborated their social objectives—all while engaged in the give-and-take of exchanging information and opinion through conversation. The fact that the great houses were the only ongoing elite social centers outside the capital at Williamsburg magnified their importance. For as centers of sociability, and in light of the extensive interests of their masters, the great houses were crucial to the operation of the communication networks that provided order and coherence in Tidewater society.

The communication networks that centered at great house dinner tables, drawing rooms, kitchens, stables, and storehouses were composed of people of all ranks, from the magnate himself down to his servants and slaves.[44] Where there were important differences in social rank, as between a master and his white servants or black slaves, the range of communication was often narrowly functional—delivering orders, passing messages, reporting on tasks, the weather, or the cultivation, harvest, and processing of crops. Masters confidently relied on the communication networks of their subordinates because they normally worked smoothly. Though the letters and diaries of great gentlemen are studded with complaints regarding lost or delayed transatlantic letters, breakdowns in the local information networks of subordinates were virtually unknown. The comings and goings of underlings, both those of the magnate himself and those of his fellow gentlemen, kept these networks open and functioning every day from dawn until dusk.

Two examples drawn from many recorded instances throughout the 18th century will illustrate the reliability of such communications. A routine case from the experience of William Byrd was multiplied countless times throughout the region and the period: Byrd sent written instructions to his overseer at James River Falls and later received word that all was well there.[45] The messages moved so promptly, accurately, and predictably that they are only worthy of comment on that account. A more unusual message came to George Washington on a stormy morning, informing him that his mill was in danger of washing out. Washington reported: "I immediately hurried off all hands with shovels & ca. to her assistance and got there myself just time enough to give her a reprieve for this time by Wheeling dirt into the place which the Water had Washd."[46] In both of these cases, one ordinary and one an emergency, and occurring several decades apart, neither gentleman doubted the reliability of his communication networks. Though the information came from a single source and lacked positive confirmation, it came from people who were trustworthy in such matters. The messages, after all, were plausible and straightforward; they covered subjects on which either the message-bearer or the one who had sent him possessed direct knowledge; and there was no motive for supplying wrong information. Under circumstances like these subordinate networks worked to masters' satisfaction.

There were, of course, occasions where self-interest and self-protection led subordinate networks to supply bad information. When provisions were stolen, an animal injured, equipment broken, a crop mismanaged, or someone got drunk or ran off, subordinates might well mislead their master. In such cases, however, they did not come forward and interrupt the master's business or leisure to bring him lies. Misinformation came when a master, cognizant that something was amiss, made inquiries. A master who questioned or cross-examined subordinates in situations like these, was already displaying an appropriate skepticism that reduced his risk of being misled.[47]

Magnates also tended to doubt some of the information their overseers furnished. They understood that it was often in an overseer's interest to conceal mishaps or misdeeds, particularly in light of the sometimes conflicting goals of overseer and master. On occasion Byrd's overseers spent more time on their own projects than Byrd's, and tension between overseer and master was common and chronic.[48] Unlike other subordinates, overseers possessed considerable freedom and were only nominally dependent on their employers. Moreover since overseers were not gentlemen they could not be expected to follow the code of truthfulness that inhered in a gentleman's honor. Like other subordinates, overseers had to be watched ordinarily, and full trust was extended only after a long proof of loyalty.

With members of their own social class, however, the English gentleman's code of honor was part of the standard of courtesy the magnates promoted and enforced. Even allowing for intense jealousies and rivalries, truthfulness was expected among gentlemen. Yet because the range of information that passed through gentry networks was so comprehensive and might be consequential—touching everything from war and peace and life and death, to the private morals of particular people, and included matters of judgment as well as fact—gentlemen paid close attention to who was providing the information and to identifying its original source. Frequently they also suspended judgment until confirmation from other sources was available.

In this context each magnate developed what may be called circles of trust—a small number of people, mostly men, whom he saw frequently and whose judgments he had grown to respect.[49] These circles of trust were much like the information networks possessed by Samuel Sewall and other Boston leaders during the same era, although in the Chesapeake there was no distinct array of prominent clergymen who were included. But as in Boston, a magnate's trusted associates were selected from among his and his wife's families, his neighbors, and his business and political associates. Judging from these circles' small size and their exclusivity, personal temperament and affinity were as important as common economic, political, religious, and social interests. For among magnates who competed actively with each other for political and economic advantage, genuine trust and friendship could never be a simple question of class, kinship, or ethnicity.

Circles of trust normally included people of roughly the same age. Though there might be significant differences of status, it is rare to see quasi-paternal or filial relationships, or those of patron and client in these circles. Brothers, brothers-in-law and uncles were most often connected in circles of trust, but the links were selective and all such kin were not included. Personality and proximity were crucial within the family as well as beyond its boundaries, for neighbors as well as political or business acquaintances. William Byrd's circle included other plantation gentry, his brother-in-law John Custis and his wife, his Uncle Philip Ludwell II, his neighbors Major Theodorick Bland, Colonel Edward Hill, Colonel Eppes, and Benjamin Harrison and his wife, in addition to the clergyman Charles Anderson and the physician William Cocke, who was also colony secretary. These men and their wives shared common general interests, but there were no particular conflicts or rivalries between them. All were literate, well-born gentlemen and gentlewomen whose tastes were compatible. None competed with Byrd in urbanity and sophistication, but all respected their friend's polite accomplishments. Such circles were seldom destroyed by conflict, and they changed only slowly as death removed their members one-by-one.[50]

Among the strengths of these circles of trust for passing information was the fact that each man not only had his own circle but, as in Samuel Sewall's Boston, was part of several other circles. As a result circles were interconnected, and news that was not confidential might maintain its credibility as it passed through extensive, far-flung, intricate networks in the thinly settled Chesapeake of William Byrd. Breaches of confidentiality seldom came to light and, when found out, had lasting consequences for the parties involved.

An episode in William Byrd's experience reveals the magnates' keen interest in maintaining the discipline of their face-to-face peer networks. At the end of 1711, Byrd opposed a plan to raise £20,000 through special taxes and had, in the course of conversation remarked that "no Governor ought to be trusted with £20,000."[51] Less than two weeks later word came back to him that this unguarded comment had been passed on to Governor Spotswood himself. Within a few days Byrd discovered it was Will Randolph who had passed the remark on to Spotswood, so Byrd confronted Randolph in a letter. The latter replied immediately, admitting in writing that he had "told it," defending himself by saying that "he thought it no secret." Byrd's reaction was to mark Randolph forever more "as a very false friend."[52] A person such as Randolph could never be part of Byrd's circle of trust nor could he, after this episode become known to Byrd's acquaintances, be part of the circle of trust of anyone who shared Byrd's perception of events.

Randolph, however, was of small consequence to Byrd; what mattered was the news from "my brother Custis who told me the Governor was angry about what I had said."[53] When Byrd called on Governor Spotswood soon after, "he looked very stiff and cold on me."[54] Byrd did his best to "say the truth" of the episode to Spotswood, but the breach of confidence was hard to repair. Byrd sent gifts of poplar and fruit trees to the governor to assuage his feelings. But ultimately Byrd only regained the governor's trust when he was fortunate enough to bring him the gift of early information, when early one morning, after learning from a captain that the English fleet had arrived, he "hastened to Williamsburg and went to the Governor with this news and was the first to tell him for certain of the fleet." That night Byrd could record with satisfaction, "I went home with the Governor to dinner and ate some roast beef."[55] The timely delivery of accurate information could restore a relationship, just as an indiscretion or misuse of information could destroy one.

For the most sensitive kinds of personal, financial, and political information the magnates' circles of trust were crucial to the Tidewater communication system. But no such selective relationships were necessary for the transfer of ordinary public news of the neighborhood or the colony, and such news could often be as important to the great gentry as the information that passed through more discreet channels. Indeed the great gentry perpetually sought information about what was happening at their own scattered plantations, throughout their county and colony, and about British culture and politics generally. Visitors to their houses, whether highborn or low, were routinely questioned, as if information was the price of their food and lodging. Though visitors often knew nothing of consequence beyond what was already known at the great house, their interrogation was an accepted routine. In such cases visitors provided confirmation of what was already known as well as reassurance that no new stories were abroad. A visiting niece, an itinerant carpenter, a teamster, or even a herdsman from another plantation all had information to impart, even if it was only that they had heard no news. In an environment where unforeseen and unwelcome news was common, like a death or the loss of a ship, the adage "no news is good news" had real meaning for those who dwelled in the relative isolation of a Tidewater mansion.[56]

Indeed in their minds the great gentry never accepted their physical or social isolation, and did their best to deny and reject it. The Horatian ideal was useful and attractive for rationalizing their separation from English society. But it was in their enthusiasm for occasions like weddings, christenings, and funerals, for horse races, fox hunts, and balls, for the festivities that accompanied the installation of a new governor or the proclamation of a new monarch, that they acted to join the islands of great house civility that were already connected through kinship, churchgoing, and participation in civil government—county courts as well as the colony legislature. Before 1750 the great gentry had succeeded in creating a polite Anglo-Virginian society that might have satisfied William Fitzhugh's longing for "society that is good & ingenious."[57]

Next to the great gentry mansions, parish churches were the most important and numerous communication centers where the magnates promoted their vision of English culture. At church they visited with others of their rank in a setting where their conduct might serve as a model to the lesser planters who accorded them deference. Though worship service provided the occasion for gathering, services were brief, and more time was spent in the churchyard conversing before and after the service than in attending the word of God. Except for a handful of the most pious gentlemen and ladies, religious needs do not seem to have been the primary motive for attendance. Indeed the most pious might sometimes stay home deliberately. As one devout gentleman noted on a Sunday: "At home reading—which is much more instructive than the sermons I hear at Church."[58] Because the clergy sometimes served several parishes, one could not even be sure the priest would show up to deliver a sermon, and the alternative, the reading of prayers by a layman, was no attraction for attendance. Since sermons by eminent English divines were commonly part of great men's libraries, and devotional manuals were even more widely available, gentlemen and their families could perform satisfactory religious exercises at home, in bad weather or in good. For in contrast to Puritan New England where corporate worship was a Sabbath day requirement, the Anglican Church—especially in the Chesapeake—was far more accepting of private services which could be readily conducted according to the *Book of Common Prayer*.[59]

Among the great gentry the motives for church attendance extended beyond worship. Church was an occasion, a time to do business—both literally in connection with their intertwined material, political, and family concerns, and more broadly in the sense of engaging in the sociability that established their identity as the rulers of Virginia society. An outsider, Philip Fithian, the tutor at Robert Carter's Nomini Hall, who on one of his first visits to a Virginia church found an advertisement for the sale of pork posted at the front door,[60] gave a vivid description of well-attended, fair-weather church services in the Tidewater:

> the three grand divisions of time at the Church on Sundays, Viz. before Service giving & receiving letters of business, reading Advertisements, consulting about the price of Tobacco, Grain, &c, & settling either the lineage, Age, or qualities of favourite Horses 2. In the Church at Service, prayrs read over in haste, a Sermon seldom under & never over twenty minutes, but always made up of sound morality, or deep studied Metaphysicks. 3. After Service is over three quarters of an hour spent in strolling around the Church among the Crowd, in which time you will be invited by several different Gentlemen home with them to dinner.[61]

The gentry socialized and talked business together before services began, then entered the church as a group and, when the service was over, came out together to resume their conversations and visiting. Though Fithian, a Presbyterian, found the mingling of religious and secular activities improper, there is no reason to view the gentry's behavior as hypocritical or, in their own terms, profane. That they enjoyed themselves and were brought up to date on the news and gossip of the parish and beyond in no way conflicted with their religious expression. It was all proper and beneficial. Attendance, it is true, was voluntary; but that did not diminish its importance. Indeed it may be that it was precisely because churches in Virginia were less intensely preoccupied with conversion and salvation than in New England, that participants could make churchgoing into such a communicative social occasion.[62] Participation by gentry in public worship, like the polite sociability with which they surrounded it, was not only exemplary for their social inferiors, it also enhanced their images of themselves as true English gentry.

Except for the absence of women and children, sessions of the county court were similar to church meetings in that the business of the court was sandwiched in between a great deal of practical sociability and, as with church, attendance was uneven and unpredictable. Usually a small minority of the justices, perhaps five out of a roster of twenty or more, heard the cases. Before a quorum was present and as the parties who had business were gathering, talk on prices, crops, hiring craftsmen, politics or religion might mix with the exchange of news and storytelling. At mid-afternoon, when the court usually adjourned, more socializing was common. As with the case mentioned earlier, when a court was interrupted by the arrival of letters, ordinarily the justices were as concerned with their private affairs as with dispensing justice.[63] As with church attendance, going to court enabled the great gentry to connect with current information networks and do business while publicly acting out their gentleman's role.

Participation in the Virginia legislature, either the Governor's Council or the House of Burgesses, represented the pinnacle of such activities for the great gentry. More than any other Virginia experience, being in Williamsburg reinforced the sense of connection with genteel English culture. Although the capital was smaller than many English county towns, it quickly came to embody a certain grandeur and refinement. At Williamsburg all of the elements associated with polite society came together in political gatherings, in dinners and balls, in drawing-room discourse and coffeehouse conviviality. By the early decades of the eighteenth century, after the construction of the new capital, the governor's palace, and the College of William and Mary, the prospects for genteel Tidewater society were being realized.

In 1724 a clergyman from England described the "City of Williamsburg" as

> a Market Town, and governed by a Mayor and Aldermen: and is well stock'd with rich Stores, of all Sorts of Goods, and well furnished with the best Provisions and Liquors.
>
> Here dwell several very good Families, and more reside here in their own Houses at Publick Times.
>
> They live in the same neat Manner, dress after the same Modes, and behave themselves exactly as the Gentry in London; most Families of any Note having a Coach, Chariot, Berlin, or Chaise. . . .[64]

The parish church itself, he pronounced, was "adorned as the best churches in London"; a dozen years later another English visitor would laud Yorktown's private "Houses [as] equal in Magnificence to many of our superb ones at St. James's."[65] By 1750 Williamsburg would be the site of elegant balls, theatrical performances, a coffeehouse, a general printing shop, a newspaper, and a well-stocked bookstore. Through the patronage of the governor and great gentry, Williamsburg society came to embody Virginia's own idealized variant of polite English culture.

The importance of this ideal for Virginia magnates early in the century is suggested by their attempt to oust Governor Francis Nicholson because, among other offenses, he did not act the part of a gentleman. A soldier of common birth and Tory attachments, Nicholson was a rude, hot-tempered, hard-drinking Yorkshireman who, his opponents reported in 1704, was unfit to be governor.[66] "Rogues, Villains, Newgate Birds, Beggers, cheats & Cowards," were Nicholson's epithets for Virginia gentlemen, "and [he said] of the Gentlewomen that they were all a parcell of **Jades, & Jilts. . . ." So far was Nicholson from polite courtesy, they complained, that "he lives in a very sorry house not worth above £10 or 12 a year," and "his furniture & attendance are miserably mean."[67] To complete the picture, Nicholson kept "very irregular hours of Eating, Sleeping & doing business."[68] Such behavior might be acceptable in a military camp, but it was no model of gentility. Apart from pragmatic political requirements for the office, what was necessary to fulfill the magnates' cultural objectives was a polished dignitary to head the emerging social hierarchy.

In Alexander Spotswood and William Gooch, who headed the colony from 1710 to 1722 and from 1727 to 1749, respectively as lieutenant governors under the Earl of Orkney and the Earl of Albemarle, the great gentry enjoyed the kind of social leadership they sought. Spotswood, at his very first meeting with his Council "made a courteous speech," and Byrd exclaimed that when Spotswood made his opening speech to the House of Burgesses he "delivered it with the best grace I ever saw anybody speak in my life."[69] In contrast to Nicholson, Spotswood entertained properly at dinner parties and balls. By his whole bearing he testified that Virginia was part of English society and not, as Nicholson's rule had implied, a raw frontier garrison.

The emergence of Williamsburg as a refined provincial capital symbolized the achievement of a polite Anglo-Virginian society. No longer were the great houses separate islands of gentility; they had become parts of a growing network of satellites, tied directly to England by the commercial and cultural cargoes in the ships that docked at their wharves, and also connected to English society through its Tidewater surrogate at Williamsburg. Controlling the government, church, and college, and setting the standards of conduct for would-be gentlemen and gentlewomen through example, by mid-century the great gentry appeared to have solved the problem that troubled their grandfathers and great-grandfathers—how to be an English gentleman or gentlewoman three thousand miles from home. Communication systems of their own devising had enabled them through travel, letters, printing, and conversation both to keep in touch with fashionable English culture and to diffuse and establish that culture among Virginia gentry.

The threat of becoming a rustic, however, remained—in Virginia much more than in England itself. Tidewater magnates knew real-life characters resembling Henry Fielding's fictional Squire Western, so they could not feel complacent. At horse races and fox hunts, at cockfights and boxing matches, at militia musters and at elections, some gentlemen descended to drunkenness and brawling unbecoming their station. Though such gentry were literate enough to carry on business and defend their interests in court, they were ignorant of history, philosophy, and letters. A boorish materialism that contradicted the courtesy manuals of Georgian England permeated the mentalities of such planters. Though prosperous, they were the cultural kinsmen of the yeomen and "buckskins" who composed the bulk of Virginia's white population.[70]

The great gentry had created a high society that made it possible to be a proper gentleman, but there was no guarantee that they or their sons and sons-in-law would measure up. On a Tidewater plantation it often took some doing to be able to picture oneself as a cosmopolitan Englishman; nor was it possible to maintain the self-image entirely on one's own. Such self-perceptions required continuous nourishment in the form of recognition and respect from the great gentry, royal officials, and polite Englishmen. A mirror of politeness was necessary, and it was elite information networks that provided that mirror. Long ago scholars pointed out that "news, literature, and personal messages from London did not merely convey information; they carried with them standards by which men and events were judged. In them, as in the personal envoys from the greater European world, was involved a definition of sophistication."[71] The gentry's information system simultaneously defined standards and conveyed sanctions within Tidewater high society.

The mirror of politeness reflected the three kinds of behavior that had been prescribed in the printed manuals of etiquette and gentility ever since Castiglione's *Book of the Courtier* appeared in the Renaissance: physical prowess as displayed in the gentlemanly arts of fencing and riding; social refinement as manifested in entertaining conversation, music, and dance in the company of polite men and women; and learning based on the classics. Of the three, two depended wholly on social information systems. Neither birth nor wealth, alone or in combination, could make a gentleman. Without particular forms of communication, gentility did not exist. This realization underlay the flowering of Tidewater culture in the 18th century, often described as "the golden age."[72]

For Philip Fithian, who came from the upper ranks of New Jersey society, where the ideal of English gentility was much less powerful, and where more bourgeois values prevailed, the Tidewater attachment to Castiglione's prescriptions stood out. Though Fithian regarded himself as a gentleman and was accepted as one in the Carters' circle, he was nonplussed because he was "presum'd to be acquainted with Dancing, Boxing, playing the Fiddle, & Smallsword, & Cards," none of which were part of his own sober background.[73] Nor did his New Jersey Presbyterian upbringing furnish sufficient social grace to be gay and amusing in company. "At home," he mused, "I am thought to be noisy enough; here I am thought to be silent & circumspect as a *Spy*—How different the Manners of the People! I try to be as cheerful as I can. & yet I am blamed for being stupid as a Nun–."[74] Perhaps he exaggerated his deficiencies, because Robert Carter, who hired him to furnish elocution, erudition, and discipline for his sons and daughters at Nomini Hall, was well-satisfied. Carter knew that his children would learn the requisite gentry social skills in his own and other great houses from the examples he and his wife, together with their circle, set every day.

New Jersey ideas of social intercourse simply would not do for the great families of the Tidewater. Social rank ruled sociability in Virginia, according to a more rigid, courtly manner than New Jersey. As Fithian observed:

In New-Jersey Government . . . Gentlemen in the first rank of Dignity & Quality, of the Council, general Assembly, inferior Magistrates, Clergy-men, or independent Gentlemen, without the smallest fear of bringing any manner of reproach either on their office, or their high-born, long recorded Families associate freely &

commonly with Farmers & Mechanicks tho' they be poor & industrious . . . we
see labourers at the Tables & in the Parlours of their Betters enjoying the advantage, & honour of their society and Conversation. . . .

But you will find the tables turned the moment you enter this Colony. . . . Such
amazing property . . . blows up the owners to an imagination, which is visible in
all . . . that they are exalted as much above other Men in worth & precedency, as
blind stupid fortune has made a difference in their property.[75]

In practice this meant that the dining rooms, drawing rooms, ballrooms, and
gardens of the great magnates were insulated from the rough manners of
farmers and tradesmen. The self-conscious effort to create polite society on
the Tidewater frontier required an exaggerated, English-style exclusiveness.
At home, at church, at court, and at public events like horse races and
muster days, the gentry were viewed by all, but they mingled with each
other. No wonder that when a common youth like Devereux Jarratt "saw a
man riding the road, near our house, with a wig on, it would so alarm my
fears . . . that . . . I would run off, as for my life."[76] The great gentry in their
periwigs were a class apart.

One consequence of their social exclusivity was the creation among them
of an environment where easy courtesy flourished. From childhood, boys
and girls learned to mix in company with ease and assurance. Liberality was
the rule of hospitality, a rule that extended beyond food and drink to conversation. To contradict or affront a member of the company was improper,
because it might be viewed as a challenge of honor. Instead humor, patience, and kindliness were expected, whether it was an exclusively male
gathering, as when public officials dined together at a tavern, or in the mixed
company usually found at the great houses. The earnest gravity and readiness to dispute that northern clergy and lawyers displayed, was alien to the
Tidewater gentry's style.

Just as equals did not directly challenge equals except within the ritualized
confines of games and contests, so the rule of cross-class interaction was
condescension and submission. Among the reasons that subordinates—from
overseers down to slaves—misbehaved surreptitiously was to avoid directly
challenging the master's authority. From a master's perspective, the discovery of covert defiance was unwelcome, but its discovery and punishment
reinforced his role in society. The appearance of open defiance, which challenged a master's stature, was much worse. More than cooperation was
required of subordinates, readiness to help and an agreeable disposition
were expected. When William Byrd's secretary-librarian dared to speak to
his master in a way that seemed surly, he was immediately and severely
reprimanded.[77] Farther down the hierarchy, slaves were expected to behave
with conspicuous deference in every transaction with their master, while he
in turn treated them with patriarchal justice and kindness.[78] Forms of speech
and conversation were everyday systems that defined social identity and

controlled relationships. Part of Fithian's discomfort was a consequence of being a kind of anomaly in a system of conventions that was different from those he had known.

Between men and women the rules were more complicated, and perhaps more fluid over time. For although male heads of household commanded their wives' and daughters' deference in a general way, this hierarchy was erased in polite society. Here women enjoyed parity with men and may even have possessed superiority owing to gender roles. In Georgian England, women were thought to be naturally more polite than men. Byrd was conventional in often seeking "the company of Women, not so much to improve his mind as to polish his behavior." The presence of women in company elevated the courtesy of all. As Byrd observed in a commonplace: "There is something in female conversation, that softens the roughness, tames the wildness, & refines the indecency too common amongst men."[79]

Byrd's comments were not merely formulaic sayings. His first wife, Lucy Parke Byrd, once reproached a gentleman visitor for swearing in company, though Byrd thought her comment unbecoming to a hostess.[80] She even chastised Byrd and a visiting clergyman for conversing in Latin, which excluded the women. It was, she said "bad manners."[81] The reprimand angered Byrd, especially since the cleric was "a man of no polite conversation, notwithstanding he be a good Latin scholar;" but he accepted his wife's correction and went on to speak English so that all could follow the conversation.[82]

At its best, polite conversation in mixed company seems most often to have concerned belles lettres, travel and social customs, and religion. When men and women read aloud together early in the 18th century their texts were chosen from among works like Jeremy Collier's *Short View of the Immorality and Profaneness of the English Stage* (London, 1698), Martin Lister's *Journey to Paris* (London, 1699), and Bishop Tillotson's sermons.[83] Yet not all their discourse was so elevated. At Byrd II's sister-in-law Custis' house, the talk was of "Mrs. Russell and the Governor, not much to the advantage of the first. My sister[-in-law] loves to talk a little scandal of her neighbors."[84] News and gossip of the great gentry were irresistible. Nor was it necessary always for the company to join in a single conversation. Though less genteel to do so, the men might talk tobacco while the women discussed something else entirely. In a family setting one could even be contentious, as when the Parke sisters, both matrons, "had a fierce dispute about the infallibility of the Bible."[85] A pattern of comparative equality between men and women is evident in dining room and drawing room conversations, even though gender distinctions were clearly defined and patriarchal supremacy was the rule.[86] Women were, after all, members of the inner circle; and in their social stature, they were joined by birth, wealth, political connections, and emotional relationships with their male counterparts.

Yet in at least one crucial way women were a class apart from and inferior to the male members of the great Tidewater gentry: women were barred from the classical education that, since it was a preparation for a public role, could only be a man's badge of gentility. A girl might be provided with a tutor like Fithian, but if she sought to learn Latin and Greek she was told "women ought not to know these things." Genteel education for women was limited to modern languages, arithmetic, needlework, and music.[87] In contrast it was classical learning that was the ultimate for achieving the status of an English gentleman. As one rich but only slightly educated Tidewater father told his sons at school in England, "how stinging is the [affliction?] when we fall into the Company of the learned, we cannot bear a part in the conversation for want of Learning."[88]

The extraordinary value of learning for establishing one's stature among the great gentry led Philip Fithian to report that in the Tidewater anyone bearing a degree from the College of New Jersey at Princeton "would be rated, without any more questions asked, either about your family, your Estate, your business, or your intention, at £10,000: and you might come, & go, & converse, & keep company according to this value; & you would be dispised & slighted if yo[u] rated yourself a farthing cheaper."[89] Fifthian, a Princeton graduate himself, was not boasting; he was astonished. At twenty-six he had no wealth and no position. As a would-be Presbyterian pastor his only assets were his education, his character, and a respectable family. Yet in spite of all this, and even with his obvious deficiencies in the arts of dancing, swordplay, and sociability, he was an eligible bachelor in the highest circle.[90] By the second half of the eighteenth century classical learning in the contemporary Augustan mode had become the sine qua non of gentility.

It was largely for this reason that the contents of Tidewater newspapers came to resemble the *Tatler* and the *Spectator* as repositories of essays and poetry rather that late news.[91] The gentry who patronized the press needed it less for news than as a stage on which they could display their learning and wit. The governor's councilors and the leaders of the House of Burgesses who, with their relatives and friends subscribed for most of the newspapers that were printed, learned about public affairs directly through participation or indirectly in letters and conversation. Their circles of trust, interconnected as they were with dozens of other circles, supplied urgent news more swiftly and reliably than newspapers could. The great gentry did not hurry to read their newspapers, whether English or American, when they arrived; they set them aside for when time allowed as leisure reading and, in Byrd's case, as background preparation before he visited Williamsburg for politics and socializing.

Yet if the newspapers were not urgent, they were nevertheless important in providing a forum for literary and political discussion and public recognition of rhetorical skills. The model of gentility that William Byrd followed early in the century, producing literary, political, and scientific essays, poetry, and even a few plays, appealed to the gentry for a long time. His works had circulated in manuscript and in London publications. But by mid-century, gazettes in Williamsburg and Annapolis provided a closer, more accessible platform. The seeds of polite English society that had been planted in the Tidewater at the beginning of the century and so assiduously cultivated for two generations, had sprouted and grown. Among the great gentry a genteel Anglo-Virginian culture was flourishing.[92]

This triumph of Tidewater gentility may be viewed in several ways. By the time that Thomas Jefferson—educated not in London, but in Williamsburg— was making his way in the 1750s and 1760s, it was certainly an objective phenomenon as compared with the sparse penetration of polite standards in the Tidewater of William Fitzhugh and Governor Francis Nicholson at the turn of the century.[93] Gentry society had risen to at least rural English standards. Yet the reality was less important than the way the great gentry viewed it. By the middle decades of the century their perspective had changed. Now established as the grandsons and great-grandsons of immigrants, they had shed the longing to return to England as more than tourists. Though the young, potentially downwardly mobile George Washington sought a career in the regular British army, wealthy young men were content with aspirations to rule the Virginia society that had become their pride.

It was under these circumstances that the Horatian model of gentility— once employed as an apologia for one's distance from the center of civilization—became transformed into the rural republican ideal. Now Virginia was viewed less as a retreat than as the center of a polished, learned, and purified society, free of the corruptions of the greatest extremes of wealth. England, once seen by Virginia gentlemen as the only place to educate young gentlemen, now became the worst place to educate them for anything but careers of extravagance and vice.[94] It was not thrift that led Robert Carter of Nomini Hall to hire a Princeton-trained Presbyterian tutor rather than an English one. Carter had his own Virginia priorities for learning, speech, and manners; he did not aim to make his sons and daughters merely English gentlemen and gentlewomen. He preferred that they become the best Virginia English.

By the 1770s, of course, the dream of English gentility was a casualty of imperial politics, and only loyalists—very scarce in the Tidewater—maintained it. Yet the ideal of the cultivated gentleman that was so important for the great gentry's identity survived. Now clad in the classical robes of Republican Rome, whence the ideal originally derived, Virginia became the new center of civilization. As a result the significance of information networks changed. The booming of guns over the Chesapeake had long signified the arrival of the British tobacco fleet; now the sound of guns announced the Declaration of Independence. Connections with England, once so highly prized as sources of political and cultural influence, now receded. In the the new order the communication networks that reached beyond the great gentry down through the lesser gentry and yeoman would be crucial. Learned cosmopolitanism, long the mark of the gentleman, would remain vital for the great gentry's image of itself. But whereas these qualities had always connected a gentleman to the sources of power in colonial Virginia, now emotional, popular rhetorical skills which could bond white people of all classes together—as exemplified by Patrick Henry—were more important.[95]

Their information networks had enabled the great gentry to meet the threat of rusticity that isolation from England had posed early in the century; but now they faced a far more difficult challenge of rusticity, a challenge to their own leadership. For a host of reasons they would not be so successful in resolving this threat. So long as the great gentry kept polite culture exclusive, the influence of boorish rustics would grow. But if they opened the doors of genteel sociability to all, they would lose it as a defining characteristic of their own class that made their rule legitimate. The problem really had no solution, though, if we are to judge by the school system he designed to pluck natural aristocrats from the masses in order to cultivate them with gentlemen's sons, Jefferson clearly understood it.[96] This scheme to retain the advantages of a learned, cosmopolitan ruling class might have solved the problem of planter rusticity in republican Virginia; but it was never tried because it lacked sufficient public support. In time the yeoman variant of the Horatian ideal would supplant that of the cultivated gentleman, and in political rhetoric rusticity would be viewed as more honorable than genteel learning. By 1840, when that scion of Virginia gentility, William Henry Harrison, was seeking the presidency, he would be represented not as a gentleman descended from gentlemen, but as a cider-drinking, log-cabin yeoman. And twenty years later he would be succeeded in the White House by a genuine son of the log-cabin yeomanry.

Chapter 3

Rural Clergymen
and the Communication Networks
of 18th-Century New England

Early in May 1770 a recent Yale graduate who was about to accept a call from the church at Danbury, Connecticut, reflected on his decision in a letter to his sister at home in Norwich:

> The Body of the People I fear are rather too close and contracted—tho' some Particular Gentlemen seem sufficiently liberal. The town is considerably large and Pleasant for a country Place. I expect you will tell me, whenever you come to see me, that the People are not genteel Eno', and that you wonder I would settle in such a Place where there are no more Gentlefolks. But Plain, honest, wealthy Farmers, I believe are generally the best People to a Minister—They are in general such kind of People as the old fashion folks at our End of the Town. . . . They are in general I believe a kind People in their Way. They don't seem altogether Agreeable at Present, but I trust I shall soon get used to them.[1]

Like literally hundreds of other 18th-century Yale and Harvard graduates who settled in rural parishes for the purpose of spreading the divine word as ministers of Christ, Ebenezer Baldwin had to adjust to his rustic community. After years at grammar school or under the tutelage of a local pastor, every clergyman had then gone on to more years at Cambridge or New Haven studying more Latin and Greek, in addition to theology and philosophy. Even though they were often no more than twenty-five years of age when they came to rural places like Danbury, they arrived as learned, cosmopolitan gentlemen, equipped not only to preach the gospel but also to serve as intermediaries between the New England cultural and political capitals where they had trained and the backwater parishes where they had now come to live.[2] Immediately, they entered a religious and secular fraternity of gentlemen, including not only the other clergy of the vicinity but the notables whose lands and trade as well as civil and military offices placed them in the first rank.

In most rural parishes the clergy occupied a special place in New England's communication system, and by their presence and stature exercised a significant influence on the passage of information into and within the community. In Massachusetts, for example, parish pulpits were seldom without a settled minister in the 18th century. Indeed fully 60 percent of the parishes enjoyed the services of a settled parson at least 90 percent of the time. Parishes that lacked a regular clergyman, those which were too divided or too poor to hire and retain a minister year-in and year-out, were few. Only 10 percent of Massachusetts parishes were vacant as much as 30 percent of the time. Since most vacancies were in small, relatively new churches, it is evident that the overwhelming majority of people spent their lives in communities where settled clergymen were ever present authorities.[3] The clerical role in the flow of information was enhanced because of its religious office and because, in some measure, the possession of knowledge itself was power. Although a rural minister's eminence derived from his office, his strategic location within the society's communication system augmented his power.

Historians of the American Revolution have understood the special power of the clergy for at least two generations. More than sixty years ago Alice M. Baldwin (herself a daughter and granddaughter of New England clergymen) emphasized the clergy's role in the patriot movement of the 1760s and 1770s. Taking her cue from the loyalist Peter Oliver's contemporary assessment of the decisive influence of the "black Regiment, the *dissenting Clergy*," Baldwin demonstrated that numerous clergymen were important advocates of revolutionary ideas in their pulpits and in print.[4] More recently Bernard Bailyn, Alan Heimert, and Harry S. Stout have called attention to the far-reaching influence of clergymen on communication in New England from the Great Awakening through the Revolutionary era.[5] In many respects the importance of the clergy for articulating and transmitting cultural ideals is widely accepted and understood.

Yet the actual extent of clerical influence, precisely where and how and why it operated, is more obscure. Biographies of particular clergymen, from Connecticut's Thomas Clap and Ezra Stiles to Massachusetts' Charles Chauncy, John Cleaveland, Samuel Cooper, and Ebenezer Gay, illumine the subject considerably, as do several works on the New England clergy as a whole.[6] Yet by tracing the activities of some actual clergymen "on the ground," as they went about their daily, weekly, yearly business, still more can be gleaned about their place in the communication systems of their localities and in New England at large during the 18th century.

Peter Oliver, the chief justice of Massachusetts' highest court who was displaced by the Revolution, was convinced that the clergy were the heart of the communication system and that they were ruinously uninformed. In one disgusted outburst he declared that New England ministers were "as ignorant as the People."[7] On this point Oliver was surely exaggerating to the point of error. Although one can be both ignorant and possess a college degree—even one from Harvard or Yale—Oliver's claim is absurd. For in rural New England the 18th-century pastor was normally the only college graduate in the parish, and he possessed an extensive network of extra-local connections.

The most important of these extra-local connections can be broadly defined as professional, and derived from participation in ministerial associations and networks of college alumni. By mid-century most clergymen were part of county or sub-county ministerial associations where anywhere from four to a dozen fellow clerics gathered on a monthly or bi-monthly basis to consult with one another on points of theology, discipline, church management, or to assess candidates for vacant pulpits. Usually these were also distinct gatherings of either Harvard alumni or Yale alumni, though in the Connecticut Valley and in New London County there were almost even numbers of Harvard and Yale graduates by 1740.[8] Indeed as of that year analysis of the distribution of clergymen according to college affiliation reveals significant geographic patterns that influenced communication networks.

Although 64 percent of all clergymen in 1740 were Harvard graduates, there were parts of New England where the Cambridge network was weak or non-existent (see map no. 1). Yale graduates, who comprised only 24 percent of the total, dominated the westernmost tier of counties running in a band northward from New Haven and Fairfield through Litchfield County in Connecticut and Berkshire County in Massachusetts. Here there were 51 Yale graduates settled, and only 8 from Harvard. In Rhode Island, with its independent Baptist origins, neither the Cambridge nor New Haven networks were strong, as non-degree-holding preachers dominated. Clerics like Newport's Ezra Stiles, who possessed a wide array of correspondents throughout New England and beyond, were exceptional. In the Rhode Island countryside local laymen handled most preaching and, partly for this reason, most Rhode Islanders remained outside the web of clerical connections and awareness. Also, their colony was accorded scant attention by the majority of rural New Englanders who never traded through Rhode Island, had no family there, and lived at a distance.[9]

The pulpits of eastern and northern New England, by contrast, were filled overwhelmingly by Harvard graduates. The Cambridge connection dominated a long, broad arc running from Cape Cod north and west through Worcester County and beyond into New Hampshire and Maine. In addition the northeast corner of Connecticut, Windham County, which had been settled largely by migrants from Essex County in Massachusetts, was a Harvard bastion. These patterns, established as they were by patterns of migration and

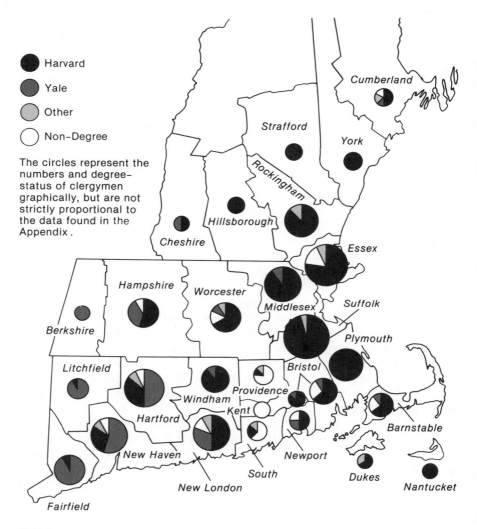

The circles represent the numbers and degree-status of clergymen graphically, but are not strictly proportional to the data found in the Appendix.

The information on which this map is based is tabulated in the Appendix.

the influence of doctrinal leanings, as well as the inertia of long-lived incumbents, changed only gradually in the middle decades of the century.

By 1770, a generation after the Great Awakening and on the eve of the Colonies' independence, significant changes had occurred (see map no. 2). The overall incidence of Harvard graduates had declined, from 64 percent to 47 percent, while the Yale-affiliated clergy had grown, from 24 to 34 percent of the total. Equally striking was the substantial increase in non-degree clergy, usually Baptists, who rose from 8 to 12 percent of the total, as well as

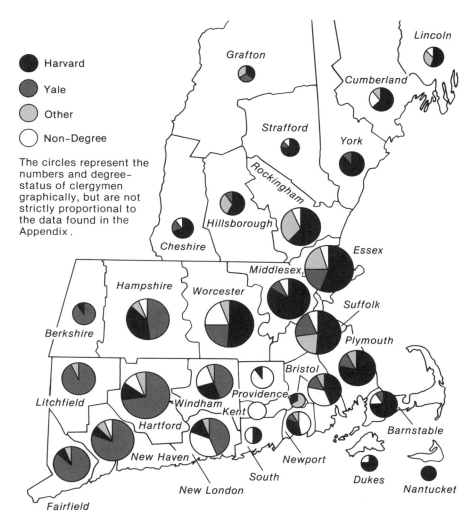

The circles represent the numbers and degree-status of clergymen graphically, but are not strictly proportional to the data found in the Appendix.

Harvard
Yale
Other
Non-Degree

Lincoln

Grafton

Cumberland

Strafford

York

Rockingham

Hillsborough

Cheshire

Essex

Middlesex

Hampshire

Worcester

Suffolk

Berkshire

Plymouth

Litchfield

Windham

Bristol

Providence

Kent

Hartford

Barnstable

New Haven

Newport

South

Dukes

New London

Nantucket

Fairfield

The information on which this map is based is tabulated in the Appendix.

the increase from 4 to 7 percent in degree holders from other colleges. What was most evident was that Yale had assumed a dominant place throughout Connecticut and in the Connecticut Valley in Massachusetts. Elsewhere the Harvard network remained, but with a notable presence of Yale graduates, so that there were New Haven connections to every Massachusetts county, four of the five New Hampshire counties, and York County in southern Maine. Equally significant, Baptist congregations, though still centered in Rhode Island, were now found in substantial numbers in bordering areas of eastern Connecticut and Massachusetts, and were scattered widely through most of New England.

Though it is impossible to measure precisely the importance of college alumni networks for communication, their existence warrants attention. As time went on, the expansion of the Yale network came to overlap Harvard's so that, wherever clergymen were doctrinally congenial, the two networks became interwoven. Indeed by the time of the Revolution, Cambridge/New Haven networks crisscrossed all of New England, except in Baptist enclaves.

Their operation was most visible in association meetings that were often de facto alumni clubs, and in the ceremonies that grew out of annual election days and college commencements. These latter events commonly drew clergymen back to their alma maters in Cambridge and New Haven. Shared participation in public ceremonies and in formal and informal dinners renewed ties to the faculty and their alumni brethren. In the cosmopolitan environment of the election and commencement festivities, not only oratory but conversation flourished. Moreover few clergymen would return home without visiting the shop of a merchant who stocked books and periodicals. Finally, when they departed after two, three, four days or even a week, the journey usually began in the company of several colleagues who conversed as they traveled on foot and on horseback. For those whose travel spanned more than one day, the homes of clergymen along the route often furnished lodgings. Such face-to-face professional connections, reinforced as they were by alumni bonds, enabled rural clergymen settled in confined parish locales, to participate in an extensive, cosmopolitan, regional network.

One measure of this participation was the authorship of published sermons during the 18th century. When one considers the period 1740–1799, for Massachusetts, the distribution of authors' home parishes is remarkably scattered throughout the province (see map no. 3). The greatest concentration was, as one would expect, in the long-settled, densely ministered eastern parishes located within thirty miles of Boston. And yet in every decade there were publications from authors who dwelled in small communities fifty or even one hundred miles from Boston. It appears that publications generally reflected population density, the number of parishes, and the length of their settlement—rather than the influence of location per se on access to the press. Over the decades this record indicates that the professional networks that extended across New England effectively integrated rural clergy with their professional counterparts in urban centers.

Family relationships within the clerical profession embedded some clergymen within these networks even more deeply. Even though it appears that during the 18th century a majority of clergy had no living clerical relatives, a substantial number had one or two, and about five percent had three or more colleagues in their own or their in-laws' families.[10] Because these clerical clans—families like the Cottons, the Shaws and the Williamses—often possessed at least one centrally located, prominent member, their

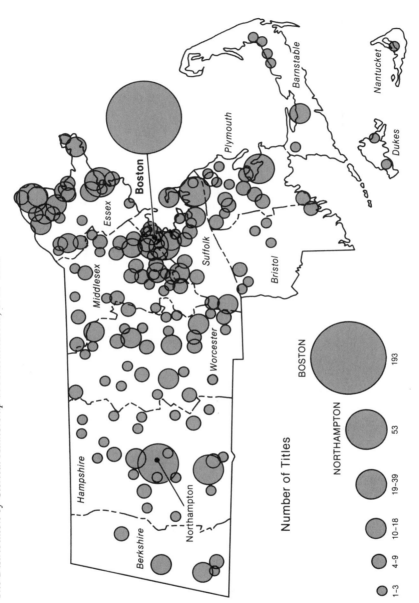

The Distribution of Clerical Authorship in Massachusetts, 1740–1799

Barnstable

Nantucket

Plymouth

Dukes

Boston

Essex

Suffolk

Middlesex

Bristol

Worcester

Hampshire

Northampton

Berkshire

Number of Titles

BOSTON

NORTHAMPTON

193   53   19–39   10–18   4–9   1–3

communication networks were even more active and extensive than the rest of their clerical brethren. Yet even the growing number of pastors who sprang from unlettered families—those whose fathers, uncles, brothers, and in-laws were all farmers and tradesmen—possessed extra-local connections that most of their parishioners lacked, because scarcely any ministers were natives of the parishes they served. Often coming from distant counties, like the Norwich native Ebenezer Baldwin who went from Yale to Danbury, they retained family as well as professional connections that connected them to wider communication networks.

In addition to these extra-local professional and family relationships, the pastor entertained out-of-town visitors several times each month, made visits within the town and beyond it routinely, periodically exchanged pulpits with neighboring colleagues, and traveled outside the county far more than virtually all his parishioners. Moreover, because of the clergy's sense of being out "in the wilderness," they actively sought to make themselves informed.[11] Visits to nearby gentry, militia officers, merchants, and justices of the peace who were returning from travels, as well as the exchange of books and magazines, even newspapers, were commonly part of the effort to remain informed and to escape their "Seclusion" and "Retirement" "when under Confinement to so narrow a Sphere of motion," as Ebenezer Parkman noted.[12] Parkman, who was a Boston native, visited his relatives and attended conventions and commencements almost every year. Each time, he returned to Westborough in Worcester County with books as well as a store of news from the metropolis. By mid-century a visitor to his study reported he possessed "a Collection of Books not inferior to the best in the hands of Any Country Minister."[13] Timothy Walker, who settled on the New Hampshire frontier in 1729, made repeated trips to Boston carrying news back and forth, news which sometimes related directly to the military security of his rural outpost. During the 1750s and 1760s Walker even journeyed to England three times on behalf of his community when his parishioners' land titles were threatened by the Portsmouth government. Admittedly Walker's travels were unique for a rural minister and Parkman's library was unusual, but to assert that the clergy were "as ignorant as the People" is to argue that their exceptional reading, correspondence, visiting, travel, and professional connections were of no consequence.[14]

What Oliver meant, surely, was not that the clergy were literally as ignorant as common folk, but that they were ignorant of politics and thus readily "duped" by a handful of Whig radicals.[15] Here partisanship ruled Oliver's judgment. Rural clergymen could not have access to the same information that was available to their Boston counterparts; nor did their calling encourage the intense preoccupation with politics that royal public officials like Peter Oliver, Thomas Hutchinson, and their Whig adversaries shared. Yet clerics did seek to be politically informed—especially in wartime—by reading newspapers, by hobnobbing with the county gentry at militia training

New England Clergyman

Ebenezer Devotion, a rural Connecticut pastor who was a contemporary of the clergy-men discussed here, personifies the ideal of the patriarchal minister whose authority is fortified by learning. The library that serves as backdrop includes over fifty bound volumes and more than a dozen pamphlets. Spine titles identify books of sermons, Biblical commentaries, and a Hebrew text, in addition to works in history, philosophy, science, law, and belles-lettres. Particularly striking is the representation of the books which are in the disarray of active use—in the pastor's hand, on the table, and in the upper shelves of the bookcase. A clergyman was expected to use his books, not display them as ornamental, leather-bound status symbols.

Courtesy of Brookline Historical Society, Brookline, Mass.

days, and by interrogating travelers. If few of them were adequately informed according to Peter Oliver's standard, it was because New England's
information flow was dominated by Whigs. One senses this particularly in
the case of a parson like John Ballantine, whose parish at Westfield in the
Connecticut River Valley had a connection to the royal administration via
the magnates of the region, the "River Gods." Ballantine himself was well-
disposed toward Governor Hutchinson and his associates, but he came to
understand events in Whig terms partly because so much of his news came to
him through Benjamin Edes and John Gill's vigorously pro-Whig *Boston
Gazette*.[16] The option of selecting a newspaper according to its editorial
stance was a luxury available to few rural ministers.

Oliver decried the "black Regiment" repeatedly, attributing vast importance to the dissenting clergy because, he said, they were "the Oracles of
their parishes."[17] Alice Baldwin collected a substantial record of their public
sermons in print and from local histories, and she identified fully sixty members of New England's black regiment.[18] This is a large number, but it is
important to note that it is less than 10 percent of the college-trained orthodox clergy as of the single year 1770 alone.[19] Considering all the clergy who
served in New England during the period for which Baldwin compiled data
(1750–1790), it appears that fewer than 5 percent of New England's clergy
left a record of public speeches on behalf of either Whig or Tory politics.
Under these circumstances one must wonder just how numerous the black
regiment actually was, and whether the power and influence of the clergy
truly made them parish oracles. Here any blanket assertion is likely to
mislead. Had the question been put to the clergymen in person, and a
comparison drawn with their 17th-century predecessors, their answer one
supposes would have been a resounding "No," since the decline in clerical
stature and influence was such a persistent element in both their experience
and their rhetoric.[20] Still, if one allows for some exaggeration on Oliver's
part, his assessment cannot be dismissed. Among the hundreds of rural
parishes there were some in which a clergyman's standing was so awesome
that his judgments could be decisive. There were a few towns like Lexington
where it was said that the Reverend Jonas Clark led the community into the
Revolution.

Timothy Walker of Concord, New Hampshire, was just such a person as
late as the 1770s. Walker, who had come to the fledgling settlement at the age
of twenty-four in 1729, had become a patriarch of near legendary stature.
Early in his tenure he had organized the defense of the little community
against Indians from his home inside a log palisade. Later, as already noted,
he went to England to arrange a successful legal defense against rival land
claimants. Personally, Walker was not only a spiritual guide but also the man
to whom his neighbors turned for business advice and to draft their legal
documents. Community ritual signified Walker's position: at the meetinghouse it became the congregation's custom to stand while Walker passed

down the aisle in his large powdered wig, bowing to his people left and right after morning and afternoon services. When Revolutionary New Hampshire created a Provincial Congress in 1775, Concord voters elected Parson Walker to represent them.[21] In the person of their venerable clergyman, Concord people found the embodiment of a patriarchal leader whose authority stood unchallenged. Walker was surely a kind of oracle.

It must have been such a colonel in the black regiment that Oliver was describing when he claimed,

> I knew a Clergyman, of some Note, in a Country Town, who went to the Meeting House where ye Inhabitants usually assembled upon their civil Affairs, & took his Seat at the Communion table; & in the Plenitude of priestly Power, declared to the Assembly then convened on the solemn League & Covenant [a patriot boycott] that whoever would not subscribe to it was not fit to approach that Table to commemorate the Death & Sufferings of the Savior of Mankind.[22]

Whether Walker or any New England clergyman actually did what Oliver alleged is uncertain; but it is not inconceivable. Some of them were awesome figures; as one of Walker's own parishioners reportedly declared: "Parson Walker was the only man the Almighty ever made that he was afraid of."[23]

Yet Timothy Walker's standing in his parish in the 1770s was scarcely typical. His contemporary Ebenezer Parkman had settled in Westborough, another frontier parish, at about the same time, but, though he expected to rule his people and to command their deference as a matter of course, he never quite succeeded.[24] When the townspeople built a new meetinghouse in the 1740s, they located it a mile away from Parkman's house, making it impossible, he believed, for him to eat dinner at home in between morning and afternoon services. No one invited him to dine, so Parkman ended up haggling in the town-meeting over whether the town would provide an allowance or reimbursement for his dinners.[25] Later, in 1775, Parkman would fight a losing battle to uphold his veto on actions of the church.[26] During the Revolutionary crisis, the freemen of Westborough spurned their parson's leadership because Parkman, though a Whig, was too cautious and too loyal. After fifty years in the parish Parkman found he was shepherd to an independent flock, and that his own position and security, even his supply of firewood, depended on his willingness to accept secular Whig oracles and accommodate his own views to those of the majority in his parish.[27]

Parkman was a learned, widely-connected clergyman who was, to judge from his reading and correspondence, no less cosmopolitan than Walker, though he had never ventured beyond New England. He had, back in the 1760s, purchased a copy of Montesquieu's *Spirit of the Laws* and had studied Bishop Hoadly's political writings to prepare for a parish sermon on the Stamp Act.[28] Moreover, like most clergymen, he occupied a central social position in Westborough's communication system. Parkman called on his parishioners regularly, visited and prayed with the sick, officiated at weddings, baptisms, and funerals, and dined with the gentry. Standing in the pulpit he read public proclamations, called for charitable contributions for disaster victims and the poor, and asked prayers for people who had special needs. Many years later a Maine villager recalled that his own minister's "long prayer was always interesting. For in it he told the congregation, through his address to the Almighty, the village news with great particularity. That prayer served all the purposes of a local newspaper. From it we learned of those who during the preceding week had been married, who were sick, who had died, who had gone on a journey, who had gone to college or come back from college."[29] Parkman, even more than the Maine cleric, was an intermediary between the people of Westborough and news of the world beyond its borders because his learning and connections beyond the parish as well as within it were so extensive. Yet he was not, like Walker, his town's patriarch or its oracle.

If there were, as Oliver claimed, some oracles—perhaps Walker, Jonas Clark at Lexington, John Cleaveland in Chebacco, as well as a handful of powerful loyalist clergymen who with their allies slowed the Whig juggernaut for a time—most clergymen held their power more tenuously and in accordance with the wishes of those "Plain, honest, wealthy Farmers . . . the old fashion folks" that Ebenezer Baldwin knew in Danbury.[30] During the Revolutionary era New England's 700 or so rural clergymen generally agreed with and accepted their parishes' views on imperial politics. They were, moreover, far more concerned about spiritual than political salvation. Later, as the war dragged on, the maintenance of their salaries in cash and in kind became a chronic preoccupation. Despite clergymen's hopeful rhetoric, few ever achieved the oracular status of patriarchs. Mostly they were paid guides, hired to help their employers along the path to salvation.

Justus Forward, the Yale graduate who had settled as a young man in the Hampshire County, Massachusetts, community of Belchertown in 1756, seems representative of most rural clergy in that his political concerns were subordinate to his pastoral ones. Less learned than Parkman, he was described by an acquaintance as "pre-eminently a matter-of-fact man."[31] Forward was an evangelical and a Whig who spent most of his time attending to the spiritual and physical well-being of his people—he was a self-taught, unpaid physician—in addition to managing and laboring on his own farm. Forward, like Parkman and nearly every other rural clergyman often interacted with his people in informal, unofficial ways. On one January day he noted routinely: "A N[umbe]r of my Parishioners about 25 gave me a spell of Chopping wood, cut up about half my wood. I made them a supper."[32] Like most, Forward was a reasonably talkative person whose days were filled with a succession of conversations as he went about his duties and chores. Routine conversations brought him news, as "from a Traveler [who] came to my House August 3d & Confirms the Account of the Fort [possibly Ticonderoga] . . . being in possession of the English," news which Forward then conveyed to others.[33] The need to confirm information before giving it credence or passing it on was an ordinary part of his critical judgment. When Forward received the "important and Interesting News of the Reduction of Havannah—of a Victory gained over the French by Prince Ferdinand—[and] of a Victory over a spanish Fleet by admiral saunders—the spanish Fleet [included] 10 sail of the Line of which twas reported saunders took 8, sunk one & one escaped," he *went on to note* that "this last Acc[oun]t, viz. of sanders proved not True."[34] As a responsible official he expected to weigh and assess the information he received, since "Pieces of News proved false" sometimes.[35] Impressing parishioners with the need to exercise similar caution was part of a minister's role. *"Give not an easy Credit to all Reports,"* a Stoughton, Massachusetts pastor admonished: "Nothing is more uncertain than common Report. It seldom speaks true; and when there is some Truth in it, it is often so adulterated with the Mixture of Falshood with it, that it is difficult to know which part to believe."[36] For this reason clergy such as Forward were especially vital intermediaries. They were recognized as discerning judges of truth and falsehood who possessed a high level of credibility.

During the Revolutionary War they used their pulpits for state and national proclamations. Proclamations of fast days and thanksgiving had a long history. Forward, for example, had led his people in giving thanks for victories in the French and Indian War; and in 1766, shortly after receiving a letter from fellow Yale alumnus Ezra Stiles, " 'congratulating you and my Country on the Repeal of the Stamp Act,' " Forward noted that, though "I had no Proclamation, but however Invited my People last sabbath to attend [a thanksgiving service]—accordingly most did."[37] Now, however, Justus Forward took to reading pronouncements of the legislature and the Continental Congress completely on his own. On May 31, 1778, for example, he concluded his sermon on a text from Jonah, and then went on to "read a Address of Congress to the people which came in Tuesday paper—made no Observations upon it."[38] As time went on Forward used his pulpit more and more in this fashion. He was no oracle, and he did not lead his parish off to battle, but he did use his influence on behalf of causes he approved.

The most striking example of Forward's exerting political leadership came during Shays's Rebellion. In August 1786, Belchertown selected Forward as its delegate to the county convention at Hatfield, and he attended for three days. He was sympathetic to the reform movement but rejected military action and opposed the closing of the court at Northampton "by a Large Mob."[39] Thereafter "the mob Party," as Forward described it, gained control of the town meeting, laid in military supplies, and selected more aggressive delegates to the November county convention. In response, the Belchertown church met and "judged the late risings in this county against Government, . . . [and] against . . . gospel rule." Forward himself "talked with Converse, one of the insurgents; he did not appear convinced."[40] In early December as "our Militia seemed eager to go" join in stopping the courts, Forward "made a speech to them persuading them to be quiet and rest the Matter with Governments and Rulers." A week later Forward read publicly the General Court's address to the inhabitants of Massachusetts, a mixture of conciliation, admonition, and defense of the government that "Took an Hour." Within the week the same address was read at the town meeting, and Forward took the message to the leaders of the "mob Party" personally in an effort to convince them to take the oath of allegiance and obtain amnesty.[41] In all of this Forward employed his clerical office and his role in the community's communication network to blunt his town's radicalism.

Thereafter he seems to have assumed a less partisan role. In 1802, for example, after reading a public thanksgiving proclamation, he went on to read a report from the Missionary Society and then "invited our people to contribute."[42] He even lived long enough to read a "Continental Fast Proclamation from President Madison" at the outset of the War of 1812.[43] Forward was by this time an avid student of foreign affairs via the newspapers. Though he was critical of Madison's policies and under no compulsion to read his proclamation, he did so because he believed it was his duty to inform the parish on public as well as religious matters.

Justus Forward's use of the pulpit in this way was becoming anachronistic by the second decade of the 19th century. Ironically, in light of Peter Oliver's and Alice Baldwin's emphasis, the Revolution undermined the authority of most rural clergymen and left them more insecure and less influential than ever before. During the 1780s and 1790s clergymen themselves bemoaned their reduced stature, and with good reason. A few retained positions of influence, but their profession and the ground rules through which it operated were changing. Though Justus Forward was able to retain his veto in church affairs as late as 1797, many clergy had lost their veto, as had Ebenezer Parkman over twenty years earlier.[44] The security of settled tenure, a bulwark of clerical self-confidence, collapsed as parishes secured the right to dismiss their ministers. The turnover of clergymen in pulpits everywhere mounted sharply, and the pattern of twenty, thirty, and even fifty years of service to a single parish that had characterized Walker, Parkman, Cleaveland, and Forward became a rare exception rather than the norm among the generation of clergymen who began their pastoral careers after 1780.[45] The sources and character of clerical authority were changing in post-Revolutionary society. Their sphere of influence, like their role as intermediaries in the New England communication system, became narrower and more specialized.

Why this was so is a complicated, many-sided story. Changes within religion leading to disestablishment and vigorous denominational competition altered the foundation on which a clergyman's authority rested within a rural community. Developments in agriculture, commerce, and manufacturing made the solitary farming pastor in a farming town a thing of the past, while the stratification of rural society became more complex. Merchants, physicians, and lawyers, often college-educated, multiplied rapidly in the New England countryside, becoming rivals to the clergy as sources of general information. In Massachusetts as a whole, clergymen had constituted 70 percent of all learned professionals in 1740, and much more outside of Boston and the port towns; but even though their absolute numbers had doubled by 1800, they now represented only 45 percent of learned professionals. Lawyers, almost unknown in 1740, became substantially more numerous than clergymen by 1820, and emerged as the leading class of public officials and community spokesmen.[46] Republican politics, built around electoral competition and calling for an informed citizenry, thrust lawyers forward, and the clergy were confined to specialized denominational subjects and moral reform. The situation Lyman Beecher found in 1798 when he settled in a remote parish on the eastern tip of Long Island he recognized as unusual; "The people are peaceable. Not a lawyer in the whole country. Industrious, hospitable; in the habit of being influenced by their minister."[47] This was what Baldwin had found at Danbury a generation earlier, and what Parkman, Walker, Ballantine, Cleaveland, Forward, and hundreds of others had found in their parishes from the 1720s through the 1760s.

But by 1800 times had changed almost everywhere, and especially in southern New England. Where Forward had been his town's part-time physician, Walker his town's part-time lawyer, and all of them part-time tutors in Latin and Greek as well as part-time farmers, now professional specialists took over. Public grammar schools, rarities in the pre-Revolutionary countryside, were increasingly augmented by private academies in every county after the Revolution. The gentry no longer sent their sons to study with the parson, and the principals of the new academies emerged as further rivals to the clergy as authoritative sources of information. Even more important, newspapers penetrated the countryside as never before. Only a dozen years after Timothy Walker became the first newspaper subscriber in Concord, New Hampshire, in 1778, a printer began publishing a paper in Walker's own parish, and two years after that a second printer and a rival paper came to town.[48] Throughout New England printers and newspapers multiplied at a geometric rate after 1780, spreading to dozens of towns by 1820. In addition, where the minister's library had often been the only library in town, now village library associations sprang up—forty-two were formed in Massachusetts during the 1790s. Post offices, which were closely related to electoral politics and printing, had been unknown in rural New England before the Revolution, but by 1820 there were 443 of them in Massachusetts alone.[49] A new communication network was emerging in which clergymen, while still important, played a narrower, less authoritative role. Where they had once been central figures in New England's rural communication network, screening and spreading a wide spectrum of secular as well as religious information from their unique position of parish eminence, now local clergymen became denominational partisans and pastors to their parishes in a restricted sense.

In the 1790s, Federalists pressed the orthodox clergy into service as allies in an increasingly desperate partisan effort to shore up the political and religious establishment. Similarly the Massachusetts Medical Society and the Massachusetts Society for Promoting Agriculture would seek to draw on the clergy's communication network to advance their programs.[50] These efforts were fruitful for a time, but their long-range consequence was to encourage the reduction of clerical influence in secular affairs. In parish after parish the authoritative clergyman like Walker was succeeded by someone who appeared to be more an advocate than an authority. His voice might command attention but seldom deference, unless he was addressing a sectarian audience on a subject promoting denominational identity. David Daggett, one of the new breed of Federalist lawyer-politicians and the nephew of a Yale president and clergyman, offered a capsule analysis of what was happening in a remarkably ambivalent Independence Day oration in 1787. Before the Revolution, Daggett claimed,

> This state, and many others, were under a most perfect aristocracy.—The name we truly disowned, yet quietly submitted to a government essentially aristocratic.—
>
> The minister, with two or three principal characters were supreme in each town.— Hence the body of the clergy, with a few families of distinction, between whom there was ever a most intimate connection, in effect, ruled the whole state. The loss of this happy influence of the clergy, in this country, is deeply to be regretted, and is to be ascribed to two causes—the increase of knowledge, and growing opposition to religion.—Knowledge has induced the laity to think and act for themselves, and an opposition to religion has curtailed the power of its supporters.[51]

As one-sided and incomplete as Daggett's assessment was, he did capture something essential in what was happening. For if a minister's role had not been quite as decisive in the 1760s and 1770s as Peter Oliver claimed and Alice M. Baldwin subsequently sought to prove, it had been uniquely important and influential in rural villages. The clergy had indeed occupied an unrivaled position as interpreters of events and as intermediaries between their villages and the events and culture beyond the parish. The revolution which they supported, however, was a catalyst promoting a political and social transformation that would in time destroy their special role as authoritative intermediaries.

When the new century opened, the clergymen of most country towns were not rooted in their parishes for life. They were no longer authorities to be consulted on every subject, nor were they regarded as the best source of information about the world beyond the township. Instead they had become denominational advocates, often temporary in residence, whose ambitions were larger than living out their lives saving souls in one small parish. As one

Andover student put it: "I hope to become a good writer and thus I can do good on a greater scale; for the press is becoming the great engine for moving the world."[52] No matter where he found his first pulpit he could use the press—always accessible to clergymen, and now with the emergence of denominational presses becoming more available than ever—to publish his way up and out in the manner of a Lyman Beecher. Where locally-patronized occasional publications had once served to consolidate a clergyman's stature in his parish, now publication was becoming a means of escape. As communities were no longer committed to a single clergyman, so ambitious parsons like Beecher were no longer committed to a single parish. Their learning and public oratory were now being compared to secular rivals, and common people enjoyed independent access to information through the press. When a minister excelled at public oratory, as was the case with Lyman Beecher, he soon departed his obscure country parish and began climbing the professional ladder to ever more prestigious, influential, and lucrative posts. More often clergymen made lesser moves within their denomination's array of missionary, teaching, publishing, and pastoral positions. From the standpoint of the New England communication system their particular movements made little difference, since their role in the diffusion of information had largely receded within sectarian boundaries. In time, as the Second Great Awakening took hold, there were important exceptions—great revivalists as well as local clergymen who reached beyond their own denomination by advocating reforms like temperance and abolition. But the public would never again adopt the old deferential ways. Now informed by abundant newspapers, periodicals, and books in addition to lawyers, physicians, schoolmasters, and politicans, the "Body of the People" that Ebenezer Baldwin spoke of were no longer "too close and contracted." Instead, their "knowledge" had indeed encouraged them "to think and act for themselves."

Chapter 4

Lawyers, Public Office, and Communication Patterns in Provincial Massachusetts: The Early Careers of Robert Treat Paine and John Adams, 1749–1774

When the Continental Congress met at Philadelphia in 1774, nearly half its members were lawyers. Thirteen years later, the majority of delegates to the Constitutional Convention were lawyers. Thereafter, as the new government took shape, lawyers figured prominently in all its branches. Massachusetts, which had sent the lawyers Robert Treat Paine and John Adams to the first Continental Congress, increasingly turned to the law profession for representatives, so much so that during the first fifty years of the new government (1789–1839) nearly two thirds of Massachusetts' congressional delegates were lawyers.[1] In the early republic men trained in law were evidently highly regarded as public officials, not only as judges but especially as representatives.

From a 20th-century perspective it may seem obvious that this should have been so. Nothing could be more rational than to put experts in charge of creating legislation, and no policy could be more prudent than to place specialists trained to understand those statutes in charge of their administration and enforcement. Yet such judgments presume a great deal, not only about lawyers but about their reputation for probity and faithfulness in pursuing the public interest. From the perspective of provincial Massachusetts the idea that lawyers should be entrusted with a preeminent role in public affairs was doubtful. This outcome resulted from the parts certain lawyers played within Massachusetts' particular configuration of information networks—local and provincial, and networks within and between social ranks.

Before the Revolutionary era lawyers were few, confined to Boston, and they seldom held any public office. From the colony's founding and for a century thereafter, no practicing lawyer was ever elected to the General Court; and after one was elected in 1738, twenty years passed before an attorney was again elected.[2] Even within the judiciary, where legal expertise might be most highly valued, trained lawyers were rarities.[3] Colonial and provincial magistrates were usually drawn from the ranks of land-owning gentlemen and farmers and from among the merchant elite, men who were well-connected to their constituencies.

Lawyers, who had never been welcome in the Puritan colony, were widely viewed with suspicion. Indeed no occupation or profession was so generally mistrusted in colonial tradition as lawyers, who were frequently berated along with usurers as parasites who preyed on their neighbors and society at large. Their emergence as a small but significant professional group dates from the 1730s. Even after the expansion of commerce created jobs and legitimacy for the legal profession, it was widely seen as a necessary evil rather than a positive good. To the degree that lawyers gained prestige and recognition during the mid-18th century—and they did—their enhanced stature was not connected to any noticeable shift in the Yankee Puritan outlook, but was rather the result of the increasing Anglicization of the upper reaches of Massachusetts society through connections with royal government and English trade.[4] During the Revolution most lawyers remained loyal to the Crown; and many abandoned republican Massachusetts in 1775–76.[5]

Yet this exodus, particularly of senior Boston and Salem lawyers, in what one scholar calls "one of the strangest paradoxes of early American history," did not stigmatize the profession as a whole, and it was to lawyers that the public increasingly turned for leadership. Even though most prominent lawyers had come down on the Tory side, there were others, often younger men, who had established outstanding republican credentials in the 1760s—James Otis, Joseph Hawley, Oxenbridge Thatcher, Robert Treat Paine, and John Adams among them. Ever since the Stamp Act resistance in 1765, the Revolutionary movement had thrust lawyers into major political roles.[6] Their rise from sufferance to prominence was already underway.

The connection between the Revolution and this emergence of lawyers was noted by observers even before the French visitor Tocqueville remarked upon it in the 1830s.[7] Usually their prominence has been seen as a logical consequence of their technical knowledge and their role in the rapidly expanding commercial activity of a growing economy. Men in no other occupation, it has been assumed, were so well suited to drafting constitutions and statutes once the British system was cast off. The fact that lawyers served as spokesmen and agents of merchants in a commercially oriented society gave their political leadership a powerful foundation.

But it is important to remember that in the new republic leadership rested as much on popularity as expertise, and anti-lawyer sentiment did not die in

1776 or 1787. In Massachusetts, lawyers were prominent targets of Shays's Rebellion, and anti-lawyer speeches rallied anti-Federalists at the Constitutional Convention in 1788.[8] As a class, lawyers served as convenient targets of popular distress in the early republic. Still, rhetoric notwithstanding, individual lawyers with local connections were elected to office repeatedly.[9]

Among the chief reasons people came to know and to support attorneys in politics was their unique placement, social and regional, in 18th-century Massachusetts communication networks. Learned and articulate, lawyers were also known to be informed about public affairs beyond parish and township boundaries. Moreover as politics based on paternalistic leadership faded, it was lawyers—more than clergymen, merchants, landed gentlemen, or yeomen—who were publicly on view as shrewd, knowledgeable agents and advocates. In light of the prevailing social ethos that idealized union and harmony, the ethos that normally guided clergymen and town officers alike, lawyers were exceptional because they were free to assert a new political role as public advocates.[10] For them, engaging in conflict violated no cherished values; it was a routine, calculated exercise. Since controversy was their business, they came to appear as appropriate agents to defend community interests as the conflict with Britain grew.[11]

Robert Treat Paine and John Adams were two lawyers who came to assume such roles. Their careers from the time they graduated from Harvard College in 1749 and 1755, respectively, until the Massachusetts General Court selected them to serve as delegates to the Continental Congress in 1774, illustrate how, as lawyers, these two brilliant young men came to emerge as central public figures in the oldest, largest, and most influential New England colony. In both cases their places as lawyers in the communication networks of the province and their towns and counties account substantially for their political prominence.

Though Paine and Adams both had kinfolk scattered through New England as a consequence of their ancestors' arrival during the Great Migration of the 1630s, neither built his career on the strength of powerful connections or family wealth. And while neither man began life poor, they were both self-made men who climbed by calculating their advancement and exploiting their opportunities. For both of them family support for a Harvard college education launched their journeys into the first rank of Massachusetts and national leadership. Yet how Paine and Adams came to Harvard, and how they achieved recognition and power were not foreordained. Law, for Robert Treat Paine, became a means for halting the downward slide of his family's fortunes, while for John Adams the law supplied a ladder upward from his respectable but modest origins. Their choice of law and their means of pursuing it reveal how the unique position of lawyers in provincial information networks enabled them to achieve legitimacy and recognition as political leaders in Massachusetts.

Robert Treat Paine was the son of a Harvard-trained clergyman, Thomas Paine, who resigned from his Weymouth pulpit in the 1730s to become a Boston merchant. By the time "Treat," as he was then called, was ready for college, at age fourteen, in 1745, his father's ventures were prospering. On paper, at least, Thomas Paine was worth tens of thousands of pounds: he owned ships, land, a Boston mansion, and a few domestic slaves. At Harvard, Treat's social status, which was enhanced by his father's college degree and wealth as well as his mother's descent from the 17th-century Connecticut Governor Robert Treat, placed him ninth among twenty-five new students. Had Thomas Paine's business continued to thrive it appears that Treat would also have become a merchant. But owing to the hazards of shipping during King George's war and post-war credit, Treat's father was deeply in debt by his senior year. Consequently Robert Treat Paine left Harvard in 1749 with the tastes and expectations of a rich man's son but without the means of satisfying them. He would have to make a career from scratch.[12]

Before deciding what to do, he took the job that was open to any impecunious college graduate as a stopgap—that of schoolmaster in a remote country town, in this case Lunenburg, forty miles northwest of Boston. Being a schoolmaster in central Massachusetts was no career for an ambitious college graduate, and, predictably, Paine soon grew restless with the social isolation it entailed. Yet Paine's first reaction to his new role, his amused gratification at suddenly becoming a learned authority among country people who valued information highly, gives an inkling of his future as a lawyer-statesman. Simply by being learned and informed he acquired instant celebrity at Lunenburg. Boarding at the home of a militia officer he reported, "in the evning great numbers of the Neighbours (i.e. 5 or 6) resorted there for the benefit of Conversation; and seeing their Schoolmaster there and so lately come from Boston too, they Questioned me on subjects relating to Marketts State Politics &c many of which Subjects scarce ever before entertain'd my mind. To all these I gave very learned and elaborate Answers, and in Short when I did nott understand the Topic I follow'd that renown'd Practice of using Words and Expressions without meaning." Though he made fun of the bumpkins, he liked being plied with "*so many* Questions" and being called "a *Philosopher.*"[13] He did not even mind his friends' raillery when they called him "the *Lunenburg Oracle,*" because the stature and authority that a learned, cosmopolitan gentleman enjoyed in the information-starved countryside was flattering to the eighteen-year-old Paine.[14]

But as the months stretched on, Lunenburg was not so rewarding as to compensate for his isolation from his adoring sisters and his college friends. "I live here almost out of the world," he groaned; so he left in 1750 for a teaching post in Boston.[15] From there he began to seek his fortune in what seemed the quickest way possible—trade. His first scheme was a voyage to the Carolinas, but he lost money on the cargo of tar he brought back and two further trips to North Carolina were no more profitable. Next he tried a venture to the Mediterranean, which proved more educational than lucrative. Before concluding that trade would not be the easy route to wealth that it had been for his father, he led a whaling expedition to Newfoundland, with equally disappointing results. Only then did he turn to law.

Although for the secular-minded Paine the decision in favor of law was pragmatic—his hobbies, clockmaking, mechanics, and physics were unrelated—it was an ideal choice. Highly articulate and fond of speaking in company, Paine was also an active reader and essayist according to current English tastes. As a lawyer he would enter a learned, liberal profession that had become lucrative in Boston by the mid-1750s and was only just beginning to penetrate the rest of the province. As he explained to his father, "I doubt not I shall get ahead. . . . If a new County be Created there must be some Lawyers and I don't doubt with diligent application to my studies I shall be qualified."[16]

Paine began his studies in January 1755 with a relative, Abijah Willard, in Lancaster, Worcester County. He supported himself by keeping school and preaching in Shirley, where the pulpit was vacant. Though no scholar of religion, he found, as at Lunenburg, he could please the country people. They did not scorn his patched, shabby college gown, nor were they aware that in the half-dozen sermons he gave them he was exhausting his theological wisdom.[17] His excursions as a preacher were welcome distractions from the dry business of studying law. As he confided to a sister, "my circumstances in Life obliges [me] to apply closer to my Secular Studies than my Inclination . . . I have no other prospects of Subsistence but the Labours of my Brain, and Necessity urges that my Gains should be speedy."[18] In spite of his resolve, however, Paine took a vacation from his law studies in the summer and fall of 1755 to join New England's expedition against the French at Crown Point on Lake Champlain. Attracted by the adventure as well as the cash payment that service as a chaplain promised, Paine returned with enough money to live in Boston as an apprentice to a leading attorney, Benjamin Prat. After that there were no more detours, and Paine was admitted to the Suffolk County bar in 1757, qualifying as a barrister in the superior court a year later. Though law had begun as a respectable meal ticket for Robert Treat Paine, he found in it a calling that suited his temperament. In court, where he would have to communicate authoritatively with his superiors on the bench while also persuading yeoman and artisan jurors, his capacity for serious learning and his glib self-assurance would win respect.

For John Adams, whose family background and personality contrasted with Paine's, the destination was the same but the journey was different. Unlike Paine, Adams was a self-critical, utterly conscientious person who measured himself according to ideal ethical and professional standards that he could never satisfy. Though less self-confident than Paine, at bottom he was far more ambitious. Where Paine's objective was respectable wealth,

Adams wanted more; and he embraced law as a learned discipline and a professional calling that held the promise of lasting fame.[19]

When John Adams was born in 1735 he was already "destined . . . long before his birth to a public Education" by a father who was, though a shoemaker and farmer, "fond of reading" and an admirer of learning.[20] Later, although Adams would speak of his parents' "Ignorance," he described his father as an ideal type of the successful yeoman who

> by his Industry and Enterprize soon became a Person of more Property and Consideration in the Town than his Patron had been. He became a Select Man, a Militia Officer and a Deacon in the Church. He was the honestest Man I ever knew. In Wisdom, Piety, Benevolence and Charity In proportion to his Education and Sphere of Life, I have never seen his Superior.[21]

With such a father encouraging a career of learning and piety in the ministry, Adams' decision to practice law was the result of much soul-searching that saw him leaning to medicine and divinity before finally deciding.[22]

At college his first inclination was toward law because, he said, "it was whispered to me and circulated among others that I had some faculty for public Speaking and that I should make a better Lawyer than Divine."[23] This inclination was reinforced by the unsentimental, inside perspective on the unsavory aspects of a clergyman's career that Adams witnessed when he returned home during college vacations. The parish was torn by dissension over "Arminianism," and he was around the house reading the conflicting newspaper and pamphlet arguments during repeated ecclesiastical councils that were held there. Witnessing "such a Spirit of Dogmatism and Bigotry in Clergy and Laity" aroused "very strong doubts . . . whether I was made for a Pulpit in such times. To be a parson would involve me in endless Altercations and make my Life miserable, without any prospect of doing any good to my fellow Men."[24] These experiences gave father and son reason enough to consider the alternatives.

Medicine was clearly one respectable option within family traditions. Adams' mother, Suzanna Boylston, was the granddaughter of a London-trained "Surgeon and Apothecary" and the niece of the illustrious physician Zabdiel Boylston, who had pioneered smallpox inoculation during the epidemic at Boston in 1721.[25] So after graduation, when Adams went to lodge with a physician while teaching school in Worcester, his thoughts turned to medicine. His landlord, who maintained "a pretty Library" of medical and scientific works, made a physician's life seem sufficiently useful and rewarding to attract Adams, who "read a good deal in these Books and entertained many thoughts of Becoming a Physician and a Surgeon."[26] Yet for a person of Adams' intense ambition and exceptional verbal and reasoning talents it was law, ultimately, that fired his imagination and drew him "irresistably." Court sessions were for him Worcester's most entertaining show, and fifty years later he could still recall the names of the learned and effective advocates he had first heard in that forum.[27]

Still, perhaps because of his father, perhaps because of traditional prejudices against lawyers—prejudices his farmer and tradesman uncles and other relatives continued to express—or perhaps because he was not satisfied with the legitimacy of his own motives, it took Adams some time before he was reconciled with his choice. In April 1756 he was still weighing the relative merits of the three learned professions. By now he had ruled out medicine, not only because of the "infinite toil and Labour" it required, but because he was disillusioned about the profession. He concluded that a physician, "if he has real Skill and Ingenuity, as things go now, will have no employment."[28] The ministry still seemed the path of virtue to him, for even though "the Divine has a Thousand Obstacles to encounter," Adams believed "he will be able to do more good to his fellow men and make better provision for his own future Happiness in this Profession, than in any other."[29] Nevertheless Adams would become a lawyer. He agreed with the conventional Yankee criticisms that a lawyer "often foments more quarrels than he composes, and inriches himself at the expense of impoverishing others more honest and deserving than himself," but he would not be that kind of a parasitic lawyer.[30] Observation of provincial politics had taught him that "Law is indeed an Avenue to the more important offices of the state," and it was just this sort of public recognition that he craved. He worried that his "Birth and fortune" permitted him "no hopes of Being useful that way," but he believed the goal itself was virtuous—"the happiness of human Society is an object worth the pursuit of any man."[31]

Several months later, when Adams at last contracted to study law with James Putnam of Worcester, he was still of two minds. Contrary to his earlier sentiments, he now confided in his diary "my inclination I think was to preach," and the chief "Reason of my quitting Divinity was my Opinion concerning some disputed Points." So as to conquer his lingering doubts about the path he had chosen he resolved "never to commit any meanness or injustice in the Practice of Law."[32] That he still harbored the "illiberal Prejudices" against lawyers that were part of his Massachusetts heritage was evident in the brave assertion he made to himself that "the Study and Practice of Law, I am sure does not dissolve the obligations of morality or of Religion."[33] At bottom what Adams sought was the secular role that his own generation was to create, wherein he could not only become prosperous but also achieve fame through public service that was morally equivalent to the ministry.

When he dreamed of his future in the 1750s Adams himself understood such hopes were fanciful. The more experienced, socially sophisticated Paine seeing the law as a passport to prestige and prosperity for someone whose assets were his wits, grasped the current reality. So did a generation of students at Harvard and Yale who opted for the law instead of the ministry in unprecedented numbers from the mid-1740s to the early 1760s.[34] Yet as it turned out, partly because of this influx of native, college-trained lawyers—many of whom were ministers' sons—the ideal of the legal profession changed. By the 1770s it was coming to approach Adams' earlier vision of public service.[35] The New England college culture that the new generation brought with them to the profession combined the ideals of Roman honor and glory with a commitment to Christian virtue. From the perspective of the older and more wordly, London-trained and immigrant lawyers who had helped create the profession in Boston, this idealistic college culture seemed a naive affectation at best. According to lawyers who remained loyal to the Crown, this idealism was a fraud.[36]

Naive and sincere or not, this culture nourished a communication network among recent graduates and formed a central motif in the early careers of lawyers like Paine and Adams. It influenced their personal development, their social behavior, and their understanding of their roles as lawyers in society. The young men who entered the legal profession in the 1750s and 1760s, while other friends prepared for medicine and the ministry, often remained in close touch, and in their letters and visits constantly sought to uphold the idealistic standards of learning, refinement, and virtue they had adopted at college. Whether they read law, medicine, or divinity, they also read Vergil and Cicero. Apprentice lawyers like Paine and Adams who were transcribing deeds and writs also copied the forms of prose and poetry of the most approved modern writers in the original essays and verse they wrote to amuse and impress each other. The consequences for the legal profession, for public life, and for regional communication patterns in Massachusetts, both among individuals and for communities, were far-reaching.

One dimension of college culture that Paine's and Adams' fellow alumni carried into their professional careers was the fraternal posture, with both the cooperative and competitive relationships fraternity embodies. Addressing each other as "Brother" long after college, they formed quasi-familial networks that, as the legal profession became formally organized, reinforced the clubby, guild-like aspirations of the bar.[37] Simultaneously they competed with each other for stature according to the values they shared—learning, virtue, and the ability to perform in public, a talent that brought worldly success in terms of clients and reputation. This competition reshaped the model of the lawyer to include virtue and public service in place of cunning, and created an information network that in its province-wide collegiality resembled that of clergymen.

The content and values of college culture that were so much more rewarding emotionally than the details of common law and techniques of pleading were intertwined. Understanding nature through scientific study, for example, was learning about the Divine creation. Pondering the orations of Cicero—a favorite among this generation of lawyers—combined lessons in rhetoric with homilies on civic virtue.[38] The object in keeping up one's learning was to maintain the identity so dearly acquired at college. Only by continuing to cultivate the studies and manners of the college man could they retain the elevated, cosmopolitan qualities that entitled any college graduate, whatever his family origin, to the rank of gentleman.[39] For those like Paine and Adams whose careers placed them miles away from Cambridge and Boston, the necessity for maintaining the college network was especially keen.

Had they all enjoyed the privilege of being Boston lawyers like the first two generations in the profession, their identities as cosmopolitan gentlemen would have been more secure. For in the first half of the 18th century, virtually all Massachusetts lawyers lived in Boston where they met together daily in coffeehouses and taverns as well as at court. Routinely mixing with the leading officials and merchants of the province, they easily remained part of a community of gentlemen, aloof from the uneducated "pettifoggers" with whom country lawyers had to practice and compete. Later, when Paine and Adams took up law, established Boston lawyers like Robert Auchmuty and Benjamin Prat were insulated from what Adams called the "tittle-tattle" of local conversation. For the lucky few who could, like Adams' classmate Jonathan Sewall, pursue a Boston and a royal office-holding career in the 1750s and 1760s, it was much easier to retain a genteel identity than for the more numerous graduates who, like Paine and Adams, ended up in Taunton, Braintree, or farther afield.[40]

When the slightly older Paine proposed a correspondence with Adams, the latter accepted enthusiastically. Echoing English writings on courtesy, Adams praised the merits of conversation, which, he said, promotes benevolence and friendship while it encouraged "Industry and Emulation, and evaporates the Spleen which we are too apt to contract, by long and close attention to Business or study." Referring to his own situation at Braintree, he complained "we are seldom so happy, as to find Company much inclined to Speculation, and as some of us, can find no Company at all, the only Method left, is that of Correspondences." Letters, Adams claimed, "have all the Advantages of Conversation, with the Additional ones of searching deeper into subjects, of crushing many vain and more offensive Thoughts, and of perpetuating such as are useful and judicious."[41] Having eagerly incorporated college culture into his own world view, Adams would not and could not be merely a lawyer. Like his peers, he sought to be a cosmopolitan gentleman. Writing melodramatically to another lawyer friend, Adams avowed that without "the Aquisition of Knowledge . . . it would be a punishment to live,"[42] and to Paine he asserted "as Nature and Fortune have conspired to strip me of all other means of Pleasure . . . the Acquisition and Communication of Knowledge, are the sole Entertainment of my life."[43] Though one must make allowances for Adams' youthful fervor, his emphasis on "the Acquisition and Communication of Knowledge" points toward the redefinition of the lawyer's role that his generation would accomplish.

Classical, philosophical, and Christian learning was ultimately what defined a gentleman in provincial Massachusetts. And among college graduates, whatever their age, their learning supplied significant class consciousness. College stamped them as cosmopolitan gentlemen who, whether obscure or prominent, enjoyed access to a network of peers who rose to stations of importance. For lawyers no less than clergy, these connections supplied avenues of information and acquaintance beyond their profession as they traveled the court circuit and when, later on, they moved into the legislature.

The role of the cosmopolitan gentleman began immediately when a college graduate was accepted as an apprentice lawyer. Class recitations and the colloquies of college clubs were training grounds for making one's way in the sometimes high-powered and often sophisticated conversations of county and province elites. Apprenticeship, which often meant moving into his mentor's home, as Adams did, included access to the master lawyer's social and professional circles, where making an impression was as much a part of one's apprenticeship as mastering the law. Since religion, natural science, and history rivaled politics as topics of discussion, the legal reports and commentaries that were the apprentice's primary study were not sufficient. To be prepared for society they must also read as the gentry read, from a miscellany of current and classical authors.[44]

Robert Treat Paine, with his cultivated Boston background and his wide-ranging experience in coastal and transatlantic trade and in the army, excelled in company. With a mixture of envy and irony Adams described him as a "universal Scholar, gay Companion, and accomplish'd Gentleman," after spending an evening with him at the home of a Worcester gentleman.[45] In such a setting, where a wife or two was often part of the company, legal knowledge had no bearing, since conversation might focus on "the present scituation of publick affairs, with a few observations concerning Heroes and great Commanders" from history.[46] In view of the French and Indian War, topical knowledge figured prominently in 1755 and 1756—"the interests of Nations, and all the dira of War, make the subject of every Conversation" in Worcester, Adams reported to a friend.[47]

Where only the local gentry were concerned, a college graduate might readily excel in company. But, when the superior court and its entourage made their circuit through the counties, the competition was keener and the stakes much higher for a future barrister. "Last Superior Court at Worcester," Adams noted that Paine "dined in Company with Mr. Gridly, Mr. Trowbridge, and several others, at Mr. Putnams, and altho a modest attentive Behavior would have best become him in such a Company, yet he tried to ingross the whole Conversation to himself. He did the same, in the Evening, when all the Judges of the Superiour Court with Mr. Winthrop, Sewall, &c were present." By now Paine, a newly admitted barrister, was capable of flying high in company. Though Adams regarded him as "impudent, ill-bread, [and] conceited," he conceded that Paine also possessed "Witt, sense, and Learning, and a great deal of Humour, and has Virtue and Piety."[48] For Adams, who lacked Paine's vivacity and social self-confidence, the strategy for impressing his elders and betters would be less adventuresome and far more circumspect.

Impetuously, Adams had indeed begun by aiming "at Wit and Spirit, at making a shining Figure in gay Company." Though "in Company with Persons much superior to my self in Years and Place," like Paine he had "talked to shew my Learning." But lacking the panache to carry off such a performance, Adams retreated "to labour more for an inoffensive and aimiable . . . Character."[49] His way of impressing leading lawyers and jurists would be solid and sedate—he would outdistance his peers by the depth and breadth of his legal scholarship. The civil law would be the key to his victory since, as he noted, "few of my Contemporary Beginners, in the Study of the Law, have the Resolution, to aim at much Knowledge in the Civil Law." When he had achieved some familiarity with Justinian and the commentaries of the Dutch scholar Vinnius, he believed he would "gain the Consideration and perhaps the favour of Mr. Gridley and Mr. Pratt."[50] Adams, who formed this strategy after many visits in his mentor James Putnam's home, some on occasions when Gridley and Prat were part of the company, had read the clues accurately. When Adams called on Gridley to seek his patronage for admission to the Suffolk County bar, the senior barrister regarded as the most scholarly of Boston attorneys interviewed Adams at length.[51] Adams then accompanied Gridley to court and observed its proceedings before calling on Oxenbridge Thatcher to seek his support. With Thatcher the conversation was indirect: "Drank Tea and spent the whole Evening, upon original sin, Origin of Evil, the Plan of the Universe, and at last, upon Law." This was the conversation of a New England gentleman that a Tidewater gentleman might see as cant. When the evening was over, Thatcher observed that Suffolk County was already "full" of lawyers, but he made no objection to Adams joining their number.[52]

Two weeks later Adams' apprenticeship formally ended when Gridley introduced him to the court, announcing that Adams had

a good Character from him [Putnam], and all others who know him, and that he was with me the other day several Hours, and I take it he is qualified to study the Law by his scholarship and that he has made a very considerable, a very great Proficiency in the Principles of the Law, and therefore that the Clients Interest may be safely intrusted in his Hands. I therefore recommend him.[53]

When the formal ritual was completed, Adams sealed his entrance into this select fraternity in the customary way by inviting the members of the bar to a tavern "to drink some Punch."[54] With that, Adams joined Paine as a practicing attorney.

The career of a lawyer, like that of a clergyman, was necessarily an exercise in communication. But in contrast to ministers, who held contractual offices of authority, with fixed stipends and captive audiences, and who spoke to their parishioners on questions of faith and morality with the admonishing voice of a father to a child, the lawyer was an ad hoc counsellor and spokesman, hired for the occasion only. When lawyers opened offices and entered practice, they needed clients immediately—people who would entrust their property interests to them, overlooking their youth and inexperience for the sake of their technical learning and verbal ability. As apprentices a Paine or an Adams strove to impress their betters in the profession and in society; as practicing attorneys it was also urgent to please the ordinary land-owning farmers and artisans of the countryside and villages. Building one's reputation and visibility, acquiring prominence and respect, were the essentials for establishing a paying clientele.

In their frustration with these realities both Paine and Adams privately wished that family wealth and connections could have enabled them simply to step into a prosperous practice as did, they imagined, some of their better situated peers. Yet in the late 1750s when they began, like nearly all young lawyers they could not expect wealthy merchant clients or lucrative and prestigious government patronage. The fact was that men like Paine and Adams had seized law as an opportunity precisely because they lacked advantages of wealth and prominent patrons. Both were attracted to the prospect of earning a living in law by the realization that outside of Boston and Salem there were few trained, college-educated lawyers; and in some long-settled counties there were scarcely any even as late as the 1760s.[55] By establishing practices in Taunton and Braintree, Paine and Adams selected locations where they could provide a new professional level of service.

Since there was no possibility of simply entering practice as a junior partner in an established firm, the first requirements for success were achieving visibility and developing a favorable reputation among local notables whose smiles or frowns often influenced their neighbors. In contrast to the young clergyman who responded to advertised vacancies in existing pulpits and who need only serve brief probationary periods before being "settled" to life tenure, the young lawyer had to create his own place in the social, political, and economic order. In making his place and building his reputation, the fledgling lawyer needed to woo and impress a shifting array of people both above and below him in the social hierarchy. He needed to be capable of talking Latin or Yankee, and prepared to quote technical treatises and cite English case law, besides referring to popular writings like Watts and Doddridge and the almanac. At the same time, both for personal and professional reasons it was important to remain current in the belletristic and philosophical college culture of one's peers. That it was necessary to engage in several levels of communication in order to build up a practice is evident from John Adams' beginning in Braintree. For him the town offered particular advantages, not only because "there had never been a Lawyer in any Country Part of the then County of Suffolk," but because he could save on expenses by living with his parents, who were eager to have him.[56] Moreover, though Adams' talents as a lawyer were unknown locally, he was a native son, known to most of the inhabitants as the promising offspring of their respected North Parish deacon and selectman. Adams' family background would disarm suspicions that in another town might taint him with the generic mendacity associated with lawyers. But just being Deacon Adams' son was not enough, as he well knew.

Young John Adams understood not only the crucial importance of recognition for his career but also that there were several paths available to achieve it—speaking, through actions, and writing. Already he had been trying to impress established lawyers "by making Remarks, and proposing Questions" to reveal his own discernment and erudition. He was also aware that it would be useful to cultivate "My Acquaintance with those young Gentlemen in Boston who were at Colledge with me," for they would build his reputation among Boston merchants, shopkeepers, and tradesmen. But in Braintree, the immediate need was to "make frequent Visits in the Neighbourhood and converse familiarly with men, Women and Children in their own Style, on the common Tittletattle of the Town."[57] Townspeople must recognize him as the person with whom they felt comfortable and confident when it came to legal questions.

So Adams, who had just recently been immersing himself in Justinian to impress Jeremiah Gridley, now set his books aside and began to make the local rounds, finding to his dismay after spending months on Latin codes, that knowing the province law of Massachusetts was more pertinent than the civil law. Instead of an evening with fellow lawyers, an evening spent at the home of a militia officer "gave me Opportunity to display some knowledge of Law."[58] A visit to a deacon's led to conversations on British politics, and on the way home to others on "Husbandry, and the Tittletattle of the Town."[59] Pursuing local visibility, Adams made himself known "as a knowing as well as a familiar young fellow" to local officials who were opinion leaders, as well as to the ordinary men and women whose gossip, smiles, and frowns could make or break his reputation.[60] To "speak and shake Hands," to inquire after wives and children, to listen respectfully to loquacious townsmen, and to "mix with the Croud in a Tavern, in the Meeting House or the Training field" were Adams' tasks. The objective was "to sett the Tongues of old and young Men and Women a prating in ones favour."[61]

Until he gained a secure following and a busy practice, Adams pursued the path of pleasing those he saw as his inferiors in learning, ability and aspiration. One spring morning, for example, he accompanied his father to an auction of leases on town lands because of what he could learn about the process and the local people, as well as to "Spread" his reputation and "lift myself into Business." Afterwards he triumphantly reported, "I was consulted by 2 Men this afternoon, who would not have applied to me if I had not been at Vendue."[62] As Adams' first cases came along, he worried over their disposition from concern at the appearance he would make. When he lost his first case before Major Crosby, the Braintree Justice of the Peace—involving damages when a farmer seized and impounded a neighbor's stray cow—Adams was acutely embarrassed. Because he had prepared a defective writ, he worried "it will be said I undertook the Case but was unable to manage it." The victor would "proclaim it," so the news would be "in the mouth of every Body . . . [and] An opinion will spread among the People, that I have not Cunning enough to cope with [the farmer] Lambert." His competitors like "Bob P[aine]" would "pick up this Story to laugh at."[63] Though the case was trivial in itself and would never be published in a newspaper, it would certainly make the rounds of the Braintree information network of households and taverns, and possibly spill beyond the town into the county as well. Harvard College, book-learning, and the respect of the Boston bar could not erase this defeat.

This early setback was actually useful to Adams, since it convinced him to redouble his efforts to earn the respect of common property holders by mastering their everyday legal issues. Along the way some of Adams' college-bred airs were replaced by a solid respect for common farmers and what they could teach him. Encouraging polite conversation was a staple of contemporary English advice literature for would-be gentlemen like Adams: books were best for instruction about the past, travel was encouraged for learning about other lands, but it was said that conversation was the key to understanding people and society. In England, in Virginia, and in Massachusetts too, this prescription applied to the drawing room, tavern, and coach conversations of the well-bred—not the discourse of common farmers. But Adams, in the course of making himself familiar and visible, discovered he was learning both about his own society and the law of Massachusetts along the way. "You may get more," he observed, "by studying Town meeting, and Training Days, than you can by reading Justinian and all his voluminous and heavy Commentators."[64] Questions put by his farmer clients "led me into Useful Thoughts and Inquiries," he noted, matters that his own studies omitted.[65] Most surprising to Adams, common people could teach him much that he had not gleaned in Worcester at the polite dining tables of the Putnams and Chandlers or at the court sessions and tavern suppers that accompanied them. On some subjects he found "that as much knowledge in my Profession is to be acquired by Conversing with common People about the Division of Estates, Proceedings of Judge of Probate, Cases that they have heard as Jurors, Witnesses, Parties, as is to be acquired by Books."[66] In cultivating the ordinary property holders of Suffolk County Adams not only achieved visibility, he acquired knowledge of common legal practices that made his professional training serviceable and effective.

The progress of Adams' reputation here was all based on local impressions and reports. On his second outing before Major Crosby, "a long obstinate Tryal . . . of the most litigious, vexatious suit," Adams was the victor.[67] Next day "the story" was already spreading: "Salisbury told my Uncle and my Uncle told Coll. Quincy." The account circulating told how "saucy" Adams had been, and that the young lawyer had "whipped" Major Crosby by reminding the old Justice of the Peace that he was under oath not to advise either party but to "do Justice equally."[68] Six months later, with more victories to his credit, Adams was confident when he again appeared before Crosby. Though he knew he was still making "Mistakes, and omissions," he also knew himself to be "more expert" each time. "I feel my own strength," Adams reported, "I see the complacent Countenances of the Crowd, and I see the respectful face of the Justice, and the fearful faces of Petty foggers."[69] By his third year in practice Adams had come into his own as a legal force in his own community. Within only a few more years he would, like Paine, be a force in the county and province. Possessing a secure local reputation based on practical results, he could now turn his attention to winning the esteem of a more cosmopolitan audience whose legal business involved tens, hundreds, even thousands of pounds.

The precise nature of the reputations Adams and Paine developed are not readily known, but their general outlines can be reconstructed from their own behavior and their relationships with lawyers and other prominent people. From their early days in Boston when they were seeking admission to the bar, both were regarded as sufficiently promising to win swift admission to the legal fraternity. Indeed Paine, who began in Boston under the patronage of his mentor Benjamin Prat (himself a student of Jeremiah Gridley), was raised to the rank of barrister only a year after qualifying for practice. That he chose to settle in Taunton in 1761 was a measure of just how discouragingly competitive Boston was for young attorneys in a hurry to succeed. At the Bristol County seat, Taunton, as at Braintree and many other towns where commercial agriculture flourished, there was a sufficient volume of business to support a lawyer. Heretofore this business had been divided among many part-time, self-taught practitioners who, with a law manual or two, were as competent as local justices required. Called "pettifoggers" by members of the bar, these men possessed practices and reputations that were purely local. The arrival on the scene of a Paine or an Adams posed a dire threat to their business.

The turf battles that pitted learned, cosmopolitan newcomers against these local practitioners were crucial to the way that professional lawyers defined themselves by exploiting their information advantages as they cultivated the people. In order to build a successful practice, college-bred lawyers like Adams had to start by creating a local base in which they sharply and self-consciously differentiated themselves from the pettifoggers. Though the lawyers ultimately won this struggle, their opponents were not helpless in their efforts to stave off professional competition. Adams, the interloper, righteously denounced the "dirty and ridiculous Litigations [that] have been multiplied . . . owing to the multiplicity of Petty foggers." To block him, Adams reported that one of these pettifoggers "set himself to work to destroy my Reputation."[70] If Adams had not actively promoted his own reputation for accessibility and competence, his local base certainly would have been undermined.

Yet attorneys like Adams and Paine enjoyed advantages that pettifoggers—a motley array of farmers, traders, artisans, and tavern-keepers—however troublesome their local gossip-mongering, could not touch. College-bred lawyers possessed outside connections and superior training that brought victories at the county courts such as the Inferior Court of Common Pleas and at the Superior Court of Judicature. Traveling the court circuits, pleading together, contesting each other, arguing in court and conversing out of it, the professional lawyers developed an understanding of each other's abilities and characters. Competition notwithstanding, they felt a fraternal solidarity. They displayed their sense of fraternity publicly in 1765 when a prominent Boston lawyer died and a group of lawyers clad in the gowns of their profession marched in the funeral cortege.[71] Expressing a guild-like mentality, Suffolk County lawyers defined their own boundaries more formally and more exclusively than ever before when, in 1766, they established new and more rigorous entrance requirements, and a lengthier period of preparation for admission to the bar.[72] Not only was there a throng of pettifoggers to hold at bay, when the bar met in July 1766 "Measures for Limitation" of their own apprentices were discussed—so much did "they swarm and multiply," that the profession was becoming overcrowded.[73]

Adams and Paine, who were very much part of this movement of professionalization, actively cultivated relationships with well-placed lawyers and judges through correspondence and socializing.[74] Adams even joined his patron Gridley in founding a sodality or reading club of half-a-dozen lawyers who met periodically in Boston in the mid-1760s. It was for this group that Adams began the research that resulted in his *Dissertation Concerning the Canon and Feudal Law,* a work that appeared in installments in the *Boston Gazette* and later won an audience in England where it was printed as a pamphlet, and which ultimately led to Adams' election to the English Society for the Bill of Rights. Here was the reputation and recognition among the learned and prominent that Adams had long cherished.

Books were crucial to Adams' and Paine's self-images and to the reputations they sought to convey to the leading men of the province. In the decades following their graduation from Harvard both men actively collected libraries of hundreds of volumes. At Taunton and Braintree, where no one else had a first-rate library, the incentive to have one's own collection was keen for those who wished, as they did, to keep up with their peers in Boston. Paine, who inherited the residue of his father's ministerial library, began with a running start in religion and theology. Over the years, however, as Paine became a gentleman of the law, he sold off some of his inherited holdings in Latin, Greek, and Hebrew, and built a more secular, polite collection to complement his law books. When he made a catalog of his library in 1768, he held hundreds of titles including poetry, belles lettres, and political essays, in addition to works in history, travel, natural philosophy, theology and law. This same list shows that Paine routinely lent books out, mostly to friends and relations living in the Taunton region, but including also clergymen, physicians, and other lawyers—including Jeremiah Gridley and his Taunton colleague Daniel Leonard.[75]

The possession of a good gentleman's library was only part of their ambition. They also aimed to command legal libraries that would do much more than merely set them off from the pettifoggers. Their aim was to be at least as well-prepared for legal research as any of their competitors anywhere. Achieving such an objective required money, time, and perseverance. Key legal works were often out of print and not readily available either in New England or in London. Help in locating certain titles was required, and so when Paine's friend, the clockmaker Gawen Brown, went to London in 1758, he carried a list of English and Scots works Paine was seeking plus £7 in cash.[76] But even searches by several booksellers did not guarantee that technical material like Sir George Croke's *Reports* could be had.[77] Yet through persistence, and working through booksellers like Jeremy Condy of Boston who traveled to England periodically to buy stock, a sophisticated, authoritative collection could be assembled.[78] Paine, who helped supply legal books to the Windham, Connecticut, lawyer Eliphalet Dyer—another future signer of the Declaration of Independence—was always on the lookout.[79] Whenever a lawyer who was possessed of a good library died, there was a rush.[80] On one occasion, when Paine swiftly purchased books out of an estate, he was later obliged to return the books because, as the administrator realized after being "spoke to by gentlemen in all parts of the province," he had to provide equal opportunities for all purchasers through a public auction.[81] Although the most widely read books and manuals were often reprinted and available, the expensive technical works that could give a lawyer a professional edge in a society that had no public libraries, could only be accumulated gradually by alert collectors.[82]

As with Paine, the goal of building a first-rate legal and political library was part of Adams' ambition from his early days with Putnam and as Gridley's protégé, a time when he had "suffered very much for Want of Books."[83] To fulfill this dream he must first be prosperous, so Adams recalled, when "in the Years 1766 and 1767 my Business increased, as my Reputation spread, I got Money and bought Books and Land."[84] Though he began in the usual way by making the rounds of Boston booksellers, Adams came to the conclusion that he must have some more regular system to provide for his needs in current publications.[85] His solution was to establish a standing order with the London booksellers and publishers E. and C. Dilly.[86] In addition to specific titles that he would request from time to time, they were to send him "every Book and Pamphlet, of Reputation, upon the subjects of Law and Government as soon as it comes out."[87] Josiah Quincy, his younger colleague with whom he had worked defending the British soldiers in the trial following the Boston Massacre, already had such an arrangement, and Adams was ready to spend up to £30 yearly—half a country clergyman's salary—so as to keep himself and his collection current.[88] Many years later Adams would be able to boast that "by degrees I procured the best Library of Law in the State."[89] For Adams, clearly, the possession of his library was an embodiment of his faith in the doctrine that knowledge is power.

Being first in activities he undertook seriously was always an important underlying motive for the adult Adams. But at another level understanding the reasons why he and the New England culture that shaped him valued libraries helps to explain the increasing legitimacy of lawyers as public servants and officeholders during the 1760s and 1770s. Adams reported that the purely selfish goals of "Fame, Fortune, and Power say some, are the Ends intended by a Library."[90] This perspective, best suited to the court culture of the Anglophile elite, would never have made lawyers like Paine or Adams suitable republican servants. Indeed under some circumstances extensive personal libraries might have stigmatized their owners, as seems to have been true for Lieutenant Governor Thomas Hutchinson, whose library was destroyed in an attack on his house in 1765.[91] There were, however, alternative purposes for a library: "The Service of God, Country, Clients, Fellow Men."[92] From this viewpoint the possession of a library would accentuate the merits of a lawyer. That it denoted the high rank of a learned gentlemen all agreed. What more it signified, whether selfish or altruistic values, depended on perceptions of the activities of individual lawyers in public settings.

Here public speaking was of paramount importance. Lawyers like Paine and Adams practiced law in the rustic courts of justices of the peace in Bristol and Suffolk counties which required them to develop a style that was persuasive to country gentry, common farmers, and tradesmen. Theirs was not one of the Boston courtroom styles; indeed, Adams derided the rhetoric of one of the most highly esteemed Boston lawyers, the pompous Robert Auchmuty. Auchmuty was "heavy, dull, insipid." His presentations were studded, Adams said after watching him in action, with "as many Repetitions as a presbyterian Parson in his Prayer— . . . Volubility, voluble Repetition and repeated Volubility—fluent Reiterations, and reiterating Fluency." Such "nauseous Eloquence" proved no barrier to Auchmuty's career; indeed, he received a crown appointment as a justice of the Vice-Admiralty Court in 1767.[93] Scorning the courtroom manner of the magisterial Benjamin Prat, the gifted and popular orator James Otis told Adams: "It makes me laugh to see Pratt lugg a Cart load of Books into Court to prove a Point as clear as the Sun."[94] Rather than follow the style of these men, two of the Province's most prestigious barristers, Adams admired the controversial

THE PATRIOTIC AMERICAN FARMER.
J-n D-k-ns——n Esq.r Barrister at Law:
Who with Attic Eloquence and Roman Spirit hath Aserted.
The Liberties of the BRITISH Colonies in America.

'Tis nobly done, to Stem Taxations Rage,
And raise, the thoughts of a degen'rate Age,
For Happiness, and Joy, from Freedom Spring;
But Life in Bondage, is a worthless Thing.

James Otises, father and son. He respected the talents of Colonel James Otis, the Barnstable patriarch who was so "sociable and sensible" that he could communicate with ordinary people. "Learned he is not," Adams recognized, "but he is an easy, familiar Speaker."[95] Much as Adams admired learning and gloried in displaying his own erudition, practicing in the Massachusetts countryside convinced him it would not do to lug books into a common court, either literally or figuratively, for persuasion must be suited to the audience.

The style of public speaking that the new generation of lawyers like Adams and Paine cultivated was direct and familiar rather than pedantic, but it was also elevated above the common tavern or town-meeting harangue. Indeed it might be likened to the evangelical style that George Whitefield had popularized throughout the colonies during their youth. In addition, college experience, and the practice of declaiming Cicero in English translation as a private exercise, colored their sense of dramatic form as well as their appreciation of selfless patriotic appeals.[96] Though Paine's prosecution of the soldiers after the Boston Massacre resulted in somewhat lenient verdicts, his oral performance was a triumph. As a friend wrote, "you attracted closely the Attention of your Audience *Ciceronian like* & Increas'd your Fame."[97] Though it was Adams' misfortune to argue the unpopular side of the case, defending the soldiers, the jury found him and his colleague Josiah Quincy persuasive, so Adams and Quincy, as well as Paine, gained recognition from this public service.

What was crucial, however, in creating the image of lawyers as public servants was serving as advocates on the popular side of an issue as Paine had done. "To have the Passions, Prejudices, and Interests of the whole Audience, in a Mans Favour," Adams recognized, "will convert plain, common Sense, into profound Wisdom, nay wretched Doggerell into sublime Heroics." Six months after the Boston Massacre trial ended, on July 4, 1771,

---

"The Patriotic American Farmer"

This print honoring John Dickinson appeared in Philadelphia in 1768 and displays the close association between the patriot-lawyer and his books. His right elbow rests on a large volume called Magna Charta; *visible on the shelves are* Coke Upon Littleton *and* Hume's History of England, *two more key authorities for American political principles. This image depicts the ideal that Paine and Adams sought to embody. In November 1767, Dickinson had written that: "I spend a good deal of it [my time] in a library, which I think the most valuable part of my small estate; and being acquainted with two or three gentlemen of abilities and learning, who honor me with their friendship, I have acquired, I believe, a greater knowledge in history, and the laws and constitution of my country, than is generally attained by men of my class, many of them not being so fortunate as I have been in the opportunities of getting information." (*Letters from a Farmer in Pennsylvania to the Inhabitants of the British Colonies, *Philadelphia, 1768, p. 3.)*
Courtesy of the Library Company of Philadelphia

Adams had his day in the sun when, at a session of the superior court sitting in York County, he successfully argued for a £10 penalty against customs officials for taking an excessive fee. Though Adams believed his performance was just average, he was congratulated effusively for "the Patriotick manner in which you conducted that Cause," and he was assured that he had consequently "obtained great Honour in this County." Indeed, as the case was ending, "a Man came running down" from the courthouse exclaiming, " 'That Mr. Adams has been making the finest Speech I ever heard in my Life. He's equall to the greatest orator that ever spoke in Greece or Rome.' "[98] It was in the prosecution of such popular causes that the image of lawyers as public servants rather than parasites took shape. Because of their strategic location in a legal system built on advocacy, certain privileged, well-connected lawyers were viewed as lackeys to tyranny, while others ouside the shadow of government patronage were seen as champions of liberty.

Heretofore, under ordinary circumstances, there had been no reason for the legal profession to take on such public importance. In the past, clergymen and magistrates had possessed a virtual monopoly on public address in a society where their voices were respected as authoritative. Other than town-meeting debates, New England had no tradition of public contention, certainly not by learned, eloquent gentlemen publicly disputing secular issues. Public controversy, when it arose, was carried on in the newspapers, in pamphlets, and from the pulpit. Until now, courtroom argument had never been infused with broad, patriotic themes designed to appeal to the many. This was a new genre—analogous to New Light preaching—created by lawyers in a forum especially adapted to their station and capacities. In 1761, when James Otis, Jr., electrified young attorneys like Adams as he argued against Writs of Assistance before a tiny audience in the council chamber, he was inaugurating a new form of public speaking and a new role for lawyers.[99] Several years later Patrick Henry's legendary courtroom declamation "Give me liberty, or give me death" acted as a similar catalyst in Virginia. Henry, like Otis, like Paine, like Adams, was paid by his clients to argue particular cases which under the right circumstances could transform lawyers into professional advocates of the public interest. In contrast to magistrates and clergymen who sought to preserve harmony—albeit on their own terms— quarrels, controversy, argument, were the lawyers' meat and drink, advocacy their calling.

Yet as important as public speaking could be—and it did thrust lawyers forward—mere histrionics and show were hardly sufficient to overcome the traditional mistrust of lawyers as a class. Securing trust was the reward of accumulated exposure in which the integrity of lawyers in private as well as public matters was tested. No community would entrust its well-being to a man of doubtful honesty or judgment, however eloquent he might be. When lawyers such as Paine and Adams emerged as public figures, they had already been tested, not just as advocates but for their prudence and integrity.

Their activities as managers and transmitters of information were important factors in the testing process. That public officials be eloquent was surely desirable; but that they be informed, discreet, and discerning in the use of information was critical. For lawyers the reputation for such conduct was a professional necessity. Possessing these attributes did not differentiate them from local magistrates and clergymen, the other key information managers in the Massachusetts countryside; but the particular networks that lawyers maintained did make them especially important in their communities as the Revolutionary era unfolded.

Lawyers' frequent contacts at the county and provincial level were of key importance. A representative to the general court traveled to Boston once a year, if that often. A clergymen met fellow clerics at monthly ministerial association meetings, but these associations operated at the county or sub-county level, and few clergymen more than a day's journey away could afford trips to the Harvard or Yale commencement more often than once every few years. Lawyers, however, were almost always on the move—hobnobbing with other lawyers or with judges traveling from Boston out into the counties in order to meet their quarterly obligations. Active both as readers and in conversation with the most highly informed people in the province on secular affairs, especially politics, lawyers as a class were uniquely situated to inform and advise the leaders of their communities on current affairs.

A close look at the day-to-day existence of practicing attorneys like Paine and Adams demonstrates both the frequency and diversity of their contacts outside their home communities. When the Court of Common Pleas was sitting at Taunton in June 1762, Adams spent three evenings socializing with Paine, the Leonards (a large family that included both lawyers and judges), and with Colonel Otis of Barnstable County.[100] Just a few days earlier Adams had talked province politics with Superior Court Justice Peter Oliver (Lieutenant Governor Hutchinson's brother-in-law) when he accompanied him to the house of his cousin Province Secretary Andrew Oliver. Peter Oliver had been critical of Colonel Otis's son James, and Adams now had the opportunity of telling Colonel Otis how he had stood up for the younger Otis. Encounters like these kept all the attorneys—and the towns from which they came—up to date on the latest political gossip. Dinners in the homes of the wealthy and great, like the Boston merchant James Bowdoin and Lieutenant Governor Thomas Hutchinson, together with tavern suppers while on the circuit, made someone like Paine highly informed both as to what was happening and how people in all walks of life perceived events.[101]

At the end of January 1768, just as Paine was for the first time being elected moderator of the Taunton town meeting, Adams was chafing at the

pressures facing the successful lawyer. "What Plan of Reading or Reflection," he complained, "can be pursued by a Man, who is now at Pownal-
borough, then at Marthas Vineyard, next at Boston, then at Taunton, pres-
ently at Barnstable, then at Concord, now at Salem, then at Cambridge, and
afterwards at Worcester. Now at Sessions, then at Pleas, now in Admiralty,
now at Superior Court, then in the Gallery of the House."[102] He seemed to
be everywhere—talking, listening, reading newspapers, taking notes. Paine,
who had no strong emotional attachment to his wife and could be happy
without her for months at a time, evidently thrived on such a regimen.
Adams, who generally brought his wife a batch of newspapers on his return
from his travels, suffered from the separations, as his frequent, newsy letters
to Abigail testify.[103]

But the traveling was only part of a lawyer's circulation. Like a clergyman, he was likely to encounter many people in different circles, even within
a particular community. Disparagingly, Adams called it a "vagrant, vaga-
bond Life. . . . At Meins book Store, at Bowes's Shop, at Danas House, at
Fitches, Otis's office, and the Clerks office, in the Court Chamber, in the
Gallery, at my own Fire . . . ," he circulated continuously, talking to everyone.[104] Indeed, it was this aspect of the country lawyers' activity that made
them such crucial intermediaries in the public information network. For they
not only carried messages across space in a swift, discriminating way, they
provided social linkage by transmitting information through much of the
propertied class—which in Massachusetts included most households.

One gets a glimpse of the routine ways in which such casual communication occurred from Adams' account of a ride from "little Cambridge" to
Waltham with "Mr. Ruggles of Roxbury, the Butcher." Though strangers,
on the road they struck up a conversation in which they discovered a family
connection. Thereafter they "talked about Family, Cattle fat and lean, and
Farms. . . . He says that Roxbury People make no Profit, by carting Dung
out of Boston." That evening at Munn's Tavern, they talked over "the
Husbandry of the [Connecticut] River Towns . . . and about Captn. Carvers
Journal of his Travels in the Wilderness, among the Savages in search of the
South sea."[105] This conversation between Ruggles and Adams is revealing.
From the butcher, the barrister learned more about subjects that were vital
to the well-being of most people in Massachusetts, farm techniques and
economics, both in Roxbury, which he knew, and in the Connecticut Valley,
which he had never seen but was soon to visit. From the barrister, the
butcher learned about a recent exploration in the North American interior.
Though the tradesman and the gentleman were divided by social rank, the
capacity of each to inform the other was mutually accepted. When political
issues were at stake such relationships were crucial, as Adams had recognized during the furor over the Stamp Act. Then, following the courts in the
southeastern counties, he learned the varying positions from town to town

on the question of whether and by whom restitution should be made for damages sustained in the Boston disturbances.[106]

The fact that rural lawyers like Adams and Paine communicated readily across social boundaries does not mean that all lawyers did. Indeed in light of the conflicting ideologies of social relations in mid-18th-century Massachusetts—Anglophile and Yankee—it would be astonishing if that were so. The Bostonian Benjamin Prat, for example, believed that gentlemen could learn nothing valuable from their ignorant inferiors, indeed the more ignorant commoners were, the better for them and for society at large. "It is," Prat declared, "a very happy Thing to Have People superstitious. . . . They should not so much as know what they believe. The People ought to be ignorant. And our Free schools are the very bane of society. They make the lowest of the People infinitely conceited."[107] Such an outlook on class relations was part of an established aristocratic tradition in England, and the social circles of those like Prat, who sought to climb the imperial patronage ladder, assumed that common people had little apart from their labors to contribute to society. The Puritan-now-Yankee heritage reflected contrary values, for even though social hierarchy was accepted, the clergy denounced superstition and taught that in order to be responsible Christians every person must be educated. Country schools and general literacy, backed by legislation, were founded on these beliefs.

When they were fresh from college and full of self-conscious Latin learning, Paine and Adams were encouraged to adopt the fashionable aristocratic outlook that was in vogue among those close to the royal government in Boston and the shire towns like Worcester and Taunton. The college culture of their peers was tinged with social snobbery, and some of the most prominent gentlemen who were their models, like Prat, cultivated a haughty condescension to commoners. But practicing everyday law in southeastern Massachusetts invigorated the Yankee viewpoint that respected and encouraged the people's thirst for knowledge. Both Paine and Adams, like many other country lawyers, had taught in common public schools, and believed in an informed public. Adams articulated his confidence in the knowledge and wisdom of the common people repeatedly—and both Paine and Adams acted on his faith more and more during the political controversies of the 1760s and 1770s.

Adams' belief in the good sense and imagination of industrious common people was rooted in the experience that began in his father's home and was reinforced by what yeoman farmers and tradesmen had taught him about his own field of expertise, the law, when he was first starting out. "Go down to the Marketplace, and enquire of the first Butcher you see. . . . Go on board an Oyster-boat, and converse with the Skipper," he told a friend, and one will find as much genius, wisdom, and common sense "as you will read in the lives of Caesar, or Charles or Frederick."[108] Profoundly committed to the doctrine of self-improvement, he believed that "a Man who can read, will find in his Bible, in the common sermon Books that common People have by them and even in the Almanack and News Papers, Rules and observations, that will enlarge his Range of Thought."[109] Common people like his father were knowledgeable within their own range of experience; and where they were ignorant it was the responsibility of the learned to educate them through newspapers, pamphlets, and face-to-face encounters wherever people gathered.[110] Adams himself offered agricultural advice in his Humphrey Ploughjogger essays, and later, in 1771, no longer the sworn enemy to all pettifoggers, he was even prepared to give one some free advice: "purchase a Copy of Blackstones Commentaries," he told a Connecticut tavern-keeper.[111] As the Revolutionary crisis approached, the engaging lawyer Colonel Otis in Barnstable in 1773 took to publicly reading "to large Circles of the common People, Allens Oration on the Beauties of Liberty," a recent Whig pamphlet which he was recommending to everyone as an "excellent" work. This, Adams believed, was entirely appropriate, though the "Tories" and superior court judges were critical of this and sought to discredit him.[112] In the Tories' view, clergymen, magistrates, lawyers—indeed, all gentlemen—should be condescending fathers directing the people, and not their intermediaries, actively consulting them and engaging them in public affairs. The fact that country lawyers, unlike their Boston and Salem counterparts, came forward to assume precisely this role helps explain the transformation of lawyers' public standing.

Indeed by the early 1770s the emergence of lawyers in town affairs was almost routine. After first holding minor town offices—Adams served on a Braintree highway repair committee and Paine was a surveyor of highways in Taunton—both gained positions of trust in their communities as advisers and spokesmen when their towns confronted imperial politics in the 1760s. Adams even gained a measure of notice among Boston Whigs as the author of the Braintree resolves opposing the Stamp Act in 1765. Reprinted in two Boston newspapers, they were widely copied by other towns. Significantly, the resolutions he drafted emphasized in plain terms the economic hardships the countryside would suffer from the scarcity of cash—a chronic complaint from farmers—as well as the expansion of the authority of the admiralty court, a grievance that alarmed the lawyer in Adams more than any other feature of the Stamp Act because it struck at the concept of impartial justice.[113] At the next election in March 1766, Adams was chosen as a selectman, like his father before him. Immediately he made inquiries to begin educating himself in detail about the schools, highways, and the poor of his town, as well as the tax assessments on the property of his neighbors. Though Adams failed in his attempt to win the Braintree seat in the General Court later that spring—owing to the popularity and unusually large number of kinsmen of the incumbent, a tavern-keeper and pettifogger—Adams did find his "Connections, with the People" increasing.[114]

Paine, who only settled in Taunton in 1761 and had no family roots there until his marriage in 1770, achieved a major role in 1768 as moderator and then as the Taunton delegate to the convention of towns, a sort of self-constituted house of representatives held at Boston to protest the landing of redcoats at the capital.[115] Later, in 1773 he would draft the town's reply to the Boston Committee of Correspondence.[116] Like Adams he had become the town's unpaid attorney, advocating town interests and prudently if forcefully expressing the town's political stance. Taunton's traditional leaders, the Leonards, included professional lawyers, but since they were allies and clients of the royal administration, they would ultimately be disqualified from town service. In 1774 Taunton and Braintree elected Paine and Adams to the house of representatives for the first time. Their peers then selected them to serve on the Massachusetts council, though their Whig politics made them unacceptable to the governor. Their next position of trust would bring them to Philadelphia as delegates to the Continental Congress. As lawyers whose careers were not built on royal patronage but who had instead counted on the patronage of the people in their communities as well as the respect of province leaders, they rose to the highest positions of republican trust.

Revolutionary Massachusetts did not turn to lawyers alone. Indeed, most of its top revolutionary leaders were not lawyers; they were merchants and landowning gentlemen, with a few physicians and manufacturers in addition to lawyers. Paine and Adams were the only lawyers in the province sent to the Congress at the outset, and over twenty years would pass before a lawyer was elected governor of Massachusetts.[117] Yet it is noteworthy that the only Massachusetts delegates chosen to serve in Congress who were not Boston residents were both lawyers. Robert Treat Paine and John Adams had risen to prominence in their own communities and among the province's Boston-centered Whig elite because they contradicted the old stereotype of the lawyer as a fee-grubbing parasite and its recent variant, the imperial sycophant. Instead, Paine and Adams embodied a new ideal of lawyers as learned public servants, the public's advisers and agents.

Their stature as republican lawyers and the definition their actions gave to their role were closely interwoven with their place in the information networks that knit Massachusetts together. Alone among the class called gentlemen, they combined a particular array of communication roles. Like clergymen they were adept at speaking in public and in private to people up and down the social spectrum. But in contrast to the clergy, they held no pulpit, no position of authority over the people they addressed, and so their techniques of persuasion had to reach head and heart, holding the attention of their audience both in the competition of courtroom argument and in the privacy of the lawyer's office.[118] Like clergymen and representatives, and others who routinely traveled beyond local boundaries, they carried information across space, but the frequency and range of their travel exceeded that of any other occupation excepting only teamsters and itinerant craftsmen. More than anyone else, it was a lawyer's business to be informed about legislative actions, official appointments, and public affairs generally, and as part of their occupation they routinely associated with others who were informed, and not just about the concerns of the merchants and gentry, but about the issues that mattered to yeomen and artisans.

Tied to lawyers' need to be informed was a desire to put their knowledge and information to a higher use than merely earning fees. Nurtured in colleges run by clergymen who promoted altruistic ideals, they appropriated the clerical concept of service in defining their professional role, and sought to devote a measure of their information advantages to informing and educating the public. Though in this they were much like clergymen, since the sources and authority of their knowledge were wholly secular, there were important differences. One could disagree with a lawyer without worrying that one's morals and even salvation were in jeopardy. Most original of all for a society that viewed conflict and contentiousness as vices, they were accepted as public combatants. Since they were not themselves invested with the magisterial authority that idealized harmony and commanded deference, they were free to challenge the authority of a governor or the Crown without implicitly undermining their own legitimacy. Becoming revolutionary advocates was an extension of their role, not, as in the case of magistrates, a reversal of it.

Yet the fact that most lawyers, and particularly the mature Boston barristers, became loyalists demonstrates that it was not legal expertise or the profession of law as such that qualified a man for public service. Instead, lawyers became legitimate public officials because of the special niche they occupied in Massachusetts' multiple information networks, a place that enabled them to cement relationships with the people of their counties and with the Boston Whig elite. Serving as intermediaries between local communities and the cosmopolitan world of imperial politics, they were ideally situated to serve as spokesmen who could speak to and for their constituents. Simultaneously serving their own and the public interest, they redefined their occupation so that lawyers could be agents of public as well as private interests.

After 1774 neither Paine nor Adams would ever return to the law full-time. Instead, by serving in a succession of public offices, they came to embody and to ennoble the new definition of the lawyer they had helped to conceive and to shape. Both continued to use their legal learning to serve the public—Paine as attorney general and judge, Adams as drafter of the Massachusetts constitution of 1780. As signers of the Declaration of Independence and as patriots whose careers coincided with the independence movement and the creation of the United States, they offered inspiration to rising generations of lawyers who emerged as public mentors and republican spokesmen in a commercial society—from Fisher Ames and James Sullivan in the 1780s, to Daniel Webster and Joseph Story twenty years later. Highly informed themselves, they worked to elevate themselves and the republic by informing and instructing the people of Massachusetts. In this way the American republic would consummate the union of knowledge and power.

Chapter 5

Communications and Commerce: Information Diffusion in Northern Ports from the 1760s to the 1790s

For centuries observers have agreed that access to information in port towns was faster and more complete than in the countryside. As was evident in Samuel Sewall's Boston, the commercial and political activity centered in ports created both the demand for developed information systems as well as the means: the frequent movement of people and goods. Indeed, as studies of information diffusion in the United States during the pre-electronic era have shown, urban centers, especially ports, dominated long-distance communications.[1] Though gentlemen like William Byrd, Robert Carter, and Thomas Jefferson created islands of urbanity in rural Virginia, and though clergymen and lawyers developed techniques for staying informed in rural New England, port superiority over the countryside for the information associated with high culture, politics, and economic affairs has always been taken for granted, and justly so.

But recognition of this basic reality still leaves much obscure about patterns of information flow within port towns and the ways in which port residents acquired, used, and transmitted information. Moreover port towns, ranging from Philadelphia, North America's largest city and sometime capital of the United States, to Marblehead, Massachusetts, a minor, provincial port where fishing took precedence over transatlantic shipping and the coastal trade, varied dramatically. Information diffusion within ports was shaped not only by the complexity and range of their social and occupational structures, but also by the number and kinds of churches and secular organizations they maintained, as well as the traditions of the inhabitants and the community. By examining actual experiences of port dwellers we can begin to discern some of the ways in which information entered and moved through such communities, and the uses to which it was put along the way.

Although the period considered here, about forty years, is relatively brief and there were no significant changes in communication technology affecting it, time is an important consideration because the 1760s and 1790s differed notably. By the 1790s London was no longer the hub of American economic and political activity and the United States possessed a national politics of its own. A related phenomenon indicative of changes in the diffusion of information was the expansion of the printing business. In 1760 there were only eighteen different weekly and bi-weekly newspapers being printed in a handful of port towns. By 1790, dozens of port and inland towns were printing 106 newspapers.[2] Moreover, the 1790s were culturally distinct from the 1760s, for by the end of the century the dynamism of the American Revolution was being infused with the energies of the romantic movement and the second Great Awakening. New ideas and attitudes as well as new institutions affected the substance and the style of communication, and perhaps also the paths along which information traveled.

No one has yet attempted a comprehensive survey of information diffusion in port towns, an effort that would entail detailed analysis of hundreds of subjects.[3] But despite the limitations of the sources and the paucity of our present knowledge much can be learned even from the experiences of a handful of men: the merchants John Rowe of Boston and George Nelson of Philadelphia; the lawyer William Pynchon of Salem and the law student and fledgling attorney John Anderson, Jr., of New York; and the artisan Ashley Bowen who worked as a rigger and sometime laborer and sailor in Marblehead. The range of their experiences as recorded in their surviving diaries and letters is limited of course, but collectively they span the years 1760 through 1798 and include thousands of daily records and hundreds of letters.[4] Taken together, they permit frequent glimpses of the movement of information in the context of particular lives. A close look at daily conversation, reading, and excursions reveals some of the ways information moved in port towns during a key era.

The two merchants we will be considering, John Rowe of Boston and George Nelson of Philadelphia, were both English immigrants who settled in America's major ports before reaching the age of twenty. Rowe, born in the West Country shire town of Exeter in 1715, settled at Boston before 1736. Bringing some property with him and retaining his English family connections throughout his life, Rowe was an industrious trader whose ventures thrived. Marrying Hannah Speakman, the daughter of an established Boston family, Rowe rapidly climbed Boston's social hierarchy. By the 1760s Rowe was a wealthy, prominent merchant who owned wharves and real estate in addition to shipping and stock. He served as a Boston selectman in the mid-1760s; he became the chief of all American Masonic lodges in 1768; and he was acquainted personally with Massachusetts' commercial and governing elite, both Whig and Tory. Generally a man of moderate, even cautious views, he was a conventional Anglican in religion but a Whig in the conflict with Britain. His surviving diary and letters span the years 1760 to 1779.[5]

Nelson, who was born in 1736 in the English midlands, came to Philadelphia in 1755. An Anglican like Rowe, he, too, married into an established family, a connection one suspects was motivated largely by prudential considerations since when he married in 1760 his wife, Sarah Tomlinson, age 50, was 24 years his senior. Compared with Rowe, Nelson's achievements were modest. In business he operated a partnership, Nelson and Fox, and later became a subordinate associate of Jacob Hiltzheimer, a Philadelphia merchant who dealt extensively in provisions and livestock. During the Revolution, Nelson worked with and for Hiltzheimer and the Congress supplying American troops. Later he became a wholesale salt and sugar dealer. Though he never approached the front ranks of Philadelphia society, Nelson served as a vestryman for St. Paul's church and as president of a mutual benefit society, and during the years for which his diary and letters survive, 1780–1781 and 1790–1792, he was a respected, long established resident.

To succeed as a merchant, access to current information was as much a necessity as capital, credit, or the ability to calculate. Early knowledge of any news that could affect prices and markets could make a man rich in a hurry.[6] Chiefly for this reason, among merchants the speed and privacy of face-to-face communication gave it priority over printing in any form. Printing was valuable of course, but it was the medium for multiple copies, especially suited to the transmission of lengthy or complicated information. Even in printing's fastest form, the handbill, production and distribution took hours. So although merchants like Rowe and Nelson supported newspapers as subscribers and as advertisers, to keep themselves informed they depended first and foremost on face-to-face socializing in their urban locations, the wharves, the taverns, the coffeehouses, and the clubs of Boston and Philadelphia.[7] In conversations they could actively and critically appraise information—checking its reliability and freshness, while comparing their own assessments to those of others involved in trade and shipping. Other merchants and their agents, naval and customs officers, as well as shipmasters were always available for talk. Since Philadelphia and Boston were both seats of government as well as trade, political news was current and available.

For merchants like Rowe and Nelson such face-to-face sociability involving information exchanges was an everyday experience. Rowe had his fingers in so many pies that scarcely a day passed when he was not meeting with other merchants and Boston notables. Sometimes he sat down to talk two or even three times in a day with a shifting, overlapping cast of fellow merchants, selectmen, freemasons, or coparishioners. His "Posee Club" was a small group of friends who met Tuesday evenings and complemented his

"Wednesday Night Club." Other evenings he might also participate with the "Charitable Society," join in an arbitration of some commercial matter, or meet with the selectmen, the St. John's Masonic lodge, or his vestry.[8] Whatever the occasion, Rowe often came home better informed than before. After an evening at the coffeehouse with the province treasurer Harrison Gray, the eminent lawyer Jeremy Gridley, the merchants Ezekiel Goldthwait and John Boylston, and a Captain Davis, Rowe came home with good news regarding the creditworthiness of a bond he was holding; "this information," he noted, "pleased me very much."[9] For good or ill, however, Rowe was almost always out hobnobbing with his peers so as to remain au courant.

Sometimes, even without benefit of the arrival of a ship from afar, the news could be momentous. On Tuesday, January 15, 1765, Boston's mercantile community was "much alarmed" because, as Rowe found out when he made his rounds of the wharves and stopped at the coffeehouse, the great merchant "Mr. [Nathaniel] Wheelwright stopt payment & kept in his room." As a result of Wheelwright's bankruptcy, Rowe realized "a great number of people will suffer." That evening after supper Rowe ventured out in the cold Boston streets to visit Mrs. Cordis' tavern where, as he expected, "the Conversation of the eve'ng was on Nat Wheelwrights affaire."[10] Rowe took the day's news calmly enough, but later that week he learned that by a domino effect John Scollay, John Dennie, and Peter Bourne had also failed, and he expected that he personally would "be a large sufferer by Scollay."[11] The next morning, Sunday, Rowe awoke "much out of order," and he stayed home from church because he found his "mind too much disturbed" by the wave of failures. On Monday, January 21, when Rowe once more went to work in his accustomed way, he found there was "A General Consternation in Town, occasined by these Repeated Bankruptcies."[12] Boston's financial calamity was, in an often used phrase of the period, "the talk of the town."

Though the information available from ordinary face-to-face merchant encounters in Boston or Philadelphia was often more cosmopolitan than what came to rural clergymen or country lawyers through incidental conversations, local concerns were nonetheless paramount. During the 1760s and 1770s, for example, Boston merchants informed one another continually on the subjects of imperial politics and administration, but their conversations were usually tied to local events. Rowe, for example, reported a coffeehouse discussion among nine gentlemen where the conversation came down to "the Seizure [of a ship] made by Capt. Folger & the reseizure of it afterwards by Capt. Hallowell." Sharp words ensued between merchants William Molineux and John Erving, and Rowe himself was disturbed by Molineux's "Indiscretion."[13] Here, as was often the case, a subject that might be cosmopolitan in another context became the occasion for expressing local hostilities.

Rowe's preference for spoken rather than printed information experience is evident even in moments when he chose to be reflective, as when after an

evening at his Posee Club he returned home to find Reverend William
Walter with whom he went on to share "two hours Conversation on the
Times."[14] Rowe liked his pastor, conversed easily with him, and admired his
sermons. But though he attended services regularly and listened to sermons
on public occasions, his reactions to them—"serious," "Judicious," "elegant," "good & sensible, Discourses but a little Metaphisical," "very long"—
reflect overall impressions rather than close scrutiny.[15] He rarely, if ever,
read a sermon and his diary and letters are almost wholly free of reference to
any printing other than handbills and newspapers.[16]

To be sure all merchants were not so. Nelson, who was a zealous Christian, read religious books and pamphlets often, and in addition he read
secular histories and biographies. But in Rowe's case a personal affinity for
socializing is evident in his frequent participation in friendly gatherings and
quasi-public dinners where he sometimes served as master of ceremonies
and led the toasts.[17] Such heavy, almost exclusive reliance on sociability and
the face-to-face encounters of his business day to supply access to information was not necessarily typical for merchants operating in late 18th-century
ports. But Rowe's experience, however exaggerated in degree, does underscore the primary, indeed crucial nature of such activities. Rowe did not
attend all his clubs, meetings, dinners, taverns, and coffeehouses alone—his
peers were out and about spending their time in the same way. Though some
certainly used books and pamphlets, even newspapers, more actively than
Rowe, it is significant that an immigrant could become a highly successful
merchant moving in Boston's highest social circles, dining with the selectmen of Boston, the governor of the province, even the commodore of the
British fleet, without being much of a reader. And why not, when Samuel
Mather, another prominent Boston merchant and scion of the great clerical
family, did not attend college and never valued learning. Of him an acquaintance reported "the information he possessed was from conversation."[18]

For merchants, face-to-face communication was paramount. Like Rowe,
the comparatively bookish Nelson "walked down Town by the Wharves to
see what was doing," and "went down to the Coffee House in the Evening,"
even if he "heard no News to be depended on"[19] since the coffeehouse
usually provided the freshest news. Indeed it even kept a blank book in
which patrons recorded news and opinions daily. Nelson, like other patrons,
consulted the "Coffee House Book" routinely, finding news of the French
fleet first reported there, as well as a critique of Pennsylvania's assembly
president, Joseph Reed, "which caused a great deal of clamour," and led
Reed to write "an Answer denying the charges."[20] Downtown, the wharves,
the taverns and coffeehouses were the key centers of information in port
towns.

Although among merchants the written word usually stood lower than the
spoken word as a means of information, this was not always the case. Where
news from afar was concerned, letters—commonly an extension of the

spoken word in their personal attributes—often played a powerful role. Because letters were nominally private exchanges between respected acquaintances they possessed a higher degree of credibility than newspapers. Moreover because every merchant had correspondents in other ports with whom he routinely exchanged letters, access to letters was widely diffused in port towns. When letters carried information that went beyond private transactions to include news of markets and public affairs as they often did in times of war or political turmoil, their contents rapidly entered and shaped the face-to-face intercourse of the trading community.

While the first reports of distant events of general concern normally came from the mouths of ship captains, the more detailed "inside" accounts came in letters, as when news arrived telling of changes in the English cabinet, alterations in Parliamentary legislation, or the siege of Charleston, South Carolina.[21] Thereafter oral transmission through face-to-face contacts diffused the news throughout the town, as George Nelson reported: "This Morning going to the Office Mr. Barge informed me that one of the Assembly Mr. Reigart had a Letter from Lancaster informing him that Green had beat Cornwallis."[22] Nelson never saw the letter and perhaps neither did his informant Mr. Barge, but the gist of its contents reached him quickly. Indeed letters bearing news of public interest were scarcely private messages at all and seldom remained confidential for very long. In March 1775 General Gage sent for John Rowe because, as Rowe put it, he wished "to see a letter I received from Thomas Griffith."[23] Evidently news of its contents had reached the Massachusetts governor by word-of-mouth and he wanted complete firsthand information. That he would send for Rowe and that Rowe would promptly comply even though he was a patriot and no friend of the administration, reveals the semi-public status that merchant correspondence possessed.

Because merchants collectively maintained the most extensive letter-writing networks of any group in addition to their highly developed face-to-face networks, they were often responsible for bringing news into a town, a colony, or a state and then diffusing it. The implications of this phenomenon for the imperial crises of the 1760s and 1770s, and for the formation of the national government in the 1780s, suggest a magnification of merchant influence going beyond their power as articulate men of means close to the centers of political action. Not only were they the chief patrons of newspapers, as advertisers and subscribers, but their strategic role in their communities' information system meant that they, even more than clergymen, lawyers, or magistrates, defined what was newsworthy and that they dominated interpretation of events.

The place of newspapers in the overall diffusion of information in port towns and among merchants was important, though apparently secondary to face-to-face contacts and letters. Although merchants were often avid newspaper readers and newspapers were a regular feature of coffeehouse furnish-

ings, the ways that Rowe and Nelson used papers show that newspapers only
occasionally contained information that mattered as much as what they
gleaned from conversations. Rowe tended to treat newspapers somewhat
casually, as when he thanked a correspondent in London for "Sending the
papers & Magazines, they Divert an hour or Two every week."[24] Rowe did
read newspapers regularly and, as was common, he sent them on to others as
sources of detailed information. After Boston's great fire in 1760, for example, he sent newspaper accounts to his correspondents to "fully acquaint"
them.[25] Yet he also sent newspapers on to others even when he believed
their contents were "of no Consequence," because they were, in any case,
entertaining.[26] As with magazines and books, their contents helped nourish
sociability.

There were, however, occasions where the news they provided could be
critical. Nelson, who went out to buy the paper even on days he was too sick
to go to the office, learned through a newspaper that Congress had raised
the duty on salt and so concluded that he, as a dealer in that commodity,
must raise his price immediately.[27] Though this was news he might as well
have received orally, for some kinds of information word of mouth was
simply inadequate. King George III's 1781 message to Parliament dealing
with the American war was an event of intense interest in Philadelphia,
however on February 6, 1781, Nelson found that though there was "a good
deal of talk about the Kings speech," he "could not meet with any Person
that had seen any thing of it."[28] In a case like this where the text was the
news, the newspaper was ideal. Two days later Nelson "went to the printing
office and got the King of Englands Speech which was taken from a [New]
York Paper brought from there by some Gentleman last Night."[29] After
Nelson read the speech—"it breaths nothing but War"—rather than having
to accept someone else's characterization of it, he could be fully informed.[30]
In such a case, where information was embodied in a text, there was no
substitute for printing, and merchants, like everyone else in port towns,
turned to the press for news.

The information networks and activities of merchants, though probably
more developed than those of other port residents, were not separate or
distinct from those of other citizens of comparable stature—public officials,
manufacturers, contractors, and members of the learned professions of medicine, law, and the ministry. Gentlemen of all descriptions participated in
clubs and committees, and coffeehouses and taverns were patronized by an
even broader range of citizens.[31] Though merchants might dominate the
information flow in a port through force of numbers and the pervasiveness of
their extra-local interests, to a greater or lesser degree their information
experiences were widely shared among the established, propertied residents.
In many respects all shared a common experience.

Yet even with all the similarities of interest and social standing that connected lawyers with merchants, there were some significant differences in

the character of their information activities. If for merchants the foremost need was to be up-to-date, among lawyers it was breadth and depth of knowledge of people and the law that was more often critical than a command of current events. While it is largely true that both merchants and lawyers competed with their peers on the basis of information, the type of information each required differed, and so did their orientation toward communication activity. Consideration of the experiences of the attorneys William Pynchon of Salem and John Anderson, Jr., of New York City illustrate some of the differences.

In contrast to Rowe and Nelson, both Pynchon and Anderson were college graduates who had been born and raised in America. Pynchon, born at Springfield, Massachusetts, in 1723, came from a family of Connecticut Valley magnates. Coming east to study at Harvard, whence he graduated in the class of 1743, he possessed numerous connections to leading Massachusetts families.[32] At Salem, the second largest port in the province, he soon became the premier lawyer. In the period 1776 to 1789, the years for which his diary survives, Pynchon remained one of Salem's leading citizens, although he was stigmatized owing to his loyalist connections and sympathies. Living a quiet life somewhat detached from the commotion of Salem politics, Pynchon was a learned, enlightened gentleman whose law practice was centered in Salem and Essex County but embraced all of eastern Massachusetts.

John Anderson, Jr., born in New York City in 1773 was separated from the Salem barrister by two generations, a substantially different background, and the far more urban environment of a port that, with about 25,000 inhabitants, was over three times the size of Salem. His father, a Scots immigrant printer who published the pro-patriot *Constitutional Gazette* in 1775 and 1776, became a prosperous storekeeper and auctioneer who was able to enroll both his sons in Columbia College in the 1790s. Though neither Anderson senior nor his wife, Sarah Lockwood (a Connecticut Yankee), came from cultivated families, the home they made together was genteel, and they delighted in encouraging music, drawing, and reading aloud in their warm, affectionate family circle.[33] The surviving diary of John Anderson, Jr., begins in 1794 when he was attending lectures at Columbia and studying for admission to the bar; it ends in September 1798 when the fledgling twenty-five-year-old lawyer and most of his family were cut down by one of the city's recurrent yellow fever epidemics.

Certainly Anderson and Pynchon had little in common. Pynchon, old enough to be Anderson's grandfather, was a traditional Anglophile gentleman who clubbed with mature magistrates, lawyers and merchants, while Anderson, a bright young "nobody" with cultivated manners and artistic interests, went around with youthful Jeffersonian Francophiles, men who were as yet only marginal participants in the city's economic and political life. Yet as remote from one another as Pynchon and Anderson were, they had much in common insofar as information networks and activities are concerned. Their experiences with reading and sociability disclose the inter-play between printing and face-to-face communication in another segment within port communities.

Notwithstanding differences in age, status, and community, like Robert Treat Paine and John Adams, and in contrast to Rowe and Nelson, Pynchon and Anderson spent much of their time reading. As might be expected both lawyers read and reviewed the legal treatises that were necessary for their occupation; but in addition both read extensively in the high cultural literary and philosophical works of their day. As if to counterbalance the specialization that technical mastery of the law required, they sought to make themselves generalists like Paine, Adams, and the Chesapeake gentleman William Byrd. Both in their solitary hours—a much greater part of their week than Rowe's or Nelson's—and when they were in company, reading and discussing each other's readings, even reading aloud, formed the core of much of their sociability. For them printed texts much longer and more complex than newspaper fare constituted the information that they prized most highly. Current events, which loomed so large in the daily information activities of merchants, were less often consequential for lawyers. As with Paine and Adams, Pynchon and Anderson would never wish to appear uninformed or out-of-touch, but every event that might make ripples in the marketplace did not concern them. Books, and to a lesser extent magazines, that conveyed the leading ideas of their era, both classical writings and those of more recent origin, were everyday concerns, not casual diversions.

Continuing participation in "college" or "gentlemen's" culture was very much easier in port towns than in the countryside because of the density of men who had the training, inclination, and resources to pursue it.[34] This concentration meant access to the clubs and private libraries characteristic of genteel urban society. Pynchon's club, which had formed during his first years in Salem and survived deaths and loyalist departures, continued through the war and into the 1780s. Though some quota of mundane chitchat and local tittle-tattle occupied their hours, each meeting was usually devoted to a single serious subject. Sometimes one member presented the material, as when Professor Samuel Williams of Harvard explained an eclipse, or "Mitchell at the Club at Mr. Goodale's . . . shews [Samuel] Johnson to be wrong as to his criticism on Addison's simile of the Angel."[35] On other occasions discussion might be based on a text which was read aloud, such as a selection from Johnson's *Lives of the Poets* or a notable sermon like Ezra Stiles' *The United States Elevated to Glory and Honor*.[36] For the members of Pynchon's club serious reading was an essential part of sociability.

In contrast to a country lawyer, however, neither Pynchon nor Anderson needed to invest in an extensive personal library so as to read widely. Pynchon, for example, routinely borrowed the works of English, continental, and classical authors of literature, history, theology, and political theory from a private Salem library. Anderson regularly drew on his friends and on an impressive array of New York libraries in the 1790s: the Public Library, the City Library, the New York Society Library, the New York Circulating Library, Robinson's Library, the college library, and the library of his club, the Horanian Society. Sometimes borrowing on his own, sometimes on another's membership, and sometimes for a rental fee, Anderson gained access to the literature, history, philosophy, and political science of his own day, as well as a measure of classical learning.[37] In contrast to would-be lawyers dwelling in most inland communities, Anderson could reach way beyond a handful of familiar texts, and way beyond the opportunities a local lawyer's or clergyman's library might afford.

Though neither Pynchon nor Anderson seriously pursued the highest traditional learning by reading systematically in Latin, Greek, and Hebrew as William Byrd had done, in many ways their reading resembled that of the Chesapeake gentry. What differentiates these lawyers at the end of the 18th century is less the substance of what they read than the ready access to books and learning that the port towns supplied. This is not to suggest that extensive reading was a routine popular activity anywhere in the late 18th century. But it is certain that for those possessing the time and the aspiration to enter the exclusive circle of genteel culture—an aspiration for lawyers perhaps even more than for merchants—the means, books, were available.[38]

If for merchants it was face-to-face communication that was paramount, and not contingent on the possession of much book learning, for lawyers, especially urban lawyers, the two modes of conveying information, talking and reading, were fused. As for everyone else in the period the mainstream of communication was sociability, and among lawyers it was reading that often propelled conversation. Trained to refine their understanding of treatises and cases through discussion, habituated to talking shop about statutes and precedents they knew through print, talking about books was not only admirable and edifying, it was familiar. Among lawyers, to be lacking in the conversation derived from books was much like being a Tidewater gentleman ignorant of horses or fox hunting. It was not that they were central to every conversation, but assumptions and references drawn from them might come up at any time. To express ignorance of the world of genteel learning was to place oneself outside the circle of conversation and so to be excluded from much of the information that passed informally among lawyers and other college-educated men.[39]

Such patterns of conduct were not simply manifestations of youthful college culture among recent alumni like John Adams or John Anderson, Jr. William Pynchon in his sixties, like Byrd at the same age, was actively reading and discussing new works as well as old classics. But unlike Byrd, Pynchon in Salem was not dependent on the society of his own dining room or library. He had not only the "hurly-burly" of court days and their dinners, he had the casual gatherings in Salem taverns, frequent visits, and the weekly meeting of his club. At the club, which met now at one house then at another, a special environment of controlled controversy prevailed among fundamentally like-minded men of roughly the same generation and social standing. Here were circles of trust akin to those of the Chesapeake gentry, where confidential information could be exchanged undisturbed by conflicts or indiscretions.

In port towns the cultivated conversation that flowered in the intimacy of gentlemen's clubs was a social institution as it was in Williamsburg and in the great houses of the Tidewater. Small and informal though they were, clubs represented an essential part of urban society for gentlemen in the 18th century. William Pynchon noted, upon returning from his club meeting one night in 1786, that his son John and his friends had begun a club, meeting at Pynchon's home. It was a poignant moment for the old man who saw his son, also a Harvard-trained lawyer, following in his own path. "Long may their motives in forming it continue, and," he wrote, his hopes reflecting his own experience, "may the advantages arising from it be as durable as I wish them."[40] The continuity between the two generations of Pynchons was more than an expression of family culture; it marked a social continuity for a type of communication that was growing and changing.

After leaving college Robert Treat Paine and John Adams had missed such clubs in Lunenburg and Worcester, in Taunton and Braintree. But for John Quincy Adams, apprenticed to the attorney Theophilus Parsons at Newburyport in the 1780s, an intimate club like the Pynchons' was his chief diversion.[41] By the 1790s in New York City and other major ports, club life was coming to include a wide range of associations, from the small, informal college-type, to more formal societies with dues, officers, and minutes according to the model of the Masons, whose lodges multiplied dramatically after 1790. Anderson, who like Pynchon had his particular small informal club, the Horanian Society, also joined a variety of other clubs. They ranged from the Athenian, where he read his essay "on the Utility of Afflictions," and debated the justice of the United States going to war against England in 1794, to the Law Society where he spoke on the desirability of democratic societies in 1795, to the college belles lettres association, the political Tammany Society, and a militia organization he helped form during the Quasi-War with France.[42] This proliferation of clubs and, more broadly, voluntary associations from the 1780s onward transformed the club tradition so that for young men like Anderson the motives for participating were quite different from William Pynchon's two generations earlier. The privacy and confidentiality that were hallmarks of the old clubs of five to ten members, gave way to a more public dimension in the larger, new style societies and associations.[43]

The multiplication of associations and the pattern of membership one sees in Anderson's experience were as yet confined mostly to ports such as Philadelphia, New York, Baltimore, and Boston. But in the succeeding decades associations would sweep over much of the United States, not only the lesser ports but inland towns as well, including many predominantly rural northern communities. Propelled by a variety of motives, among which the drives for self-improvement and self-promotion were prominent, and sustained by changes in the economy and society, forming and joining associations would become a 19th-century American obsession as farmers, mechanics, apprentices, and women became engaged in wide open clubs devoted to improvement and advocacy. Why all this should have happened will be considered in a later chapter. What needs to be emphasized here is the interconnection between reading and conversation among men who defined informed conversation in terms of extensive reading in the high cultural texts of the period and who required such reading and conversation for their well-being.

For the port-dwelling lawyers Pynchon and Anderson and their circles, the need for this kind of informed discourse, as opposed to the more practical orientation of the merchants Rowe and Nelson, can be understood partly as a question of status. Among merchants wealth and social rank were so closely joined that learning was merely ornamental. Among lawyers, however, prestige was more closely tied to learning. During the era when Pynchon's standards were formed, the greatest Boston lawyer was Jeremy Gridley, who had climbed to the top through his conspicuous learning rather than any superiority of family, connections, or wealth. Encouraging young John Adams to value knowledge more highly than wealth, Gridley preached the ruling values of his profession while he also exemplified them.[44] Since colleges and clergy maintained the same priority for learning over wealth, the message to lawyers, and indeed anyone concerned with social approval and rank, was to read and be learned.

In addition, however, there were particular reasons for lawyers' special connection with extensive reading and learned conversation. First, as has been already noted, there was the question of lawyer legitimacy—less important in Salem and New York than in the countryside, but real nevertheless. Pettifogging lawyers and rapacious fee-grabbers were social scapegoats; but lawyers who cloaked themselves in a mantle of conspicuous learning won respect. There was also the question of appearances. If a lawyer showed himself ignorant on matters of genteel learning, his knowledge of the law might be suspect. Since young lawyers newly in practice often had time on their hands while they waited for customers, reading could improve the passage of time. Moreover, given the ponderous quality of most legal treatises, reading history, philosophy, science, religion, and belles lettres was entertaining as well as instructive. In contrast to legal works which could fuel conversation only with other lawyers, it was just this sort of general reading that enabled them to talk knowingly with other gentlemen.

The realization that it was functional for lawyers to read extensively in the high culture of their day is not surprising in light of the time they devoted to such non-legal reading. If this kind of reading and conversation had been damaging to their careers, it would not have been so prevalent. Yet to explain their behavior wholly in functional terms is to overlook important motives that were rooted in personality and culture rather than careerism. For as one probes the diaries and letters of late 18th-century lawyers, meeting them in private and in public settings, at home and in court, at the office and in their taverns and coffeehouses, it is evident that the legal profession drew into its ranks men who found learning rewarding in itself. Too secular and often too skeptical to become clergymen, law was the only other occupation where reading and disputation exercised and enlarged a practitioner's powers. As lawyers they could be paid well for doing what they enjoyed. Making letter-perfect copies of writs was no one's idea of fun, but the "culture" of lawyers, who spent hours in reading and discussion, appealed to men who delighted in the Enlightenment's cornucopia of knowledge.

At a deeper level the individual impulse to command learning was connected to a personal sense of power. For some people wealth was paramount, for some salvation, for some the ability to heal. Though motives are normally blended, considering Pynchon and Anderson as well as Paine and Adams, it appears that all took special satisfaction from the sense that by using their minds they were most fully realizing their faculties as human beings. Employing their minds so as to understand the realities of human life in its natural and historical setting gave them a sense of exhilaration. They bought books and patronized libraries for many reasons; but the most fundamental was the feeling of empowerment that book-learning could provide for people of their disposition.

The significance of personal temperament as well as social circumstances for the diffusion of information is vividly illustrated by the activities of Ashley Bowen, a Marblehead, Massachusetts, artisan who dwelled in this modest, fishing port for all of his life. Marvelously well-informed and systematic concerning some kinds of knowledge, Bowen was wholly ignorant regarding others. Examination of Bowen's communication experiences suggests that in his case class, culture, and occupation were more important than location or literacy for information diffusion; but it also underscores the fact that individual preference could also play a key role in the diffusion of information so as to counterbalance the influence of class and location.

Bowen himself, born in 1728 to a respectable and rising Marblehead family, spent his life on the working men's side of the divide between gentlemen and commonfolk. Though Bowen's father, Nathan, who had come to Marblehead from a Boston countinghouse, was a schoolmaster, notary, pettifog lawyer and justice of the peace, who amassed a significant estate by the time of his death at age 80 in 1776—more assets than John Adams senior— Ashley Bowen went to sea as a thirteen-year-old boy.[45] Whether he was unsuited to schooling and unruly, or whether his parents hoped he would make his fortune as a mariner, is unknown. What is known is that after twenty-seven years sailing all over the Atlantic and Caribbean and rising from cabin boy to merchant captain, and including some service in the Royal

Navy during the attack on Canada in 1759, Bowen settled in Marblehead in 1763. Though Nathan Bowen was a man of means with an appointment as a notary and justice of the peace, Ashley Bowen earned his living as a rigger and sailmaker for Marblehead's fleet. His was a career of downward mobility in which high culture had only a limited role, chiefly in his worship activities in the modest Anglican church his father had joined, St. Michael's. Bowen was literate, kept a journal, and drew pictures of ships and diagrams of rigging. On occasion he composed witty, sardonic verse. But he lived in a social milieu that had little need for his high level of literacy. Bowen's literacy level would have been valuable in the gentleman's world, but in his own circle it was superfluous.

Bowen's surviving journals, which span the years 1766 through 1795 (with some interruptions), reveal a highly localized environment where face-to-face encounters supplied virtually all the information Bowen sought. Here the sociability of the workplace and the neighborhood was the major conduit of information. Conversations with employers, neighbors, and fellow workers kept Bowen well-informed within the narrow, somewhat specialized range of his own concerns. "Tis said," "rumor of," "we hear" "they say," "talk of" are the common ways Bowen recorded his knowledge of events.[46] That knowledge was spotty indeed when it concerned events which had no immediate affect on either the Marblehead peninsula or its shipping. On September 5, 1770, for example, Bowen heard, accurately, that George Whitefield was preaching in Salem.[47] Several years later, however, Bowen and his neighbors could only "suppose the new Governor is come" from the "great guns" they heard firing from the direction of Boston, 12 miles across the water;[48] and when cannon were heard again two weeks later, Bowen had no explanation for it.[49] Later, in September 1774, at the time of the Powder Alarm, a false alarm which led tens of thousands of minutemen to march on Boston and an army of three thousand to gather on Cambridge common, two days afterward Bowen knew only that there were "three thousand men somewhere."[50] When news traveled by water, carried directly to Marblehead by ships' captains and crews, as with reports of the Battle of Bunker Hill, Bowen was much better informed.[51] But when it came overland, as it had two months earlier on April 19, 1775, Bowen reported only that there was "a hubbub about soldiers. News from afar talks of war."[52] Bowen's face-to-face networks were inconsistent and unreliable when the subject was extra-local, making him substantially less informed than a merchant such as Rowe or Nelson, or a lawyer like Pynchon or Anderson.

Whether the primary cause of Bowen's ignorance was the defects in his word-of-mouth networks or resulted from his own personal indifference to outside news is a matter of conjecture. Given the daily traffic in and out of Marblehead, it seems likely that had he chosen to spend the time necessary to obtain better information of outside events he could have been more fully and accurately informed. But Bowen's interests were more basic: he wanted to know what ships entered Marblehead, when they sailed, and what work was being done on them. For information of this sort in which his livelihood was at stake, Bowen's face-to-face networks provided swift, accurate information. On this subject his knowledge was encyclopedic.[53]

Bowen was also well-informed on local church affairs, and not only his own parish. He generally knew when a clergyman from outside the town visited or when a new minister was installed. Indeed regular church going and occasional family visiting were just about his only diversions from work during the years when he was fortunate enough to be fully employed as a rigger. In Marblehead's bad times of smallpox epidemics and economic depression he had more time for church and family as he foraged around town looking for labor.[54] During these times of underemployment and unemployment Bowen's face-to-face networks apparently diminished as his contacts with merchants and shipmasters became more intermittent. Except for the rare mention of naval actions during the Revolutionary War, his world seems to have been bounded by his family, neighborhood, and church.

Though Bowen was highly literate and found the time and place to maintain his journal no matter how poor he became, reading played only a very specialized role in his life. The one book that Bowen read carefully was the *Book of Common Prayer,* a sacred text furnishing comfort and protection. During the crisis of 1775–1776 when Anglicans in Marblehead were under suspicion as Tories, Bowen, fearing that a crowd might destroy St. Michael's *Book of Common Prayer,* used the time available from the disruption of shipping to make a manuscript copy of the sacred book which he hid away for safekeeping.[55] In light of the harassment loyalists in the town encountered, the destruction of the Royal Coat of Arms in St. Michael's interior in 1776, and the violence that Marblehead had witnessed during the controversy over a smallpox inoculation hospital a few years before, Bowen's worries were not wild or fantastic. What the episode demonstrates is just how essential the reading of a particular text was for Bowen's well-being. In contrast to merchants and lawyers, extensive reading, whether in books, magazines, or newspapers, did not concern Bowen. Being generally informed or mastering a body of knowledge through books did not interest him. Bowen did not trouble to use his face-to-face contacts to glean the news of distant capitals from mariners returning from New York, Philadelphia, and across the Atlantic. Even news from Boston, Salem, and Portsmouth was normally beyond his purview.

Bowen's parochial perspective and the fact that he was highly informed on local matters that directly concerned his work, family, and religious worship, did not simply reflect the insularity for which Marblehead was well-known among cosmopolitan visitors.[56] Like other ports it had its shares of merchants, lawyers, and college men by the 1780s and 1790s, and one of its merchants, Elbridge Gerry, for whom Bowen occasionally worked, represented Massachusetts in the Continental Congress.[57] Though Marblehead was certainly a more provincial place than Rowe's Boston or Pynchon's Salem, the explanation for Bowen's limited participation in the information networks of the day was not his geographic location; nor can it be attributed solely to his modest social rank. For with Bowen's learning and intelligence, and during the many days he was unemployed, he could have borrowed reading materials from his fellow church members, from town officials who knew him, and from the merchants and captains who entrusted their ships to his rigging skills. Although his social place impeded access to extensive reading, it was not an insurmountable barrier. Bowen did read newspapers occasionally, and he usually knew when a handbill was circulating. Since the key news in newspapers and handbills spread more swiftly through face-to-face networks anyway, even without reading Bowen could have been more broadly informed if he had exploited his own network more actively. Evidently Bowen was content to dwell in a world of more closely bounded information.

Here Bowen's perspective seems to have been connected with his own acceptance of having slid into a humble rank. His father was, he said, "Squire Bowen;" and he called his father's associates "the Quality."[58] But even though Bowen took notice of gentry events like the Harvard commencement, he knew he was common. On the day after the announcement of his second marriage to Mary Shaw, the illiterate widow of a poor fisherman, Bowen noted wryly that for the moment he was "a sort of a gentleman."[59] Elsewhere his sense of the social distance between himself and "the quality" was expressed in his derision toward Marblehead's "inoculation gentry," the gentlemen who had backed the smallpox inoculation hospital.[60] Although Bowen was linked to gentility through his father and perhaps also by his writing and drawing skills—both polite accomplishments—he had renounced all pretensions of that sort. When he wrote a satire it was not to amuse or impress his club or a circle of newspaper readers; it was for his private diversion. When he wrote a letter there were no literary flourishes; he confined the contents to the essentials. Just how basic Bowen's life was is suggested by the plight of the sixty-year-old father of four in 1788, a year when what little employment he could find was "common work" at 5 shillings per day.[61] Ten days before Christmas, a holiday for Anglicans, Bowen noted "no shoes, no Church. Poor, poor, poor times!" Downcast, he wrote for help to his brother-in-law Moses Porter, twenty miles off in Boxford. The next day "Brother Porter" came to Marblehead with a pair of shoes for each member of Bowen's family and 20 shillings and 8 pence in cash.[62] Bowen thanked God and Brother Porter for their goodness. Gentility was far from his mind.

Considering all the circumstances of Bowen's life—his many years at sea, his struggle to support a family with a continuing succession of wives (three) and children from the 1760s into the 1790s, all on a rigger's earnings in a port disrupted by warfare and economic vicissitudes—one can hardly wonder that the information that concerned him most was highly practical and centered on local matters. It was not that he was indifferent to the greater world of Massachusetts, the United States, and Europe; it was simply that he felt no need to be broadly informed, and whatever information happened to come his way casually was good enough.[63]

In this context it is significant to note that Bowen was a sociable person and a good storyteller, according to the Salem clergyman William Bentley who knew him in his old age. Though he found the seventy-eight-year old Bowen narrow and opinionated, Bentley enjoyed his company and particularly liked Bowen's stories of his days as an assistant to Captain James Cook, under whom Bowen had served in the Royal Navy in 1759, long before Cook's fame as an explorer.[64] For Bowen, of course, these were not cosmopolitan conversations; they were detailed reminiscences of his life long ago. Bowen, pleased to be noticed by Bentley, one of the most learned and cosmopolitan Americans of his generation, made no effort to take advantage of this connection to enlarge his own knowledge of the world. Instead the old mariner, by now a source of oral history, spoke and the erudite Reverend Bentley listened and learned. At Bowen's death in 1813 Bentley memorialized him as "my old friend. . . . The same firm man. With all his prejudices & with sacred attachment to British everything, Navy, Church, State, so much did he love the memory of 1759 & his intimate friendship with Cooke the Circumnavigator."[65] Bowen was, said Bentley, "a man of strong but uncultivated mind," whose "probity . . . has always been admired."[66] Bentley's remarks and Bowen's journals point to a connection between Bowen's artisan status and his locally-centered information activity that was reinforced by a temperamental desire to turn away from the new and the different in favor of the familiar.

Though Bowen dwelled in a port town where visitors were entering and leaving by land and sea daily, apart from his knowledge of harbor activity his personal information flow was much like the countryside, where most information passed by familiar face-to-face networks in conjunction with newspapers and books. Indeed the differences between port towns and the countryside were often only differences of degree—port residents had more personal contacts, more occasions for interaction, more collective rituals like church services or funerals, and easier access to printed goods. Moreover even ports like Salem, Boston, and Philadelphia could be small communities insofar as information diffusion was concerned.

One sees the small community within the major port in numerous instances. In Boston John Rowe moved swiftly to scotch a rumor some people had "wickedly & Maliciously spread" about him and was satisfied when he "got the first of them to Acknowledge it to be a lye," so that a signed declaration could be used, as he put it, "to Clear my Innocence."[67] At Philadelphia, as in the countryside, people found each other by making inquiries through networks of acquaintances. As Nelson reported, "Mr. John Lisle came to my house and enquired where Mr. Jones lived that came in yesterday Evening from Charles Town & I went with him to Mr. John White for information who directed him to Chesnut street."[68] In Salem "the town talk" might concentrate on a particular breach of courtesy, such as "Collector S. Webb's doings and rudeness in seizing the Widow Pickman's furniture for taxes," or focus on a ceremonial social event like the visit of the Marquis de Lafayette, which left "each circle, club, and tea-table in Salem," Pynchon noted, "finding and proving and disputing as to neglects and affronts respecting the entertainments and ball for the Marquis."[69] In the 18th century the face-to-face information networks that underlay community life operated in much the same way whether in ports or in the country.

Yet information diffusion in port towns was in some ways so unlike the countryside as to lead to distinct patterns of behavior that may be best described as urban. Urban communities in the late 18th century, which were all ports, possessed institutions and customs that affected both face-to-face and printed modes of communication directly. The result was that port residents, whether merchants, professionals, or artisans, were all exposed to unprecedented quantities of information, with a frequency not available elsewhere.

The single most tangible difference was the ready availability of printed goods, especially books. The port towns all had libraries of some description available to some or all of their residents.[70] Most often they were private, gentlemen's libraries, but there were also commercially operated rental libraries, and more rarely, free libraries for mechanics or the general public. In addition there were merchants who imported and sold a variety of titles that went beyond the devotionals, hymnals, and schoolbooks of the country store. Books were a luxury, generally costing from a day's to a week's wage for a common laborer; but they were not scarce commodities. As a consequence port dwellers enjoyed more choices in their reading matter, and were more likely to express their individual taste in reading. Rather than having to settle for whatever came to hand, as John Adams did when he was away from his own library, or else, like Adams, having to spend a fortune on books, a Pynchon or an Anderson could read widely with ease. In the port towns the decision to read books extensively or to read them scarcely at all, like Rowe and Bowen, was a consequence of individual preference and social milieu, and not an issue of availability as it was even for prosperous people who lived in the countryside off the main trade routes.[71]

This discriminating access to books for port residents was matched by a greater independence from newspapers. Ironically, though newspapers were printed locally and imported directly, and so were cheaper, fresher, and more readily available in ports than elsewhere, port residents were less dependent on them for information than rural residents because of the efficiency of urban face-to-face networks.[72] For even though most information flowed through limited networks of known associates—and not randomly from person to person like a contagion—the port towns had such dense,

interconnected, and overlapping networks that information of keen importance to each person was likely to come more swiftly from conversation than
a newspaper. Newspapers, after all, were only printed once or twice each
week, and they were based on information that had accumulated from letters, formal proceedings, word-of-mouth reports, and other newspapers. As
we have seen earlier, newspapers were superior to face-to-face networks
only when precise detail was important, as with extended, complex messages. Partly for this reason newspapers were loaded with speeches, laws,
treaties, and essays. They served partly for genteel entertainment and partly
for reference. Paradoxically, for the port residents who were their primary
patrons and consumers, newspapers were seldom most urgent for news.

A further irony was that newspapers in great ports also came to carry
information that in a smaller community would have travelled by word of
mouth. In Philadelphia, for example, a butcher advertised the date that he
planned to slaughter a steer. Such notices made a part of the newspaper a
bulletin board for a community that was too large and complex to carry such
particular information via word of mouth beyond a small neighborhood. A
Philadelphia reader who was looking for fresh meat might find this notice
more "interesting" than the weeks-old report of foreign news that filled
three columns on the front page, whereas a reader fifty miles inland would
find no interest in the butcher's notice, since even if the notice was timely he
would not have gone to Philadelphia to buy fresh meat. Under these circumstances it is easy to understand why newspapers often possessed a low level
of salience for many people much of the time. Their unique strength was that
they made relatively short official texts available; but for many in their
potential audience all they provided was stale news, details, and irrelevant
commercial notices. Given all the alternative means of information available
in ports, newspapers could only play a modest role.

The Revolution and the creation of the national government, however,
were instrumental in augmenting the importance of newspapers in the communication activity of the port towns. Not only were there more and more
frequently published papers, but judging from the diaries and letters of the
people considered here, they were read more often and more actively. The
conflict with Britain and independence gave rise to a raft of significant texts,
from Acts of Parliament and official colonial resolutions to polemics like
John Dickinson's *Farmer's Letters,* to accounts of battles and diplomatic and
political maneuvers.[73] Since newspapers were the prime vehicles for official
texts, controversial argument, and detailed reports of distant events, the
appetite for papers intensified. The fact that the scope and complexity of the
commercial activity that supported newspapers increased simultaneously,
helped to consolidate their enhanced role. Whatever the limitations of newspapers, in the 1780s and 1790s they were a larger presence in the information
flow of port towns than they had been earlier.

Nevertheless it was the density and variety of occasions for exchanging information face-to-face that set the port towns apart from the countryside. Here there were markets and shops, taverns and coffeehouses, and the sociable workplaces of two dozen crafts, where a barbershop could serve as "the Fountain Head of Politics for the most grand Disputations."[74] Here the multiplicity of churches and benevolent societies, clubs and libraries, legislatures and courts, all provided opportunities for exchanging information and enriching the substance of what passed between people. Theatricals, concerts, circuses, Independence Day festivals, the visits of dignitaries like George Washington and the Marquis de Lafayette, the funerals of prominent residents like Andrew Oliver in Boston and Benjamin Franklin in Philadelphia, were all events that brought people together and created opportunities to converse. In such a setting information traveled rapidly among the different media—printing, letters, oratory, and conversation—to all the streets and neighborhoods. In addition, for urgent news of general interest there were handbills and, more rarely, posters. Under these circumstances, simply to live in a port meant that everyone, even a person like Bowen who had no special interest in general news, would be exposed to major currents of information. For a person such as Anderson, who was eager to participate in all the cultural activities New York City offered in the 1790s, and who enjoyed the leisure to do so, living in a great port became a kind of education in itself.

But if ports were, broadly speaking, information "hothouses" which facilitated information diffusion among all their residents, it is also true that the size and character of the port, and the class and occupation of inhabitants—together with their individual preferences—affected their information activities profoundly. Philadelphia, a center of both continental and provincial politics, a metropolis for printing as well as trade, was much more of an information "hothouse" than Salem, where the county courts met and printing was strictly for Salem and its neighbors. Whatever news concerned the government of the United States was accessible to George Nelson by a walk downtown—and when he had no more urgent business he would spend a few hours listening to debates in the Pennsylvania assembly or the congress of the United States. When a celebrated preacher like the Universalist Elhanan Winchester visited town, Nelson or Anderson could hear him speak, borrow or purchase his works for further reading, and perhaps even engage him in private conversation.[75] William Pynchon, by contrast, at best got news of the Massachusetts or United States government secondhand, days later; and the number of luminaries passing through Salem, let alone the availability of their publications, was not to be compared with Philadelphia, New York, or Boston.

Yet because of community size and economic and ethnic complexity, the information networks of the great ports were more often specialized, not only by class but by neighborhood and type of activity. Nelson, for example, engaged in elaborate conversations about the supplies and prices of salt, a narrow, technical kind of information that was concentrated in a network of importers, wholesalers, and bulk consumers.[76] Though comparable topics of information and the specialized networks in which such information traveled existed everywhere, their numbers and relative importance were magnified in the great ports. In a Salem or Marblehead, like a country town, once information entered one network it was more likely to be dispersed throughout the community because sheer size and complexity did not create impediments, and common interests like shipping or fishing created porous, overlapping networks among different neighborhoods and social strata. At the same time higher levels of ethnic homogeneity and residential stability made networks more inclusive than in the great ports.

It is also likely that in places like Philadelphia, New York, and Boston in the 1780s and 1790s the sheer abundance of information that was becoming available made specialized networks more necessary than heretofore. The problem for a salt dealer like George Nelson was not to glean some news of business and the world, but rather to choose the news that affected the price of salt from among the wealth of reports and bulletins available to him in conversations and in print. By going downtown and speaking with other buyers and sellers of salt, Nelson informed himself and reinforced a specialized network. In the great ports the need as well as the availability of such specialized networks surpassed the lesser ports. Though compared to the countryside, all ports were information hothouses; the ways in which they functioned varied substantially.

Yet judging from what we have seen of Rowe and Nelson, Pynchon and Anderson, and Ashley Bowen, occupation and class counted for even more than the particular kind of port. The information activities of merchants and lawyers overlapped of course, as did their social stature, but merchants' marked emphasis on face-to-face communication supplemented by letters, where lawyers drew much more heavily on books, had significant implications for their respective social roles. Merchants, perhaps more than they realized, dominated perceptions of contemporary affairs as a consequence of their intense concern with current events; while lawyers, like clergymen, acted as custodians of cultural traditions—seeking to guide society according to the lessons of history and philosophy.

To an ordinary workman such as Bowen, the primary usefulness of information lay in maintaining a family's material and spiritual life. Unconcerned with influencing his fellows or making a mark in any public role, the information that mattered to Bowen came from his family and acquaintances in and around Marblehead, and the *Book of Common Prayer*. Being well-informed in a broader sense was not important to Bowen. He was interested if news came his way, and owing to the hothouse effect, his casual conversations probably included cosmopolitan information about overseas matters more frequently than if he had been a country blacksmith; but for Bowen, cultivating such knowledge served no practical or psychological need. Evidently only those whose livelihoods depended on being informed or who sought to be genteel actively pursued current events and general knowledge.

By the 1790s in New York City a pattern of increasingly private, exclusive behavior is evident that would intensify the effects of specialization and stratification on the movement of information. What was happening is symbolized by the way that John Anderson, Jr., and his friends participated in the city's Independence Day celebration in 1794. The festivity was a great community enterprise capped by speeches and a parade in which city officials and residents marched in groups according to their office, occupation, or another corporate identity such as fire company. In the celebration the city's specialization and stratification were simultaneously recognized and subsumed in a great collective experience in which residents joined together, each in his or her appropriate station. Yet Anderson and his friends, though they might have joined in the parade, viewed it as outsiders. They rented a rooftop, bought ice cream and punch, and viewed the whole spectacle from above.[77] They were not strangers. Doubtless they recognized many of the marchers, and they may have waved and called out to them. But in obtaining their own private vantage point set off from the crowd and in making the affair into a private party, they were insulating themselves from the common experience and creating a private enclave. In itself this was not wholly new when one considers the long-standing vitality of clubs, but to treat a community festivity in such a private way pointed toward the separation of private and public experience that would grow in the 19th century.

What this meant for the diffusion of information is not entirely clear, however it does point to more sharply defined boundaries between people, and hence more clearly defined and distinct information networks. In contrast, in 18th-century port towns—great ones such as Philadelphia, New York, and Boston as well as lesser ones like Salem and Marblehead—the high density and overlapping quality of information networks carried information efficiently and helped integrate the diverse elements of the community. The challenge posed by great size, increased specialization and stratification, and the separation of public and private experience, were only beginning to affect communication networks and the diffusion of information. In the decades after 1820, as the availability of print and long-distance communication increased and local organizations multiplied, a new configuration for the diffusion of information would emerge.

Chapter 6

Information and Insularity: The Experiences of Yankee Farmers, 1711–1830

Warm sunshine and fresh breezes blowing off Long Island Sound made June 30, 1747, an ideal day to harvest hay at New London, Connecticut, and that was exactly what the sixty-nine-year-old farmer Joshua Hempstead was doing. It was all routine until, Hempstead reported, "I acidentally Stuck my pitchfork into my left Leg a little above my shoe Lappet." Still, he continued stacking. "It proved Exceedingly painful in the night," however, so although the sun shone brightly the next morning, Hempstead "Lay by most of the day lame." But he went back to the task as soon as he could: "toward night I Stackt some hay."[1] In July this was the life of a New England farmer, young or old; and whether in 1740 or 1840 thousands of men like Hempstead were bound to the same demanding discipline of seasonal work that tied them to the land that they owned or rented. Viewed from a distance, they seem much like peasants caught in an endless, repetitive cycle of local experience. Planting, cultivation, and harvest, animal husbandry, making and breaking tools, cutting and consuming cord upon cord of firewood, they ate and slept and worked from generation to generation, raising and burying families, chores without end.[2] Thomas Gray, a gentleman poet, separated from such farmers not by time, as we are, but by social rank, expressed a similar view more picturesquely in his "Elegy Written in a Country Church-yard":

> Oft did the harvest to their sickle yield,
> Their furrow oft the stubborn glebe has broke;
> How jocund did they drive their team afield!
> How bow'd the woods beneath their sturdy stroke!

> Let not Ambition mock their useful toil
> Their homely joys, and destiny obscure;
> Nor Grandeur hear with disdainful smile
> The short and simple annals of the poor.

With sympathetic condescension he explained the parochial ignorance of plowmen for whom, alas, "Knowledge to their eyes her ample page/Rich with the spoils of time did ne'er unroll."[3] To many observers then and now, these were the insular conditions of peasant life in the encapsulated communities of the rural past.

To some degree, these images conveyed in Gray's "Elegy" reflect realities. On the day in June 1750 that Gray was poetizing, Hempstead, and many like him, were doing local errands, surrounded by familiar faces and situations.[4] For them information regarding high culture or the outside world was of much less immediate concern than information on the weather and the wide range of personal and local events that dictated the schedule of their labor and determined their paths of duty and opportunity every day. But Gray's perspective and the view of Yankee farmers as peasants is incomplete because it obscures the more dynamic, heterogeneous, even cosmopolitan elements of experience that shaped farmers and their communities in colonial America. Close observation of farmers' lives reveals an interplay between routine, quotidian local events and the occasions where information from the world beyond the town and county entered their experience, giving the lie to the image of timeless inertia that makes outsiders' visions of rustic life so appealing and romantic.

Certainly farmers dwelled within circles of familiar people, places, and events most of the time, and they and their outlooks were influenced by these circumstances. Yet they never deliberately insulated themselves from the world beyond their localities—indeed they were normally eager to learn more about it. Most provincial of all American provincials, and sometimes sensitive on this point, farmers could spend a whole string of days in touch only with their own household or perhaps only with neighbors who were equally isolated. As a result farmers, in contrast to urban artisans, could never assume that proximity would keep their word-of-mouth sources of information abreast of consequential matters. They recognized that they must seek out news and knowledge. The ways they went about it and the kinds of information they sought reveal profound continuities in New England farm life, as well as changes wrought by commercial and urban development in tandem with improved transportation.

Farm families were the most numerous among New England inhabitants and were also the most varied with respect to wealth and residence. Working on lands that ranged from the worn-out, sloping, marginally productive, and inaccessible to the flat, rich, loamy acres of the mid-Connecticut River Valley—land that was just as accessible to markets as the environs of New

England's many saltwater ports—farmers could be poor or prosperous. They might be transients who paid barely any taxes, never held office, and dwelt at the fringes of their communities both literally and figuratively. Or, like Joshua Hempstead, they might be longtime residents whose offices as select-men, militia officers, and deacons placed them at the center of community life. Owing to such wide variations in their condition and geographic loca-tion, their social roles had many and complicated dimensions.

In the North, generally farmers ranked beneath the gentry, merchants, and professionals who led society and articulated its cultural standards. At the same time farmers normally stood higher than many artisans and most laborers who, with few exceptions, lived an almost purely local and private life under modest circumstances. Because farmers usually became property-holders at some stage in their lives within a society where property conveyed political stature, and because they were frequently rooted in a particular community with their kinsmen, they often attained positions of responsibil-ity within their towns. As justices of the peace, representatives, militia offi-cers, as selectmen, deacons, tax assessors and probate agents, they partici-pated in a colony-wide system of laws and forms and paperwork, just as gentlemen, merchants, and professionals did. Yet at the same time they remained men who worked with their hands indoors and out and who, like artisans and other laboring men, relied more on their mechanical skills and physical strength for their livelihood than on their literacy, verbal skills, or the possession of fresh news and knowledge of high culture and public affairs. Though farmers were generally sociable, literate, and preferred to be informed, their daily lives were organized around the urgency of timely planting and harvests. The small crises of animal husbandry, of flooded fields and broken fences, took priority over nearly every other kind of information—whether local gossip, high politics, or salvation, whether com-municated orally, in a letter, or in print. The most critical store of informa-tion for farmers was experience, accumulated and hoarded up over many seasons from childhood on. Perhaps for that reason their orientation toward outside information often seems closer to that of artisans and laborers than to that of gentlemen, merchants, clergymen, and lawyers. Access to outside information was not critical for their day-to-day operations nor for their stature as farmers. Only when they entered into public life did circumstances change; and since holding office was mostly voluntary, concern for informa-tion beyond direct experience was evidently more a matter of personal aspi-ration, taste and temperament among farmers than for most other men.

I

The aged Joshua Hempstead who stuck himself with his pitchfork in 1747 was just the sort of farmer who for many decades had taken an interest in external as well as local affairs. For though his fields and woods supplied his principal livelihood, Hempstead refused to limit himself to farming. Like many other farmers he possessed skills which he used to supplement his income, vary his work, and to keep himself fully employed and engaged in the life of the community. Only the range of his talents was extraordinary— carpentry on ships and houses, inscribing gravestones, surveying land, the drawing of wills, deeds, and common writs, as well as occasional sailing and trading ventures. He really was a jack-of-all-trades. Hempstead's multiple practical and personal skills and the sizeable property that he was able to accumulate encouraged his fellow townsmen to entrust him with their public business. A 1678 native of New London, and a grandson of Robert Hempstead, one of the town's original settlers, by his mid-thirties Joshua Hempstead was serving as a selectman and on various town committees concerned with, among other things, the selection of a schoolmaster. Later on Hempstead would emerge as the farmers' champion in town affairs and as a representative to the Connecticut legislature.[5] A New London historian exaggerates only slightly when she writes, that by the time Hempstead was in his fifties, "he generally held three or four town offices; was justice of the peace, judge of probate, executor of various wills, overseer to widows, guardian to orphans, member of all committees, every body's helper and adviser, and cousin to half of the community."[6]

As may be apparent from this catalogue of Hempstead's activities, he was a sociable and practical person, not introverted or bookish. His diary, a massive document that ran from 1711 to 1758, supplies a record of his activities and the events that came within his purview, not the inner reflections of self-conscious piety or the detailed observations of a literary person. Religious devotions never played much part in his life—he was not admitted to church membership until he was forty-eight-years-old—and he spent little time on reading. Though he was literate and active as a record keeper and draftsman, he was not a reader. Years went by without any mention of a book, a sermon, a newspaper, or even an almanac in his diary.[7] At his death the inventory of his property included an extensive list of tools and livestock, but only a few books—three bibles in various states of repair and a couple of volumes of law.[8] Printed matter occupied only a marginal place in Hempstead's life because the dominant way that he obtained information beyond his own direct observations was through word of mouth. His only exposure to the formal world of ideas came when he listened to pulpit oratory.

Hempstead had his fingers in a lot of pies in and around New London, and he prospered; yet he was never so well-off as to adopt a life of gentlemanly ease, free of manual labor. He and his people were farmers; indeed among the eighty-five New London natives who graduated college from 1693 to 1850, not one was named Hempstead—a coincidence perhaps—but one that suggests that Joshua's lack of gentlemanly aspirations may have been part of an enduring family culture.[9] Characteristically, on October 28, 1758, though he was eighty-years-old and suffering from a pain in his bowels, Hempstead "was most of the Day Stacking Corn Topps. . . . I handled Every Shef & Stowed them away . . . [it was] night before wee had done."[10] Hempstead, who could afford to rest from his lifelong labors and who would be resting in his grave eight weeks later, believed in what he was doing. Farming was his calling.

Most likely it was because farming was his primary occupation that the information that most often concerned Hempstead was local in both origin and consequence. It included the health and travels of his relatives and neighbors, their births, marriages, and deaths, news of their livestock and crops, transfers of property, damages from storms and fires, and a daily weather record drawn from his own and others' observations. Hempstead's immediate neighborhood and his activities within New London defined the circle of inclusion, which extended several miles from his home farm. Because he had family in the nearby towns of Groton and Stonington, and acquired a farm in the latter town, he obtained the same kinds of information from distances up to fifteen miles away, though only sporadically and incompletely. His capacity to be regularly and thoroughly informed was limited to the laboring circuit of New London farming which meant trips "to town," "to [church] meeting," and among neighbors who worked for one another, renting each other's draft animals, equipment, and skills. From a gentleman's perspective the information obtained might be regarded as merely "the short and simple annals of the poor" who would never read from the "ample page" of knowledge; but for those who dwelled within this world exchanging all of this information, these annals were neither short nor simple. Dry facts recorded in Hempstead's diary marked the achievements and failures of Hempstead's neighbors and kin, their virtues and vices, God's blessings and His admonitions. For Hempstead they constituted a record and a guide to the shifting pattern of relationships—familial and communal, economic and political—of the people with whom he lived. To be ignorant of these matters in an interdependent community assured one's exclusion from community decision making and risked the failure of one's agricultural endeavors and the well-being of one's family. "The short and simple annals" were of no interest to an outsider, but they were necessities for Hempstead and lesser farmers in New London and New England generally.

Had such local matters constituted the entirety of Hempstead's access to information, then the image of encapsulated rural life set apart from general affairs would be accurate. In fact, however, though Joshua Hempstead neither could nor would ever be so well-informed about events beyond his locality as within it, he was always cognizant that New London was part of a transatlantic society where religious and political controversy as well as international warfare exerted powerful influences on events. Moreover this consciousness was evidently widespread, because Hempstead's word-of-mouth networks—people he met by chance in town, at church, as he went about his ordinary farming and civic affairs—kept him sufficiently informed so that he seems never to have felt the need to subscribe to a newspaper, and he seldom if ever read one. This was as true in 1711 when, after carpentering on a ship and stopping at a militia officer's house he came home with "ye sad news of ye English Canada fleet," as it was in 1757 when his son, who had been out mowing hay, returned with the news that "before sunrise a Post came from the Govr. & Informs that fort Wm. Henery is Invaded."[11] Such news was almost always available at public occasions like church, court, and town-meetings, where many people assembled including the town's clergymen, merchants and magistrates—its most highly placed, cosmpolitan, and best-informed residents.

Information about the world beyond New London did not come with every trip to town or every time Hempstead or his sons went out mowing or to track down a stray animal; but it did happen with some frequency, just as visitors to the farm, neighbors and relatives, sometimes brought information to his door. On the rare occasions when a post-office rider stopped at Hempstead's farm to feed his horse, Hempstead received payment in news as well as cash, as in 1712 when the "Post from hartford" brought "ye Sad news of ye Death of ye [colony] Secretary."[12] Post riders and indeed all travelers were routinely pumped for information as they passed through the countryside. They complemented the resident clergymen, magistrates and merchants, as well as circuit-riding judges, ship captains and sailors, teamsters and drovers, who kept local word-of-mouth networks supplied with a diet of general news. The information was not necessarily accurate or timely, but since it seldom demanded any action from local people, that made little difference. Its crucial importance lay in the fact that it connected the great world which lay beyond daily experience with the farmers' own local affairs. Significantly, the contours of the great world that circulated via word of mouth were provincial, centering on the colonies and their imperial links. In contrast to newspapers, which paid attention to European affairs and to literary and scientific high culture, the word-of-mouth networks limited diplomatic news to that which immediately concerned imperial war and peace; news of monarchs passed only when succession to the British throne was at stake.

In Joshua Hempstead's case, as with the other farmers considered here, letters and personal travel also played a significant role in enriching local information networks. Nearly all of Hempstead's letters were from relatives—a younger sister who had moved to Maryland and whom he visited once; a son who shipped aboard a vessel trading with "Martineco" in the West Indies; and with Long Island kinsmen. The information was primarily personal business but could also include military news and reports of health and economic conditions. Hempstead's own travel was also quite limited, a few trips to New Haven and Hartford and a single trip to Boston and another to Maryland in the course of a lifetime. But travel also

enhanced his information network and that of his neighbors because contacts once made might be refreshed by message-bearing third parties years
later. Hempstead was no cosmopolite, but this sometime agent of Winthrop family interests was no bumpkin either. On his Maryland trip, made
during his seventy-second year in 1749, he proudly noted that in New
Jersey he "waited on Govr. Belcher & Recd. a Letter etc. & had an hours
Conversation very free & familiar about ye affairs of our Govermt for near
40 years past & his thots of time to come & other private affairs. his
Excellency Treated me with much Respect & Invited me to Stay all night &
dine with him on the morrow, . . . but I told his Excellency I should Loose
my company if I stayed & must be Excused."[13] Belcher, a native of Massachusetts and its governor from 1731 to 1741, doubtless enjoyed the opportunity to reminisce with a substantial Yankee yeoman, and his gracious condescension made the visit memorable to Hempstead for whom such exalted
company was rare indeed. Before the month was out he would be back in
New London attending to his seasonal chores—"at home haying most of
the day."[14] Travel beyond New London county and the receipt of letters
were events that allowed him to set his local experience in a broader
context.

For one brief period in Hempstead's life, when the notorious, seemingly
deranged New Light preacher, James Davenport, came to New London,
local events assumed general importance, and Hempstead and his neighbors
were situated at the intersection of local and cosmopolitan news. The stories
of Davenport's antics that circulated throughout the colonies, particularly
the book-burning episode of March 6, 1743, often originated in New London
where they circulated in local face-to-face networks just as they were entering general colonial word of mouth, letter, and newspaper accounts. The
proximity of such notable events was distracting, and took people away from
their routine labors. As early as April 1741 Hempstead went on two consecutive days to hear the Pennsylvania revivalist Gilbert Tennent preach, and in
the following month he heard James Davenport twice. By early June 1741
there was a great revival in New London, "the greatest Success Imaginable
& beyond what is rational to Concieve [sic] of it. . . . Never any such time
here & Scarce any where Else."[15] And so for a time it continued. But
Davenport and his most enthusiastic followers were a peripatetic group, and
after their departure the revived community settled down.

When Davenport and his companions returned in early 1743 there was
another climax of interest in religion which culminated in the bonfire of
"corrupt" books and other worldly vanities. During this episode Hempstead
was away on a visit to Long Island, but after he returned he went once more
"to hear Mr. Davenport," whom he with the other justices would later try
for the book-burning. Hempstead's account of this experience conveys his
preference for the familiar rational, systematic mode of preaching:

[Mr. Davenport] was scarcely worth the hearing. the praying was without form or comelyness. it was difficult to distinguish between his praying & preaching for it was all Meer Confused medley. he had no Text nor Bible visable, no Doctrine, uses, nor Improvement nor anything else that was Regular forenoon and the Last Sabath before by Report was of ye Same peice though not on the Same subject for then it was the hand of the Lord is upon me over & over many times; then Leave of & begin again the Same words verbatim. now it was (in addition to telling of his own Revelation & others Concerning the Shepherds Tent & other Such things) he Calld the people to Sing a New Song &c forevermore 30 or 40 times Imediately folowing as fast as one word could follow after another 30 or 40 times or more & yn [then] Something Else & then over with it again. I cant Relate the Inconsistance of it.[16]

From Hempstead's perspective there was nothing to be gained by listening to such effusions. Yet it was only after hearing Davenport in 1741 that Hempstead first began to evaluate the sermons he heard instead of just taking them in. Now he began to note that this preacher gave two "Excellent Discourses;" that one "Repeated an old Sermon," and in 1745 Hempstead actually took time off from haying so as to hear the great English evangelist George Whitefield preach four times. In contrast to Davenport, he concluded, Whitefield was indeed "an Excellent preacher."[17]

Because he happened to live in New London, Hempstead could, without leaving his usual haunts, witness all of the most celebrated evangelists of the Great Awakening—Tennent, Davenport, Whitefield and, on the day of Davenport's trial, Jonathan Edwards.[18] As a result Hempstead became an informed observer of the great revival and a more critical, discerning judge of pulpit oratory than he had ever been before. In this case as in others, he and his neighbors who had flocked to hear the famous preachers, could understand their own local experience in the context of general colonial affairs.

Local circumstances varied, of course, but farmers who lived inland were equally touched by the Great Awakening and cognizant of its greatest preachers. Like Nathan Cole, a farmer who lived a dozen miles northwest of Middletown, Connecticut, they could follow word-of-mouth reports of Whitefield's preaching at Philadelphia, Boston, and elsewhere, so that on the October morning Whitefield arrived at Middletown he was greeted by a throng of 4000 people. Cole himself reported that "all along the 12 miles" he traveled, "I saw no man at work in his field." Instead as he approached Middletown he heard the "low rumbling thunder" of horses hooves and witnessed the great "Cloud of dust" they raised as the "Steady stream of horses and their riders" poured into the village.[19] Without printed handbills or organized publicity, face-to-face encounters had brought word of Whitefield's spiritual celebrity into the houses of Yankee farmers. Whether inland or at New London they were provincial people no doubt, but they were not isolated rustics encapsulated in a timeless agrarian idyll.

In 1726, during a town conflict, Hempstead had emerged as a leader among New London farmers, and it is important to remember that for him as well as his neighbors, farming was the primary livelihood, which made local information paramount.[20] It was only because they lived around New London, a saltwater port with ties to Boston, Newport, and New Haven, where the frequency and freshness of contacts and information from the great world was superior to most inland locations, that the participants in Hempstead's word-of-mouth networks could be relatively well-informed. Whether it concerned religious controversy, military affairs, or word of some calamity, the news came to New London. Five days after a fire swept Boston in 1711 killing almost a dozen people and gutting 100 houses, Hempstead learned of the disaster at church.[21] Similarly, news of war and peace or the arrival of an imperial notable was signaled by cannons booming within earshot of New London farms.[22] Welcoming an imperial officer was of no practical interest to a farmer such as Hempstead; but because his farm was near one of the colony's chief ports, such information was available. Because New London was a potential target for attack during the several wars with France, war news possessed special urgency. Indeed the town-meeting repeatedly petitioned the colony legislature for help in fortifying the harbor. Location as well as occupation and social rank clearly affected access to information. For farmers and tradesmen, the site of their residence was especially significant since their occupations—in contrast to merchants and professional men—never required them to maintain connections or correspondence with associates beyond their localities.

II

Living in a community that was relatively isolated from the information flow generated by commerce and colonial political affairs made access to outside information more difficult, as is evident in the experiences of Matthew Patten, Abner Sanger, and Samuel Lane, two New Hampshire farmers and a tanner whose lives overlapped Hempstead's generation. Like Hempstead, all three relied chiefly on word-of-mouth networks for information, but Bedford, Keene, Dublin, and Stratham—all inland towns—were closer to the periphery of colonial settlement and more distant from the thoroughfares of trade and communication than New London. As a result it appears that though these countrymen learned about outside affairs less often, for them gaining information was a more self-conscious, deliberate activity than it was for Hempstead. It is noteworthy that after the Revolution, when newspapers became more widely available, two of the three became subscribers; they were concerned enough about extra-local information to pay for it.

Samuel Lane, who was born ten miles south of Portsmouth in the coastal town of Hampton in 1718, moved a few miles inland to the neighboring town of Stratham in 1741 to make his career.[23] Like Hempstead he was not only a farmer, and though he operated a farm throughout his life, as early as the age of twenty-five years he declared that farming was no longer his "principal business." Instead he made most of his living as a tanner, shoemaker, and whip maker, with some occasional earnings from surveying. In contrast to Hempstead, who was a farmer first and last, Lane was eager to escape the life of the soil; and if he had been blessed with a father like John Adams', he might have gone to college. His yearnings were revealed at age twenty when he identified himself in his journal as "Samuel Lane (not) Master of Arts (nor yet) Studient in Physick & Astronomy."[24] Later, when he matured and prospered, Lane would become a selectman, a deacon, a town clerk, a justice of the peace, and, in 1775, a one-term member of New Hampshire's provincial congress. Though he was not so prosperous as Hempstead, in his old age he would have the satisfaction of knowing that his grandson Joshua Lane was graduated in the Harvard class of 1799. As a farmer and tanner in Stratham, New Hampshire, Lane's opportunities for gaining information were relatively few; but his ambitions and achievements were substantial.

Like everyone else in Stratham, most of Lane's information came from local word-of-mouth sources and concerned local affairs. Lane's tanning business put him in close touch with farmers in Stratham and neighboring towns, but only occasionally with a Portsmouth merchant. His constant diet was local news and gossip as in New England farming communities everywhere—the "short and simple annals" of Gray's elegy. But such local horizons and limited information did not satisfy Lane and, blessed with a constitution that enabled him to get along on less sleep than most, he often lit a lamp at night and read.[25] Indeed Lane could have been the model for the ideal farmer of Timothy Dwight's *Greenfield Hill,* "a farmer, who steadily did what was called a good day's-work, and yet employed several hours every day, in reading."[26] Unlike the plowmen of Gray's elegy, Lane pursued the "ample page" of knowledge, engaging in a decades-long process of self-education that gradually made him something of a Yankee gentleman.

Exactly how and when Lane acquired his reading matter is largely a matter of conjecture, though scattered clues and the list he made late in life of 307 books he owned indicate substantial clerical influence. Certainly the titles, mostly religion and history together with reference works and textbooks, suggest a collection whose seriousness was more similar to the didactic social libraries founded at Durham, Guilford, Lebanon, Pomfret, and Woodstock in Connecticut from 1733 to 1745 than the fashionable libraries of Virginia gentry.[27] Here were no gentlemen's magazines, no *Tatler* or *Spectator,* and the only novel was that clerically approved, all-time American favorite, Daniel Defoe's *Robinson Crusoe.*[28] Into the desk and bookcase he bought in 1760 he placed the most widely read authors in New England. Isaac Watts, John Bunyan, Cotton Mather, and Jonathan Edwards were predominant in his collection, which he seems to have acquired mostly from the 1760s onward.[29] His strategy in inflationary times, to invest in land rather than leather or money-at-interest, had paid off; and he came to be regarded as one of Stratham's leading men, known for his fondness for "society and edifying conversation, as well as of reading" and for his "large acquaintance with men both in civil and religious stations."[30] By the 1750s when his church elected him to the post of deacon and Governor Wentworth appointed him to be a justice of the peace, Lane was closer to the cosmopolitan audience of Gray's "Elegy" than he was to its bucolic subjects.[31]

Yet in spite of the learning he achieved and the material accoutrements of genteel status he acquired, Lane remained a man who lived by the sweat of his brow, handling livestock hides, and doing farm labor.[32] Indeed even when he was past seventy years and his strength was failing, he still worked in his stinking tanyard, and he would labor at harvesting hay until he was past the age of eighty.[33] Such experiences always framed his perspective in evaluating outside information. When, for example, in 1794 he read a newspaper account of the terror in France, he drew a farmyard analogy to describe the awful work of the guillotine by remarking that the revolutionaries "make no more Difficulty in Cutting off their great Mens Heads, then we do of a Sheeps head."[34] By this time Lane, who first mentioned seeing a newspaper in 1752, was a regular reader who extracted a miscellany of military, diplomatic, and political news, as well as statistics on population and epidemics and, in August 1793, the practical information that "Hay [is] Exceeding Scarce in every part of the Country."[35] Lane, the self-educated farmer-tanner whose affinity for information and learning was more a matter of temperament and taste than utility, was eclectic in his approach. Combining his knowledge and understanding of the local world of direct experience with an awareness of the wider world based on more than a smattering of knowledge of current events, history, and religion, Lane surmounted the limits of his location, origins, and livelihood to become a Yankee gentleman, albeit one with calloused hands.

The extensive use of print that Lane employed to enter the world of high culture and cosmopolitan knowledge indicates what was possible, not what was typical. Even Dwight in the *Greenfield Hill* idyll had allowed that he only "once knew a farmer" of bookish habits.[36] The common experience was more like Hempstead's, though perhaps because inland New Hampshire was more isolated than New London and because print became more abundant as time went on, printed matter seems to have played a larger role in the lives of Matthew Patten and Abner Sanger.

Patten, a year younger than Samuel Lane, was born in Ireland in 1719 and emigrated with a brother as a young man to the area in southern New Hampshire known as Souhegan-East, which later became Bedford.[37] Rapidly adapting to the frontier and settling when hunting and trapping for meat and fur as well as fishing still supplemented farm income, Patten, like the others, was something of a jack-of-all-trades. He made tools and buckets, carved gunstocks, built and sold furniture, and surveyed land in addition to drafting legal forms and letters for less literate neighbors. Because he was one of the more accomplished people in his fledgling settlement and a regular churchgoer who helped raise the meetinghouse, Patten was elected town clerk in 1756.[38] By this time he was married to Betsy Macmurphy, another Scots-Irish immigrant, who bore him four children, three living. When his children were young and after they left home he hired men and women to help in harvesting his wheat, oats, rye, and flax[39] though, as he noted on July 28, 1766, "my little boys and Betsey and I Reaped 5 stooks and 7 Sheaves of Wheat."[40] As was true everywhere, the farm was a family enterprise in which, from an early age, the children worked as they were able. By the mid-1760s Patten had emerged as Bedford's leading man—its first selectman as well as town clerk, fence inspector, and appraiser of damages.[41]

Although at one level Patten's stature in his community derived more from his mastery of local affairs than from any familiarity with high culture or outside events, by Bedford standards Matthew Patten was cosmopolitan. Every few weeks he traveled on his own or others' business to other towns in the region and occasionally he visited Portsmouth, Newburyport, or Boston. Indeed he was in Boston during the great fire of 1760 "that Raged to a great Degree and . . . Demolised 5 or 6 acres." And on his return he fed detailed news of the event into local information networks.[42] Patten also wrote a substantial number of business letters, perhaps one per month, frequently on behalf of his less literate neighbors. On July 22, 1760, for example, he wrote two letters, one on his own and the other for Madam Goffe.[43] As town clerk he served also as a kind of community scribe who, for a fee, drafted deeds, advertisements, and legal notices so that occasionally words that he had composed found their way into the classified columns of a newspaper. There is little evidence that Patten himself read a newspaper with any frequency, but he did purchase an almanac in some years and he was also a reader of books.[44] He made himself a bookcase to hold his small collection, which apparently included religious works and a few law manuals. As selectman and town clerk, written communications, where a precise text mattered, as in legal documents and public proclamations, played a substantial role in his experience.

Yet in Patten's daily routines it was physical labor and face-to-face encounters that prevailed overwhelmingly. Patten was not bookish or cosmopolitan in his preoccupations, and did not stay up nights reading. He was informed on the major events of the day such as the earthquake of 1755 (which was felt at Bedford), the English victory at Quebec in 1759 which was celebrated by a colony-wide day of thanksgiving, and the Stamp Act of 1765; moreover he attended church services regularly and paid attention to the preacher's text for the day. But farming was his chief concern. On the day that he wrote the letters including Mrs. Goffe's, his main activity had been mowing and raking hay with his son Jonas and catching thirty-six pounds of salmon with Samuel Paterson.[45] Like his neighbors, Patten's life was ruled by the common cycle of seasonal labor in southern New Hampshire. January through March, when the ground was hard, was his time for logging. Plowing and planting dominated April and May, with a respite from field work in June when fishing, often with seines at Amoskeag Falls, was Patten's most productive activity. July and August were harvest months, with processing and storing the harvest and slaughtering as the main chores for September and October. Before the ground froze, October and November were a time for plowing and sowing, and then, until logging began again, Patten made firewood out of the tree tops and waste timber that had been felled the previous year. Interspersed as time and weather allowed, he ran surveys, made wooden barrel hoops (as many as fifty per day), made utensils and furniture for home use and for sale, composed and copied letters and documents, and carried out his various public offices. During most of Patten's life these tasks, usually in the presence and with the help of others, bounded much of his access to and interest in information.

But the American Revolution interrupted these patterns of experience and required Patten and his neighbors to be more cognizant of events and information beyond their locale. For Patten, an experienced town leader now in his fifties, the Revolution began in the summer of 1774 when, responding to the call of local Committees of Correspondence for a fast day, he disavowed the loyalist tendency of his Bedford minister, who refused to observe the fast, and instead took his family to neighboring Derryfield where they were instructed in the theme of repentance.[46] That winter Patten served on a committee to draft instructions for the Bedford representative, and in the spring of 1775 he was drawn into an even more active role. When news of the fighting at Lexington and Concord arrived in Bedford on April 20, Patten was at the center of town consultations. The next morning his son John and two of his nephews set off to join the patriot army near Boston. Thereafter Patten became enmeshed in the mobilization of the region, serving as a delegate to the provincial congress that year, as a representative to the General Court for Bedford and adjoining Merrimack in 1776 and 1777, and in 1776 as a member of the state committee of safety. He was also appointed as a justice of the peace and a judge of probate by the new state regime.

As a result, Patten was thrust into a role where being informed regarding extra-local and general affairs became his duty, and official messages came to him unbidden, as when he "was wakened in the morning by Mrs. Chandler's coming with a letter from the Comitee of the Provincial Congress."[47] In July 1776 it was not good enough for him to simply know by word-of-mouth the fact that the United States had declared independence. Perhaps that was why Patten bought a printed copy of the Declaration of Independence following a meeting of the committee of safety at Exeter.[48] People would ask Patten what exactly was going on when he returned to his district and he would have the text to show them and to read publicly.

Sadly, as Patten was returning home with the Declaration of Independence in his pocket, he was told that one of his sons, the boy who had enlisted after Lexington and Concord and who had recovered after having been "shot through his left arm at Bunker Hill fight," had died in the retreat from the abortive attack on Quebec. When Patten reached his house his wife was waiting with a letter from their son Bob, who had been with his brother when he died a month earlier. For once Patten exploded with anger and grief: his John had been cut down "in the prime of life by means of that wicked Tyranical Brute (Nea worse than Brute) of Great Britan he was 24 years and 31 days old."[49] When Patten recovered his equilibrium he scoured his own purse and borrowed cash from his kinsmen and neighbors so that he could go to Ticonderoga to bring Bob home for a furlough.[50] If the harvest suffered, and it did, so be it. For a Yankee farmer like Patten a revolution, a war, and a son killed while serving the cause warranted interruption of regular duties.

Fourteen months later, after the continental Army forced the surrender of General Burgoyne's army at Saratoga, the war receded from Patten's region and life returned closer to normal. By the war's end in 1783 the experience of the now sixty-four-year-old Patten resumed its old course except that now, as a justice of the peace, his official duties gave him responsibilities throughout Hillsborough County, not just his town. Unlike Samuel Lane who had become a regular newspaper reader, Patten went back to his local orientation, taking cognizance of the outside world only on the occasion of some major event or the statewide proclamation of a day of fasting and prayer. Living in Bedford, a farm community of fewer than 500 people at the time of the Revolution and which lay on no major thoroughfare, Patten was on the periphery of information diffusion in the early national era as he had been in colonial times.[51] Though Patten never sought isolation, he lived with a degree of it that Lane never accepted.

Abner Sanger, a day laborer and farmer who spent most of his life at Keene and Dublin to the west of Bedford, was a generation younger than Lane and Patten and, in his mature years, neither prosperous nor a major local officeholder. Born in the hill town of Hardwick in central Massachusetts in 1740, Sanger came to reside at Keene together with his twin brother Eleazar, his parents, and his sister Rhoda in 1753.[52] At the outset of the war Sanger, like Patten's son John, immediately marched off with a local company (and a borrowed musket) to the siege of Boston following the Battles of Lexington and Concord. But he soon grew disillusioned with the "United States of Rebellion" or the "Divided States of America" as he later called the new nation, and, with his brother, refused to sign the patriots' boycott association in 1776.[53] The following year Eleazar fled to Long Island, leaving a wife and children behind. Abner, who was not yet married, after twelve weeks imprisonment as a suspected loyalist at Charlestown, New Hampshire, stayed on in Keene with his mother and sister, where he operated a forty-acre farm and hired out as a farm worker in the neighborhood. Though living an intensely localized existence in which a circle of perhaps one hundred or so people figured regularly, superficially Sanger resembled the plowmen of Gray's elegy. Nevertheless word of mouth gave Sanger a modicum of information about the outside world, and because he read books and newspapers, exchanged letters, and even drafted letters for others, Sanger was less isolated and uninformed than one might suppose. Certainly he was no cosmopolite; he told the time by reading the angle of the sun, not the face of a clock.[54] But the experiences of Abner Sanger suggest how deeply the general culture penetrated the ordinary existence of even remotely situated New England farmers.

In contrast to Hempstead, Lane, and Patten, Abner Sanger was neither notably ambitious nor hardworking. During his bachelor days especially, which lasted until he was forty-five years old, Sanger seems to have always found time among his chores and errands for conversation and social drinking. On the afternoon of July 2, 1782 he visited Abijah Wilder's new house where he ran into Silvester Tiffany and passed "an hour with him about females, also about Masonry and etc."[55] Three days later, after finishing a job hoeing someone else's corn, "we drink toddy at night—plenty."[56] Several days later on a cool, blustery morning, Sanger declared a holiday for himself and went to the Cheshire County courthouse in Keene, to watch the blocking of court sessions by a crowd of debtors. Finding a friend among the spectators, they went to "Eames's tavern and drink together." Though the weather had now turned fair, "from about noon I spend until dark," a good seven hours.[57] The following Tuesday afternoon Sanger also took off: "I go to David Nims's to drink. There is only Ruth Lawrence and Nab Nims's at home. Ruth and I have some talk. . . . Unction's wife come along and desired me to call at her house when I went home. . . . We spent until sundown talking about her." Sanger happily passed the hours gossiping with neighborhood women. Later two men joined the conversation and he learned the interesting news that cattle to supply the army and to pay New Hampshire taxes had arrived in town.[58]

At this stage in life, being a bachelor, the focus of Sanger's local information was often female. During the summer of 1782 he was evidently involved with several Keene women. Sometimes he stayed with Poll Bailey at night; sometimes he stayed with Rachel Morse. At least once, after spending the night with Poll Bailey, he visited Rachel Morse the next morning.[59] Nor did he confine himself to these two only. He also visited Poll Washburn and Pat Skiner; "I help fix their loom," he said.[60] So conspicuous were his comings and goings that he himself became a subject of gossip as he reported, "Mr. Farr tells me that Esther Scovill was affronted about my going to see Rachel

Morse and Polly Bailey."⁶¹ At this time the woman he would ultimately marry, Elizabeth Meed, was just 15 years old.

Intriguing as these fragments of local love life are, they should not lead us to the conclusion that Sanger's world was wholly private. Women, who mostly stayed close to home, were seldom conduits of public information; but when Sanger was out and around town he was always alert for news. To someone of his common rank and who held no public office, the news came irregularly, almost at random. Yet through a mixture of word-of-mouth and newspaper reports Sanger, like others in Keene, maintained a grasp on public affairs. In September 1776, for example, he and his brother went to a neighbor's "to grind our seythes and read newspapers," borrowing Abijah Metcalf's periodicals as readily as his grindstone.⁶² Similarly, before he spent an hour-and-a-half "shutting up hogs" for the tavern-keeper Alexander Ralston, he passed most of the morning reading Ralston's newspapers.⁶³ When he was visiting another one of his many employers the newspapers were delivered at nightfall, so Sanger stayed on: "I hear them read, then come home."⁶⁴ For a farm laborer like Sanger, who had work to do every day but whose access to fresh newspapers was restricted to a few times each year, newspapers were seductive. "Afternoon I go over to old Benjamin Willis's to cut wood," he noted in February 1782, "but spend all the while until night reading in his newspapers." A week later would be time enough to attend to Willis's firewood.⁶⁵

There were, however, word-of-mouth sources of information on public affairs that sometimes drew on newspaper accounts and were sometimes wholly independent of the press. For Sanger such reports arrived without any regularity whatsoever. A man might come home from Northfield, Massachusetts, with news of the depredations of the Hessian troops, another might come from Connecticut with reports of French aid to Congress, while a third local traveler might return from Boston with a still wider range of reports.⁶⁶ One day Sanger might go up the main street in Keene and hear only of local doings, or he might, as on November 26, 1779, learn of the Comte d'Estaing's "defeat at Savannah."⁶⁷ At work the talk would be about a neighbor's livestock or, as in November 1777, when Sanger was working for the tanner, Thomas Baker (sometime selectman and justice of the peace), news would be passed of Washington's and Howe's armies at Philadelphia.⁶⁸ News came at random. Thus, near the end of August 1782, he happened to meet a man on the bridge over Keene River "that tells me there is talk of peace." Later that day, while he was "dragging old flood-wood out of the saw mill creek," he inquired of a passerby, a "Londonderry man" who told him "there [is] much talk of peace with Britain."⁶⁹ Similarly in October, while he was digging potatoes, "Ralston come along and tells me that their talk was that Governor Hancock of Boston was dead."⁷⁰ In the first two cases the information was accurate, and in the third it was mistaken. Either way, however, it became part of Sanger's consciousness. Though he had no systematic means of being publicly informed, his perspective embraced the nation. Years later, when he was a husband and father in nearby Dublin, he would subscribe with a post-rider to receive a weekly newspaper.[71]

Sanger also grasped the opportunities for other kinds of information that were available through word of mouth. A few days after Ralston told him of Hancock's death, Sanger called on Captain Stiles whom he found "at work on Ralston's horse-frame." For two hours they talked, and in the process Stiles explained to Sanger "how to cast interest."[72] Later on, after a young lawyer moved into a part of Sanger's house as a tenant, Sanger agreed to pledge fifty acres to the lawyer in exchange for help with various court proceedings "for and against me . . . and to tutor me there in."[73] As local and earthy as Sanger was, he wanted to be informed concerning business and legal matters of personal consequence as well as on news of the outside world. Though Sanger neither sought nor attained the learning of a New Hampshire gentleman, he was not quite the simple plowman either.

For someone like Sanger, residing near the periphery of American settlement, who held no public office and whose social rank was modest, information beyond what was generated locally represented something of an achievement. Learned people were few in Cheshire County and not always accessible. The fledgling lawyer would share his learning for a fee and, when he chose to, Sanger could hear Parson Aaron Hall of Keene weekly and sometimes more often.[74] But such people were not his companions at work or recreation, and he did not enjoy access to their learning or their outside networks on a casual basis. Sanger also had access to relatively few books—about two dozen during the years 1774–82 and 1791–94—and their use by Sanger and others who shared them and even copied them, suggests a general scarcity in Keene in the 1770s and early 1780s.[75] He learned about "the art of dyeing out of Farr's book called *Art's Masterpiece*;" and since the book was borrowed, he spent the better part of two days making a handwritten copy of the text for later reference.[76] Similarly, he also spent parts of fifteen days copying whole sections out of a borrowed three volume edition of *The Ladies' Library*, a collection of ethical essays first published in 1714. He also shared the few books he possessed, and on a Sabbath when they did not attend church, Sanger visited with his tenant's wife, with whom he read a "treatise upon virtue" from his volume of Bishop Joseph Butler's *Analogy of Religion*, a book which he had acquired from a local physician in exchange for carting hay the previous year.[77] Never especially pious or bookish, Sanger nonetheless owned and used books in a setting where for most people, as for him, the few titles that were readily available passed from hand-to-hand.

Among such people letters came infrequently and so their interest and impact were magnified accordingly. Because Sanger was fully literate and some people, usually women, were not, he sometimes played an intermediary role similar to Patten's for less literate neighbors. A woman whose husband was absent came to Sanger with his letters and left them with him, asking the farmer to write a reply on her behalf. Sanger's own sister-in-law could not correspond either, so when he received a letter from her husband he invited her to "come to hear brother Eleazar Sanger's letter read."[78] The importance a letter could command is dramatically illustrated by a month-long episode in the summer of 1794, when Sanger was farming in Dublin, ten miles east of Keene. Sanger had learned sometime in June that a letter from his brother was sitting in the Boston post office, so early in July he asked Captain James Adams, a local storekeeper, to pick it up for him on his next trip to Boston. But by the time Adams arrived in Boston, Sanger's wife's cousin, Benjamin Johnson, had picked up the letter for Sanger. Consequently for a time the letter was lost, last said to be headed for Keene. On Sunday, July 27, Sanger journeyed "to Keene inquiring for the letter . . . at all the public houses and others to and through Keene Steet," all to no avail.[79] Finally, ten days later, Sanger's own son walked in with the letter; it had been handed to him by Captain Adams' brother Eli.[80] Sanger never commented on its contents, which probably dealt with personal business, but the considerable effort that he and others made to retrieve it is indicative of the importance people placed on such communications. Many hands were involved in transmitting this single letter, and though delivery could be prompt and reliable between some locations, efforts like this one were not remarkable.

The path of Eleazar Sanger's letter, from St. Johnsbury in northern Vermont to Boston and then back to Dublin—from one outlying town to another through a distant central place—reveals a basic feature of peripheral rural localities like the New Hampshire towns. Though isolated from all but their neighboring communities, they frequently maintained active communication with Boston, which was their link to other rural places. Although their social and economic interests and their physical proximity might seem to put them closer to other peripheral communities than to centers like Boston, the information they craved beyond local experience, and their commercial connections to the outside world, ran through Boston. By the 1790s Sanger, with a post-rider delivering his weekly newspaper, could nourish regularly that yearning to know about more than the world of his family and community.

III

Such developments should not, however, suggest that improvements in New England's information networks reduced the importance of the immediate local world for Sanger and other farmers. Their activities and livelihoods were still so bound up in their localities that concern for information beyond the requirements of farm and community remained largely a matter of per-

sonal preference. The career of a contemporary of Sanger, the farmer James
Parker of Shirley, Massachusetts, illustrates precisely this phenomenon.[81]
Born in Groton, Massachusetts, in 1744, Parker moved to a small but well-
situated forty-acre farm in neighboring Shirley in 1765. There, though 40
acres was normally barely enough to survive, his labor, discipline, and management skills enabled him to prosper in farming much as Lane's efforts had
led to success in the tanning business; but unlike Lane, Parker kept himself
comparatively aloof from town business, rarely holding any public office
although, by his forties, he became just the sort of prosperous, respected
farmer who commonly became a town officer or church deacon. Parker,
however, was not so disposed and only served as a selectman for one year
(1782–1783) and as a town meeting moderator just once.[82] In old age he
accepted an honorific appointment as a justice of the peace, but he never
actually carried out the duties of the office.[83] Parker's Revolutionary War
service was limited to thirteen days starting with the battles in nearby Lexington and Concord, and a two-month stint during the siege of Boston in
February and March 1776. Parker paid attention to public affairs and was a
partisan at various times; but his chief concern was to cultivate his own
garden, which he did assiduously, ultimately rising to gentlemanly stature
and sending two of his four sons to Dartmouth College.

The town of Shirley, a community of some 700 hundred people at the time
of the Revolution, was located thirty miles northwest of Boston.[84] It included fertile lands and was close enough to a commercial center to permit
market farming to flourish; thus it was a good place for a man of Parker's
ambitions. Indeed Parker was able to raise tobacco there for a time, before
turning to hops on a regular and profitable basis. Inland it certainly was, but
for trade and communication it was much more advantageously situated
than Keene or Bedford, New Hampshire. Though it did not lie on a main
thoroughfare, and had been hopelessly rustic by the standards of a Harvard
graduate like Robert Treat Paine, in 1755 travel to Boston from Shirley and
neighboring towns was common and even frequent in the late spring and in
the fall. Consequently though Parker's access to information about the great
world was more restricted than Hempstead's at New London, it was superior
to that of the New Hampshire farmers, so his participation in information
activities reflects even more fully his personal preferences.

For Parker what appears most noteworthy is the development of those
preferences as time passed, and particularly as he assumed the trappings of
gentility. During the 1770s and much of the 1780s it is evident that Parker
read little, and when he did it was usually a newspaper and on rare occasions
a sermon.[85] News of the war, particularly, was of great interest to him and
while the information that was available from word-of-mouth sources was
sufficient for the early years of the conflict, in June 1778 he felt sufficiently
prosperous to contract for a subscription to the *Massachusetts Spy* published

at Worcester by Isaiah Thomas.[86] Though "a great many flying stories consirning the Army" passed through Shirley, Parker was eager to obtain the fuller, more detailed accounts of state and national politics and diplomacy, as well as battles, that the *Spy* provided.[87] In contrast to the aspiring Samuel Lane at the same stage in life, books and the historical, political, and philosophical literature associated with high culture, did not concern him.

During the 1780s, however, Parker's style of living began to change markedly. When he had moved to town in 1765 he lived in a modest, two-room farmhouse. Nine years later, with a wife and three children with him in the household, he added a lean-to at the rear, making a third room.[88] Parker's wintertime coopering and schoolteaching enabled him to accumulate a few amenities such as "a new red jacoot" in 1774, but it was not until the war inflated agricultural prices that Parker really prospered.[89] A fourteen-dollar pocket watch in 1776, the newspaper in 1778, a second watch, a beaver hat, and some ribbon that he purchased in 1782 were signs of Parker's new found prosperity. The turning point came at the end of 1784 when Parker bought a second farm and moved into its larger, more commodious house. Now he bought his mother a gold necklace when he made a trip to Boston; and he sent his eldest son James to New Ipswich (New Hampshire) Academy.[90] Though other farmers were suffering in the mid-1780s and Shays's Rebellion would find sympathizers in Shirley and Groton, Parker's prudent husbandry, shrewd management of tobacco and hops as well as ordinary crops, and his fortunate investments in land enabled him to assume genteel status. By the 1790s he had clad himself in a velvet jacket and breeches, "Bought silk for two Gounds" for his daughters, "papered my east room" and furnished it with a desk and a clock.[91] Father of six daughters and four sons, he had come a long way from a two-room house on a forty-acre farm.

Under his new circumstances Parker found it unsatisfactory to rely only on neighborhood word of mouth as he went about his duties; nor was a newspaper sufficient. So Parker entered new social and information circles that placed a wholly new set of demands on his store of knowledge and required him to change. In the two years 1792 and 1793 Parker joined the Freemasons and became a student of Masonry; he became a founding proprietor of the Shirley library society; he started to attend Harvard commencements; and, having become a church member in 1789, he began to attend ordinations in neighboring towns.[92] These social circles brought him into the information world of high culture, and now Parker enjoyed access to more cosmopolitan word-of-mouth networks than he had ever before experienced. At the same time, however, because he was mixing with college graduates, professionals, gentlemen, and their imitators, he had to turn to books to attain the requisite quotient of cultural literacy. So he became a reader and owner of books, and within a few years the erstwhile cooper ordered a cabinetmaker to make him a bookcase to house his growing collection.[93] By

1798, when he entered his fifteen-year-old son Daniel in Dartmouth College, he was prepared for the high point of the journey: "I supt with the President," he proudly recorded.[94]

As Parker was expanding the range of his reading matter and social circles he also took advantage of the increasing variety of public oratory that was becoming available. During his first twenty years in Shirley, like the other inhabitants, he had been exposed only to the pastor's regular preaching, except on the few occasions when he attended a funeral in his native town of Groton. Even the Revolution had only generated a brief flurry of oratory, chiefly in the form of sermons directed at the minutemen early in 1775. Parker was interested enough during the winter months to go to Lunenburg to hear the Reverend Zabdiel Adams in January 1775, and to attend a similar occasion where the Reverend Samuel Dana spoke at Groton in February, before hearing his own pastor, the Reverend Phineas Whitney, address the Shirley minutemen just three weeks before the Battles of Lexington and Concord.[95] But thereafter there was a long period when the only occasions for oratory were regular preaching and funerals. Indeed so far as Parker was concerned the only unusual oratorical event that he witnessed for over a decade was not a public address at all but a ceremony of the "Shaking Quakers" that he saw in the neighboring town of Harvard after the harvest in 1781.[96]

Shays's Rebellion, however, generated political oratory that reached people in all parts of Massachusetts and from then on, as Parker was becoming a gentleman, he took up the advantages that a changing society was providing, both within Shirley and as far away as Boston. On January 1, 1787, Parker attended the special town-meeting called to hear the Reverend Whitney read the recent address of the General Court to the people of Massachusetts, dealing with the problems of public debt, taxes, and Shays's Rebellion. This forty-page document, which was evidently read publicly in most towns, may have been the first formal secular oratory ever voiced in much of the state.[97]

Parker heard it in his hometown, but now, in keeping with his new gentlemanly ways, he was traveling with some frequency to ceremonies where both secular and religious oratory figured prominently. In 1792, for example, he attended ordination ceremonies in nearby Westford and Harvard, where he listened to special ordination sermons and responses.[98] The following year he joined in the Freemasons' celebration at neighboring Lancaster where he heard the Reverend William Emerson preach.[99] He also attended the Harvard commencement in 1793, a great festival of oratory, some of which was in Latin.[100] Later, in October, Parker was back in Boston for Governor John Hancock's funeral, another rhetorical effusion.[101] In the space of a few years he was hearing more oratory apart from regular preaching than he had heard in his entire life.

As time went on, such occasions were multiplying for Parker as for everyone else. George Washington's death at the end of 1799 generated a flood of public oratory in memorial services throughout the United States. Towns all over New England recognized Washington's passing, and in Shirley, Parker was present among his neighbors to hear the Reverend Whitney's "oration sermon" delivered on Washington's birthday in 1800.[102] Parker's more cosmopolitan stature was evident in his attendance two years later at Boston's Independence Day ceremonies where he listened to a patriotic address by the Reverend William Emerson, whom he had heard nine years earlier at Lancaster.

Yet because New England was becoming more diverse, even people who stayed close to home began to experience choices with regard to oratory. Secular orations remained scarce, particularly in the countryside, but evangelism and the multiplication of sects introduced variety into places like Shirley. In 1803 a "methodus preacher" was active in town, according to Parker, who joined his neighbors at the schoolhouse to hear him.[103] In 1814 a Universalist came and Parker twice attended his sermons before the town voted to deny him "the Use of the Meeting House."[104] When diversity was not available in Shirley, there was always the Shaker community service a few miles down the road at Harvard.

Between 1765 and 1814 both Parker and Shirley had changed, though it was Parker, who became a gentleman and lived to vote for Andrew Jackson in 1828 while his neighbors were voting for Massachusetts' native son John Quincy Adams, who changed more.[105] Using the opportunities that his prosperity and the republican era offered to surmount the parochial influences connected with dwelling on an inland farm, Parker fulfilled his private ambitions. Success, not farming, was his calling, and he used his resources and the occasions the times afforded to lift himself and his family to a position of affluence and gentility.

IV

Some of the changes evident in Parker's life, as well as continuities reaching back to Joshua Hempstead's day, are revealed in the experiences of Thomas Benjamin Hazard, a Kingston, Rhode Island, farmer and artisan who was a dozen years younger than Parker and lived from 1756 to 1845.[106] In contrast to Parker, Hazard's circumstances put him on a course of downward social mobility, and his own seeming indifference to worldly achievements kept him in modest circumstances throughout his life. Yet because of his family background, perhaps, he maintained connections to the cosmopolitan centers of Newport and Providence throughout much of his life, so that the high culture of Atlantic merchants intersected with his own networks of local information. His family culture encouraged some acquaintance with learning, though his occupation and stature made no such demands.

Hazard's father, a direct descendant of one of Rhode Island's first settlers, was a fourth son whose father was unable to launch him into prosperity. His mother, whose identity is uncertain, was connected to comfortable Newport families. Because both of his parents died during his childhood, Thomas B. Hazard was raised as an apprentice to John Hull, a Tower Hill blacksmith. During the Revolution his oldest brother Benjamin was captured by the British and died aboard a prison ship. However another brother established a farm in Kingston. His sister, Nancy Hazard Tanner, settled in Providence, about a day's journey to the north.

After Hazard completed his apprenticeship, he lived a peripatetic life for several years, boarding with relatives and employers in Worcester County, Massachusetts, and at various Rhode Island locations. He did day labor for farmers, cultivating land, mowing hay, harvesting potatoes, corn, and beans, as well as making nails, parts for farm equipment, and kitchen implements. In addition to hunting small game and fishing, in his spare time he read advice books like "the young mans Best Companion," and popular works in religion, philosophy, and history.[107] During an eight-month period from September 1780 to May 1781 he read in no less than eleven different books, including "a collection of Prose and Verse for the youse of Skools," "a moral Essay of Paine," "Reflections on Courtship and Marriage," "Theory of the Earth Concerning the conflagration," and works by Robert Barclay, George Whitefield, and two Quaker authors.[108] Hazard was an observing Quaker who was evidently engaged in a course of self-education somewhat more modest than the ambitious Samuel Lane and James Parker, but nonetheless earnest indeed comparable to the readings of Abner Sanger while he was doing day labor before his marriage. Hazard's purchase in December 1780 of "Bales Dickshonnaryes" expressed his needs.[109] Hazard was confidently literate, writing and receiving family letters routinely, even drafting them occasionally for others; but the limits of his formal education were obvious in his phonetic spelling, which was idiosyncratic even by the casual standards of the day.[110]

After October 1783, when he married Hannah Knowles of Little Rest (Kingston), which lay on the Boston Post Road, his attention to reading subsided, and thereafter he seldom picked up a book. A year later their first child, Benjamin, was born. By now Hazard and his wife had moved out of the Knowles homestead and into a small farm nearby which Hazard rented. Here Hazard, who was operating a blacksmith shop and farming for his father-in-law and himself, would become deeply enmeshed in a face-to-face world of local information which, in spite of its proximity to Newport and Providence, until the early 19th century was only occasionally touched by word of mouth or printed information from the great world beyond.[111]

As Hazard worked in his shop, went about his farm errands, and attended Quaker meetings, the information that came to him was usually local and, whether local or distant in origin, often possessed a strong "human interest" element. High culture or even general political and economic information of a mundane sort was scarce. In the early 1790s, for example, when the French Revolution, European diplomacy, and fiscal politics in Congress were commanding the attention of merchants and lawyers in the port towns, and of Samuel Lane in Stratham, New Hampshire, the talk in Hazard's shop was of a "black man Dropt Dead yeasterday in old Elisha Wattsons field," of a child burned "so bad that thay believed it to be adiing," and of how "Robert Babcock kild an Ox yeasterday by driveing to heard."[112] The tenor of local conversation is suggested by reports of a swarm of bees and of "Several Sheep bitt by Doggs."[113] Even when information from farther afield passed through the neighborhood it often possessed the same personal character, such as news of a disastrous gust of wind at New York that "kild and Drownded 25 people," or word brought by a visitor that "goviner Greens Wife and John Cases Wife both of Est Greenwitch died in one day."[114] Except for the occasion where Hazard went with his brother to find out about reports of smallpox in the area, the information that passed through Hazard's word-of-mouth networks was not necessarily useful or elevating; but it was diverting.[115]

That Hazard needed inexpensive diversions at this point in his life is suggested by the fact that in December 1794 this thirty-eight-year-old father of three children could not attend religious meetings because his shoes were too poor[116] His situation was not as desperate as Ashley Bowen's had been six years earlier in Marblehead, because Hazard owned property and could feed his family; but spending money on recreation or leisure was beyond his present means. Possessing decent shoes was important to him because listening to Quaker oratory was one of his few diversions. Hazard did not visit taverns or listen to the formal sermons of the clergy, but over the years he heard a variety of Quaker orators, including Isaac Hicks and a number of other Pennsylvania and British Friends, at monthly and quarterly meetings.[117]

In the next decade, however, Hazard's fortunes improved substantially. He was still a farmer and blacksmith, making soap, plowing, sowing, harvesting, and crafting nails and tools on his anvil, but now, with his wife's inheritance, he was enjoying prosperity. When he sent his son, Benjamin, to the pier at Newport in March 1806 to pick up sand and iron, he also sent along a bushel of white beans to pay for a pound of chinese tea and some sugar.[118] And in June he had a bonnet made for his daughter Hannah, and he bought her some calico.[119] The following year he would purchase a four-dollar looking-glass.[120] Hazard was still engaged in a good deal of barter—he traded a mink skin he had trapped for flour—and he continued to exchange his labor with his neighbors; but he lived with greater leisure and ease than in years past.[121]

Hazard did not, however, turn to reading as he had in his youth. Instead he took time for public affairs, emerging as a "country party" political leader in the Kingstown community of Little Rest. Consequently he became part of a statewide political network that brought him to a new plateau of information beyond the incidents of farm, shop, and meetinghouse. On April 14, 1806, after working in his shop, beating some of his flax, and putting meat up to smoke in his chimney, he "received a Letter from Providence [signed] by a number of men wishing me to support Richard Jackson for Goviner."[122] It seems unlikely that Hazard supported the Federalist Jackson, and in August he dined with the Republican Governor Isaac Wilbour and traveled with him to Providence.[123] The emergence of competitive electoral politics in Rhode Island drew Hazard, and with him many of his neighbors, into a more extended, cosmopolitan communication network even if their own priorities and outlook remained staunchly local.[124] Indeed at the beginning of 1807 Hazard, once an almost purely locally oriented Quaker, took the step of writing to his Congressman at Washington, DC.[125] Later that year Hazard was elected to the Rhode Island legislature on a statewide Republican ticket.[126]

Rhode Island, with 72 deputies and 10 assistants for about 75,000 inhabitants, was small in population as well as territory; even so Hazard's two years of service in the legislature enlarged his experience significantly.[127] He dined with governors and corresponded with congressmen;[128] he traveled to Providence and Newport the fast way—by packet boat—instead of overland;[129] and when the Republicans launched a newspaper at Newport in March 1809, Hazard paid a dollar (a day's wages) to subscribe.[130] In many ways Hazard's life was unchanged—the labors of his shop and farm were much as they had been for twenty-five years, but now that he had been an actor in state politics he possessed a knowledge of events and a perspective that could never be so locally centered as before.

For Hazard it is impossible to measure such changed perspectives with precision, but a few examples drawn from his later years when he continued to live as before, suggest their dimensions. In the 1790s and earlier, whenever he referred to a black person, he used the old-fashioned terms, a "negar" or a "black," but by the 1820s Hazard had adopted the new vocabulary of race and was referring to men and women "of color."[131] In the past he had paid no particular attention to national elections, but now he began to record the local vote for the United States Congress.[132] And by 1820 he was even paying attention to a holiday that had no place whatever in the New England of his younger days—Christmas.[133] Moreover, although from the age of seventy or so the range of his activities and acquaintances was diminishing, he took a steamboat to Newport in 1827 and, though he never rode on one, a dozen years later, at the age of eighty-three he walked to a railroad depot to view a railroad train.[134] Indeed in his late seventies and early eighties he borrowed newspapers, attended a "Babtiest" meeting, visited a steam-powered factory, and went to listen to a visiting lecturer.[135] Learning about the outside world and new technology was important to Hazard, wholly apart from any occupational requirements or social ambitions. And by the 1830s, even in a declining agricultural community like Little Rest in the town of South Kingstown, such information was accessible, even to someone born in another era and preparing not for life but for death.

V

Combined, the lives of Hempstead, Lane, Patten, Sanger, Parker, and Hazard spanned 177 years from 1678 to 1845. Because they all farmed they shared common experiences—plowing, tending livestock, harvesting hay, digging potatoes—experiences that were much the same in Hempstead's youth as in Hazard's old age. Indeed it was this seemingly timeless aspect of their lives, combined with their concern for the here and now of each crop, that gives Gray's elegy its resonance as an impression of rural reality. Nor is Gray's depiction of farmer ignorance—"Knowledge to their eyes her ample page / Rich with the spoils of time did ne'er unroll"—wholly misleading, since none of these men attended college or read very widely by the standards of Augustan England. Networks of local information combined with the knowledge drawn from direct experience, not books, supplied most of their sustenance.

Yet Gray's image is finally deceptive, not only because of its genteel romanticism but because the society wherein New England farmers dwelled was based on an economic and political configuration and a collection of social assumptions and attitudes markedly different from English pastoral ideals. The world of New England farmers, whether Hempstead and Hazard near the sea or Patten and Sanger at the edge of the up-country frontier, mixed agriculture and the stability of a deferential social order with commerce and the fluidity and competition that accompanied a broad distribution of landed property and political enfranchisement. Rural people were not in truth insulated from external affairs either in their consciousness or as a matter of practical fact, nor were they content to dwell wholly within a local sphere. All of the farmers considered here were assisted by their neighbors and by society more broadly in learning about the world beyond their neighborhoods.

Beyond these common realities, however, there were important differences. Location, wealth, the time in which they lived and their individual talents and aspirations all mattered. Lane, born in 1718, and Parker, born in 1744, demonstrate that it was possible for inland farmers who aspired to genteel status to achieve the learning and conversation of Yankee squires in the second half of the 18th century. Blessed with ample portions of health, stamina, foresight, and good fortune, their assiduous labors and rising land prices gained them prosperity and the time to enter public life and genteel voluntary associations, as well as to read books, magazines, and newspapers. At the same time there is reason to believe that although such a course was possible, it was unusual. Such prosperity and aspirations toward assuming the mantle of gentility and high culture, while common enough among merchants and lawyers, were not typical of farmers. Hempstead, two or three generations earlier, had no such ambition, though he might have had the means. Immensely well-informed in practical matters and town affairs, he left high culture to the clergy and gentry, pursuing for himself only the goals of salvation, public service, and family security through agricultural prosperity. Patten, the same generation as Lane and who also sat in New Hampshire's Revolutionary government, was like Hempstead and Sanger and possessed neither the means nor the appetite for social climbing. Hazard, whose family connections ran up into Rhode Island's elite, was similarly accepting of his social place and, apart from his early foray into self-education, set such notions aside as he matured.

Indeed one striking feature of all these farmers who were content to be farmers—Hempstead, Patten, Sanger, Hazard—was the way that they used their literacy. Instead of employing it as an avenue to high culture, they read and wrote so as to carry out private and public business—keeping accounts, corresponding with family, securing their property, staying abreast of the law and current affairs, and helping their neighbors with the same tasks. As diarists they were doubtless more reflective and used their literacy more actively than most—but even their diaries, which record details of weather and farm accounts, have a decidedly practical cast. These farmers used their literacy much less for recreation than to serve concrete objectives and, except for newspaper reading, general information was seldom one of them. Instead, for most information they relied on direct observation, their own or that of others', and word-of-mouth reports. Word of mouth was relatively swift, its bearer could be questioned, and it arrived in a familiar vocabulary and context. There is no evidence that many New England farmers born before the Revolution read Lord Chesterfield's advice in favor of sociability, but their society intuitively valued direct observation and conversation as principal sources for information and learning.

Indeed it was these ingrained habits that agricultural reformers sought to alter by turning farmers toward print in the first half of the 19th century. Almanacs of the day, a popular medium that reached into farm households on a truly massive scale, preached the doctrine that farmers especially should live by Bacon's dictum that "Knowledge is power," and explained that accumulating knowledge was an essential use of literacy. "Every Farmer should have a book for inserting all these useful hints, which are so frequently occurring in conversation, in books, and gathered in the course of his reading, or in the practical management of his farm," counseled the *Christian Almanack* for 1828.[136] Conversation and observation were not to be supplanted, just supplemented by reading and writing. Robert B. Thomas's *Farmer's Almanack* for 1836 advised in February, often a slack time and a period for indoor labors, that: "A book is a very useful article in a farmer's family. Suppose, now that you procure Fessenden's New England Farmer to amuse youself with these long winter evenings? This would set you thinking to some profit."[137] Speaking to farmers, the almanacs touted reading for utility and practical advantage, not moral improvement or high culture.

Here newspapers, because they were now cheap and widely available, were recommended as particularly valuable to farmers. In 1834 one farmer's testimonial declared, "I take the newspapers, which always contain something instructive, and give some useful information. They are a cheap and easy vehicle of knowledge."[138] Robert B. Thomas went right to the heart of the issue in urging print as the most efficient means of being informed. The farmer's "love of home," he argued, "is his safety:"

> He must guard against contracting a fondness for being off, off; ay, off from the place of his business, the place of his interest, the place of his family, the place of his love. Call me away from the enticement of the idle and the time-spendthrift. Yonder is a horserace that draws its thousands. . . . Is there a gathering at the village tavern? I hope there are no farmers there. *Loafers* can never be farmers. Yet "some love to roam;" some love just to take a little trip down town, or over to the corner, or to Trundlehead's mills, to see what's going on. But they will "hang on;" and this makes a bad case of it. Now, there is no need of going from home to find out the news. The way to have this accomodation is to take a newspaper, and then the news will come to you, even to your very door; and your family will also receive a benefit in reading the paper. Look to it.[139]

The pattern of behavior that Thomas was cirticizing, while explicitly reminiscent of Abner Sanger during his bachelor days in Keene in the 1770s, also represents an attack on the whole 18th-century mode of merging sociability and information networks. Thomas declared reading print to be the preferred mode of transmitting information not out of any concern for complicated texts or refined arguments, but because print, the newspaper, could do what word of mouth had always done before but with a saving of time that made it more economical than "free" word of mouth. Thomas's challenge pointed toward America's future; for farmers raised before the Revolution, it represented a distant vision.

Farmers' experience of literacy had never been as an alternative to word-of-mouth and local networks, but as a way to supplement personal interaction and, less often, as a means to rise into the world of high culture. Like Gray's plowmen they had all known the repetitious tyranny of farmyard chores, but unlike the peasants of poetry, their consciousness moved beyond such tasks because of the information about the world beyond their horizons that word of mouth and public speech, travel and observation, and letters and printing had provided. Conscious of issues of international war and peace, of doctrinal controversies within the Christian church, aware of national politics, of antislavery and temperance, they viewed their own local existence from a broader perspective.

Chapter 7

Daughters, Wives, Mothers: Domestic Roles and the Mastery of Affective Information, 1765–1865

On Saturday, June 18, 1774, tutor Philip Fithian was startled by an episode at the Chesapeake mansion of his employer, Robert Carter.

> 'Squire *Lee* call'd in, & brought a late London News-Paper in which we are informed that another Act of Parliament has pass'd taking from the People of Boston all power of trying any Soldier, or Person . . . for commiting any Crime; & obliging all such offenders to be sent home for legal Tryal. . . . He informed us likewise that last Saturday in Richmond (our neighbour County) the people drest & burnt with great marks of Detestation the infamous Lord *North*—Mrs. *Carter,* after the 'Squire left us quite astonished me in the Course of the evening with her perfect acquaintance with the American Constitution.[1]

After listening silently to the men's political discussion and withholding comment until the privacy of her family was restored by Squire Lee's departure, Anne Tasker Carter had revealed a political learning and acuity that surpassed Fithian's. His surprise is noteworthy because he had known for months that she was intellectually sophisticated; indeed her husband had remarked that "He would bet a Guinea that Mrs. Carter reads more than the Parson of the parish!"[2] But Fithian had never heard Mrs. Carter speaking on political subjects. Social prescription, which made public affairs an exclusively male subject of discourse, had hitherto concealed the reality that this plantation mistress was an informed and astute political observer. Since the colonial ruling gentry, and the Carters in particular, generally lived according to the approved British conventions—it was only after Squire Lee left that Mrs. Carter made her confident foray into constitutional debate—the episode reveals that even at the highest, most self-conscious level of society, there was some tension between the conventional view of politics as an exclusively male branch of information, and actual behavior. Indeed a few years later an outraged daughter from Charleston, South Carolina, articulated the tension precisely, complaining that "the men say we have no business with political matters . . . it's not our sphere! . . . [But] surely we may have sense enough to give Opinions . . . without being reminded of our Spinning and household affairs, as the only matters we are capable of thinking, or speaking of, with justness or propriety."[3]

Among ordinary Northerners the same incompatibility between women's real lives and what was prescribed for them by moralists was also evident. A generation after the Carter incident and 600 miles to the north in Salem, Massachusetts, Unitarian clergyman William Bentley recorded a telling encounter between an ordained clergyman and a matron of the artisan class. According to Bentley, the Reverend Peter Sanborn, a Calvinist evangelical, told his congregation that the recent deaths by lightning of the Lynn artisan Miles Shorey and his wife were owing to the fact that

> The man [was] a Sabbath breaker, & that he was at work at his trade on the Sabbath on which he suffered. This was reported to Mrs. Breed, the mother of Shorey's wife. . . . Mrs. Breed made it her business to call on Sanborn & *she could out talk any man*. She finally persuaded him to contradict the fact, that he had said anything implying any such charge against Shorey & wife & then she obtained vouchers for the good conduct of Shorey.

Thus Mrs. Breed not only vindicated the reputations of her unfortunate daughter and son-in-law, but also maneuvered Sanborn into punishing himself by telling a second lie to quiet the first. For after she obtained his written declaration that he had never made such accusations, as well as testimonials to the "general sobriety and virtuous conduct" of her deceased children, she brought them to the *Salem Register* to print. As a result Sanborn was left having "to vindicate himself to his parishioners," the very people who had first reported the precise words of which he now claimed to have "no recollection."[4] Mrs. Breed's revenge, adroitly employing the press to expose Sanborn's mendacity and abuse of clerical authority, made a mockery of the old shibboleth that women should "suffer and be still." As in the case of Mrs. Carter, Mrs. Breed's actions suggest that although society assumed that there ought to be a distinct and subordinate sphere for women regarding information as well as most other aspects of life, reality was more complicated. Social prescriptions were surely influential in determining the kinds of information that women and men sought, as well as what was accessible to them; but the information they acquired, employed, and passed on to others was also affected by a host of other factors, personal as well as social, economic as well as temporal.

Before exploring the interplay between prescription and reality in actual women's lives, let us consider the ruling social assumptions that shaped white women's roles.[5] These standard expectations, chiefly concerning property-owning households, but drawing on generic perceptions of women's nature, were largely drawn from contemporary English society, where the home had long been regarded as women's proper and exclusive place. Domestic production, which in common households meant preparing food and making clothing and other textiles, and in wealthy households required supervising servants and doing fine needlework, were basic female responsibilities. In addition, of course, all the tasks associated with childbirth and the first years of nurture of children, both girls and boys, belonged to women. When children passed beyond the toddler stage, girls were to become their mothers' apprentices, just as boys were to follow their fathers. Mothers were their daughters' role models from their earliest years, as each generation passed on the skills and lore of womanhood required for household production, child care, and family nurture in general.[6] For when family members, including servants, fell ill, practical responsibility for care belonged to mothers, literally from the cradle where they swaddled their babies, to the deathbed, where women prepared the dead for the grave.

Though advice books aimed at women on household management were printed as early as the 16th century, until they began to be widely distributed in the 1830s, the usual assumption was that the information women needed to fulfill all these tasks came primarily from direct experience and face-to-face conversations. The network of instruction did not depend on literacy, but instead on the tutelage of mothers and the larger circle of female neighbors and kin in surrounding households, to whom daughters were sometimes apprenticed. Since, as with men's work, many women's jobs promoted the collaboration of women from several households—for sewing, food preparation, childbirth, and sick care—ordinary experience was believed to supply adequate instruction.[7]

Above and beyond these varied and demanding domestic duties, custom dictated that—for the sake of their own souls as well as their families'—women even more than men should be pious Christians. Both in actual practice (women's entry into church membership was normally two or three times greater than that of men) and in theory (women were said to be more emotional than men), there was supposed to be a special affinity between women and piety. To the extent that prescription matched reality, one reason may have been the exceptional power for women of the Christian message of resignation. Women found particular comfort in the doctrine of resignation because it supplied a justification for submission and reconciled the differences between their assigned responsibilities and the authority and power they exercised. For although in the final analysis the immediate care and well-being of their families was their responsibility, both tradition and theory placed husbands in authority.

At most, women could act as "deputy husbands" according to law and custom. Daughters, wives, and mothers were always at least nominally subordinate to the man who headed the household of which they were a part. For even though men's occupations often placed them outside the home much of the time, they were supposed to be its rulers, agents of the state, as it were, for maintaining the order, regularity, and productivity of families. Though women's sphere was firmly domestic, women were not to rule the home. Political power, whether by the hearth, at the town-meeting, the county court, or the capital—and even in the parish—was intended exclusively for men. As Elizabeth Cady Stanton observed, "for all the information she [woman] might desire on the vital questions of the hour, she was commanded to ask her husband at home."[8]

These expectations regarding women's sphere and their domestic roles were broadly sanctioned and remarkably durable through the 18th and much of the 19th centuries. Yet they were never entirely fixed, and between 1765 and 1865 clergymen and moralists, some of whom were women, modified the common prescriptions so as to accomodate enlightened republican and romantic ideas. The evolving perceptions of women's roles called for a real, if limited, female cultural enfranchisement in which literacy was required of all women, not just the upper class, and morality became a transcendent responsibility.

The belief in female literacy which had been building in America throughout the 18th century, emerged full-blown in the 1790s when the ideal of republican motherhood was articulated.[9] To rely only on female word-of-mouth networks or even the instruction supplied by fathers, brothers, husbands, and the parish clergy was no longer sufficient. Women were expected to read so as to become more broadly educated, not just in practical subjects such as arithmetic and grammar, used in running a household and instructing small children, but also in more general areas like geography, astronomy, and even history. Whereas the custom of relying on face-to-face exchanges had meant that most women were largely confined to local information networks, at least for direct access to information, literacy was intended to encourage entry into the realm of cosmopolitan information via newspapers, magazines and books. Before the Revolution, when Robert Treat Paine married the semi-literate Sally Cobb, social convention had been relatively indifferent if not actually hostile to female learning—John Adams' wife, the learned Abigail Smith, was exceptional—for women's place was understood to be in the home intellectually and psychologically as well as physically. Afterwards, in the new republic, it was the Sally Cobbs who became unusual in the North, as a new convention was formulated that required literacy and encouraged schooling for girls. As a result, by 1830 northern women in various ranks closed the literacy gap that had often divided their mothers and fathers in the past.[10]

There were objections from moralists, especially conservative clerics,

along the way. Reading, and particularly novels, encouraged emotionalism—even passion—and distracted women from their work. Facetiously, a Yankee satirist asked:

> And why should girls be learnd or wise,
> Books only serve to spoil their eyes.
> The studious eye but faintly twinkles
> And reading paves the way to wrinkles.[11]

His jest reveals that while society was moving toward the encouragement of women's reading, including the use of libraries and the formation of women's reading clubs, there was also some reaction.[12] No single voice spoke for everyone, and ambiguous, even contradictory counsels were expressed.

Partly for this reason, and partly because of the emerging ideal of the republican mother, female literacy became conventional by close association with family moral development. Whereas 18th-century fathers had exercised chief responsibility for the morality of their households, during the Second Great Awakening a new consensus took shape which assigned children's moral instruction to mothers rather than to fathers. To inculcate virtue in the home became women's highest calling, and placed on them significant responsibility for the entire moral order.[13] If women were ignorant and illiterate they could only fail. They must read and be informed to instruct their children.

While the ideal of father reading—especially the Bible—to the entire family remained secure, a prominent teaching role was assigned to mothers and daughters in which literacy was essential. Thus the emerging pattern of the 1820s and 1830s, where young women moved out of their homes to teach school prior to marriage, was only logical in view of this idealized women's sphere. That they also were engaging in cottage industry and moving into textile mills in factory towns, not only reflected economic necessities but also social rank and the traditional idea of women's work as spinning and weaving. According to the older view, however, even if women produced for the market they should remain at home—making butter and cheese, sewing clothes, weaving straw hats, sewing shoe uppers—keeping their hands busy, and not by turning the pages of a book.

In time, however, the ideal of universal female literacy prevailed, so that

---

New England Primer

This illustration from a New England primer (New Haven, 1830) depicts the idealized genteel republican mother instructing her son and daughter in reading. That this instruction is being done in the home represents a continuation of the long-standing practice of treating literacy as a family responsibility. The larger windows that were put in post-Revolutionary houses helped provide reading spaces.
Courtesy of the American Antiquarian Society

"The Temperance Home"

This scene in a prosperous home of 1850 depicts the traditional, patriarchal use of books in the family. A grandfather reads to his wife, children, and grandchildren, nine people assembled during the daytime, probably the sabbath. This image in which a patriarch employs books to impart information to his family represents an ideal that was familiar to Samuel Sewall in the 17th century as well as Calvin Fletcher in the 19th century. It is taken from The National Temperance Offering *(New York, 1850).*
Courtesy of the American Antiquarian Society

the only significant strictures remaining on women's cultural enfranchisement concerned definitions of suitable reading. Here the doctrine of separate spheres continued to exercise a significant influence on women's consumption of information. Although the republican ideal sought to make all branches of information accessible to men, some, it was argued, were either dangerous for women, as with romances, or useless, as with politics.[14]

Of course however powerful and intrusive the strictures placed on women of all ranks, they could be challenged, as the examples of Mrs. Carter and Mrs. Breed illustrate. Indeed social conventions could always be breached with impunity when conditions were right. The wife or kinswoman of a leading political figure might engage in drawing-room political discourse and even newspaper controversy, as in the well-known cases of Abigail Smith Adams and Mercy Otis Warren (James Otis' sister), both highly informed analysts and commentators on public affairs.[15] Prescriptions could not control Abigail

Adams' or Mercy Warren's behavior any more than Mrs. Carter's or Mrs. Breed's when the circumstances of a particular woman's life—who and what she was, when and where she lived—provided opportunities to contradict society's rules. Yet the strength and influence of social prescription was magnified because of the legal and economic dependence of the vast majority of women, whose central responsibilities were domestic. These realities shaped their consumption of information and their roles in its diffusion.

This understanding underlines the complexity of analyzing the roles women played in the diffusion of information. As with men, their experience was dictated by the era of their birth and their stage of life. It was influenced by their family origins, their education, and the circumstances of their own adult family—especially motherhood and their husband's occupation and social status—as well as where they lived. Moreover particular variables, such as the incidence of disease in their families and the specific personalities of the fathers and husbands under whose legal dominion they lived, shaped vital elements of their experience. Nonetheless, because of the power of gender roles, white women shared a wide range of experiences. Womanhood virtually always dictated a domestic occupation, so women's access to information and their participation in communication networks was shaped in distinctive ways; even though, as with men, the information women acquired and passed on to others depended on personal preferences as well as social circumstances.

Women were also linked together up and down the white social spectrum by the institutions of marriage and maternity, possibly the greatest watersheds in their lives, when normally they left their families of origin and exchanged the status and responsibilities of a daughter for those of a wife and mother. A small but growing number of women never married or bore children, and some spent decades in widowhood rather than remarry. However, it was expected that all daughters should become wives and mothers as in fact most did. As a result the kinds of information that were accessible to women and which they sought to command were distinct from men. We can begin to grasp some of the differences by considering the experiences of several daughters, wives, and mothers at various stages of the life cycle and across the century from 1765 to 1865.

During the years of early adulthood before marriage Candace Roberts, Mary Guion, and Lucy Breckinridge, born between 1781 and 1843 and dwelling in Connecticut, New York, and Virginia, kept private diaries that span the years 1800 to 1807 and 1862 to 1864. It is their experiences, supplemented by the diaries and letters of several other young women, that supply the foundations for what follows. That the experience of each was unique in key ways should go without saying; what is remarkable is that the information activities of these three daughters—so different in background and circumstances—should have so much in common.

The humblest of the three was Candace Roberts, born in 1785 into the family of a Bristol, Connecticut, clockmaker, Gideon Roberts, and his wife Falla Hopkins. Candace Roberts' father practiced a craft he had learned from his father, one of the first settlers of Bristol, and which he passed on to his sons Wyllys and Titus. Though rooted in Bristol, his travels peddling his wooden movement clocks took him as far south as Pennsylvania.[16] Respectable but of modest means, Gideon Roberts could give his second daughter Candace some schooling in the new republican mode, and at seventeen she was studying geography, historical biography, and moral essays. She even had a try at public speaking, when, as she put it, she "went down to the south school to speak my piece."[17] Though Roberts passed most of her days doing household labor—washing, carding, sewing, knitting, and baking—her preoccupations suggest genteel aspirations. In 1801 and 1802 she made and accepted visits frequently, attended several balls, paid a good deal of attention to her clothes, and at least once spent four hours curling her hair.[18] But her family was too poor to keep her at home as she would have preferred, so when she was eighteen her father sent her out as an itinerant painter of tinware and clock faces. Her job was to embellish the severe, black roman numerals of clock dials and the drab surfaces of tin trays, teapots, and boxes with colorful vignettes of birds, flowers, and fruits. As part of her pay she boarded for weeks at a time in the houses of clockmakers and tinsmiths within a day's journey of her home. As a result, Roberts took part in the table talk and workroom conversation of many more households than most women her age, and she developed a wider network of acquaintances than young women who moved directly from their father's to their husband's house.

Yet because of the force of social conventions as well as her own temperament, these experiences did little to enlarge her knowledge of the world around her. Though she had been gregarious enough at home, where she was an insider, singing at social gatherings and making friends easily among her peers, living as an employee in another's house was constricting. A respectable employee was hired to work, not talk, read, or visit. A respectable woman, Roberts could not saunter down to the tavern for companionship in off-hours like a journeyman, and because she was an itinerant, she could not become involved in the female networks emanating from the churches. The conditions of her work encouraged introspection and loneliness.[19] Her sense of her situation was summed up by an episode one Sunday in 1804 when, as she put it, "I met with great mortification at meeting today, being something of a Stranger and not taking the seat which I ought to."[20] Thus she moved from one household to another, never quite fitting in and indifferent to much of what passed around her, whether at Andrus' in Farmington, Harrison's in Waterbury, or in Plymouth at Eli Terry's. Instead of local, national, or world news, the information Roberts craved dealt with her own emotions and relationships with others. Next to her own feelings of solitude, the gossip of local courtships, the turmoils of town politicians and the victories of Napoleon, were merely chatter, remote and uninteresting.

Roberts gave no more serious attention to newspapers than she did to the conversations that surrounded her in the homes of her employers. Instead she exchanged letters with her siblings and friends, attended church services, and read books—mostly novels. Born in an era when the novel was enjoying a great surge of popularity, especially among young women, Roberts took particular comfort in the companionship of novels which assuaged her loneliness during her time away from home. Though fictional, they were informative as well as "entertaining." They clarified and reinforced her own sentiments while teaching her to view reality in romantic categories.[21]

In the widely-popular *The Children of the Abbey,* a 600-page book, which she read twice in the space of sixteen months, Roberts discovered "the most beautiful characters and the most infamous characters," a simplified view of human behavior that both inspired her and gave her an escape from the mundane clockmakers' homes where neither the most beautiful nor infamous dwelt.[22] *The Romance of the Forest,* an adventure that ended happily with the marriage of the heroine, supplied the same kind of nourishment.[23] From reflective essays Roberts took information that functioned similarly as when, browsing in a general store, she picked up *The Influence of Solitude Upon the Human Heart* and after reading a few pages "found every word touched my heart, and led me into gloomy reflections concerning my situation."[24] What other titles she might have picked up in this particular store is unknown, but in the best stocked country stores of the era she would have found an array of textbooks and references, Bibles and devotional works, advice books ranging from home medical manuals to Lord Chesterfield's *Principles of Politeness,* examples of history, Latin classics in translation, and a handful of poems and novels such as Edward Young's *Night Thoughts* and Daniel Defoe's *Robinson Crusoe,* in addition to compendia of belles lettres like *The Ladies' Library.*[25] The fact that Roberts opened up *The Influence of Solitude* and found it deeply affecting suggests much about her use of print; its primary function was to inform and sustain her emotionally.

Indeed it is not too much to affirm that the chief function of literacy for Roberts was to nourish her sense of identity and her emotional well-being. Caught in circumstances where she reluctantly left "the pleasing society of my parents Brother and sisters" to work for the Eli Terrys of the vicinity, people who could treat her visiting friends with "the greatest indifference," she maintained her relationships and sense of inclusion through correspondence.[26] The information contained in the letters Roberts received and sent did not concern business or practical matters, nor were they in any sense "newsletters" that could be passed from hand to hand to bring their readers up-to-date on local events. Instead they were private, personal missives that invited the reader to share the writer's experience and which reasserted bonds of affection and inclusion. After reading a friend's letter, Roberts exclaimed, in language that might have come from a romantic novel, "O what endearing lines how it enlivens and expands the heart, to hear the sentiments of Friendship flowing from the lips or pen of one we esteem."[27] Roberts' phrase "lips or pen," conflating conversation and letters, is a reminder that for her as for many 19th-century women letters were surrogates for visits, occasions when information on thoughts and feelings enabled friends and relatives to nurture emotional relationships.[28]

Life provided no romantic, happy ending for Candace Roberts. At her father's direction she continued her work in the vicinity of Bristol until her untimely death in December 1806. In retrospect what seems most significant about her experience is that, in spite of her reading, travel (including trips to New Haven and Hartford), correspondence, and conversation, she never strayed from the domestic hearth psychologically or extended her interests beyond the arena of sentiment that was fashionable among her female peers. Because of her gender and her acceptance of the doctrines of subordination and separate spheres, notwithstanding all the possibilities for information that were available in New England at the opening of the 19th century, Roberts lived in a kind of voluntary seclusion. As an artisan's daughter her choices were few, and she followed the path of prescription, the path of least resistance, in contrast to Mrs. Carter and Mrs. Breed. Their challenges to convention were rooted in a mastery of information about the self and society that were part of a maturity rarely found in men or women of twenty-one years. But in Roberts' case personal temperament played as much of a role as her gender and social class did, as is evident from the experiences of other daughters whose lives were equally constricted, though by different social circumstances.

One was Mary Guion, the daughter of a prosperous farmer at Bedford in Westchester County, New York, at the southwestern boundary of Connecticut. Her diary, which she began early in 1800 when she was eighteen-years-old and continued until late 1807 when she married Samuel Brown, reveals a person no less influenced by fashion and prescription than Roberts, and even more limited in some ways since, except for a single trip to New York City, she never left home before her marriage. But in contrast to Roberts, who as an itinerant craftswoman was thrust into the lonely status of an outsider, Mary Guion was always surrounded by family, friends, and often suitors. For this reason, not only temperament, reading became for her a way to enhance her sociability among men and women of various ages and not, as it was for Candace Roberts, an alternative to the sociability she missed.

The substance of the information that engaged Mary Guion was essentially affective, the same as for Roberts, who was, after all, a contemporary dwelling within the same region. Indeed the same novel that so absorbed Roberts, *The Children of the Abbey,* Guion noted, "sent me to rest with my eyes drowned in tears."[29] Novels, essays, verse, and an occasional sermon comprised virtually all of her reading. On those occasions when Mary Guion did look at a newspaper, it was not necessarily to learn about public affairs but because a suitor, her future husband, "brot a news paper for me to read and pointed out one particular paragraph to me" which dealt with the choice of a spouse.[30] As with Roberts, Guion's domestic situation encouraged her to confine herself to the women's sphere, the private world that treasured piety, sentiment, and beauty. And like Roberts, Guion sought to conform to prescribed conventions, not challenge them.

Yet Guion's experience demonstrates that exactly the same kinds of information that could nourish interior emotional life and supply a common culture among women could also provide for sociability between women and men in a social class that was only slightly more elevated than the skilled artisan's. In the Guion household Mary's reading enabled her to engage in adult conversation with family members and friends, and to listen appreciatively to the polite palaver of the petty gentry. For Roberts reading was chiefly confined to the Sabbath; but for Guion, who spent much of each week scrubbing floors and milking cows as well as spinning and sewing, it was an everyday activity which she cultivated because, she believed, "I can be receiving instruction & improveing my mind from some authors." Recognizing that she was no beauty—to her regret there were "others where nature had been more bountiful of her favors [and] is Deckorated in a crowded Ball room & admird by every eye"—she would use books to make herself "more agreeable in company."[31]

That Guion was working to establish herself securely in polite society through reading is evident in her observations. One evening, for example, when a Mr. Pixley visited, she joined him and her father.

in the Parlour [where] the Spectator was lying on the table[.] the discourse than ran upon Books wich is always very entertaining to me[.] . . . he appeared to be very well informd in books wich I always do admire to see in any person and I believe he does to for he spok highly in favour of reading and how advantageous it was to any person when in Company where the discourse ran upon Books[.] & in such refind Company you may be sure my Evening past agreeable.[32]

In contrast, when the family visited another neighbor, "the time past away," but Guion would have liked just as well to have stayed home alone, since "the Company they was so very Illiterate."[33] Indeed even at home there was no assurance of polite conversation. A visitor who arrived one evening while she "was siting on the stoop with father" engaged him in conversation that was "similar to farmers about their stock & the produce of their fields." She stayed "as a silent Spectator & heard them with the greatest attention but," she said, "at length growing weary of hearing a conversation in wich I could not claim part I went in the house." Unlike the polite discourse of books, which could connect the male and female spheres, talk of livestock and tillage was for men, and Mary Guion neither would nor could join in.[34]

In Guion's milieu, close to the lower boundary of genteel manners, where if the father slaughtered a hog the women were busy afterwards preserving everything but the squeal, novels were emerging as secular texts that both men and women could discuss.[35] The genre was still criticized; indeed, one of Mary's Sunday callers, frustrated that she preferred to read silently than to socialize with him, "began to talk against reading such Books a Sunday;" but there were other men who found novels an ideal medium for bridging the gender gap.[36] When she visited Mr. Miller, she found a man who "reads a great deal & like myself likes to discourse upon what he's read," and with novels they were on common ground. Before Guion left, she was delighted because they "had time for a smart confab [on] the Children of the Abbey wich he had read & I am now reading [It] seamed to engross the greatest part of our discourse."[37] On another occasion, when she was dining with Mr. Isaacs, who, like her father, was a member of Bedford's social library, the subject of novels was raised "wherein his Lady and I both joined in opinion that we liked reading them too well but that we thot people might very much improve the understanding by a serious attention to them." Among such people novels, like textbooks, treatises, and sermons, were didactic works which, though sometimes so compelling as to distract from one's duties, were instructive for understanding sentiment, relationships, and morality.[38]

Mary Guion's aspirations for gentility were probably much like Candace Roberts' had been in the days before she left home, when she too could be occupied with her appearance, her clothing, and the dances she and her friends grandly called "balls." But because Guion's family prospered—her elder brother bought his own farm with £700 in 1802—they could acquire the trappings of gentility. Guion's access to polite reading matter, from the *Spectator* on the parlor table to the novels in the village library, though similar in kind, was greater than Roberts'; and it was the possession of this kind of information and access to polite conversation that were the hallmarks of genteel status. The reinforcement Guion's home provided was less a matter of leisure than a sign of familial aspiration. When Mary and her sister were working with their hands, their younger brother Tommy read aloud to them.[39] Her older brother praised her reading and writing, and when he went to New York he sent her a letter of advice which she cherished, and when he returned he brought her a book as a present.[40] Such encouragements, enabling her to command the body of information required for gentility, assured the fulfillment of her hopes.

For Lucy Breckinridge, living sixty years later and five hundred miles to the south and west in the Valley of Virginia, acquiring gentility was never an issue. Born in 1843 as the sixth child (third daughter) of one of Botetourt County's richest planters, Cary Breckinridge and his wife Emma Walker

Gilmer, Lucy was a granddaughter of General James Breckinridge, a William and Mary graduate, Virginia legislator, and four-term United States Congressman during Madison's presidency. Her father, also an alumnus of the college at Williamsburg, threw his energies into plantation management and, after inheriting half of his father's 4000-acre estate and gristmill, multiplied his assets so that by the time of Lucy's seventh birthday he owned 131 slaves, more than all but one of the county's planters.[41]

But though Lucy Breckinridge was separated in time, place, and social rank from Candace Roberts and Mary Guion, she too was a daughter whose obedience to her parents was dictated by law as well as custom. And as with Roberts and Guion, a domestic role leading toward marriage and motherhood was prescribed for her. Nearly all the information to which she enjoyed access, whether through conversation, observation, or letters, through public speech or printed matter, focused on private life—especially social manners and personal emotional states—thereby reinforcing the central doctrine of separate spheres. So well schooled was her society in the idea that women must dwell in a private sphere that, while the public actions of Union and Confederate men were wreaking a havoc that included the battlefield deaths of two of her brothers, her own consciousness was focused on domestic affairs. Indeed, even in the fully developed information environment in which she dwelled, where newspapers and letters were delivered to her home, Grove Hill, almost daily, and where she had the run of the family library as well as the company of cultivated friends and relations, she remained socially sequestered, so that only on isolated occasions and without aid or encouragement from others did her actions defy the ruling prescriptions for women.

Lucy Breckinridge was a naturally inquisitive person, more sophisticated and robust intellectually, more detached and critical than Roberts or Guion. But like them her aspirations for self-improvement focused on self-knowledge and understanding human nature more than on religious piety. The diary she started in August 1862 after the death of her favorite brother John, when she claimed to have "no inclination to read anything but the Bible and the newspapers," began in an artificial, epistolary form, influenced no doubt by such works as Samuel Richardson's novels or *Mrs. Rowe's Letters*.[42] Yet, as the weeks went by, she often forgot her imaginary correspondent, an older friend she had named "Harriet Randolph," just as she laid aside her plan to read only Scripture and battlefield reports. Instead she recorded her daily rounds of reading, letter-writing, working (chiefly sewing and knitting), and socializing with family, friends, and two fiancés, one of whom, the Texan Thomas Jefferson Bassett, she married in 1865. Her log of how she spent her time reveals that, though her family's stature and wealth provided access to a broad spectrum of information, her rural location at the Grove Hill estate near Fincastle meant that the only public speeches she heard were the sermons of a few Episcopal, Presbyterian, and Methodist clergymen. The theater, concerts, public festivals, and voluntary associations—educational, philanthropic, missionary, and reform—were all outside her experience. As a result conversation, her own and others' letters, and reading supplied virtually all of Breckinridge's information.

In conversation and letters her sources were more often female than male, and reinforced the pattern of separate spheres. Frequently the topics were people and common experiences. News of friends and relatives, their health and sentiments, and happy occasions like betrothals or mournful events such as deaths all passed routinely among Breckinridge's female circle of sisters, friends, and cousins. Her mother, whose managerial responsibilities for the Grove Hill household kept Mrs. Breckinridge occupied much of the time, was an honored member of this circle; and Lucy treasured the mornings or afternoons once or twice a month when her mother was present. Usually they all did handwork while they talked. Letters and printed matter, a newspaper, a magazine, a book, could enter into these conversations as when a passage was read aloud, but some letters were treated as private, and reading among these literate, privileged women was characteristically a silent, solitary activity.[43] Subjects like history and natural science—which Breckinridge never seems to have read—were at no time part of their conversations. Politics and religion were almost equally absent, except for personal comments on the merits of local preachers and news of the fortunes of the armies in which their kinsmen served. If they were inclined toward abstract discussion the subject was always a suitable perennial topic relevant to all participants, like the moral qualities of men and women or the advantages of matrimony versus maidenhood.[44]

When men were part of the social circle, as they often were in the evenings, patterns of conversation changed, and Breckinridge sometimes found opportunities to participate in the male sphere, if only silently and vicariously. When a former tutor visited, "Brother Gilmer and himself got to discussing the doctrines of the different churches," and Lucy was an avid spectator. Later she made detailed notes of their arguments, concluding with reference to predestination that "I have never met anyone yet who could throw any light on that subject."[45] Two days later, when a Virginia cavalry commander was visiting her brother, she again listened as the two "talked politics." Once more, she found, "I learned a great deal that I never knew before, for instance that Calhoun was not a secessionist but a revolutionist." Afterwards the two men talked about Swedenborg and his theories, which their silent observer found "very beautiful."[46] Here Lucy Breckinridge was being introduced to an education akin to Mrs. Carter's in which the overheard conversations of men, supplemented by access to a library, might lead to mastery of male subjects like politics or comparative religion.

Significantly, there is no evidence that men at Grove Hill ever included women directly in conversations on such topics. Indeed conversations between men and women here rarely started with novels—that meeting ground of Mary Guion's set; instead, men usually condescended to converse on subjects from the female sphere, familiar people, places, and sentiments, as well as potentially flirtatious topics like the desiderata for a spouse. The difficulty of finding mutually interesting topics is evident in Breckinridge's account of a visit from her fiancé, Thomas Bassett, whom her sister helped entertain, so that "in spite of . . . Mr. B.'s numerous anecdotes relative to hogs, dogs, cats and other animals, we spent quite a happy day."[47] Though Bassett could on occasion discuss novels in mixed company, reading did not evidently furnish the prospective couple with much common ground.[48]

That they did not have books in common is significant in that Mr. and Mrs. Breckinridge regarded Bassett as a suitable mate for their third daughter, even though she was bookish and they had raised their own sons to be comfortable conversing about books with their sisters. Evidently the concept of separate spheres enabled the senior Breckinridges to view the cultural gap between Lucy and Thomas Jefferson Bassett as of secondary concern. That the gap was real, however, is evident from Breckinridge's readings in contemporary literature and several secular and religious classics. Bassett's anecdotes collected from observing "hogs, dogs, cats," his "domestic conversation," drew on a body of information about behavior, motivation, sensibility, and society that was worlds away from Breckinridge's mentality.

Lucy Breckinridge's reading, about two-thirds of which was fiction, went well beyond sentimental tales to include the most sophisticated English literature of the era. During the early 1860s she read a galaxy of the best recent works by Edward George Bulwer-Lytton, Wilkie Collins, Thomas De Quincey, Charles Dickens, George Eliot, William Makepeace Thackeray, and Anthony Trollope. The social commentary of Victorian England, she found, illuminated her own world. Trollope's *The Bertrams,* for example, was "very interesting . . . as the characters remind me of people that I know, and it is very well written."[49] She expressed her critical judgment when she read lesser works like the American Mary Virginia Terhune's *Alone* which, though "quite an interesting novel," she found "not very well written."[50] Such observations were not the stuff of parlor repartee, intended to show off her literacy; they were wholly private or at most shared with her sisters to assist their reading choices.

Though novels by English and American women were part of their reading—Mary Elizabeth Braddon, George Eliot, Margaret Oliphant, Julia Pardoe, Terhune, and Augusta Jane Wilson—in contrast to the information she and her friends exchanged in conversation, which came largely from other women, the predominant authors she read were contemporary English men whose view of the suitable roles for men and women reinforced American conventions.[51] While by their own conduct and topics of conversation Virginia gentlemen told them indirectly to respect the separate spheres, the books women like Breckinridge chose for instruction and entertainment dealt with emotional and social relationships and so underscored that prescription.

Occasionally, however, when Breckinridge moved from contemporary authors to the 18th century, or strayed across the English Channel to a French author, the familiar conventions faced unsettling challenges. Perusing a volume of Smollett she picked up in the family library, she entered a now-forbidden social environment: "I enjoyed today reading some in a very bad book, *Peregrine Pickle* [1751]. It is very funny and interesting, but I cannot bear to read anything coarse, so I won't finish it."[52] Breckinridge's self-censorship is a measure of the degree to which she had internalized the rules of femininity by the age of twenty-one years. Earlier her self-consciousness had been aroused reading Jules Michelet's book on women, *La Femme* (1860). "I do not like that kind of reading," she confessed; "it scares me of myself, and makes me rebel against my lot."[53] She sought information in books, but more for the sake of enlarging and strengthening her understanding of reality than for challenging it.

The Grove Hill library, which contained a core of titles commonly found in an early 19th-century gentleman's collection, sometimes supplied her needs. Here she found Plutarch's *Lives,* though she "never could get entirely through it," as well as the classic London periodicals, Joseph Addison's and Richard Steele's *The Spectator* and Samuel Johnson's essays in *The Rambler.*[54] Now well over a century old, these one-time gentlemen and ladies' magazines with their essays on politics, biography, and belles lettres remained sufficiently fresh and rewarding to invite Breckinridge back to them repeatedly. Indeed she evidently read these 18th-century periodicals more frequently than any magazine of her own day.[55] Perhaps equally significant was the fact that when she sought religious comfort, in addition to the Bible she most often turned to the "Sermons on Human Nature" that the Anglican cleric Joseph Butler had published in 1726. She found them "so hard to understand that I have to study them very carefully," but some of their subjects—self-deceit, compassion, and resentment—touched precisely what was on Breckinridge's mind.[56] Across fourteen decades Butler's counsel remained useful and current. Perhaps it was because women's roles and religious affinities remained more stable than those of their male counterparts, but they seem to have more often maintained the older pattern of reading "steady sellers" like John Bunyan's *Pilgrim's Progress,* Edward Young's *Night Thoughts,* and even Thomas à Kempis' *Imitation of Christ,* as well as Butler.

Two Butler sermons that Breckinridge contemplated, "Sins of the Tongue" and "Forgiveness of Injuries," sometimes had very precise applications.[57] "Girls will tell everything they hear," she fumed after an episode where an intimate conversation "overheard" between Breckinridge and her first fiancé was repeated.[58] "She [Jennie Miller] had better warn her friends of her too acute hearing. Of course, she has told everyone! I'll remember!" Because the idea of private conversation was well developed by the mid-19th century, especially where sentiments between lovers were concerned, she pronounced that Jennie Miller was "dishonorable."[59]

Among daughters, who were at a stage of life where they were often self-conscious about their own thoughts and prone to speculate on their marriage prospects, there was an especially keen awareness of the idea of private information in relation to domestic life. For them and their male and female friends' conversations, diaries, and letters might be confidential, not because of reasons of state or commercial advantage as in the Boston of Samuel Sewall and John Rowe, but for the sake of personal feelings which, by the beginning of the 19th century were just as important from the perspective of those concerned.

Earlier, though there were certainly important exceptions, personal communications had not been routinely regarded as privileged. In 18th-century taverns, for example, people felt free to listen to the conversations of others and to enter into them with questions and comments. Even sealed letters were opened and resealed in transit, sometimes with a postscript added by the person who was transmitting the letter on to the next hand.[60] Diaries also possessed an ambiguous status until the first half of the 19th century. Some, like those of Anna Green Winslow, a Boston teenager in the 1770s, were composed with a view to sharing them with parents as a kind of accounting of personal development over time; and certain diaries such as Isaac Mickle's Philadelphia diary of the 1840s included portions intended to amuse an audience of friends.[61] But others were strictly private, as with William Byrd, who, though certainly the master of his domain, found that the only way he could be sure of the privacy of his diary—which included an accounting of his sexual activity—was to write it in a shorthand cipher. Mary Guion's expectations as a daughter in a household with an older brother reveal the anxieties that the issue of personal privacy created during the transition from the more corporate sensibility of the 18th century to the highly individual, more romanticized consciousness of the Victorian era so clearly articulated years later by Lucy Breckinridge.

Mary Guion's account of her feelings on the subject of privacy reveals how information about the self and one's sentiments was becoming privileged, albeit with some difficulty:

I was a Scrubing the floor[.] James was In the study he steps in the Parlour & said to me Polly I never knowd you kept a Journal befor[.] I made no answer thinking he had read it & they many things the Book contains fild me with confusion[.] but I believe he had not but only said so as a kind of asking my liberty & from my silence he took concent for he went to reading it[.] some time after my Curiosety drew me into the Parlour & thro the door I saw him reading this Book[.] I wishd then I had never wroat it . . . so I said James you do very wrong[.] I never intended anyone should read that[.] he answered Ive read the 3 first leaves & can see no harm in it[.] I shoud like very much to read it all. I said Id rather give a doller than have you[,] so I stept up to him to shut the Book and said you must not—but he is Considerable of a student and I supose had a very great curiosoty to know the contents. I said no more but I realy have felt a kind of feebleness & trembling thro shame ever since.[62]

The fact was that although Guion intended her diary to be private and had composed it confident in that assumption, and even defended her right to privacy, in the end she yielded to her brother's superior learning and social status at the expense of her own embarrassment and individuality. Being a daughter and a younger sister made self-assertion, even control over one's own diary and aspirations, a formidable challenge in the early republic.

One sees echoes of these themes in Breckinridge's letters. An active correspondent who sometimes wrote as many as half-a-dozen letters in a day, Breckinridge overcame her physical isolation at Grove Hill by keeping in touch with friends and relatives frequently. Indeed Monday through Friday, and sometimes even on Saturday, someone from the household—her father, a sibling, or a slave—brought the mail and the newspapers from the Botetourt County Courthouse three miles away. Every week she was pleased to receive a letter or two from a married sibling, a cousin, or a friend, and in these letters the sociability and personal intimacy that were so much a part of genteel women's culture was maintained at a distance.[63] By saving the letters she received and rereading them in batches Breckinridge could visit vicariously those who were separated by distance or death.[64]

The importance of letters for a family like the Breckinridges was magnified by the Civil War and the fact that there were always one or two brothers in Virginia regiments, even after two were killed in 1862 and 1864. In July 1864, with military action encircling the county, the mail was cut off for a week at a time when, Breckinridge noted, "receiving the mail is the only important event of our lives."[65] Under these circumstances some letters were private, and some were not. Those containing news of the well-being of family members were shared aloud, while those devoted to personal sentiments remained private. But even letters that were read retrospectively for sentimental reasons might be part of a social exchange, as when about a year after her sister-in-law Fannie Burwell Breckinridge died, Lucy "read a good many of Fan's letters" to guests who shared with her "alternating moods of joy and sadness" in the "talent and liveliness [that] was lost in her death." Lucy Breckinridge and her peers believed in privacy, but it was not absolute. Indeed in the view of evangelicals, the private letters of the deceased could even be published if that would serve the noble goals of Christian sentiment. An etiquette stemming in part from romantic novels defined the parameters of privacy.[66]

One important time when as a daughter Lucy was reluctantly forced to accept this social reality was after her older sister Elizabeth leaked word that

"The Love Letter," by Thomas Sully, was used as an illustration to accompany a romantic poem in The Gift: A Christmas and New Year's Present for 1837 *(Philadelphia, 1837). "Let me read thy thrilling strain!" the poet asks. Here the connections between young women, letters, privacy, and sentiment are explicit as the beautiful semi-nude subject reads in bed before the miniature image of her lover. The poem's closing line,*

> *From thy page my soul is drinking*
> *Drops of pleasure's honey-dew,*

reinforces the sensual connotations of the love letter.

Lucy and Captain David Gardiner Houston had become engaged. Her parents believed Houston to be an unsuitable match and persuaded Lucy to break it off, which she did with mixed emotions. Until the outcome of this affair was settled, Lucy reported that "Pa opens all my letters," including those from Houston.[67] As a daughter she recognized that her own secret commitment to marriage had been illegitimate, for when parental authority was at issue there was ultimately no privacy.

Nor did Lucy or the other Breckinridge girls find anything dishonorable in perusing the personal letters of Union soldiers that happened to fall into their hands: "we amused ourselves reading some Yankee letters that Capt. Harris captured."[68] Because these were the letters of strangers, indeed enemies, the ordinary rules did not apply. In the domestic sphere of 19th-century women, certainly for Guion and Breckinridge, that which concerned the heart and mind—the sentiment and reason that defined the innermost self—was privileged information. However the letters of strangers could be treated casually, for amusement, like conversations overheard in a public place. And if the Breckinridges were violating the Yankees' privacy, so much the better; it was a small act of hostility against an enemy that was invading their land.

The case of the Yankee letters, like the episode where James Guion read his sister's diary, illustrates the fact that the privacy of no written communication can be absolutely secure. The shredding of letters for reasons of state is an old story; indeed, when Samuel Adams was serving in the Continental Congress in the summer when fireplaces were cold, he used scissors to make confetti out of letters that he tossed to the winds so as to assure the secrets of his correspondents.[69] But when Lucy Breckinridge sought to guarantee ultimate privacy she resorted not to a scissors but to the ritual of burning the letters she had exchanged with her betrothed.[70] This act, replete with romantic suggestions of purification and sacrifice, was also an assertion of autonomy that assured her that neither her parents nor her siblings would ever have unbidden access to the thoughts she had chosen to convey to her future husband. Only the destruction of letters or a diary could secure absolute privacy; and by Lucy Breckinridge's era references to the burning of intimate correspondence were almost so common as to be a typical ritual.

Considered together, the experiences of Roberts, Guion, and Breckinridge sustain the view that prescription and reality were closely entwined for many daughters in the first sixty years of the 19th century. In conversation, whether among other women or with men, approved conventions were reinforced just as they were bolstered by the male and female authors they read. Challenges to social prescription appear rarely and only when women allowed their own direct observations of reality to dictate their views as with Mrs. Carter and Mrs. Breed. Though such occasions might be few in Lucy Breckinridge's experience, they could burst upon her consciousness with unexpected power. At the end of 1864 she suddenly discovered she was, as she put it, "a true abolitionist in heart." What brought her to this remarkable assertion was not a book, not a conversation, but a small drama she witnessed while visiting at the home of her eldest sister, Mary Ann Breckinridge Woodville. Here she saw her nephew "Jimmy chasing poor, little Preston [a slave] all over the yard with a great stick, and Sister not making him stop but actually encouraging him. I never shall forget Viola's [Preston's slave mother] expression of suppressed rage—how I felt for her! My blood boiled with indignation." Though Lucy did not challenge convention by confronting her sister then and there—she was, after all, a guest in her sister's home and Jimmy was not her own child—she did resolve that "*my sons had better not beat a little servant where I am!*"[71] In this assertion Breckinridge remained within the female sphere of child-rearing, but she was also newly politicized in the manner of readers of *Uncle Tom's Cabin.*[72] Breckinridge could draw this antislavery lesson from direct observation because her own sensibility, developed in the same home as her sister, had also been nurtured on novels which expressed a social conscience, such as the works of Charles Dickens and Victor Hugo.[73] In this context, and not only with respect to romantic fantasies, the dynamic, potentially subversive implications of novels for traditional arrangements were manifest. Novels conveyed information and messages about values and behavior that, as Mary Guion had asserted, "might very much improve the understanding," and so alter conventional beliefs.[74]

Daughters were not, of course, their own masters, and they were subject to powerful indoctrination in prescribed female roles. But the information environments that enabled them to read and to discuss their reading allowed them to cultivate domestic values which offered avenues for change. Personal experience, conversation, and reading could be mutually reinforcing so as to alter prescription in subtle ways that could ultimately lead a loyal daughter of the Confederacy to declare herself, if only in the privacy of her diary, 'a true abolitionist in heart." In contrast, married women, whose prescribed roles entailed greater authority and responsibility, had less occasion and perhaps less need for reflective, sentimental reading. Although still formally subordinate to their husbands much as daughters were to fathers, wives could exercise substantial autonomy depending on the calling and character of their husband as well as their own occupation and temperament. Consequently, though they too were primarily concerned with affective information, the experiences of wives differed significantly from those of daughters in ways that we shall examine in the lives of Martha Moore Ballard, Mary Vial Holyoke and Sarah Hill Fletcher between 1760 and 1824.

The prescribed social standing of a wife in early America was always and necessarily ambiguous because she was simultaneously regarded as a responsible adult, a "deputy husband," and a person with few rights at law who was normally excluded from property-holding and all public roles.[75] Her actual condition could vary radically from the egalitarian, companionate marriage that Abigail Smith Adams enjoyed with John Adams for fifty-four years, to the legally sanctioned tyranny that husbands such as Henry Beekman Livingston exercised for decades over Nancy Shippen, and Pierce Butler maintained in the mid-19th century over Fanny Kemble, who before her marriage had enjoyed a phenomenally successful theatrical career.[76] Aware of these divergent possibilities from their own observation as well as from novels, daughters like Lucy Breckinridge contemplated marriage with a mixture of expectancy and apprehension, understanding that even with the best of husbands and a relationship based on mutuality, the transition from daughter to wife and mother encumbered a woman with new and weighty cares and risks. "I never saw a wife and mother who could spend a day of unalloyed happiness and ease," Breckinridge observed, declaring with finality that even with "an immense amount of love" a wife's lot meant "trouble and suffering."[77] Children, a household, and a husband all made demands of an urgency, extent, and complexity that far exceeded the responsibilities of a daughter.

One consequence of this transition from daughter to wife was a shift toward information activity that was less intensively centered on the self and relationships and more likely to embrace the community and business affairs that engaged her husband and family. Whether daughter or wife, the woman's sphere was domestic, but a wife's role often promoted wider information perspectives than a daughter's. As her husband's companion and associate she assumed an outlook different from that of a daughter. Whereas a self-involvement nourished by sentimental, imaginative literature was legitimate for daughters, whose responsibilities were chiefly personal, the business of a wife concentrated on the well-being of a husband and family and so information about other people engaged wives continuously. For them being informed about the society beyond the self, knowing the family, the household, and the community, was an essential part of daily life.

The experience of Martha Moore Ballard, a Hallowell (now Augusta), Maine, midwife, demonstrates some of the possibilities of a wife's role, although the fact of her dual occupation, wife and midwife, meant that independent of her husband and family she developed an unusually wide circle of acquaintances, especially among women.[78] Ballard, born in 1735 in Massachusetts and married in 1754, lived in the town of Oxford near the borders of Connecticut and Rhode Island before 1777, when she and her husband Ephraim migrated to Hallowell, a Kennebec River town on the central Maine frontier which had been settled in the 1760s. There he operated a sawmill and supplemented the family income by surveying land, while she ran their household and delivered babies two or three times a month. By the 1780s the Ballards had three sons and three daughters who ranged in age from Jonathan, born in 1763 and who became a farmer, to Ephraim, born in 1779, who was ultimately apprenticed to his brother-in-law, a joiner. Long before the family moved to Maine they had lost two daughters in childhood just nine days apart. Ballard's diary, which was similar to a farmer's in that she kept an account of her work as well as of personal events, covers the years from 1785 until the month of her death in 1812. The record she made of her activities reveals a woman who was highly informed on matters that touched her own experience but who was also cognizant of society beyond her own domestic sphere.[79]

As might be expected of a woman whose time was under constant claim by others, most of the information she received and passed on was by word of mouth. Obliged to feed and lodge loggers who hauled timber to the Ballard mill, and called out of her home at any hour of the day or night for the delivery of an infant, all in addition to the routine responsibilities of feeding and clothing her family, she had few occasions for reflective reading or purely social intercourse. In contrast to Candace Roberts, Mary Guion, and Lucy Breckinridge, Ballard could seldom use her literacy to supply emotional reinforcement, genteel lessons, or social insight. In her diary she kept track of her life, her family, and their doings, while her reading, which was almost entirely restricted to Sundays, offered religious instruction when attending church was difficult.

The information Martha Ballard acquired and conveyed dealt mostly with persons, not business, political, or religious affairs, and made her something of a community resource for gossip in the growing but still thinly populated, comparatively isolated Maine interior of the 1780s and 1790s.[80] Present each year in at least two dozen homes where she spent long hours in the company of other women gathered to assist in childbirth, Ballard became acquainted with hundreds of the settled families residing in Lincoln County. Moreover because of her medical competence people brought her information regarding illnesses and injuries so that in time she accumulated an encyclopedic knowledge of the individual well-being of hundreds of people, knowledge that in its encyclopedic character resembled the rigger Ashley Bowen's intelligence concerning the condition of ships moving in and out of Marblehead harbor.

To some extent, such information came to her not because she was a midwife but simply because it was the common grist for conversational mills. When a Captain Stackpool visited in July 1790, there was no particular reason for his imparting the news "that Sherebiah Town expired last evening . . . that a Mr. Lues was killed by a limb falling of a tree; that a man at Penobscott hanged himself and another at Boston shott himself."[81] These were merely mildly sensational stories that compelled a measure of human interest. Similarly, when word spread of a local romantic imbroglio, resembling a contemporary novel—"Mr. Smith was gone away, and 'tis feared desires to deprive himself of life on account of Polly Hamlen's refusing to wed with him"—Ballard, like everyone else in Hallowell, heard about it. Indeed at church the following Sunday she found "Smith and Polly Hamlen are all the conversation at present."[82] Four days later a man informed Ballard "he had heard Smith had hanged himself."[83] That a man, rather than a woman, conveyed this news to Ballard had more to do with the fact that she was the wife of the sawmill operator, than because she was a midwife. Yet there was a whole miscellany of information—about wounds inflicted by tools, about burns, falls from horses, and woodsmen's injuries—that came to her because of her medical relationship to the community. People sought advice, reassurance, or simply understood that such information was of interest to her, in the same way that the weather was always interesting to farmers.

Ballard also took note of news of general human interest that circulated through the county. Information touching on criminal misbehavior, such as the arrest of a forger, a husband's abuse of his wife, the punishment of a thief, was of no concern to her as a midwife, but neighbors, her sons, her husband, brought such news into her house. Once the sensational news of a gentleman's axe-and-razor murder of his wife, six children, and his own suicide, thrust the seventy-one-year-old Martha Ballard into the center of a hideous scene because she was a neighbor and a medical practitioner. Two neighbor wives awakened her at three o'clock in the morning on July 9, 1806, with word that Captain James Purington had killed his family and himself. After her eighty-one-year-old husband, Ephraim, had gone to Purington's to assess the situation and returned before sunrise, they went together "to behold the most shocking scene that was ever seen in this part of the world." They stayed to help clean up the disaster. Indeed, Martha Ballard worked all day washing the corpses and preparing them for burial with linens she had brought for the purpose, while, as she labored, "many hundred persons came to behold [this] horrid spectacle."[84] Within hours, news of the awful sensation had spread like a contagion through the countryside. The next day Hallowell was thronged for the funeral, and Purington relatives lodged with the Ballards.[85] Though Ballard had often learned of lurid criminal events by word of mouth, on this occasion she was at the center of an information tumult unique in her experience.

It is significant, surely, that all the news of the Purington murders and suicide came to her either as a firsthand witness or via word of mouth, and that the event attracted hundreds of people to the scene and to the funeral through the same means, without any printed broadside or newspaper to pass from hand to hand.[86] Residents of Hallowell like the Ballards had been newspaper readers since the end of the 1790s at least—Martha Ballard had spent a full day in January 1799 "putting the newspapers in regular order and sewing them"—but urgent news and the information affecting Hallowell people most directly usually came via chains of oral diffusion.[87]

There was, however, a gender distinction in the ways that public information moved through society. For although Martha Ballard traveled more extensively and enjoyed a wider acquaintance than many men and most women, where the public side of the community's information was concerned, her husband was usually her key source. In the movement to dismiss the Reverend Isaac Foster, for example, Martha Ballard was vitally concerned and a staunch supporter of the beleaguered clergyman, but it was her husband who kept her informed at key junctures.

Foster's ouster evidently began with a defamation case at the beginning of 1787 when a Captain Sewall and his kinsman Thomas Sewall leveled a number of charges at their pastor, including an assertion that he did not respect the Sabbath and had violated it by commanding his servant to labor on Sundays. Ephraim Ballard called on Thomas Sewall "to converse with him concerning [the] ill he is accused of spreading," hoping to reconcile the conflict. But when Ephraim reported the substance of his interview to Martha she noted it had been fruitless.[88] Several days later, when the Sewalls were tried "for defaming" Foster, Martha attended the trial with another wife and co-parishioner; then, after the Sewalls were found guilty, she called on the Reverend Foster to pay her respects. The contention did not end there, however, and almost two years later Ephraim Ballard came home from town meeting with the news that a council was being created to consider Foster's dismissal.[89] Once more Martha Ballard attended the trial, in this case a clerical council "to hear the evidences examined."[90] One month later Ephraim brought Martha the final verdict from the town meeting, "that the Rev'd Mr. Foster should not preach in the meeting-house anymore."[91] Martha Ballard had been thoroughly engaged in the struggle on behalf of the Reverend Foster and fully informed by her husband, though as a woman she could not participate in the key decisions. Here her relationship to her husband made her an insider, even if she could not cast a vote on Foster's behalf in the town-meeting.

But if Martha Ballard's access to public word-of-mouth information was normally through her husband, her midwife's practice gave her medical information that did not come from him. Ballard never claimed to be a learned person, and when a problem lay beyond her experience or did not respond to treatment, she was quick to recommend someone of greater skill or knowledge. Only in emergencies when the patient was in danger would she venture beyond familiar boundaries.[92] She did not study books; she listened, and watched, and experimented. From a physician she learned doses of "cream tartar, niter and senna."[93] From an old woman she learned a "syrup of vinegar and onions, and a decoction of gold thread and shumake berries."[94] At the age of sixty-six she witnessed the dissection of a corpse "which was performed very closely."[95]

That Martha Ballard does not appear to have employed any of the well-known medical manuals is surprising in light of the fact that she read newspapers and sermons routinely and earned enough from her practice—£15 to £20 per annum in the 1790s—to have been able to afford at least one such book.[96] Possibly she did in fact use a medical manual but did not record its use in her diary. However, it is also plausible to suppose that after delivering hundreds of babies—over 400 by 1791—she felt there was not much to be learned about obstetrics from books, and she generally left other serious ailments to physicians. Indeed, as with daughters, she seems to have used her literacy more to satisfy personal needs than to advance her husband's or her own business. Her diary did serve as a work log, and in it she kept track of payments; but it was not a ledger. She devoted it mostly to personal, family, and community doings. Moreover the letters she wrote and received dealt almost exclusively with family news. It was, she wrote, "refreshing to hear of the health and prosperity of my dear connections who are hundreds of miles from me."[97]

Even the newspaper, which enabled her to follow public events such as state and national elections, was a source for her of family news, as when she learned of an uncle's death as she was "perrusing the newspapers" one winter's day.[98] She was not necessarily indifferent to public affairs, but they were the domain of men. On Independence Day, for example, it was her husband and sons who went to the village to hear the orations and march in partisan processions, while she stayed home visiting with her daughters and grandchildren and attending to chores.[99] In contrast, she rarely missed an opportunity to listen to a sermon, and carefully kept a record of their texts. For Ballard, who dwelled in a world which revolved around the health and well-being of individual people, it was religion and piety, not politics, that supplied understanding and a sense of order. That politics and the public world were for men and that household affairs and caregiving for women she never doubted.

When Ballard passed her seventieth birthday and old age sapped her strength and capacity for work, the extensiveness and scope of her information networks contracted, but the character of the information she encountered remained appropriate to a wife. Her husband, who turned eighty in 1805, continued to bring home descriptions of orations he heard, now Masonic as well as patriotic and political, in addition to bringing "wood on his shoulders for the fire."[100] Occasionally she still went out at night to supervise the delivery of an infant.[101] But she also suffered the melancholy of reduced activity. There were days when they both felt "feeble," and in addition, having launched their sons and daughters on modest though respectable paths, they sank into poverty.[102] Their children might provide small luxuries—a new snuff box, an almanac—but in 1810 their cow was seized for nonpayment of taxes, and Ballard lamented, "what are we to do, God only knows."[103] Although the parish provided some charitable help, her chief joys were her grandchildren—"it is as a cordial to have a child come to see me," she wrote.[104] Yet there were days when that also could be too much, as on a Sunday when she was "unwell, but have had the noise of children out of 5 familys to bear; some fighting, some playing, and not a little profanity has been performed."[105] In spite of her advanced years Ballard was still in the situation that Lucy Breckinridge understood to be the natural condition of a wife. From Ballard's perspective, having noted the fifty-sixth anniversary of her marriage to her "dear companion," there was no regret, simply the desire for a measure of comfort before crossing over to the next world.[106]

The earthly world that Martha Ballard inhabited was rustic and austere, although by the end of her life the town of Hallowell, which had been made a county seat in 1799, was entering an urban stage. Her own parish even enjoyed a visit from the Reverend William Ellery Channing of Boston and President Jesse Appleton of Bowdoin College.[107] Still, by comparison, the society in which her contemporary Mary Vial Holyoke dwelt was cultivated and luxurious. As the wife of the Salem, Massachusetts, physician Edward Augustus Holyoke, the eldest son of a Harvard president, she enjoyed the amenities of wealth and social prestige in a flourishing port town. Mary had been born into the family of the Boston shopkeeper, Nathaniel Vial, in 1737, and only moved to Salem in 1759 when Dr. Holyoke remarried after the death of his first wife. There she spent the remainder of her days, traveling only within Massachusetts, mostly to Boston and Cambridge, and bearing twelve children between 1760 and 1782, six of whom survived infancy.[108] Her extant diary, which begins seven weeks after her marriage in 1760 and continues until sixteen months before her death in 1800, parallels Martha Ballard's in many respects. It too chronicles a life within the domestic sphere, though in a different milieu, while further illuminating the character of a wife's participation in the diffusion of information.

For Mary Vial Holyoke the move from Boston, New England's largest seaport, to Salem, which with some 4500 inhabitants in 1760 ranked fourth below Newport and Marblehead, was certainly a step toward rusticity.[109] Salem was both smaller and more puritan and provincial than Boston. Yet compared with Hallowell, Salem was the vanguard of fashion and closely connected with province and transatlantic information networks. Salem ships traveled all over the Atlantic, and salutes fired in Boston Harbor were signals for Salem as well. Living in Salem and married to a physician who made house calls to the town's highest and lowest families gave Mary Holyoke access to a great variety of information. What she regarded as significant reveals how her genteel perspective shaped her reception and transmission of information.

Holyoke's attention to "social news," the visits and entertainments of her community's elite, is much like that of Lucy Breckinridge nearly a century later. When she took note of a barbecue where she was among fifty guests or recorded a dancing "assembly" at the schoolhouse chamber, it is evident that social standing, not age or marital status, explains much of her interest in this information.[110] Her own identity and social standing was based on how she navigated in polite society, and knowledge of such occasions was as necessary for Mary Holyoke as the neighborhood gossip of property, marriages, and deaths stored up by farmers was to them, or the news of ships to marine tradesmen, and the knowledge of families, pregnancies, and health was to Martha Ballard. This would be as true for Holyoke at the age of sixty-one, when a ball was held in honor of President John Adams' birthday, as it had been when she first arrived in Salem as a bride.[111]

Closely associated with this kind of "social" information was news of the various public entertainments and visiting lecturers that passed through Salem from the 1760s and 1770s onward. Though she could not attend all such events, each one was noteworthy in a community whose leading inhabitants aspired toward urbanity. The public reading of a play called "The Provoked Husband," the performance of operatic songs by an itinerant Englishman, a lecture on electricity, were all part of polite society and palpable evidence that Salem shared in Boston and even London culture.[112] For a woman of Holyoke's stature, as for men of the same rank, it was important to be conversant with this sort of genteel public events.

In contrast, when it came to public affairs relating to provincial or imperial politics, there was no such expectation for genteel any more than for common women. Through her husband, through conversations with visitors and neighbors, and through newspapers, Mary Holyoke might have been almost as politically informed as Mrs. Carter, or even Abigail Adams, and Mercy Otis Warren. For even though Edward Holyoke was a physician and not a politician, much current information was available in Salem to a literate woman who moved in elite circles. Yet Mary Holyoke's knowledge of political affairs was haphazard and uneven compared to her command of social events. Indeed, it was chiefly when a political occurrence was memorialized with a public social occasion, as with Salem's fireworks celebrating the capture of Havana in 1762, the "Rejoicings for the Repeal of the [Stamp] Act" in 1766, and the festivities for the ratification of the United States Constitution in 1788, that she paid attention to public affairs.[113] Less conspicuous though equally important events like the signing of the Declaration of Independence made little impression on her.[114]

In this the elevated Mrs. Holyoke was, like the common Mrs. Ballard, typical of most women who, with their husbands, did not regard politics as women's concern and were content to be ignorant of public affairs. That Abigail Adams and Mercy Otis Warren were so fully informed was exceptional, and largely a consequence of their particular domestic situations, dwelling with husbands whose companionship engaged them in public affairs. For even Samuel Adams, perhaps the ultimate contemporary example of a politically preoccupied husband, felt obliged to apologize for violating the conventions of gender relations on the rare occasions when he appended a political paragraph to a domestic letter to his wife.[115] If conventions were to be broken so as to enable women to become politically informed and engaged—which did happen with some frequency in elite families—it was often somewhat covert and assisted and encouraged by a father, a brother, and, most important, a husband.

In Holyoke's case the information outside the women's sphere that her husband most often shared was medical, and even this was not wholly outside the domestic arena. For a woman to possess statistical information on the incidence of smallpox in Boston and the extent of inoculation at Cambridge was unusual, although it was routine for wives to inform themselves on health subjects and to follow the spread of contagions through word-of-mouth and newspaper reports.[116] Moreover in most families it was wives who provided medical care in the first instance. Consequently, the increased access to information that Holyoke enjoyed through her husband's professional knowledge did not set her apart decisively from other matrons. Indeed, her gossip with them, when it did not concern "social events," touched on the same sorts of affective and personal matters that were the focus of Martha Ballard's conversation—family, friends, and neighbors, together with local anecdotes of special human interest.

The information that passed in these conversations was almost wholly domestic in nature. During the Revolution, it is true, war reports were conveyed—as when "our People" took possession of Boston in March 1776 or when seven years later there was "News of Peace"—but in peacetime almost the only exceptions were anecdotes about criminals and local disasters.[117] When a boat capsized in the harbor drowning ten Salem residents in 1773, and a fire consumed thirteen buildings in town the following year, everyone was impatient to learn what had happened more swiftly and in greater detail than any newspaper account could provide.[118] In such cases it appears that husbands were more interested in news of the mechanics of the accident—how and why it occurred—and wives with tidings of the human consequences, of broken families and homes destroyed. These differences were rooted less in prescription than in social experience. Women's preoccupation with home and family, made information pertinent to their own involvement in the daily needs of children, husbands, relatives, servants, and apprentices, their chief concern.

As a result there were fundamental continuities in the information experiences of wives and mothers from one generation to the next. As they moved from youthful marriage through matronly maturity to old age some of their capacities and duties changed, but the domestic role that defined how they spent their working lives endured. Doubtless this is one reason why by 1800, forty-one years after Mary Vial Holyoke came to Salem, her information experiences remained much as before. The town of Salem had changed; it was larger, more prosperous and decidedly more urban and heterogeneous than it had been in 1760. Religious sects and meetinghouses had multiplied as had secular entertainments—lectures, performances, and exhibits of curiosities ranging from a mechanical automaton to an Indian elephant. Yet, although Salem was now spruced up with sidewalks and streetlights and even supported a bookstore, its urbane appearance and mentality did nothing to alter Mary's status as Dr. Holyoke's wife, as a mother, and now as a grandmother. It was this social position that assigned her to domestic duties as well as providing her with an entrée into Salem's wealthiest families. Salem now provided more balls and genteel public entertainments than ever before, so news of such events more often passed between her and her daughters and their acquaintances; while more newspapers brought an increased frequency of sensational human interest reports as compared with the previous generation. But the overall character of her experience remained the same—information concerning the family and locality dominated her field of vision.

For Sarah Hill Fletcher, who was born in 1801 in the frontier region of Mason County in northeastern Kentucky, life was never so settled nor gender roles so refined. Though Mason boasted an unusually large number of settlers from the northeast, including perhaps fifty New England families, and became known as "the best schooled county" in Kentucky, it was more like Ballard's Maine than Holyoke's Salem.[119] During Sarah's girlhood her family, of mixed Virginia and Massachusetts descent, moved to Urbana on the central Ohio frontier, and it was there that she first met her future husband, Calvin Fletcher, who was teaching while studying to become a lawyer. Four years later they married, and in October 1821 the twenty-year-old bride and her twenty-three-year-old husband moved to the new community of Indianapolis in central Indiana. Henceforth Sarah Hill Fletcher would stay put, traveling only to visit relatives. She spent most of her time managing the household, where she bore and raised eleven children before her death in 1854. Her diary and letters, which center on the years 1821 to 1824, provide only a glimpse of her days as a young wife, before maternal responsibilities engulfed her.[120] Yet they offer a distinct perspective on women's information experiences from a point midway between the youthful womanhood of daughters like Roberts, Guion, and Breckinridge and the mature matronhood of Ballard and Holyoke. Here the significance of the transition from daughter to wife and the interactions between prescription and reality are illuminated.

Sarah Hill's tutelage under Calvin Fletcher began in the schoolroom, where he was her instructor, and this relationship, where husband played mentor to wife, continued to influence much of Sarah Hill Fletcher's reading and conversation after their marriage. Indeed, she may well have commenced her diary at her husband's recommendation. Calvin Fletcher, an ambitious, mostly self-educated Vermont farm boy who confided that "of all fears that of poverty I most dread," went west to seek his fortune.[121] He aimed to climb to the top of Indiana society, and he sought to make his "bashful" bride into an accomplished companion as well.[122] Thus he deliberately erased part of the boundary separating the male and female spheres by encouraging his wife to emulate his own rudimentary gentleman's education through the study of rhetoric, poetry, science, geography and travel books, as well as arithmetic and Chesterfield's ubiquitous advice on courtesy.[123] In contrast to daughters such as Roberts, Guion, and Breckinridge who all read contemporary novels avidly, the only novel Sarah Fletcher read between 1821 and 1824 was Oliver Goldsmith's picaresque morality tale, *The Vicar of Wakefield* (1766), and the chief poetic work was James Thomson's *The Seasons* (1726–1730).[124] Both books, while suitable for either sex, were commonly found in the gentlemen's social libraries of the late 18th century in New England.[125] The only work she read that was specifically directed to women was a compendium of extracts from English magazines called *The Western Ladies Casket,* which was "edited by a lady" at Connersville, Indiana.[126] That virtually all of Fletcher's reading was supplied by her husband is suggested not only by the paucity of popular novels but by its distinctly secular caste. The sermons with which a wife such as Martha Ballard or a daughter like Lucy Breckinridge retreated, books that furnished a pious alternative to novels, were not part of Sarah Fletcher's reading diet, although she attended church and regarded herself as a Christian.

The same pattern is evident in Sarah Fletcher's attention to current political events as reported in "noose papers" and her command of the vocabulary of business deals pertaining to land, logging, contracts, and prices. Indeed, it appears that in the interval between marriage and the birth of her first child, frontier life often made Sarah her husband's companion at labor, as at their first harvest in Indianapolis where together, she wrote, they "geathered our Beets carrots and Potatoes. In the Eve butchered a pig."[127] Three days later they collaborated in building a corncrib to store their crop.[128] At this point, early in her first pregnancy, her physical condition did not yet confine her within the woman's sphere, and social convention was more readily ignored perhaps on the frontier than in a settled community by a couple whose goals included gentility. In public, as at the town's Independence Day celebration in 1822, the women were separate from "the men [who] had a barbacu & dind inder the green sugar trees," but at home it was different.[129]

The connection between Sarah Fletcher and her husband during the first year of their marriage was so comprehensive that, except for the letters she exchanged with her female relatives and friends, she cut herself off substantially from female information networks as she developed her own increasingly genteel standards. Although her neighbor Elizabeth Nowland was friendly and taught her to play dominoes, Sarah found her company "not so pleasant as I could wish for," because Nowland "did not converse much upon any thing much."[130] Fletcher's expectations were being shaped by the reading her husband encouraged so that, when, two weeks after reading in "Earl of Chesterfields Letters to his Son," she "attened a quilting" she commented that "there were several ladys who were formaly from Kentucky & I think in there descorse a mong the Females they use a gradeal of vulgarity."[131] Such a judgment coming from a Kentucky native who found Betsy Nowland's company most satisfying when they were visiting in a rough-hewn tavern "where," she remembered "we had plenty of cyder to drink," reveals that Sarah's gentility, such as it was, reflected the influence of her Yankee husband and his books.[132]

The degree to which Sarah Hill's marriage to Calvin Fletcher had made him, though just three years her senior, into her full-time instructor for the upward social climb was demonstrated at a visit to the home of his new law partner, B. F. Morris, the county recorder of deeds and the man whom the legislature had elected as its agent to sell Indianapolis city lots. Here, Sarah reported, "I did not injoy myself in the least altho I might appea[r]ed to do so." The problem was not her hostess, "a very sociable woman;" it was her own sense of insecurity in meeting her husband's expectation that she appear as a genteel, worldly woman: "Mr. F. was present a great part of the Eve which rendered me quiet unhappy & imbarast thinking he was mortified at my actions."[133] Her husband, who had spent some evenings at "a debating school,"[134] was pulling himself up; but of her own accomplishments she testified: "I made no convercesion and [was] trembleing fearing there mite be some question asked that would expose my ignernce." Because her husband had "taken a greateal of pains with me," she felt she had let him down.[135] In fact, however, Calvin Fletcher was very pleased with his wife, a woman who could help him dig potatoes, dress a hog, build a corncrib, and live with him in a "cold," "poor," rented cabin seventeen-foot square—while also studying and learning because she shared his "thirst for improvement."[136]

The Fletchers did not defy the conventions of separate male and female spheres—there was never a deliberate confrontation—they simply ignored them as it suited their convenience, while also conforming pragmatically as occasion warranted. Because Sarah Hill Fletcher stopped keeping a diary within a year after the birth of her first child on April 15, 1823, her subsequent experiences are accessible only through her husband's diary, an inadequate source.[137] However, her own diary during the first months of her son's life, as well as her husband's record, suggest that a return to a more thoroughly female sphere began with the arrival of the women who assisted her in childbirth. It was not only a question of giving up outdoor physical labor with her husband, it was also her reading and socializing that changed. Indeed, as her husband began to prosper and to be more occupied by his legal practice he moved into a more distinctly male world, while she was becoming part of a matronly circle. That they were now moving toward separate spheres was evident by the first day of 1824 when Sarah, "very much against my will," accompanied her woman friends to hear preaching in the evening, while Calvin, against his better judgment, went to the tavern to see a "theatrical performance" that he felt wasn't worth the price of admission.[138]

Five years and three more children later, their information activities began to converge once more, though in ways that were significantly different from the first years of their marriage. Calvin no longer assumed the mentor's role supplying Sarah with reading. As always he read extensively, but she, thoroughly occupied with her domestic and maternal duties, read little and no longer concerned herself with impressing "society" for her husband's sake. Their common concerns—now child rearing and the Methodist branch of Christianity—brought them into conversation and reading that joined the male and female spheres. While at the same time each was ever more rooted in the informational sphere of his own sex. For Calvin it was legal and political affairs, real estate and farming that absorbed most of his waking hours, hours he spent in the company of other men and their organizations.

Sarah, in contrast, was preoccupied with domestic concerns and spent most of her days with family, neighborhood women, and female charitable and sewing societies. Enjoying a goodly measure of health and prosperity, the mature matron Sarah Hill Fletcher assumed a role that was fully consonant with social prescription.

Although the experiences of six women spread across one hundred years can only suggest possibilities, the records supplied by these daughters, wives and mothers reveal that social prescription and the actual circumstances of their lives were mutually reinforcing, and exerted a profound impact on their information networks, their conversation and reading. The idea of separate spheres for women and men, wherein some kinds of information were seen as particularly appropriate for one sex and not the other, was powerful because parents and children, husbands and wives, internalized these ideas and demanded conformity to them in their own and other's behavior. As a result, gender roles circumscribed the cultural enfranchisement of women that female literacy and the general encouragement of women's reading and voluntary associations fostered. A kind of segregation of men and women, reinforced by economic roles shaped information diffusion, with domestic and affective information being women's special province. The separation was never absolute; indeed, it was expressly tempered by courtship, parenthood, and common religious activities. Yet for most of the social scale women spoke mostly with other women, shared the same sorts of reading matter, and heard public speeches only from a preacher. Departures from this almost universal pattern came less as challenges mounted in deliberate defiance of convention than as unusual personal behavior, such as the political literacy among elite women that was sanctioned by their husbands, Mrs. Breed's defense of her deceased daughter and son-in-law, or Calvin Fletcher's sharing of everything from books to business affairs with Sarah Hill Fletcher before her long term of motherhood began.

Normally women's reading was not the same as that of men at anytime during this period. Though there was some overlap, and most of the authors women read were in fact men who wrote for mixed audiences, the emphasis for women was clearly on private experience, especially sentiment and morality, whether expressed in novels or treatises on religious affections. In the 1850s New England's most famous female author, Harriet Beecher Stowe, reported that when her mother was raised at the end of the 18th century:

A small table under the looking-glass bore the library of a well-taught young woman of those times. 'The Spectator,' 'Paradise Lost,' Shakespeare, and 'Robinson Crusoe' stood for the admitted secular literature, and beside them the Bible and the works then published of Mr. Jonathan Edwards. Laid a little to one side, as if of doubtful reputation, was the only novel which the stricter people in those days allowed for the reading of their daughters: that seven-volumed, trailing, tedious, delightful old bore, 'Sir Charles Grandison,' a book whose influence in those times was so universal, that it may be traced in the epistolary style even of the gravest divines.[139]

History and politics, the Latin classics, natural sciences, and theological polemics were for men, for whom argument and conflict were appropriate. Piety and devotional religion where peace and harmony ruled, were for women. Though piety was prescribed for both sexes, and both men and women were expected to attend church, the normal situation can be inferred from the New London farmer Joshua Hempstead when he remarked, "Thin Congregation. No weomen," on a Sabbath in 1748 when wicked northwest winds were driving the fallen snow in great drifts.[140] Normally the church's most numerous constituency, women were absent only because of the fierce weather.

Sharing a limited range of reading, venturing out of the domestic circle on their own only to attend church, a library, and women's voluntary associations—and being primarily absorbed in the duties of home and family—except for courtship, women spoke mostly to other women about common experiences. There were, however, some significant differences in the conversational activities of matrons and daughters beyond the fact that parenthood and household management concerned the one and personal development and courtship engrossed the other. Following the Revolution, the prescription for all white Americans, female and male, was a more refined, elevated conversation befitting a virtuous citizenry. For daughters, as we have seen, this was particularly stressed by those who would educate the future mothers of the republic.[141] A new, enlightened republic standard aimed to make daughters more rational and cultivated than their mothers. Consequently there was real tension between older, more practical expectations for daughters and the fashionable aspirations of the new era. Robert B. Thomas, the editor and publisher of the widely read New England *Farmer's Almanack,* framed the issue in a humorous vein in 1838 when he counseled:

> The fashion of keeping a girl at school all the time is a most miserable one; for the preceptress, or school dame, is generally a despiser of common sense, and would think it degrading in a lady to know how to cook a dinner of pot-luck. Do not take offense my fair pedagogues; I would by no means offend true delicacy. But, tell me, seriously,—do you not think it an indictable offense for any one to talk, before the ladies, about fried pork and parsnips, bean porridge and buttermilk?[142]

There was a hard edge to Thomas' jocularity which reflected a backlash against the efforts of women like Mary Guion and Sarah Hill Fletcher to achieve genteel standards and a reverse snobbery toward the manners of such well-born women as Lucy Breckinridge. Matrons had been more practi-

"The Novel Reader"

The idea that novels could exercise a pernicious moral influence, especially on women, is evident in this image of a tradesman's wife who has neglected her domestic duties because she is entranced by a novel. This caricature, which appeared in The Winter Wreath *(New York, 1853), called attention to the fact that some women were spending too much time reading novels.*

Courtesy of the American Antiquarian Society

cal in the past, Thomas seems to say, and it would be better if girls were raised to repeat their mothers' experience rather than to repudiate it according to fashion. The new standard seemed to insist on too much schooling and too much reading.

Novels, especially, were said to launch flights of fantasy away from the ordinary burdens of life. Moreover they served as agents of change, promoting social sensibilities that might not be merely more refined but that led girls to expect companionable husbands and, as with *Uncle Tom's Cabin,* a society that was more just and compassionate. Perhaps because male supervision of daughters was somewhat attenuated—fathers invested more of their parental supervision on the education of their sons than of their daughters—the latter became extensive novel readers in the first half of the 19th century. In contrast, wives were usually a less promising audience both because their duties allowed them fewer discretionary hours to give to reading and because of their husbands' influence on their reading choices. That a man whose wife read novels could never amount to much was the message of a popular print as late as 1853. Entitled "The Novel Reader," it depicts a family in disarray as, at fifteen minutes past noon, a dog makes off with the dinner meat, a cat feasts on the milk supply, and the tradesman husband and the children protest because the midday meal is unmade while mother, ignoring the chaos, sits entranced by her novel.[143]

Obviously such a print would have been meaningless if, in fact, large numbers of wives were not reading novels in preference to assiduous performance of their chores. That they did so in spite of contrary prescriptions and the day-to-day demands of their families illustrates their ability to ignore social prescription, challenging it tacitly, perhaps even guiltily, as with Mary Guion, who liked reading novels "too well."[144] The matrons of the 1850s, after all, had been the daughters of preceding decades who had learned to turn to novels for instruction and improvement as well as solace and escape. The implications for such behavior were profound.

For the direction of social change was to increase women's participation in information networks beyond the domestic circle and reduce the dependence of daughters, wives, and mothers on husband and family for information beyond their immediate observation. "Young ladies are no longer dependent upon the other sex for literary information," declared a writer in a woman's magazine; they could now "converse with as much facility upon the merits of modern writers as the male portion of the community." The availability of printing and the emergence of women's associations supplied the broad spectrum of women who saw themselves as middle class with opportunities that began to parallel those which men had enjoyed in preceding generations.[145] That such a momentous change was socially acceptable was largely owing to the vitality of the doctrine of separate spheres. By assigning men and women specialized roles and prescribing appropriate information activities to accompany those roles, female identity, and therefore male identity, was preserved in the Victorian era. Much as doctrines of racial segregation followed the abolition of slavery in the North after the Revolution and in the south after the Civil War, so the idea of separate but equal gender spheres palliated adjustment to women's new roles as they gradually evolved during the 19th century.

Chapter 8

William Bentley
and the Ideal of Universal Information
in the Enlightened Republic

When the Reverend William Bentley died at age sixty in 1819 he was a famous man, a scholarly celebrity. Recently honored with a doctor of divinity degree from his alma mater, Harvard, his eminence had long been recognized by election to leading American learned societies: the American Philosophical Society, the American Antiquarian Society, and the Massachusetts Historical Society. To John Adams, Bentley was "Doctor of Physics, Dr. of Philosophy, Dr. of Laws, and D.D."[1] Proficient in some twenty ancient and modern languages, a keen student of philology, scriptural criticism, and human and natural history, Bentley was, with Thomas Jefferson, one of the great polymaths of the early Republic. Indeed Jefferson, seeking the best scholars to guide the University of Virginia, invited Bentley to become its founding president. For breadth and depth of learning Bentley, whose personal library of 4000 volumes ranked with America's greatest private collections, had few peers.

Yet Bentley's legacy to 19th-century scholarship was astonishingly meager for one of such immense, widely recognized learning. Bentley's name appeared on the title page of merely a compilation of hymns and a handful of routine pamphlets, talks he had given as a guest preacher and at ceremonial occasions. He was not the author of a single book among the thousands he possessed, and though he was more learned than the college professors of his day, he trained only a handful of students, mostly teenage girls whose domestic careers assured their obscurity.[2] Bentley founded no school of thought and left no lasting monuments to his extraordinary learning. According to his will, even his library was divided after his death. Such an end for one of the early republic's most erudite and benevolent scholars seems paradoxical.

Bentley attained eminence, but in the long run his influence in the society which nourished him and in which he flourished was evidently slight. By the 20th century, indeed, Bentley was remembered as little more than a quaint Salem, Massachusetts, clergyman, the author of a voluminous personal diary chiefly of interest to historians.[3]

The paradox of Bentley's eminence-sans-influence has several dimensions. Though he was "a noble speciman of humanity," as one of his neighbors put it, he was also a man of many "eccentricities."[4] One of the most significant, in contrast to clergymen who sought influence through careerist climbing, was his fixed commitment to his first church settlement, Salem's Second (East) Congregational parish. There, as a religious liberal, a Unitarian who believed in the complete humanity of Christ, he set himself apart from his orthodox peers in Essex County. A Jeffersonian Republican in a denomination and region dominated by zealous Federalists, he was so irregular that he was shunned for years by some of New England's leading men. Since none of the New England colleges, and certainly not Harvard or Yale, were kindly disposed toward outspoken Jeffersonians, Bentley's political and theological beliefs narrowed his prospects for personal or institutional influence.

Yet there are broader reasons, deeply rooted in the history of 19th-century culture, that help to explain why this exemplar of informed, enlightened republicanism should so swiftly have faded from memory. Bentley was the quintessential generalist in the takeoff era of the specialization of knowledge, when experts were emerging in all fields—from archaeology to zoology. What was awesome erudition in Bentley would be viewed as dilettantism a generation or two later. His influence and fame were transient because Bentley devoted his life not to original or creative thought or even to some scholarly edition or compilation, but to the acquisition and transmission of knowledge broadly conceived. Bentley was a collector, preserver, and transmitter of information. Sharing the Enlightenment perspective of the far more creative Benjamin Franklin and Thomas Jefferson, secular men who went beyond scholarship to become central participants in the politics of their time, Bentley, as befitted his clerical profession, was, though partisan, an observer who sought to embody and promote the ideals of the Encyclopedists, of achieving comprehensive knowledge. For William Bentley, being informed came very close to knowing everything about everything—not only the high culture that came from books and periodicals, but also the information that came from direct observation of flora and fauna and earth formations, from inspecting roads and bridges and manufacturing processes, and from studying human nature as manifested in the ceremonial artifacts of other cultures as well as in the intricate relationships of his own parishioners. By embracing all knowledge and refusing to specialize, Bentley won the plaudits of his own age but guaranteed his future oblivion.

The chief practical use Bentley made of his information, though laudable from a republican perspective, further contributed to his transient celebrity. For Bentley was a journalist almost as much as a clergyman, and he drew on his extensive reading and his wide circle of acquaintances and correspondents to produce biweekly news digests for Salem newspapers for nearly twenty-five years. Combining a phenomenally acquisitive and retentive mind with a generous disposition and an ideological commitment to an informed citizenry, Bentley delighted in sharing his information. A model popularizer dedicated to using his own learning to better educate the public, by means of the newspaper he became a one-man adult education institute. But his columns, like most journalism, commanded only ephemeral interest. When Bentley died, both his columns and his influence ceased. Ironically, this immensely learned clergyman has been recognized more as a journalist than as a scholar or divine.[5]

Yet however slight the recognition and influence that have been associated with William Bentley since his death, the fact of Bentley's fame in his own time is convincing evidence that though he personally was exceptional, Bentley embodied some of the central values and cultural motifs of his era. His faith in an informed citizenry, equipped by knowledge not only for self-government but to elevate American moral, cultural, and material life, was one of the great aspirations of the early republic. In Salem, the prosperous port town where he dwelled from 1783 onward, patriotic celebrations, improvement-minded voluntary associations, schools, and libraries all testified to the pervasiveness of this ideal. Bentley was at odds with many of Salem's leaders on national politics—especially foreign affairs—but his hopes for Salem and for American culture were widely shared.

Moreover Bentley's cosmopolitanism and optimism were well-suited to Salem during the generation following the Revolution. Though the town's population growth during Bentley's era, from around 8000 to 13,000 people, was modest compared to that of the nation as a whole, in wealth and urbanity Salem attained a golden age.[6] It was a dynamic community, where the physical environment was remodeled according to rational and progressive principles. New streets and new wharves, new public and private buildings, and a new attention to urban refinements like streetlights, sidewalks, and street signs, the planting of shade trees, and the park-like fencing and grooming of the commons expressed the new urban spirit. The affluence that sustained these improvements came from the East India trade, from trading with a Europe that was almost continuously at war and, during the War of 1812, from privateering. Merchants, ship owners, and captains did best of course, but prosperity flowed through the community generally, touching families involved in the maritime trades, all branches of construction, and the artisans who crafted consumer goods. In contrast to Ashley Bowen's nearby Marblehead during the same era, when even among the able-bodied there was persistent poverty, the Salem poor were mostly people who were aged, disabled or widowed by accidents or alcohol. Salem was a rich community.

Though Bentley was not himself much interested in money except to buy books and to assist the needy, he certainly found the cosmopolitanism that commerce and wealth promoted congenial. From the 1790s onward Salem boasted concerts and theater performances in addition to fashionable assemblies and balls. With visitors from all over the Atlantic world passing through the town, and Salem ships trading regularly to the Baltic, the Mediterranean, and to the China Sea, Bentley enjoyed indirect access to much of the world.

Yet as cosmopolitan as Salem was, the town's saltwater gentry were also somewhat ingrown, cliquish, and often divided amongst themselves over religion and politics in a censorious partisanship that was manifested in rival newspapers, clubs, and neighborhoods.[7] The town's clergy could scarcely remain aloof from these conflicts, so Bentley's place in Salem's information system was influenced not only by the great Federalist-versus-Jeffersonian debates, but by the myriad differences between orthodox and evangelical Calvinists, deists, Unitarians and Universalists, and Baptists and Anglicans. Since Bentley neither trimmed nor concealed his own views—though he tried to be understanding and generous to all viewpoints—he was also an engaged partisan. Salem in Bentley's era was large enough to contain great diversity among its inhabitants but small enough so that they interacted in a personal setting.

In this regard Salem during the last decades of Bentley's life was similar to Boston as it had been when he had lived there as a young boy in the 1760s. Bentley was born in 1759, the son of the carpenter Joshua Bentley and his wife Elizabeth Paine Bentley, the daughter of a prosperous merchant. William, however, was not raised in the straitened circumstances of his parents' and younger siblings' home, but in the prosperous North End household of his maternal grandfather, William Paine. There the youth was prepared for Harvard at the Boston Latin School, which he entered in 1773, just as revolutionary politics in Boston were coming to a crisis. His college years, although punctuated by the blockade of Boston and formation of the Continental Congress in 1774, and by the commencement of hostilities in 1775 and the Declaration of Independence in 1776, led not to military enlistment but to a career in the ministry via the common route of several years' service as a Harvard tutor. Coming to the East Parish in 1783 to assist the Reverend Joseph Diman, Bentley entered an urban community which, while smaller and more provincial than Boston, resembled the capital in its diversity, sophistication, and commercial vitality. These were the attributes of Salem that attracted Bentley and bound him to it. For though he was a convinced Christian and a masterful interpreter of Scripture, his interests and temperament were secular and worldly. He acted out his piety in social ethics rather than introspective devotions; and critical analysis was more to his liking than the rituals of faith. Bentley was a student of Christianity, but he was also a student of comparative religions, archaeology, anthropology, and history.[8] For him

Salem and the East Parish were a convenient venue for being both a practical Christian and a student of God's handiwork in all its manifestations.

Moreover in the leading families of the East Parish—the Crowninshields, Fiskes, Gibauts, Hodges—William Bentley, who never married, found an emotional home among people who became his companions and friends. Their business, which brought them into contact with Russia, Sweden and Germany, Britain, Holland and France, Spain, Portugal and Italy, as well as the East Indies, encouraged an enlightened cosmopolitanism that fostered Bentley's tolerant perspective of mankind. Though Bentley was far more of a free thinker than his leading parishioners or the rest of his parish, overseas experience had tempered local prejudices, and Bentley's evident unselfish devotion to the well-being of his people encouraged them to accept Bentley even when they differed from him.[9] The fact that he never made an issue of his clerical authority or carped about his salary, paid or unpaid, set an example of forbearance that characterized the East Parish during the decades that Bentley headed it.

Bentley's symbiotic relationship with the Salem community was acted out in many ways. That he, as a clergyman, was also a school committee member, a mainstay of the Salem Female Charitable Society, and attended militia musters regularly was by no means unusual; but that he joined the Union Fire Club, the Marine Society, and the Freemasons, were marks of his thoroughgoing entry into Salem's secular sociability. As bookish as Bentley was, he was also sociable, turning up at assemblies and balls, at the theater and concerts, and in the summertime joining in fishing and sailing excursions, picnics and beach parties. Having no family of his own in Salem, Bentley was included in the many organized and casual activities of his friends in respectable Salem society.

Considering Bentley's extensive socializing and the conscientiousness with which he performed his pastoral duties—writing two sermons each week and visiting in the households of his parish—the breadth of Bentley's knowledge and of his writing is remarkable.[10] It is true that he enjoyed more discretionary time than most clergymen, since in contrast to rural ministers he had no farm to operate for his support, and unlike nearly all his peers he lived as a boarder in his parish and so had no family and household of his own to maintain. Still, Bentley did not just collect books, periodicals, and newspapers; he read them critically. And he wrote tirelessly in his notebooks, in his diary, in the church records, and, of course, the newspaper. Bentley's "glancing eye and quick perception enabled him to run with rapidity through a book," one of his friends reported. Blessed with an extraordinary memory, outstanding diligence, and great "wit [and] originality of ideas," Bentley, superbly suited as he was for pastoral sociability, was even more gifted as a scholar.[11] Over the years the people of the East Parish came to cherish the outspoken, controversial, and eccentric pastor who flourished in their midst. Bright, energetic and generous, cheerful and companionable,

Bentley was, like many of the curiosities he collected for his cabinet, a rare specimen.

Although Bentley was extreme, even compulsive in his quest for universal information, his parish, contemporary journalists, and his learned peers respected his efforts and achievements. Grounded as his efforts were in the republican idealism and the enlightened Christianity of the day, they were part of the broadly based movement toward a more thoroughly informed and educated society that was leading Congress and the state legislatures to support public educational institutions and to create a comprehensive postal system wherein the distribution of newspapers and periodicals was subsidized.[12] Thus Bentley became the personification of a key aspect of the republican dream, and he pursued the goal of knowledge in the long-prescribed manner, making his pastoral career a vehicle for conversation, reading, and in a small way travel.

Though Bentley was living during a period of dramatic expansion of information systems such as the postal system, the press, and public oratory—and indeed of information itself—he became conscious of these developments only in middle life, long after his own information habits were set.[13] His were the traditional ways of college students who attended lectures and sermons, read and took notes on their reading, and engaged each other and their tutors in conversation. At Salem Bentley had relatively few occasions to attend instructive lectures and sermons—he was usually holding forth from the pulpit himself—however reading and conversation were central activities, and in both he was voracious and purposeful.

The most remarkable features of Bentley's conversation were the topical range and the variety of persons with whom he spoke. Depending on whom he was with, Bentley could find a way to converse seriously on any subject because he was always eager to learn about other people and their affairs. If he spoke with a fisherman, he probed for information about fishes, their sizes, varieties, how they were caught, and their market price. If with a joiner or a blacksmith he sought to learn the details of their craft and how they conducted their business. No person, male or female, black or white, and no subject was beneath his interest and attention. Employing the liberty that went with his gentleman's rank, Bentley felt confident to approach virtually anyone; and his condescension was flattering and friendly enough that men and women of common status responded.[14]

Most often, however, his conversations were with men elevated above the common sort. Bentley's two "inner circles" of companions, one in Salem, the other in Boston and Cambridge, were distinct and did not overlap. In Salem he visited frequently with leading merchants and captains who were members of his parish. Among them he formed a Sunday evening club of eight (including himself), whose conversation was almost entirely secular.[15] From it Bentley, who never sailed as far as Portsmouth, New Hampshire, or traded so much as a packet of pins, became well informed on a wide variety of worldly subjects. Their talk ranged from particular discussions of ship construction and the details of theirs and others' voyages, to what goods were selling in distant markets and to matters of trade policy and international relations. From these men Bentley even gleaned descriptions of the languages and mores of the people whose distant ports they and their subordinates visited. This circle enabled Bentley to become expert in commercial matters and well-informed regarding the overseas interests of his community without venturing outside his own parish. That many of these conversations had no bearing on high culture or public affairs, not to speak of religion, seems never to have troubled the liberal clergyman. Raised as he was in a merchant's household, Bentley respected the knowledge and prowess of men of affairs whose information was often fresher and more direct than what Bentley could glean from print. Moreover what he learned from his merchant friends was not available in any library. This small circle within his own parish enabled Bentley to extend vicariously the range of his own experience so that he could speak as an informed man of the world, both in the pulpit and in the press.

What Bentley brought to his group of merchants and captains, in addition to his considerable skills as a raconteur and conversationalist, was a sense of respect and approval as well as his own wealth of information. Some of this was practical in the most immediate sense, since he could and did prepare documents for them in virtually any language and translate any foreign documents they brought to him.[16] At another level Bentley was also their teacher, and they sought his advice as to what books to read aboard ship during their extended voyages. Since William Bentley was one of the great bibliographers and bibliophiles of his day he could always respond to their inquiries as to what histories, travel essays, and treatises in religion and natural philosophy would be accessible and informative.[17] Just as they educated him in practical affairs, he guided their entry into the world of high culture.

Because Bentley was largely separated by his politics and religious doctrine from the clergy in Salem and the neighborhood and since, as he noted, "I have no literary men in my society," for learned discourse he relied mostly on a circle of Boston and Cambridge friends.[18] These men, especially the Reverend James Freeman of Boston's Episcopal Stone Chapel and James Winthrop, son of the Harvard scientist, were lifelong friendly spirits with whom he exchanged letters, books, and objects of interest, and with whom he visited several times annually. With them and a handful of others he could converse "freely," by which he meant unself-consciously, on sensitive religious topics without having to worry about the consequences of expressing unorthodox views. In this conversational circle—whose coming together was more of an event for Bentley than a matter of routine—public ceremonies like the Massachusetts election sermon in May, or the Harvard commencement in July, often supplied occasions for a meal and an overnight visit.

At these gatherings of learned "literary men" the information they exchanged touched on the affairs of churches of all denominations, Harvard College, and religious, historical, and scientific subjects. Their discourse might be lofty or miscellaneous, pedantic or even gossipy. At its best Bentley and his friends were stimulated and "amused" by "rich and very engaging conversation."[19] There were also disappointments, as when "a trifling dispute upon the facts of the Crucifixion destroyed the enjoyment" of a Cambridge dinner.[20] And sometimes, but for the manner of their speech, the information was the stuff of village tittle-tattle—the birth of a child to a clergyman's wife six months after the wedding, and the accusation of forgery against a Harvard mathematics professor.[21] Unlike his visits with his merchant friends in the East Parish, Bentley's conversations with fellow scholars provided more in the way of intellectual reinforcement and personal companionship than they did information. For scholarly information the central sources were printed. What conversation with his learned intimates supplied was informal commentary on printed materials and, more important, a sense of being "in the know" on scholarly and professional matters.

Both of Bentley's inner circles of conversation were active. He talked with some of his merchant friends several times a week, and he saw or corresponded with his learned friends monthly. These circles mattered most for his personal well-being; but it was a miscellany of encounters with people who were not close to him personally that were even more frequent and probably more important as sources of information. People of many nationalities and religions passed through Salem, and because of his reputation for languages and non-sectarian hospitality, they were usually directed to Bentley. At his home in Salem he interviewed American Indians and East Indians, Catholics, Muslims, and Parsees as well as all the Protestant denominations. He dined with Spaniards and Portuguese, Frenchmen and Hollanders, Italians, Greeks and Algerians as well as various Britons and white West Indians. For a person of Bentley's global interests these meetings supplied spectacular opportunities for learning about the languages, culture, flora, fauna, and geography of the world.

It was satisfying, of course, for Bentley to interview his friend Captain John Gibaut on his return from the Adriatic and to have from his hand letters written in Arabic and Persian, just as it was rewarding to have eyewitness descriptions of Bengali funeral practices from his friend Captain Benjamin Crowninshield;[22] but actual conversations with foreign visitors provided Bentley with information at firsthand on whatever subject he pursued. Living in Salem enabled Bentley to speak directly with Dutch diplomats and French West Indians, or even with an Italian graduate of the University of Genoa.[23] Because of Bentley's well-known interest in and mastery of languages, his study was a magnet for foreigners passing through Salem, and he took advantage of his situation to add to his store of knowledge.

Since Bentley was not only a linguist but also an advocate of religious tolerance who believed that anyone who was "pure from guile, peaceable in his life, gentle in his manners, easily dissuaded from revenge, with an heart to pity and relieve the miserable . . . [was] the man of religion . . . after God's own heart," his study was also a way station for representatives of exotic religions, from the liberal Swedenborgians to the conservative Roman Catholics.[24] Indeed his role in fostering New England Roman Catholicism is notable in light of his own distance from its doctrines and rituals. Bentley assisted New England's first native-born Catholic missionary, John Thayer, who camped with him for a few days in 1790 when Bentley could find no Salem Catholic with whom to board the missionary. Thayer, a Bostonian convert to Catholicism who had traveled in Europe and trained for the priesthood at the University of Paris, supplied information on his church that Bentley could not have obtained from reading, though to Bentley's discomfort Thayer used Bentley's lodgings to store a supply of over 400 tracts and devotionals as well as rosaries and vestments while he went off to Maine.[25] Years later Bentley would assist the Spanish consul in Boston and the Boston priest, the Frenchman Dr. Francis Matignon, in arranging Salem contributions for the Catholic Church in Boston, believing "we ought to do everything which can encourage the liberality of France & Spain, by which the Protestant religion may be more fully tolerated."[26] It is no surprise then that when John Carroll, the United States' first Roman Catholic bishop, visited Salem Bentley had the opportunity to converse freely with him "on all subjects as a man of literature."[27]

For William Bentley the chance to engage a bishop or a high government official in conversation was special. Not only did it flatter his sense of importance to converse with John Hancock or Elbridge Gerry, with congressmen and jurists, it was also interesting, not so much for the substance of information that was conveyed as for the accents and inflections with which remarks were delivered. The subjects of conversations, other than inconsequential small talk, were mostly on public affairs of a sort that was usually available from Bentley's word-of-mouth or newspaper channels. But at dinners and in drawing rooms Bentley could form judgments about persons—their intellects, dispositions, and moral qualities. Moreover the familiarity these conversations created led Bentley to think of himself as an insider among the ruling mercantile elite, even when the Federalists were in power. This sense of being part of the ruling class would shape Bentley's approach to the diffusion of information both as a preacher and as a journalist.

Yet it is a striking feature of Bentley's sociability that for all his hobnobbing with the mercantile elite and the notables of his county, state, and nation, Bentley maintained vigorous conversational links throughout his parish, embracing the poor, the old, the sick, and the forlorn as well as those who prospered. Bentley not only gathered information about his parish from such people; with their help he also compiled a wealth of genealogical and antiquarian information about Salem families, buildings, neighborhoods, and economic life. Bentley's paternalism and condescension was so effective precisely because he came to his people as a minister who would not only instruct but who would also listen and be instructed. Just as he was eager to record the oral history of Ashley Bowen's Quebec exploits with the future Captain Cook, so he was eager to record the stories of other humble people on the subjects they knew best. He did not know how or if ever he would use all this information—though he did complete the first part of a "Description and History of Salem"[28]—however he was as committed to compiling and preserving this kind of human information as he was to collecting data on flora and fauna, and perhaps even as devoted as he was to building a comprehensive library. For Bentley, in keeping with his era, believed in the knowledge and wisdom comprehended in the book of experience, and in the legion of his conversations he studied that book assiduously.

The one route to knowledge that Bentley stinted on was travel. "His people were his life," he was reported to have said, and he would not leave them, especially when he could make so many and varied overseas journeys vicariously through his mariner friends.[29] One reason Bentley was such a compulsive seeker after knowledge through conversation and reading was because of the actual, physical parochialism of his life. Though Bentley was aware of improvements in the ease and frequency of travel, noting in 1814 that "formerly . . . a man who had been by land through our States or any one of them was consulted as an Oracle. But now . . . many have passed the whole length of our Atlantic coast," he still remained close to home.[30] He witnessed thousands of ships depart from Salem harbor, but he himself never sailed more than fifteen miles out to sea. On land he barely left Massachusetts, journeying twice to nearby New Hampshire, once to collect an honorary degree from Dartmouth College and once on the way to Massachusetts' eastern district of Maine. Bentley never set foot in New York, Pennsylvania, or Virginia; indeed he did not travel as far south as Rhode Island or Connecticut. Curiously, this most liberal, enlightened, and cosmopolitan of Yankee clergymen—the master of twenty languages—was in fact an insular provincial as well.

Yet when William Bentley did travel, even if only to Ipswich or Haverhill within his own Essex County, he was a close observer of the people and landscape, and he gathered information along the way. Making inquiries of men and women, even of girls and boys, he wanted to know the dates of settlement and the names of early settlers, about the kinds of rocks, the cultivation of farms, and whatever manufacturing and commerce took place. His observations were so detailed that he noticed alterations in the landscape when they occurred, and, of course, sought information on them as well.

The fact that Bentley bound himself to Salem, Boston, Cambridge, and Essex County, and published accounts of his locale for the Massachusetts Historical Society collections in addition to donating early Massachusetts portraits to it, should not mislead us as to the limits of his interests. For Bentley's contributions to the Society also included exotica from around the globe, such as a hundred-pound oyster shell from Sumatra and a rhinoceros horn from Africa, as well as ethnographic objects from the Pacific, head ornaments from Hawaii, and Eskimo boots from Alaska.[31] Bentley's local interests did not signify narrowness; they represented a part of his tireless effort to achieve comprehensive knowledge. For Bentley travel supplemented conversation in learning about his local world. To learn about distant worlds beyond the horizon or long past in time it was reading that overshadowed other sources.

Bentley was a spectacular reader. Gifted as he was in speed of comprehension and in languages, Bentley's capacity for reading surpassed most learned professionals, whether clergymen, lawyers, or physicians. However it was the way that Bentley used his special aptitude that reveals his romantic, republican ambition for comprehensive knowledge. Rather than making himself the most learned and well-read specialist in his profession—the sort of aim that propelled Robert Treat Paine and John Adams to amass large libraries—and in contrast to the old gentlemanly ideal of polite learning in classics, modern literature, history, and natural philosophy, Bentley sought to know every branch of every subject, including contemporary medicine and law, fiction, journalism, and technology. It was not that Bentley believed he would actually achieve such comprehensive mastery—his resources of time, money, and ability, he recognized, were limited. Instead it was the vision that attracted Bentley. The ideal of acquiring universal knowledge is evident in his remarkable collection of books.[32]

Starting with an ordinary student's library, no inheritance, and on the strength of his clerical salary and through gifts and trades, Bentley developed his collection into one of America's great private libraries. By 1787 he had almost 700 volumes and by the time of his death the library contained about 2000 titles comprehending 4000 volumes; it was larger by 500 volumes than William Byrd's great library, and was reputed to be second in size only to Thomas Jefferson's magnificent collection.[33] To describe Bentley's collection, and how he amassed it gradually, is to appreciate the dimensions of his information dream and just how accessible its realization could be in the early republic. For one who pursued it aggressively and unremittingly there were great opportunities, even on a clergyman's salary.

Bentley's library was predominantly a collection of new books, that is books that were published after his graduation from college in 1777 (see table 1). Of these, the largest number dated from the decades 1790 to 1809, roughly the peak years of his acquisitions, when he obtained an average of

Table 1. Titles in Bentley's Library Identified by Year of Publication

Years	Number of Titles	Percent	Cumulative Percent
1500–1549	5	0.25	0.25
1550–1599	23	1.15	1.40
1600–1649	82	4.11	5.51
1650–1699	145	7.26	12.77
1700–1709	35	1.75	14.52
1710–1719	53	2.65	17.17
1720–1729	68	3.41	20.58
1730–1739	69	3.46	24.04
1740–1749	67	3.36	27.40
1750–1759	82	4.11	31.51
1760–1769	136	6.81	38.32
1770–1779	151	7.57	45.89
1780–1789	162	8.12	54.01
1790–1799	235	11.77	65.78
1800–1809	287	14.38	80.16
1810–1819	175	8.77	88.93
Unknown	221	11.07	100.00
Sum of titles	1996		

Note: The actual number of titles would be greater but for the fact that pamphlets were gathered in untitled, undated bound volumes. Many of the works were multivolume editions.

twenty-six titles each year. At the same time, however, Bentley sought many older books. By the time of his death he owned almost thirty books dating from the 16th century and over 200 from the 17th century. The possession of some of these old books may be explained by Bentley's antiquarian interests, but more often they represent either classic texts like Cyprian's works (in a 1593 edition), or treatises such as John Selden's *Dominion of the Sea* (in a 1652 edition) that were not otherwise available. The economics of publishing being tied to current markets rather than scholarly needs, key works were often available only in editions that were a century or two old. In this respect Bentley's mixture of old and new books was characteristic of all good libraries of the period.

The distribution of countries of origin in Bentley's library was, in contrast, unusual for an American in that a high proportion of the books, over 40 percent, were printed neither in Britain nor the United States (see Table 2). The collection was further distinguished because among Bentley's foreign books the largest number were German publications (40 percent), and French books (22 percent) and those of the Low Countries (Netherlands, Belgium, and Luxembourg) lagged behind (14 percent). The explanation of the German origins of so many books is partly owing to Bentley's interest in

Table 2. Titles in Bentley's Library
Identified by Country of Publication

Country	Number of Titles	Percent
England	600	30.06
United States	408	20.44
Germany	317	15.88
France	170	8.52
Low Countries	110	5.51
Scotland	59	2.96
Switzerland	35	1.75
Italy	24	1.20
Ireland	17	0.85
Spain	15	0.75
Other European	22	1.10
Non-European	17	0.85
Unknown	202	10.12
Sum of Titles	1996	99.99*

*Owing to rounding.

German philological and philosophical works and also because of Bentley's twenty-year correspondence and book exchange with professor C. D. Ebeling of Hamburg, who provided many of these German books.[34] Equally unusual was the fact that his library contained books from well over a dozen foreign countries. In this respect the library was a reflection of Bentley's linguistic talent and his drive for information from all quarters of the globe.

The languages in which Bentley's books were printed reinforce these perceptions and reveal the depth of his scholarship. Although most of the books were in English, large proportions were in the classical languages of antiquity, in German, and in French, and there were also some in Spanish, Italian, and a handful of other European and Middle Eastern languages. What is evident from this distribution analysis and from Bentley's impressive array of dictionaries and other critical and technical aids is not only his serious scholarship but also his broad interest in all sorts of contemporary writings, even including light, romantic French and German novels. Viewed in its entirety the library appears to combine the collections of the gentleman, the cleric, the lawyer, and the physician, with additional practical material directed toward merchants and manufacturers.

But while Bentley's collection displayed this comprehensive quality, it was obviously strongest in his principal areas of interest. Although his collection of thirty-seven law books was larger than most lawyers possessed, just as his forty-six medical works comprised a better library than most physicians had, in these subjects Bentley's ambitions were limited. In contrast, his array of 395 theological works and 225 volumes of the classics bespoke his desire to read and possess everything valuable in these fields. Bentley wanted all the sources and all the key commentaries; and where controversy flared, Bentley wanted every argument even when, as with Ethan Allen's *Reason the Only Oracle of Man* and Thomas Paine's *Rights of Man,* he scorned both the author and text.[35] Here, in areas of lively contemporary interest, Bentley felt he had to be able to form his own judgments independently.

In some great libraries, it appears, the act of collecting has been more important than the actual reading of books, but in Bentley's case, though he was an avid collector, he used the books he assembled. His pattern of reading, which ordinarily relied on setting aside about twenty-five hours a week, was certainly intensive as well as extensive. He filled at least nine books with his manuscript notes on a dozen different subjects, and though it is impossible to know which of his 4000 volumes he merely skimmed, it is safe to assume that he read virtually everything cover to cover, except for his dictionaries, lexicons, digests, and other reference works.[36] For the comments Bentley made on his reading in his notes, his diary, in his letters, and in his newspaper columns, reveal a mind that could grasp virtually any subject and evaluate critically an author's ideas. Moreover his assessments of bookstores and libraries displayed his own desire to go beyond "the common demand" in books.[37] Of the 286-volume library of a Newburyport clergyman that was auctioned in 1804 Bentley noted matter-of-factly that, though "not a considerable library in Europe," it was nevertheless "greater than is commonly found among our most eminent divines in America," and was actually better than any he had seen outside Boston, even though it lacked a Greek Testament, was short on Scriptural criticism, was missing any modern commentaries, and included no American history.[38] When in 1813 Bentley viewed the auction list of the nearly 1000 books that had belonged to his deceased friend the Reverend John Eliot, his judgment on the collection expressed his own values:

> I doubt whether Dr. Eliot ever added fifty Volumes to his father's [also Rev. John Eliot] Library, excepting the many pamphlets which were put together. Not a political work is in the whole Collection & not one splendid edition of any Classic. Not a Lexicon of any Language beyond those of the Schools & not a Theological work of the present Generation. No Collation of the Old or New Testament. No Polyglott, no Ecclesiastical History, & no Collection of History. Nothing like system upon any one point in the whole Catalogue, & a total absence appears of the modern Literature of Europe. Not even a Review has served to notify the progress of Letters in any Kingdom.[39]

Much as Bentley admired Eliot's moral qualities as a friend, he could not praise him as a scholar, and his library—mostly inherited—confirmed his estimate.[40] Bentley collected and read broadly among the oldest and best as well as the newest and most controversial and, privately at least, he judged others by his own standards.

Given these ideals, Bentley's own acquisitions required careful management. Bookstores were of little use: as of 1792 he believed "there is not a proper bookstore on this side of New York."[41] Later on the situation would improve, first in Boston and later in Salem, but for Bentley book purchases were mostly a matter of direct imports through his ship captain friends, and through auctions. In Boston, "usually at Election & Commencement time," when the town filled with college graduates and others who aspired to polite learning, serious book auctions were held at which books outside the common run were available.[42] Some of Bentley's books came from such sources, although Bentley's Salem friends carried his purchase orders to Europe and also brought him gifts. For example Captains John Gibaut and Benjamin Hodges could be relied on frequently for French, German, Swedish, Danish, and Russian titles—books that in some instances perhaps no other American possessed because no one else was as ambitious as Bentley to follow the progress of contemporary European intellectual thought.[43] Bentley did not deliberately create a singular collection of books, but because of the scale and intensity of his drive for comprehensiveness—which rejected the dilettantism of the era—the extended boundaries of his library and not just its size set it apart from those of other clergymen and professionals.

One further way that Bentley gathered information was through correspondence. His letter-writing was partly an extension of conversation, and it was also in some ways a substitute for travel. To the degree that Bentley used correspondence to develop his library and to collect information on people, places, and things, it enhanced all his means of learning—listening, direct observation, and reading. The full scope of Bentley's correspondence cannot be known absolutely, but he certainly exchanged letters with at least 400 people, and perhaps as many as 500 or 600 correspondents.[44] The surviving Bentley letters range from two-line local courtesy notes to six-page descriptions of natural and social phenomena thousands of miles away; and among his correspondents were parish women and old salts like Ashley Bowen, as well as foreign professors and philosophers, and presidents of the United States. His correspondents wrote from Canada to Ohio to South Carolina, and from across the Atlantic, the Baltic, Mediterranean, and Caribbean seas.

The richest of Bentley's incoming letters were packed with information Bentley had solicited. From old-timers like Ashley Bowen there were accounts of people and places, including genealogies and original documents.[45] Notables like John Adams and Thomas Jefferson sent Bentley their judgments on historical events and other learned topics.[46] Still others, like ship captains and overseas mercantile agents, or Salem men who had settled distant lands, supplied Bentley with contemporary descriptions of faraway places.[47] In a significant number of cases Bentley's only contact with his correspondent was through letters. That limitation did not hinder the development of long and fruitful exchanges where, as with Professor C. D.

Ebeling in Hamburg, mutual regard and usefulness were high. For Bentley, letter-writing was simply an extension of his other activities, and through letters he did favors and received them from the same kinds of people with whom he conversed. He sent out long, newsy accounts, and received them.[48] He supplied others with facts just as he solicited them. And for building a library, any serious library, correspondence was crucial. Whether he used traveling acquaintances to bear his letters and parcels or, as was less frequent, employed the postal system, Bentley's correspondence displayed his thorough immersion in the collection and diffusion of information.

The distinguishing mark of William Bentley's quest for information was not his excellent conversation, his voracious reading, or his "iron memory"—it was the boundlessness of his interests.[49] Not only did he seek to achieve competence in all branches of the learning of high culture, he also pursued current events, practical affairs, and the mundane details of life in his town and parish. Obviously Bentley was not a master of all knowledge: Ashley Bowen knew more about Marblehead shipping; George Nelson followed salt prices more closely; and John Adams, Robert Treat Paine, and William Pynchon had mastered the technicalities of Massachusetts law in a way that Bentley never attempted. Yet Bentley was familiar with all these subjects. Because he listened and asked questions, because he read and observed, he was almost an expert at almost everything, and he could speak and write as an initiate on these topics, and on any other that mattered to his contemporaries.

Bentley was, without question, far better informed than he needed to be for his occupation and social status. Although his vast erudition and compendious knowledge were sources of personal prestige, they were also superfluous in a real sense. Bentley was not a better pastor for his people because he could read Swedish or identify the birds found on the Pacific coast of North America. But his learning made him a resource of local and ultimately national renown, and from the early 1790s onward he began to place his learning in the service of others. He became, after a fashion, not a wise man or an oracle, but a walking encyclopedia who was available to his friends for private uses and to the nation as a whole for public purposes. Though he was a clergyman first, he became a one-man information service.

Bentley was a generous person and so in the first instance he used his learning on behalf of his friends and parishioners. Like the rural clergymen Timothy Walker, who attended to his parish's legal affairs, and Justus Forward, who looked after the sick, Bentley gave assistance to those who had need for writing letters and petitions, and for translating documents from or to English. The letters and petitions he drafted—for example on matters of property, inquiring for news of far away relatives, seeking alterations of roads, or a favor from Harvard College or the governor—might have been done by any clergyman or lawyer.[50] And most of his translations, done in French and Spanish and dealing with business and political affairs, could also have been done by others, though perhaps not so easily.[51] Sometimes, however, Bentley's unusual learning was employed, calling on his Dutch or Swedish or Arabic. The most celebrated example was when Secretary of State Albert Gallatin, called on Bentley to translate the credentials of the Tunisian ambassador.[52] Bentley may have been the only American equipped to do this service.

But such occasions, where practical demands were made on Bentley's learning, were sporadic. Doing private favors, even for the secretary of state, hardly justified Bentley's relentless pursuit of information. Yet it was by responding to one such request by William Carleton, a fellow boarder at Mrs. Hannah Crowninshield's house, that led to Bentley's journalistic career, a career which put his encyclopedic learning at the public service with few interruptions for twenty-five years. Carleton, who took over the *Salem Gazette* in October 1794, knew from his landlady's dinner table how thoroughly Bentley kept himself informed and how engaging his discourse was, and so he invited him to produce a news summary for his paper.[53] Thereafter twice each week, Bentley prepared a digest of the most important foreign and domestic news, including mention of outstanding scientific discoveries, events in the educational world, and notable books. Seeking to inform readers and to explain events, he tried to avoid partisanship and argument. Bentley the journalist strove to promote the informed, enlightened public that was crucial to the vitality of the American republic and to the progress of humanity.

Bentley's news summaries gave him a secular pulpit in which he could deliberately set aside controversial religious subjects and instead indulge his penchant for worldly knowledge. It was hard to construct a sermon around the Peruvian condor, but in the newspaper he could describe it thoroughly.[54] He could give an account of Harvard College's "cabinet of ores and minerals," and report on Paul Revere's bell foundry.[55] Moreover among the audience of the *Salem Gazette* and the *Impartial Register* there were many readers who eagerly read Bentley's analyses of European military and diplomatic affairs. These essays, usually the main portion of his summary, were grounded in history and illustrated by original documents which Bentley himself had often translated. His news summaries, which numbered in the thousands, represented a journalistic innovation that supplied the public with a new level of education on diplomacy and public affairs.[56] In these summaries Bentley wanted to get beyond "the conversation of the day, or the reports of the passing moment," to enable his readers to grasp "the causes which produce interesting events."[57] Surrounded by transcriptions of public debates and Bentley's own translations of state papers, foreign treaties, newspaper reports, and letters from foreign observers, Bentley used his column and the newspaper generally as an agency to elevate the understanding of "all classes of readers."[58]

Bentley did not consciously editorialize, but his own progressive, optimistic values found expression in his choice of subjects and in the tone of his descriptions. In commencement season he gave favorable notice to advances in higher education just as, at other times, he approvingly reported the erection of new churches and the expansion of Christianity in North America and around the world. Though accepting of all denominations, his European essays welcomed the decline of government-supported religious establishments. Bentley's enlightenment Whig outlook pervaded his political description and analysis, and must have reinforced the political beliefs of many readers. In his news summaries the horrors of war and the terrors of fanaticism provided object lessons for Americans. Though Bentley was no narrow nationalist, the dream of American exceptionalism—of a United States set apart from the war, corruption, and tyranny of the rest of the globe—was an underlying theme of his journalism.

Fundamental to Bentley's conception of the information system of a free republic was the ideal of non-partisan journalism. Consequently he was deeply troubled by the sensational invective style that the Federalist-Jeffersonian debate generated. Since the central purpose of a free press was "diffusing useful knowledge," he maintained that a newspaper ought to be "the friend of truth and knowledge." But under the influence of faction the American press was being subverted, becoming "the vile slave of falsehood, of slander, of guilt." During the mid-1790s Bentley believed that the freedom of the press was being pushed beyond the boundary of liberty and into the destructive netherworld of licentiousness that had degraded French revolutionary politics. The spirit of faction was perverting the republican ideal of the press as a vital public service, so that it was becoming "a licentious Press . . . an enemy in the bosom of any nation." Bentley proclaimed his editorial vision in mid-1796, a time of severe partisanship, vowing to "communicate everything to the public, which has in our judgment truth, happiness, usefulness, or good government as its object."[59]

Later, after Americans had drawn back from the abyss of vituperative journalism, Bentley became more concerned about the substantive quality than the potential viciousness of the press. In 1803 he concluded that "the increase of Gazettes is excessive." There were so many, and they appeared, disappeared, and changed venue with such velocity that they seemed quite literally innumerable. Nor were American periodicals rising to a British or European standard. "We have not one good Magazine in America," he complained: "That in Boston called the Weekly, I find to be Tea table business. The Quarterly is not of great fame. The missionary magazines appear feeble in their first numbers. New York Medical Repository, & Literary review are the best periodical publications I have seen."[60] What Bentley was beginning to perceive was the divergence between the ideal of excellence which was a central part of his republican vision, and the leveling effects of the popularization of information that was inherent in the multiplication of newspapers and periodicals, and even in his own news summaries.

Bentley never lost his faith in the efficacy of the diffusion of useful knowledge. But the more he witnessed the explosive growth of the popular print media, the more sober became his view of the consequences. By 1816, when he had long since ceased fulminating over the evil tendencies of faction and had resigned himself to a certain mediocrity in American journalism, he contemplated the inherent limitations of newspapers in the formation of public opinion. Whatever usefulness and high moral qualities which he ascribed to news and informing the public, it was evident that much of journalism was merely "public entertainment," and as such, insignificant trivia was coming to dominate the press. "The great number of newspapers," he recognized, "put in circulation every incident which is raised in every local situation . . . so not a fire, an accident, a fear or a hope but it flies quickly throughout the union." The result was a degradation and a trivialization of public opinion. How could thoughtful analysis of foreign affairs and national politics compete with the dramatic human interest stories that were becoming so plentiful? What Bentley bemoaned was that "the public mind is already unaccustomed to weigh these things," to differentiate between the specific and the general, between the ephemeral and the long-lasting.[61] The ability of learned gentlemen and clergy like himself to serve the public interest by sharing liberally their useful knowledge was being overtaken by competition. A shadow was falling across his own bright hopes for a free press as the foundation of an informed population. Indeed in an era when information and the media presenting it were increasing at an explosive rate, Bentley was unrealistic to have supposed that multitudes of citizens would have the inclination and ability to inform themselves broadly according to the ideal of the genteel cosmopolitan.

It was probably inevitable that as he grew older William Bentley felt some disappointments. Himself a paragon, indeed the epitome of informed republicanism, he lived to witness a variety of social developments deflect and forestall the public realization of the ideal to which he devoted his life. As a brilliant eccentric who made himself one of the most thoroughly informed people of his time, Bentley was a kind of extravagant embodiment of many of the central themes in the early republican ideal. The romantic audacity of his drive for comprehensive knowledge was closely tied to the attempt to create in America the perfect republic. According to the ideal, the arts and sciences, religion, and all learning would flourish under the aegis of liberty. In practice this meant the creation of learned societies, colleges, and academies, and building a foundation of public schools and a free and numerous press.

This general view, like Bentley's private vision, had been influenced by the Renaissance ideal of a society guided and instructed by liberally educated scholars. In the Anglo-American enlightenment the objective was to know mankind and the environment in which he lived.[62] Thus Bentley's wide-ranging interests in biology and geology, in human cultures, their languages and religion, in astronomy and meteorology, were all part of this dominant belief that through systematic inquiry an understanding of man's true nature and his place in the cosmos could be achieved. The Christian formulation of this outlook was that one studied God through his works.

What tied William Bentley to republicanism specifically and not just to the high culture of the Enlightenment was the range of his interests and his reasons for pursuing them. The high culture of Enlightenment gentlemen was broad indeed, but it did not concern itself with local matters as such, nor with the mundane, day-to-day lives of common people. In the minds of the gentry, high culture—their culture—was set apart from the vernacular world of their subordinates, except insofar as genteel standards trickled down the social hierarchy. In contrast, though Bentley shared many of the prejudices of the genteel, he aimed to know everything, and so in collecting Essex County lore, in reading the entire gamut of what came off the press, and by interviewing common people of both sexes, he overstepped the boundaries of high culture. Bentley's goal was to learn more than a clergyman, a lawyer, a physician, a professor or a gentleman, indeed more than all combined. The early American republic did not scoff at such soaring ambitions, it inspired and promoted them.[63]

Bentley's uses of his learning further mark him as a republican man of letters. For instead of confining himself to the milieu of scholars and clerks and specialized audiences, he chose to be a popularizer. To devote such erudition as Bentley's to newspaper journalism had heretofore been a kind of blasphemy to the temples of learning. But in the new republic, where the well-being of the state and society were believed to rest ultimately on an informed and virtuous citizenry, Bentley's journalism was an extension of his ministry in the East Parish to the public at large. By spending endless hours in the pursuit of information, gathering it, ordering it, and then filtering it so as to include whatever "has in our judgment truth, happiness, usefulness, or good government as it object," and excluding everything else, Bentley put his learning in the service of a secular republican ministry.[64] Moreover, in an age of scissors-and-paste journalism, where Bentley's unsigned digests and commentaries might appear in newspapers and journals throughout the United States, he was indeed serving the republic. Bentley admired erudition and pursued it avidly, but for him the proper purpose of learning and of making oneself informed was to elevate mankind and society. Trained as he was among the first generation of college men and clergy in the new republic, Bentley chose to uplift Americans not only from the pulpit, but also through the press.

There were, of course, many others who brought a sense of altruism into the journalism of the period, including other clergymen. What sets Bentley apart was his encyclopedic learning, his commitment to universal information, both private and in his newspaper columns. For with each year that passed the movement toward specialized journalism gained momentum, making Bentley's endeavors more and more anachronistic. Sectarian papers and magazines, partisan newspapers, professional journals, literary periodicals, and other special interest publications were multiplying so rapidly as to create a kind of information explosion that no individual, not even William Bentley, could hope to master. His struggle from the 1790s onward to collect all sorts of information, to sift it, and to order it for his readers, was heroic. Indeed he recognized and addressed one of the republic's most critical problems, the creation of an informed public in an era when the volume and variety of information were expanding dramatically.

For an individual to have mounted such an effort was, in the end, hopeless in practical terms. Indeed the whole idea was rooted in a republican utopianism that was more appealing than it was realistic. If at the level of 18th-century local politics the concept of an informed public was realistic, at the level of state and national affairs such a prospect was already in question during the controversy over the United States Constitution in 1787 and 1788. For optimists like Bentley, the newspaper seemed to offer a solution that would permit a broad public to command cosmopolitan knowledge, but by the time of his death in 1819 even he harbored grave doubts. And after Bentley no one would seriously attempt to do single-handedly what Bentley had done as a pastoral sideline. The age of the universal scholar in service to the republic was brief.

Yet the ideal of an informed public that Bentley pursued continued to animate American society long after he had passed from the scene. A staple of American politics, it was embraced by a wide range of reformers and improvers who believed that the good society was founded on a properly informed citizenry. By the time of Tocqueville's visit, when the perception of the power of public opinion had become commonplace, printing and oratory were bombarding Americans in myriad forms and were creating the self-intensifying competition for their attention and consciousness that Bentley had only begun to sense. Since he was born and raised in an era of relative scarcity of information, a time when it was quite common to go through a period of days and weeks when people agreed there was "no news," the idea of achieving a comprehensive mastery of information did not seem too audacious to the remarkably gifted Bentley; and the preparation of news digests for public consumption was almost his civic duty.

But as time went on and systems for creating, processing, and distributing information became more and more specialized and competitive, Bentley's efforts came to appear increasingly superficial and ephemeral. Probably Bentley was more learned and better informed than anyone anywhere had been a century before he lived, however in the century after his death his ambition came to be viewed as romantic, futile, and perhaps pointless. But for Bentley, who had known both the world of information scarcity and the world of its superabundance, the life that he devoted to collecting conversations and printed matter, to sifting them and putting his knowledge to public use, embodied a republican strategy to encompass both worlds.

Chapter 9

Choosing One's Fare:
Northern Men in the 1840s

By the time of William Bentley's death at the end of 1819, the information systems that Americans employed had passed several critical milestones and what may be called the information revolution was well underway. Whereas printing centers had been confined to a handful of port and capital towns at Bentley's birth in 1760, now they were scattered throughout the settled landscape and even the frontier. Numbers of newspapers had multiplied, from 17 to 518, and partly to facilitate the distribution of those newspapers and the exchange of information between them the new republic had created an extensive postal system that already reached into some 4500 counties and townships by 1820, and 13,500 by 1840. By this time improvements in transportation had speeded the movement of information dramatically, so that news which had required weeks to pass from one end of the nation to another in 1790, now moved in days.[1] Secular oratory, often possessing political content, had been unknown in Bentley's childhood, but now it had become routine, especially at Independence Day celebrations. Political party organizations, Masonic lodges, and a host of other male and female voluntary associations, both inclusive and exclusive, were spreading across the landscape.[2] Something that might be termed a "comprehensive" marketplace for information was coming into being, one that supplied learned, scientific, and technical information, even musical scores, for audiences high and low, expert and amateur, as well as a full range of religious and imaginative literature that was designed and packaged to satisfy all sorts of reading tastes. And although Bentley lived to regret the trivialization that he believed was overtaking the popular press, as a journalist, Freemason, compiler of religious music, and advocate of public education he had been in the vanguard of the information revolution, promoting its success.

Yet some of these developments were only just emerging by 1820. One generation later seedlings that had begun to sprout at the time of Bentley's death had burst into full bloom, and some of the features characteristic of America's 19th- and even 20th-century information systems were evident: a multiplication and specialization of information forms and sources, together with a vigorous commercial influence and orientation. Abundance and the necessity of actively selecting what to attend and what to ignore in a burgeoning, competitive marketplace, meant that individual preferences ruled the acquisition and consumption of information. The choices that people made were, of course, subject to social and cultural influences—of occupation and rank especially—but they were made individually in an environment where a wide range of printed matter, public oratory, associational activities, and even theatrical performances were available and within the reach of a vast number of patrons.

How and why people embraced these opportunities, integrating them into their lives and thereby sustaining the whole process, is the subject of this chapter. Already scholars have revealed much about the agents of this information revolution which coincided with the industrial, transportation, and market revolutions. Studies of printing, journalism, literature, popular entertainment, and the lecture system have explored the reasons that so much information came to be available; while works on political parties, reform organizations, and the flowering of middle-class culture have provided insights into the social functions and consequences of that information.[3] Rich and persuasive as much of this scholarship is, however, much of it operates at a level of abstraction and generality somewhat removed from personal experience. Consequently we remain uncertain as to precisely how the information revolution became incorporated into the whole spectrum of individual experience for consumers of print and oratory, and for participants in, for example, electoral campaigns and temperance reform.

Here, as elsewhere, one may begin to grasp what was going on by exploring individual experience. In the 1840s, the segment of the population most thoroughly involved in the whole gamut of these activities was northern, white, Protestant, and male, and tended to dwell in cities and towns rather than on farms. Such people were free to read whatever they wished, to attend any sort of public or quasi-public meeting unescorted, and to spend their resources with considerable discretion. For these reasons, chiefly, the experiences of four northern white men will be explored here. These men— a lawyer's clerk, an engraver/illustrator, a cabinetmaker's apprentice, and a lawyer/banker/farm-owner—differed in their origins and social status, but all saw themselves as respectable members of America's loosely defined and highly variegated white, Protestant middle class.

Let us begin by visiting Isaac Mickle, a wealthy young man dwelling in the environs of Philadelphia, a person whose tastes and talents made him a kind of ultimate consumer and participant in the information market. An only child born in 1822 into a long-established Camden, New Jersey, family, Mickle was raised by his mother and his uncle who, following the death of Isaac's father within a year of his birth, formed a household together. Isaac's mother indulged the boy, cultivating his verbal and literary skills from his earliest years. On Isaac's third birthday she started a library for him, grandly calling the collection the "Washington Library;" and when he reached the age of twelve she promoted him to the "presidency" of this collection of over one hundred volumes. Ever after Mickle was an avid bibliophile.[4]

Tutoring for the lad began when he was six, and by the time he was eleven years old he was attending boarding school. Already his elegantly drafted letters were sprinkled with Latin and French quotations, and he later read both languages routinely. Mickle's formal education ended at age eighteen, following several years of schooling at academies in southern New Jersey. Soon after, in May 1841, Mickle began reading law at the office of his uncle's friend, Colonel James Page, a prominent Philadelphia Democrat. Here he stayed for three years, reading law, doing errands, writing local New Jersey history, and engaging more and more in partisan journalism and Democratic politics. In 1843 the twenty-one-year-old Mickle was active in the movement to reform the New Jersey state constitution, and in the following year, after he passed his bar exam with distinction, he attended the Democratic National Convention as a reporter-editor for the Camden *Eagle.* In 1845 he published *Reminiscences of Old Gloucester,* a local history based on archival records and personal testimony. Later he purchased and edited the Camden *Democrat,* and served as collector of the port of Camden, a patronage plum from President Franklin Pierce. But what might have been a notable career was cut short by tuberculosis, and Mickle died in 1855, predeceased by two sons and survived by a wife and two daughters. Mickle's diary, journal, and letters, which span the years 1837 to 1845, supply a vivid picture of the young gentleman as a lawyer's clerk.

For Mickle, making choices where money was only a secondary concern was part of his upbringing. Though his uncle urged him to become a farmer, he chose to study law because, he believed, this was the chief route to "civil honors."[5] Though he could have attended college and once considered enrolling at Princeton, he preferred to remain in Camden, a town of some 3400 people, just a ferry-ride away from Philadelphia. At Camden he could retain his circle of local friends while simultaneously entering daily into the rich, urban society of Philadelphia. Here he could read virtually any book, periodical, or newspaper, listen to any lecturer or orator, view any play or performance, visit any church, or attend the debates of courtroom or barroom. In short, this talented and privileged young man could take his pick from a full selection of information possibilities.

Mickle's appetites, in this regard, were considerable, as is suggested by his interests in journalism, politics, literature, and law. Only a few kinds of information were of no concern to him, and though he scorned popular novels and largely ignored the physical sciences and engineering, he was inclined to sample almost all the formats in which information was distributed, whether in print, in speech, or in public performance.

A member of no church and essentially secular in his orientation, Mickle was nonetheless fascinated by what went on in Camden and Philadelphia's many churches, from the manners of the worshippers to the texts of the homilies. The best part of life, Mickle believed, was taking in information and sharing it with others. As he put it in a notice he prepared for launching a debating club, "The Henry Institute, . . . may at once enlarge our Knowledge and, by enabling us to impart it, add to its value." In phrases that had become hackneyed by the 1830s, he asserted that "taciturn men . . . are the enemies of society," and "the worth of Knowledge, like money, depends upon its circulation."[6]

The principles which seem to have ruled Mickle's perspective were rooted in the tradition of self-improvement. The genteel side of this tradition had been made popular by Lord Chesterfield's letters to his son,[7] recommending reading, travel, and conversation as the paths to refinement, cultivation, and wisdom.[8] Mickle, who first read Chesterfield at age fifteen and who, after his second reading three years later, noted that "in many things Chesterfield speaks like a man of sense," sought to inform himself and develop his own capacities through precisely these means—reading, travel, and conversation.[9]

A more comprehensive, explicitly democratic exposition of the self-improvement ideal to which Mickle's entire generation of northern white men subscribed was offered by the Unitarian, William Ellery Channing, whose lecture to Boston's young workingmen in 1838 was entitled *Self-Culture*. Characteristically, the clergyman elevated his subject above merely temporal worldly success: "self-culture . . . [is] the care which every man owes to himself, to the unfolding and perfecting of his nature."[10] But in addition to the moral and aesthetic dimensions of self-improvement, Channing pointed to reading, politics, conversation, and speech. "In the best books," he asserted, "great men talk to us." In addition, the republic, through its broad participation, was "a powerful means of educating the multitude. It is the people's University."[11] Perhaps even more important was the "power of Utterance" because, Channing explained, conversation advances intellectual development.[12] Moreover, in recognition of the competitive, hierarchical dimensions of the republic, he noted that "social rank" depended on speech. To converse "with respectable people," he recognized, "we must speak their language." Here lay the path of "social advantage," so he recommended that "the power of utterance should be included by all in their plans for self-culture."[13] Although Channing directed his advice toward common men who were without wealth or privilege, his was precisely the doctrine that Mickle embraced. This ideal of self-culture or self-improvement comes closest to explaining the ways in which Mickle participated in the world of information exchange.

In assessing Mickle's behavior, however, it would be a mistake to ignore the value he placed on pleasure and entertainment. When he read Molière's *Bourgeois Gentilhomme,* he laughed over it "more than will answer me for a week."[14] He found Samuel Butler's Restoration-era satire *Hudibras,* though "not without its faults," "witty" and worthy of being "read often, and read every time with increased pleasure."[15] His library was not a collection of religious or didactic works; it most resembled the library of a classically educated gentleman—strong in English, French, and Latin literature, history and philosophy, with only a handful of novels "such as *Don Quixote, Gil Blas, The Last of the Barons,* and some of [James Fenimore] Cooper and [James K.] Paulding's writings." He viewed most novels with a lofty disdain, and patronizingly declared to a young female cousin that "the great mass of such literature ought to be burnt by the common hangman."[16] Though he was barely familiar with the popular genre, he was so committed to notions of self-improvement that he accepted the conservative platitude that such novels could only corrupt rather than inform or elevate the understanding of their readers.

Yet although Mickle's nurture had made him genteel and elitist, he was also a self-conscious Democrat who, aspiring to civil honors, believed that the ultimate object of his own self-improvement was to serve others. Mickle, like William Ellery Channing, was convinced that class boundaries must not block the circulation of knowledge. At the age of sixteen years Mickle was already helping artisans such as his friend, Samuel Foster, a harness-maker's apprentice, to speak with "respectable people" by instructing him on English grammar.[17] The Henry Institute, which he organized at age eighteen included thirty-two members, eighteen of whom were artisans.[18] This club nourished Mickle's Democratic condescension, for here he heard a carpenter speak "brilliantly, with a stirring account of the wrongs of the red man." Conscious of his own advantages, Mickle was especially impressed because he had seen the speaker "composing at night in a carpenter shop, with one dim light set upon the best desk he could procure, to wit, a workbench." Here was a lesson in self-culture that was both a comfort and an admonition to Mickle, who reflected that "to assist such as he was always to me a source of pleasure; and I have the satisfaction of knowing that though I myself neglect my books too much, more than one friendless carpenter boy has had access to them."[19] Indeed in at least one case, after a neighbor apprentice was supposed to have gone to bed, Mickle would secretly admit him by the window of his attic study, and then "sat up till the night was far advanced, instructing him in the little I knew, and listening to the good stories which he used to tell so well."[20] The sociable exchange of good stories and book-learning enriched both young men.

For Mickle these activities and the political path to civil honors were linked in several ways, direct and indirect. "The beginning of my politics," as Mickle put it, was when he composed a speech for the shoemaker and unlicensed rum-seller Joseph Weatherby to deliver at a town caucus: "I wrote it on his lap-board, not with an awl it is true, but with a thing that was little better. He was perfectly satisfied with it, and promised to learn it by heart."[21] This kind of political action was unusual for Mickle, but it was consistent with his pattern of education and influence through mingling with common people. On the evening of New Year's Day in 1841, for example, Mickle "stepped around to John Baxter's tailor shop, which is the headquarters of a clique of young men of a certain class [mostly members of the debating club] with whom I choose to become just so intimate, and no more."[22] Three weeks later Mickle visited Joseph Weatherby's, another social center where, as Chesterfield had advised, much could be gained from observation. Mickle described the shoemaker's shop as a place "where about a half-dozen men resort nightly to spend an hour or two, in telling what wonders they have seen in their past lives. One of their number, a blacksmith, had traveled extensively in the South, and so provided a full description of Virginia's geologically formed natural bridge, including its rough dimensions, physical features, the graffiti attached to it by neighboring youths, and his own judgment "that the pictures in the geographies . . . are good representations."[23] A month later when Mickle dropped in again, he was rewarded with "some queer ghost stories."[24] Mickle was not, as he saw it, simply idling away his time in this kind of sociable recreation. Books were only one source of knowledge. As he remarked after a visit to Weatherby's, "I often pick up in my wanderings about town, items of information. . . . A shoemaker's shop sometimes holds more than lasts and awls."[25]

A few months later, however, when Mickle took up his clerkship in Philadelphia, his nocturnal visits to craftsmen's shops ended, most likely because they seemed inappropriate for an ambitious lawyer's clerk. Still, Mickle remained eager to learn what ordinary people had to say, especially on politics. One summer evening as he was walking in Camden he stopped to chat with his neighbor and fellow Democrat, James Duer, "a shoemaker loco-foco" who engaged him in conversation about President Tyler's veto of the bank bill three days earlier. "Friend Duer," Mickle noted, "notwithstanding he exhorts sometimes at the methodist meeting, considers the death of Harrison as a Providential interference to relieve our country from the curse of a national bank; and in thus believing his pious wife, who was sitting in the door, likewise joined." Though Mickle found this notion "ridiculous," he took it in with interest and without expressing his own view.[26] Similarly, when he passed an evening at Delacour's drugstore in Camden, "where a party of men meet every night, to tell jokes and discuss questions of all kinds," he found the conversation "edifying" whether or not he agreed with the views that were expressed. Mickle was convinced that passing his time this way advanced his own development, since "there really is a good deal to be learned in the 'intellectual conflict' of such places and such men."[27] Among a mixed array of artisans and apprentices, shopkeepers, clerks, and an occasional clergyman, he was being educated in the republic at large,

"Waiting for the Stage," an 1851 painting by Richard Caton Woodville, presents a view inside a tavern where three men are waiting for their transportation. Two play cards and talk, while a third stands over them reading a newspaper. An open decanter of wine is on the table. Tea is warming on the stove, and to the right is the bar. Sociability and information exchange were central to the experiences of men like Mickle, Weaver, Carpenter, and Fletcher in the 1840s.

In the Collection of the Corcoran Gallery of Art, Museum Purchase, Gallery Fund, William A. Clark Fund, and through the gifts of Mr. and Mrs. Lansdell K. Christie and Orme Wilson

what Channing had called "the people's University." He was gaining the "knowledge of life" that Chesterfield pronounced "is best learned in various companies."[28]

The style of conversation favored by Mickle and his associates was, from Mickle's accounts of it, clever, spirited, and mildly competitive, rather than solemn. In some respects they departed from the models of sociable discourse prescribed by the manuals of the day. The admonition that "in public never differ from anybody, nor from anything. The *agreeable* man is one who *agrees*," was prudent; but it did not accord with the need to both sharpen and display their wits felt by the men in Mickle's circle.[29] They did tend to subscribe to the view "that conversation is the best which furnishes

"Camp Meeting"

Gatherings of the sort depicted in this 1830 print became common in the United States during the first decades of the 19th century. Here were assembled men, women, and children, families as well as individuals, from various social ranks, who might spend hours or days participating as auditors, worshippers, and orators. On the periphery are some who appear to be spectators rather than participants. The voluntary quality of such a communication experience is suggested by the intensity of some participants and the casual inattention of several spectators.
Courtesy of the Library Company of Philadelphia

the most entertainment," but they rejected the idea that this could be achieved by calling on one's conversational partners for "the least exercise of mind."[30] Being agreeable merely, however acceptable socially, did not comport with their notions of self-improvement.

Since Mickle was headed toward law and politics, the arts of arranging information so as to persuade were particularly important, and he sought out a variety of opportunities to polish his skills. Not only did he continuously participate in one or two debating clubs, regularly listening to the arguments of other young men and making presentations of his own every month or so, he also attended public lectures frequently. In Philadelphia during the 1840s an inexhaustible, encyclopedic array of possibilities enabled Mickle to satisfy his aspirations for knowledge as well as amusement. He paid to hear speakers from all over the United States and from Britain who lectured on religion and philosophy, medicine, chemistry and physics, history and geography, politics and reform.[31] In addition Mickle availed himself of the churches and meetinghouses of Camden and Philadelphia, where he heard almost every variety of Protestant sermon, as well as the services of Catholics and Jews. In taking in all this information his aim was not to attain some sort of comprehensive knowledge, it was to deepen and enrich his understanding of people and their natural, cultural, and social environments. With this kind of knowledge he could shine in company, in journalism, and in public affairs.

The law office, similarly, was more than a narrow, technical classroom. Colonel Page's office was one large room, divided in two by folding doors. Behind doors that were sometimes open, Page did business, and in front of them Mickle, two junior lawyers, and Page's elder brother had their tables. On one ordinary day Mickle counted fifty visitors entering the office. Conversations on private and public affairs were so incessant that it took Mickle awhile to learn to read in this distracting setting. Page's prominence brought "lawyers, politicians and other public men, from Governors and Senators down to pot-house brawlers about the rights of man" into the office with some frequency.[32] Here he met "Senator [James] Buchanan . . . a large, grey-haired, queer-looking man, remarkable for a very deliberate manner of speaking," as well as ex-President Martin Van Buren.[33] Among many others, Mickle was introduced to the historian George Bancroft ("a fine looking man, but wears spectacles!") and the philosopher Orestes Brownson.[34] Mickle later used these introductions to call on Brownson at his suburban Boston home and, during a trip to New York state, to meet with Van Buren for a "short interview" on "political affairs."[35] Most important of all, in Mickle's view, was the example of his mentor, Colonel Page, "a clever and an honourable man," possessing "a fund of original wit, from which he is ever willing to draw for the amusement of a public meeting or a private circle." Indeed, Mickle observed, whenever Page rose to speak publicly, "his audience began to shrug with satisfaction at the drollery they anticipate."[36] So exemplary was Page's integrity, generosity, and commitment to democracy, in addition to his "ever ready wit," Mickle concluded at the end of his training that "had I never opened a law book at all, my tutelage would have been invaluable." Quoting an aphorism drawn from St. Paul, he was convinced that "as 'evil communications corrupt good manners' so intercourse with men of the stamp of James Page elevates . . . pleases . . . strengthens . . . [and] refines."[37]

As Isaac Mickle recognized, becoming informed by observation in company and learning directly through emulation were no less important than gaining knowledge via print or formal lectures. But in 19th-century America, being a gentleman in society was more complex than it had been when Chesterfield penned his advice. Mickle appreciated just how problematic it could be since outside his study hours and office time, and beyond his respectable debating clubs, lectures, and church meetings, he was drawn to bars, billiard halls and, rarely, brothels. Some of his peers moved "at once in the highest and lowest circles of society," so Mickle, who as a gentleman-in-training scorned provincial prudery, sometimes found the boundary between vice and virtue difficult to locate.[38]

According to one Philadelphia advice book, "the gentleman and man of the world" must "accomodate himself to every grade of persons and every class of customs and doings"—counsel that Mickle tried to follow. Yet he wondered whether "if thrown into company with the gay, and even the intemperate and dissolute, he should appear to be one of them." As one who sought civil honors as a loyal Democrat, Mickle could not deny that "every one who mingles much with the world or has extensive dealings with men, is liable to be thrown among coarse and irregular persons whom he is obliged to conciliate, and who will laugh him to scorn if he carries with him into their company . . . a refined and fastidious taste and style." Mickle had grown to understand that the realism of such advice made it impossible to dismiss. No one could deny that if a man went "to a county court or a state legislature, or among bankers, or brokers, or aldermen; in short, into any rank of society beneath the highest . . . he will be distanced very speedily and thrown *hors du combat,* unless he can drink and roar and talk roughly." Yet Mickle could not accept such advice. To acquire influence by mingling in male society on these terms was humiliating.[39] Perhaps it was for this reason especially that Mickle idolized Colonel Page. Page could mix with all companies without shedding his dignity; he could move affably among the vicious without engaging in their vices.

There was, however, one set of people with whom Mickle could most cheerfully associate, genteel women who, according to convention, would refine his sensibility and elevate his morality. As with other types of company, the eighteen-year-old Mickle deliberately set out to cultivate female connections. The "society of the ladies," he and a male friend agreed, would preserve their morals.[40] Months later, when Mickle took stock of his activities, he was pleased that all the lecture and churchgoing that he had done accompanied by women, all the debate club exhibitions in their presence, and all the parlor visiting and strolling in female company had not been mere gallantry, it had also been efficacious.[41] Genteel women, it seemed, taught refinement and courtesy through their conversation and deportment just as surely as Colonel Page taught the ways of cutting a path among men. In the right settings, it seemed, even flirtation could be part of Isaac Mickle's program of self-culture.

Yet although widespread, commonly accepted opinions and values shaped Mickle's experience and made him almost the ideal type of the self-improving young man of the 1840s, he was also distinctive in important ways that are apparent when his experiences are compared with those of Matthias Shirk Weaver. Weaver, a young free-lance engraver and illustrator, of mixed Anglo-German ancestry, was making his way in Philadelphia's art world just as Mickle was entering law and politics. Born in 1816 at New Holland in the Pennsylvania Dutch country about fifty miles west of Philadelphia, Weaver had learned some German as a boy, before his family moved to Springfield, Ohio, in 1831. After attending an academy at Canton in the northeastern part of the state, Weaver worked on his father's farm and taught school. In 1838 he moved to Philadelphia, enrolled in the Philadelphia Academy of Arts the following year, and became an engraver of lithographs. During the years covered by his diary, 1840–1843, Weaver eked out a modest living (supplemented by cash from his father) by drawing anatomical plates for the books of several medical professors, and taking miscellaneous commissions.[42] Weaver was interested in politics and, following his family's preference, worked on behalf of the Whigs in 1840. As to church affiliation, he "did not much believe in an outward profession of religion," and held that no creed was vital.[43]

Weaver and Mickle attended some of the same Philadelphia spectacles, listened to a few of the same famous lecturers, and in their different debating clubs, argued over some of the same topics; but though Weaver drew a portrait of Mickle's uncle and one of his cousins, the two apparently never met.[44] Indeed though they inhabited the same Philadelphia, they approached it from different circumstances. Not only was Mickle more wealthy, vivacious, and gifted verbally than all but a handful of his peers in and around the metropolis, he also enjoyed a wide network of personal and family connections that made him an insider who always felt at home. Weaver, in contrast, was always a migrant to Philadelphia who possessed only one or two relatives in the vicinity, and he always felt himself something of an outsider in the great city, even after he married and set up housekeeping there.

In addition there were notable temperamental differences. Mickle was an extrovert. Whether in a debate, calling on a "great man" such as Ralph Waldo Emerson, delivering a campaign speech in a tavern, or passing judgment in politics and literature, he displayed a self-confidence that would have seemed mere arrogance in someone less gifted verbally. Weaver, more of an introvert, could only fantasize about calling on the great Charles Dickens when he visited Philadelphia, and he only expressed his views on literature and politics in private conversation and in his debating club. For Weaver was striving to adopt an urbane gentility that was alien to his background. To him, Ohio was home—"Ohio folks are the best friends in the world," Weaver exclaimed after almost three years in Philadelphia, the "city of Brotherly hatred."[45] When he married, his choice was Eliza Burgert, "a Buckeye girl."[46] Later, after seven years in Philadelphia, he would return with his wife and children to Springfield, Ohio, where two years later in 1847, he died of a lingering illness. However stimulating he found Philadelphia, Weaver never became fully acclimated to the urban, cosmopolitan world.

Yet whatever the social and temperamental differences that separated

Weaver and Mickle, the young engraver was no less committed than the lawyer's clerk to the goal of self-improvement. His response to a lecture on habits was a resolution "to eradicate some of mine—and form others new & Better."[47] When he considered the standard debating topic of whether character depended on circumstances or not, he concluded firmly that, notwithstanding the influence of situation and environment, "Man may form his own character."[48] Six months later, when he began his diary for 1842, his motto was "Ich Kann" (I Can), and he placed these words at the front of the little book as a daily reminder.[49] The pursuit of an essentially secular self-culture brought Weaver actively into the marketplace for information.

For Weaver, as was generally the case, there were no clear boundaries among recreation, entertainment, and information. All three tastes might be satisfied by lectures, books, and newspapers, by debating and literary clubs, and by theatrical and musical performances, as well as by social visits. What was important to Weaver, however, was that information be the first priority. "My time is passing very unprofitably as regards moral and intellectual advancement," Weaver complained after visiting ice-cream gardens twice in one week. "I mingle too little with knowledge-seeking young men," he confessed, so he decided to "join some literary association."[50] Soon after, he joined the William Wirt Institute, a social library and debating club with which he remained associated throughout his time in Philadelphia.

Although to pursue his occupation as an engraver, wide knowledge and what Channing called "the power of utterance" were not absolutely essential, they were vital to Weaver's own self-esteem. The fact that his Pennsylvania Dutch speech was "rather vulgar" was embarrassing, as was his inattention to "how I express myself in conversation."[51] Such self-consciousness was characteristic among aspiring country people who sought careers in the cities. "I did not feel the want of the art of Speaking and writing Correctly until since I came to the City," noted another man in like circumstances, before comforting himself with the thought that "many men have risen to influence and usefulness and seats of honour who have been as ignorant at my age [twenty-four years]."[52] What these young men were recognizing was that being uninformed, what is today called "cultural illiterate," was a social liability.[53] Weaver remarked that a "person is more prized as a companion and receives more credit in society who is informed (tho superficially) on many subjects."[54] It was largely for this reason that he read natural science, history, and biography, for when his peers were conversing on the greatness of Napoleon, Cromwell, and Caesar, he wanted to hold his own.[55] Without information he could not even maintain a respectable stature at his boarding-house, where an argument over such topics as whether civilization increases crime occurred as a matter of course.[56] Competing in a social setting where innumerable young men sought to carve out a distinct place in the world, and where not even Isaac Mickle possessed sufficient wealth, connections, and talent to satisfy his ambitions without the ardent pursuit of self-culture, the ability to command information together with "the power of utterance" seemed to be the keys to success. Both were accessible to young men of even modest means through the multitude of information activities that were flourishing in the 1840s. Weaver's conclusion after struggling to make his way in the city for more than two years, was that, in the end, "knowledge is the key to distinction."[57]

The chief sources of knowledge for Weaver, as for Mickle, were printed goods and the mutually reinforcing face-to-face experiences in conversation, club meetings and lectures. Though much was made by authorities such as Chesterfield about the importance of travel as a source of information (Weaver even "made a speech before the 'Socials' " arguing that traveling, not reading, was "the best source of knowledge") in fact travel literature, which was widely read in popular editions, not travel itself, was the more important source of information for Weaver and Mickle.[58] Though both men traveled—Weaver back and forth to Ohio on two occasions (once via New York state), and Mickle in New Jersey and Pennsylvania, and to Baltimore, New York, and New England—these were primarily recreational jaunts. Avid knowledge-seekers like these two could not help picking up information along the way, but chiefly they sought the pleasures of visiting family and friends. They also sought the sensations of viewing sights such as the awesome natural wonder Niagara Falls, which both visited, or the prospect of Boston from the state house cupola—where Mickle was struck less by the view than by the "insolent" behavior of the black sightseers and the Yankee tolerance of it.[59] Neither Weaver or Mickle regarded their travels as yielding much information or improvement as compared with their other activities.

Though more accessible than ever before, letter-writing, like travel, had ceased to be a key source of knowledge. Whereas letters had once been vital sources of information on events beyond one's locality, and had taken on in some cases a quasi-public quality since they might be opened and read as they passed from hand to hand, now their contents were almost exclusively devoted to personal concerns, and any tampering with them was a federal offense. If Weaver or Mickle wished to share public news with distant correspondents, and they did, they simply put a newspaper in the mail. Because Congress had set postage rates so as to favor newspapers, they could send one anywhere in the United States for one-and-a-half cents, half the cost of sending a one-page letter forty miles.[60] It is no wonder, then, that the only information they normally received and sent via letters was personal, not the sort of knowledge that would enhance their ability to cut a figure socially.[61]

The pervasiveness of these patterns, in which printing and face-to-face activities operated as the chief sources of information, with letters being devoted to private business or personal affairs and travel often becoming a recreational activity, is underscored when we consider the experiences of Edward Carpenter, a New England cabinetmaker's apprentice. Although Carpenter entered the information marketplace from a very different vantage point from either Mickle or Weaver, he engaged himself in it in much the same manner as the urban members of his generation. Though self-culture did not always mean quite the same thing to a self-conscious mechanic who did not aspire to civic honors, he sought out information aggressively within the constraints of very meager earnings so that, notwithstanding the physical and social distances that separated him from the two Philadelphians, he was shopping in the same marketplace. That he made somewhat different choices as to what information to command was more a function of culture and aspiration than location or wealth.

Edward Jenner Carpenter was born in 1825 in Bernardston, Massachusetts, a town of some 800 people on the rim of the Connecticut River Valley just south of Vermont. His father was a self-taught school teacher and physician from Vermont who married a woman from a local farm family.[62] The eldest of seven children, Edward was sent for a time to a nearby academy to follow the English course, however there was never enough money to provide him or any of his four brothers with more in the way of formal schooling, so all the boys were apprenticed in neighboring Greenfield, two as cabinetmakers, and three as shop clerks. When, at his father's suggestion, Edward Carpenter began a diary on his nineteenth birthday, in August 1844, he was already two years into his apprenticeship and thoroughly settled in Greenfield where he would serve out a full seven-year term. Subsequently Carpenter left the trade of cabinetmaking which was becoming more and more a mechanized, factory-style business, and moved north to Brattleboro, Vermont, where he became a newsagent and stationer who sold and delivered newspapers and periodicals. At the time of his diary, 1844–1845, he was not affiliated with any church. Though not yet of voting age, he was, however, a Whig partisan.

Like Mickle and Weaver, Carpenter was attracted to the mass media, both printed and spoken. But Carpenter had to budget every penny, so when he laid out twelve-and-a-half cents on a physiology lecture he did not feel free to spend a quarter on a concert. Since mass communications were substantially marketplace commodities, money mattered, though not as much as cultural preferences. Sharing reading matter with fellow apprentices and exploiting opportunities for free information and amusement, enabled the young Greenfield "mechanic" to exercise choices much as Mickle and Weaver did.

The limited importance of wealth in determining the possibilities is striking when a comparison is drawn between Mickle's situation at the most privileged end of the social spectrum, with Carpenter's much more common circumstances. Before entering the law office in 1841 Mickle listed his key information sources:

The Washington Library, the Henry Institute, and the Camden Literary Association. By paying four dollars a year to the last of these I have access to about twenty-five of the best periodicals of this country and England. The newspapers which are taken by our family of three, are *The Saturday Courier* and *Pennsylvanian,* of Philadelphia; the Trenton *Emporium;* and the *Mail* and *Democrat,* of Camden: weekly; Kendall's *Expositor,* Washington: iregularly; and *The Spirit of the Times,* Philadelphia: daily. In addition to these I receive every few days from some old schoolmate papers from all parts of the country.[63]

Such extensive access was quite beyond Carpenter's pocketbook; nor did he enjoy as much discretionary time as Mickle. But neither was he starved for print or public speech. Carpenter subscribed to a county temperance monthly, *The Hampden Washingtonian* at seventy-five cents per year and the New York monthly *Despatch* at twenty-five cents annually.[64] He, too, exchanged newspapers with old schoolmates and relatives scattered around the country, receiving newspapers once or twice a month from as nearby as Bellows Falls, Vermont and Springfield, Massachusetts, and as far away as Indiana, Michigan, and New Orleans. In addition, Carpenter borrowed periodicals from his bosses, other apprentices, and from a Greenfield printing office, where an apprentice friend gave him access to exchange newspapers.[65] If the *Saturday Courier* came promptly into Isaac Mickle's home, it also reached Edward Carpenter, though later and with less regularity. One Sunday in March 1844, for example, Carpenter noted, "I staid in the shop in the forenoon & read some old *Saturday Couriers.*"[66] Mickle's access to printed goods was broader and more systematic than Carpenter's, but the latter also enjoyed a wide range of choices.

The exercise of personal preference, while socially influenced, is particularly evident in Carpenter's fascination with popular fiction—a taste shared by neither Mickle or Weaver. For Carpenter avidly bought, borrowed, and read precisely the class of fiction that Mickle so haughtily dismissed. Moreover for the cabinetmaker's apprentice such reading was an engaging form of self-improvement.[67] In March 1844, he reported reading "a story called Easy Nat or Boston bars and Boston boys. It is the life of three boys during their apprenticeship. One of them was Easy Nat who was led into drunkenness and all sorts of dissipation by his brother apprentices & afterwards became a Washingtonian [temperance advocate] & the other apprentice set his masters house on fire & then cut his throat." Sensational it was, but Carpenter also drew from it a moral lesson: "This shows the evil of drunken Companions."[68] He also preferred to learn history through fictional sources: "I bought a day or two ago a novel call Attilla the King and I have been reading [it] tonight." So absorbing was it that the next evening he noted, "I have been reading Attilla till I can hardly think of anything else."[69] Carpenter's reaction confirmed a journalist's declaration: "Do you wish to instruct, to convince, to please? Write a novel! Have you a system of religion or politics or manners to inculcate? Write a novel!"[70] Carpenter did read books that supplied factual information directly, such as a biography of Sir William Wallace, the hero of medieval Scotland, George W. Kendall's account of his Santa Fe expedition, a history of the United States, and a geography textbook, but scarcely with the same level of enthusiasm.[71] Never self-consciously "intellectual" as Mickle was, nor troubled, like Weaver, by the impact of his conversation on his standing among his peers, Carpenter and his fellow apprentices reveled in the attractive, entertaining packages that the information marketplace supplied.

Where Carpenter's access to information differed most markedly from Mickle's—and where his experience was closer to Weaver's—was in the extent of face-to-face contacts supplied by his dwelling and place of work. The Page law office was an information-rich environment that provided Mickle with access to news concerning local, state, and national politics, reform movements, and the whole gamut of contemporary cultural activity. Weaver, whose workplace was often his boardinghouse room, had a speaking acquaintance with no more than seventy-five to one hundred people in Philadelphia, including his landlady and fellow boarders, other artists, members of the William Wirt club, his aunt, several young women with whom he attended sermons and lectures, and his washerwoman. His customers stretched over three years were fewer than entered the Page law office on an active day and included two medical professors, a shopkeeper, a black Masonic lodge, and several portrait subjects, including a "n-gg-r [sic] preacher," with whom Weaver conversed reluctantly.[72] Only on Weaver's annual visits to Ohio was he surrounded by an extensive network of acquaintances.

Carpenter's situation in the village of Greenfield was similar. In contrast to Mickle, who stayed at the Page office about thirty hours per week, Carpenter's work confined him in the shop for roughly fifty hours each week during spring and summer, and something over sixty hours a week in fall and winter. Usually there were only two apprentices, one journeyman, and the two bosses present. Once every six months or so an artisan from the nearby town of Colrain came to spend a few days painting chairs in the shop.[73] Customers came from time to time, but the bosses spoke with them, and all Carpenter could glean from what he overheard had to do with furniture, payment, and personal matters. The most cosmopolitan experience Carpenter recorded was a short stint when a German cabinetmaker worked in the shop. From him he learned "that in Germany every man when he is 20 years old has to become a soldier, & serve till he is 26, & he says his mother will have to pay $500 towards supporting the army because he came away." Carpenter reflected, "we Yankees should think that rather hard."[74] His only other conversations with non-Yankees were with a "John Bull" artisan who sold him a razor, and when he and a few friends visited a black man's barbershop to hear a "rale nigger fiddler."[75] A person who had seen distant places or who held unfamiliar ideas, like people with unusual experiences, were not part of a workplace where Carpenter overheard business discussions of his bosses as well as the family news of everyone in the shop. Since Carpenter's own father, uncles, and brothers stopped in every week or so, Carpenter's shopmates learned equally about the health, careers, and marital plans of his family. The daily round of face-to-face contacts in the shop reinforced localism and the stratification associated with family and occupation.

Carpenter's free time brought him more cosmopolitan and improving information even though he confined his associations mostly to a circle of a dozen or so fellow apprentices. Much happier in their company than on his visits home to Bernardston, where he found "I was homesick before night for there is not so much going on here as in Greenfield," they spent every evening from mid-March to mid-September in conversation, playing cards and on outings.[76] Much of the activity was physical—swimming, "wicket-ball," barnraising, country walks, and dancing—and conformed to ideas on health that were being promoted by physicians and moralists of self-culture. In addition, they attended lectures on a wide range of subjects to enrich their knowledge. Touring experts spoke on "Geographical Geology," honey bees, phrenology, and human physiology, among other topics. Though admission charges kept Carpenter from attending every lecture, the first in each series was usually free, and all subjects were viewed as appropriate and accessible to all social ranks in Greenfield.[77]

For artisans like Carpenter the openness of the information marketplace to all "respectable" people was especially important because social boundaries limited the passage of information between the genteel and working men. Though Greenfield was less stratified than Camden or Philadelphia, there were no young gentlemen like Isaac Mickle in Greenfield who mixed with and instructed the apprentice artisans in Carpenter's circle. Interclass conversational networks were few, and Yankee mechanics, self-consciously rejecting the pretensions of their "betters," developed feelings of solidarity. For if Carpenter and his friends could not converse with "the aristocracy" of Greenfield on an equal footing, they would not converse with them at all. Carpenter was convinced that "the big bugs," as he often called them, spoke of people like him as "the rabble;" and when in July 1844 the "big bugs" had a picnic and dance from which they excluded the working men, the latter "staid outside & made such a noise they could hardly hear the music."[78] A local debate over "Which have done the most good Lawyers or Mechanics?" could be decided only one way, with Carpenter siding emphatically with the majority in favor of mechanics.[79] Since Carpenter was the son of a physician and had been enrolled at an academy, the fact that he identified himself wholly with the artisans reveals the intensity of the division. The split, which was rooted in the two different visions of self-culture that Channing's lecture had yoked together—the one competitive and hierarchical, the other co-operative and egalitarian—intensified the importance of the public media, since they were accessible to all on a near equal basis. Money mattered, of course, as did location; but among northern, white, Protestant men, personal taste, cultural influences, occupation, and stage of life were more important for shaping face-to-face information networks as well as for broader participation in the information marketplace.

The impact of stage of life particularly, and the extent to which the information marketplace was influenced by the self-culture of young men and women is evident when a comparison is made between the experiences of the youthful Mickle, Weaver, and Carpenter, and an older man such as Calvin Fletcher of Indianapolis, Indiana. Fletcher, who was introduced in chapter seven ("Daughters and Wives") as the husband and teacher of Sarah Hill Fletcher, had been a vigorous participant in self-culture activities in the 1820s when he was forming himself into a gentleman and lawyer through a program of reading, writing, and debating.[80] But by the 1840s Fletcher, who was born in 1798, was a prosperous and prominent leader in Indianapolis preoccupied with public and private business, and less concerned about his own culture than that of his eleven children.

Fletcher's rise was itself testimony to the accessibility of information and learning in the early decades of the century if one was, like Fletcher, prepared culturally. For Fletcher, who was born and raised in central Vermont, came from a family that, though declining after the Revolution, valued knowledge as well as industry. His father, a native of Massachusetts, though studious was a failure at farming who managed to support the family, more or less, as Ludlow town clerk and with the fees he garnered as a justice of the peace although, Calvin recalled, he drank too much. Calvin, the eleventh of fifteen children in a strictly Sabbatarian, orthodox Congregational home, attended local schools during the occasional weeks they were in session and worked the family farm until he was seventeen years old. He then set out on his own, working, and spending his earnings on a few months at a Vermont academy. Early in 1817 he left Vermont and, after staying with Massachusetts relatives, quit New England for Ohio where, at Urbana, he would begin a diary that spanned five decades, and teach school, read law, gain admission to the bar, and marry Sarah Hill. In 1821, the newly married Fletchers moved to Indianapolis, the new state capital, where Calvin, calling himself a "Gentleman of the Bar," immediately compiled and published a legal handbook, *The Indiana Justice and Farmer's Scrivener.* Within a year he was riding the court circuit as an attorney, and within five years he was elected to the Indiana senate, where he twice won reelection before resigning in 1833 to pursue his private interests. Thereafter as a lawyer, land speculator, and banker, Fletcher became a rich man, a leader in the Whig party and the Methodist Church, and a public advocate of temperance, Sunday schools, and progressive farming. When he died in 1866 he was one of Indianapolis' first citizens, patriarch of a large family, and contributor to many good causes.

For a man of affairs such as Fletcher, face-to-face sources of information were most important, and he had many hundreds of non-family acquaintances. In contrast to younger men like Mickle, who were actively developing their acquaintance networks, Fletcher was at a stage in life where he had no desire to extend his face-to-face contacts. Exchanges of information and sociability were so much a part of his daily affairs that he welcomed his few opportunities for solitude. As a bank president and director he had regular meetings with colleagues as well as frequent conversations with dozens of people regarding business, currency, and credit. As a farm owner and operator he supervised his own employees and made frequent visits to his tenants and to farmers who were fattening livestock for him. Though he largely withdrew from the practice of law in the mid-1840s, he continued to attend court sessions periodically. Such occasions, and transactions where he was buyer or seller, meant that over the course of a month Fletcher might speak with several hundred people as part of his occupation. In addition, though there was overlap, his work in the Methodist Sunday schools and his consultations with politicians on partisan and legislative affairs extended his circle. The fact that he often traveled in Indiana brought him into contact with the life of the road—teamsters, travelers, and the people who worked in and patronized the hostelries along the way. Though in the 1820s as a young man Fletcher had actively sought to broaden his information network by developing his sociability, by the 1840s that had ended. Indeed when the governor interrupted him with political business on an otherwise quiet Sunday at home, Fletcher was annoyed rather than honored.[81] As for debating and literary societies or the clubby conviviality of mechanics—that was for younger men who were without public responsibilities or domestic concerns.

The kinds of information that Fletcher acquired in all these encounters touched on virtually every conceivable subject, from the most ephemeral to the truly eternal, from the minutiae of local incidents to matters of cosmic importance according to Fletcher's scale of values. What Fletcher found most valuable in face-to-face exchanges, however, was information that was not available to him from reading, the pulpit, or the lecture platform. Thus he collected practical information about the credit-worthiness of particular people and the reliability of certain banknotes, for example, or inside facts about Indiana political affairs and participants. He could and did read newspapers and listen to speeches to acquire a sense of public opinion in a general way, but talking face-to-face with people in various circumstances, both people he knew and strangers, supplied a more concrete sense of the way people judged the economic, political, religious, and cultural issues of the day.

During the presidential election of 1844, for example, while Mickle was delivering Democratic stump speeches in southern New Jersey, while Weaver was designing a banner for the Whigs in Philadelphia, and Carpenter was avidly following news of Whig successes in the press, Fletcher was warily observing the political excitement in central Indiana. Although he

"Arguing the Point, Settling the Presidency," by Arthur Fitzwilliam Tait, dated 1854, is set in New York State's Adirondacks in the fall. For men it was attractive and legitimate to interrupt work to socialize over politics. The basket of kindling chips and the split wood lying on the ground suggest that the farmer was getting wood for his wife's cooking when he was distracted by a visiting hunter carrying a recent newspaper. This scene is emblematic of the separate spheres of work and sociability for men and women that channeled the diffusion of information.
Courtesy of the R. W. Norton Art Gallery, Shreveport, La.

was a committed Whig, Fletcher believed that "the subleaders of each party here are mostly unworthy men," and he was troubled by the demagogy and partisanship that seemed to prevail.[82] Traveling in the neighborhood around Indianapolis in July 1844, he noted "nearly every house had a pole erected—Ash is Whig—Hickory Democrat or Polk."[83] By the autumn "evry child we met would hollow for Polk & Dallas or Clay & Frelinghyson. . . . Evry wagoner & at evry cabin from men women & childrin I received the salute as I have in all my travels this fall—Huza for Clay or huza for Polk. Teamsters have it written on the wagon covers. . . . Evryman has his mind made up yes evry woman & child."[84] Because Fletcher was skeptical of the motives and merits of both parties, he found such full-scale partisanship worrisome, especially after reading press accounts of the riots in Philadelphia that summer; emotional partisanship might lead to public disorders. It was here, through such direct, face-to-face experiences that Fletcher became more fully informed about the character of the body politic.

Because Fletcher, like Mickle, was broadly interested in society he savored information that came to him by chance on the road, such as a brief synopsis of the Shaker religion gleaned from an elderly man, or the description of Missouri supplied by another traveler.[85] Such information was not necessarily rare or even unusual, and Fletcher might have learned as much from a newspaper. But the face-to-face experience added a personal dimension that made an impression. Fletcher, after all, could question his informant so as to satisfy his particular queries. Unlike reading, these encounters were interactive.

It was this interactive aspect of conversations that made them most meaningful. In conversation Fletcher, like Mickle, Weaver, and Carpenter, could measure and clarify personal values in relation to social attitudes. Information was not just exchanged, it was analyzed, evaluated, and incorporated into one's outlook. Fletcher, for example, had a long conversation one afternoon with his former law partner on the relative merits of "riches" as opposed to "a good name." Though their discussion topic has the ring of a debating club exercise in self-culture, it was part of a personal quest for morality among men who had plenty of experience with temptation and who were, indeed, seeking to acquire both riches *and* a good name.[86] On another occasion, when a Methodist clergyman called at his office, Fletcher brought the man home to tea, and was treated to a firsthand account of the recent New York meeting of the Methodist General Conference that had divided over the issue of slavery.[87] Like the younger men, Fletcher continued to turn to newspapers, periodicals, and books for information, though now it was less to "keep up" with or impress others so as to move up in the world, than to satisfy his own curiosity. Indeed as he entered his forty-seventh year he recognized that he was spending less time on work and more time on reading and reflection so as to cultivate his own mind.[88] Fletcher had read Channing's lecture on self-culture less than a year after it appeared and he had taken the message to heart.[89] He did not aim to become a scholar or attain comprehensive knowledge—he hoped within a few years to quit business and "change my pursuits to those [of] agriculture & spend my days in peace"—but he did want to extend his range of experience and deepen his understanding.[90] Reading works in biography, history, and travel, in addition to the Bible and doctrinal and devotional books, exhausted the time this busy man set aside once or twice each week for reading.

Though Fletcher read extensively, completing perhaps a dozen books annually during the mid-1840s, in addition to perusing the *North American Review, The National Intelligencer* (a Whig paper published in Washington), and an Indianapolis paper, he also read intensively and repeatedly in religious works and a few biographies.[91] He dipped into his biographical dictionary frequently, and reread Plutarch's lives. So impressed was he with Plutarch's life of Pelopidas, that after finishing a second reading, he passed it along to his eighteen-year-old son.[92] To enable Fletcher to clarify and organize his knowledge while he was accumulating it, he spent five dollars on *Lyman's Historical Chart; Containing the Prominent Events of the Civil, Religious and Literary History of the World from the Earliest Times to the Present Day,* and put it up in the family sitting room.[93] Fletcher, characteristically, engaged in reading not as an amusing way to pass the time, but for long-term improvement.[94] Through reading he was acquiring knowledge and cultivating wisdom rather than merely consuming ephemeral information.

Lecture-going, such a significant activity for Mickle, Weaver, and Carpenter, played little role in Fletcher's life, though he did attend his church regularly and also took a professional interest in political rallies and campaign speeches. When Fletcher was not at work or engaged in a voluntary service activity like teaching or running his Methodist Sunday school, he tried to stay home. If young men eagerly went out four or five nights each week, Fletcher did not. He preferred to acquire and organize information from reading, not lectures. It was not that he was indifferent to "the power of utterance;" he recognized its importance and only regretted its abuse by practiced orators like the Democrat Lewis Cass.[95] Indeed on his arrival in Indiana, Fletcher had been "difident to the extreme when I first began to speak," though he realized quickly that "a lawyer here must become a good advocate or speaker in public." In contrast to New York and New England, where "any man can be a good lawyer without saying a word," in Indiana he found he was dealing with people who were "bold & independant in their sentiments as to public men or measures." So he developed his own oratorical abilities, particularly honing his skills at "Irony & sarcasm."[96] Now, however, he took a more detached view of public speech; it was a crucial political skill, but not for him a prime source of either advancement or knowledge.

Letters, which were also important to Fletcher, played the same specialized role for him as for others. Most of his correspondence dealt with business or family matters, though the letters he exchanged with his brothers in New York and Virginia also contained descriptions of people and society in Indiana, as well as Fletcher's political views. Though he seldom wrote long, discursive letters to his brothers and adult sons, when he did they had the quality of conversation, or rather monologue, and provided substantial information, albeit from a frankly personal viewpoint. Comparing Fletcher's correspondence of the 1820s with that of the 1840s and 1850s, it appears that even after postal service improved and rates on letters were reduced, so many other vehicles of information had become available to him that the functions of letters were narrower and more specialized. Even in Samuel Sewall's Boston a century-and-a-half earlier, letters had mostly concerned business and personal matters; now they rarely mentioned anything else. By the middle of the 19th century the ways of acquiring or transmitting public and private information were so numerous and inexpensive, that selective and specialized patterns of use were reinforced. The overlap between printing and letters was vanishing as letters became a wholly private medium. Only the overlap between letters and conversation remained. For Fletcher's Indianapolis was no longer on the frontier, and like the rest of the northern states generally, it was integrated into the national information marketplace.

This national marketplace provided a vast spectrum of information possibilities for Mickle, Weaver, Carpenter, and Fletcher—more than they could possibly exhaust. Abundance meant not only that they must allocate their time between the sociability of clubs and conversations, attendance at lectures and performances, and reading, but that they must choose among numerous possibilities within each of these forms. For Mickle and Weaver their Philadelphia location meant that on any given day or evening there were at least several options for each activity. But even for Carpenter, located in an inland village, there were always choices: Should he stay in the shop and read? Should he go to a lecture or a concert? Should he go out visiting, or stop at the printing shop where he could converse with his friends, while also browsing the newspapers? Back home in rural Bernardston there were fewer choices, both because less was going on and because he was constrained by family obligations to do chores and visit with his relatives. Even in Bernardston, however, there was always a variety of reading matter.

The fact that Mickle and Fletcher were wealthy certainly gave them a wider array of choices in the marketplace. In contrast to Weaver and Carpenter, for them cost was not a significant factor, either in attending public performances or in acquiring reading matter. Yet in light of the whole gamut of possibilities, it would be misleading to emphasize wealth as the factor differentiating the experiences of these four men. For insofar as print and public performances were concerned—the mass media—accessibility was their distinguishing feature. Geographical location and wealth made for some differences, and those who produced and marketed information aimed at various segments of the population, but collectively newspapers, magazines, and books, like religious and political oratory and instructive lectures, were common genres aimed towards and available to everyone from the lower middle class of apprentices and artisans up through farmers, merchants and manufacturers, and professionals. All were shopping in the same marketplace, choosing from an often bewildering, repetitious array of possibilities.

Under these circumstances personal preferences were crucial for determining the acquisition of information, though often they remain difficult to explain. There were, of course, practical reasons that influenced Mickle, Weaver, Carpenter and Fletcher to make the choices they did. As one scholar has noted: "Like no other class in history before them, Mid-Victorians dealt in words. . . . Those armed with words would get ahead in the new society; the inarticulate, barely literate, and foreign speaking would not."[97] Evidently, at some point all four of these men were conscious of this reality. For the politically active lawyers Mickle and Fletcher, recognition of this fact shaped their development as they sought to master "the power of utterance" and to make themselves widely informed as well as widely acquainted with other people. In the case of the engraver Matthias Weaver, although the recognition was explicit—"must take care how I express myself in conversation" and "knowledge is the key to distinction"—the practical need to command language was obviously less urgent than the need to achieve a mastery of images through the cultivation of his artistic, spatial, and manual skills. Nevertheless because as a free lance he had to converse with a middle-class, often professional clientele, the self-culture he pursued in reading, lectures, and his library-debating club were all advantageous for his career. For a cabinetmaker's apprentice like Edward Carpenter, extensive reading, attendance at lectures on physiology, or witnessing the debates of a local club—all of which were part of his routine—were hardly central to occupational advancement although, as with Weaver, such activities could enhance his conversation with customers if he became the master of a shop. When Carpenter ultimately left his manual trade to become a retailer of newspapers and periodicals, his experiences with mass communications in fact proved important to his vocation. That preferences were shaped in part by occupational needs is borne out in varying degrees by all four men.

Yet as Carpenter's preferences led him from a skilled manual craft to work as a newsagent, it is clear that the primary rewards of information activities were not material and practical, but psychological. These men read, or listened to lectures, or joined with others to participate in meetings during their discretionary time because, with few exceptions, they found satisfaction in these activities. Mickle and Weaver, who were more self-conscious than the others, said so explicitly in their diaries. And although Fletcher and Carpenter wrote of their feelings less often, their behavior, how they spent their time and money, conveys the same sense. The common thread that runs through all their reactions, from the effusive, vivacious Democrat, Isaac Mickle, to the sober, orderly Whig, Calvin Fletcher, was Channing's most elevated idea of self-culture as the obligation "every man owes to himself, to the unfolding and perfecting of his nature."[98] These information-related activities were a form of socially approved recreation that everyone believed would add to the knowledge, experience, judgment, even wisdom of participants. Words imparted lessons. The drama and musical performances cultivated sensibility. In contrast to such rough recreations as drinking, gambling contests, and fighting, these activities made Mickle, Weaver, Carpenter and Fletcher better people, or so they and millions of others believed.

That such word-centered activities would be socially approved and build self-esteem was partly rooted in the Protestant heritage. When Fletcher was reading the Bible or religious commentaries, and when he or others went to listen to a sermon, this was surely the case. More broadly, the whole pattern of seeking information on one's own through reading, listening, and associational activity can be understood as archetypically Protestant. In addition, however, there were other sources of support for these activities that were specifically connected to early 19th-century America. One was the legacy of the Revolution that had created the ideal of the informed citizen who was knowledgeable about political doctrine and public affairs. Newspaper reading was not merely a pastime; it had become a duty. Writing in the 1780s, Jefferson had maintained that everyone must have "full information of their affairs thro' the channel of the public papers, and . . . those papers should penetrate the whole mass of the people."[99] Civic culture and public policy vigorously endorsed such information-building activities.

At a deeper level the Revolution had unleashed social aspirations that were associated with learning. "The great law of subordination," Daniel Defoe had long since recognized, called for keeping people ignorant; and one opponent of American independence had even argued that popular ignorance was a positive social good, "the only opiate capable" of enabling common folk "to endure the miseries" of life.[100] When republicanism swept this worldview aside, the conviction had grown that everyone should have access to learning; and schools, lyceums, libraries, and debating clubs were the common mechanisms adopted to promote general knowledge. Such learning also connoted gentility and was linked to the spread of genteel social forms across the country, in dress, housing, furnishings, and forms of address, as well as in the multiplication of institutions like the Masonic order, academies, and colleges. This "democratization of gentility" helps to account for the popularity of Lord Chesterfield on the art of conversation and for the need to speak knowledgeably about Cromwell and Napoleon that an engraver such as Weaver felt.[101] By engaging in information activities Americans were leveling up, bringing themselves up towards a traditional standard of gentility. The alternative, to close themselves off and to avoid refined sociability, books and periodicals, lectures and public meetings, was to become an ignorant, disreputable boor.[102] In such a social and cultural environment Mickle, Weaver, Carpenter, and Fletcher eagerly embraced the information opportunities surrounding them.

In some ways the abundance of communication activities and the extent of participation made for a truly democratizing experience. The scene on an American canal boat or railroad car of the 1840s where "a great many newspapers are pulled out, and a few of them are read. [Where] everybody talks to you, or anybody else who hits his fancy . . . [where] politics are much discussed, so are banks, so is cotton," suggests their impact.[103] Compared with colonial America, the access to information that a cabinetmaker's apprentice enjoyed, notwithstanding his minor social status and peripheral geographic location, was egalitarian. The fact that there was no great gap between what Carpenter could read on a Sunday in the Greenfield cabinet shop, and what was available to a wealthy and prominent community leader like Fletcher, or a cultivated Philadelphian like Mickle, is one measure of the democratizing consequences of mass communications. Similarly, while the differences in reading among the four men were significant, they were not of the same order as the division between ordinary people of the colonial era—men who read common texts like the Bible intensively—and the colonial elite—the Sewalls and the Byrds who enjoyed access to an extensive range of publications.[104] By the 1840s it was evident that the communications revolution had confused old distinctions between common local folk and genteel cosmopolitans.

Yet the diaries also reveal that the new plethora of mass communications may have created some distinctions and perpetuated old ones. For if local magnates were no longer the chief opinion leaders in their communities and the principal gatekeepers regarding news of the world beyond, they were replaced not by a wholly popular, democratic information system but by a new, impersonal, market-oriented elite that defined the substance of public information in all its forms, oral and printed.[105] Moreover the new communications environment in which all were encouraged to participate created a kind of information competition in which people of education, wealth, and social rank enjoyed distinct advantages. The apprentices with whom Carpenter associated could only suggest titles of popular novels for him to read; and novel-reading would not advance Carpenter's cabinet-making career or enhance his social status. But Mickle's colleagues and companions could advise him on readings that would not only cultivate his mental abilities but increase his professional and social position. While people like him and Fletcher, who were secure in their sense of social importance, could converse on an equal footing with great men—a governor, a senator, an ex-president, a philosopher—people like Carpenter, and probably Weaver as well, would always feel themselves outside the circle of communication privilege. They might read the same newspapers and hear the same speeches, but, when it came to face-to-face encounters, social rank counted. Who you were remained at least partly a function of who and what you knew. The information revolution had opened up a competition for knowledge to multitudes but not on an equal basis.

Still, notwithstanding the existence of inequalities, the generous access to information was exhilerating. Not only did it build a sense of urbane self-assurance, it also bred the feeling of independence. Instead of being obviously and directly dependent on public officials and social superiors for information about the world beyond one's community, men could acquire information on their own in the marketplace, more or less on an equal basis. To choose what information one wanted, as well as when and in what form to acquire it, strengthened one's sense of autonomy.

Choosing the medium as well as the message was all-important. True, the information conveyed in a speech might be accurately recorded in a newspaper; but to listen to a speech amidst a multitude of spectators was different than reading a newspaper report. Content did not necessarily vary from one medium of information to another, but orations, lectures, and performances, like clubs, sociability, and reading were different kinds of experiences. Reading, though it could be a social activity, was usually a solitary experience, a form of private escape from the sociability that went with living and working in close quarters. Conversely, the other information forms provided an escape from solitude as well as the constraints of household and family society. Because temperaments, like occupations, social ranks, and family situations varied, one of the attractions of the comprehensive information market was that it provided an all-embracing array of possibilities respecting the form and content of information experience. Individuals could vary their personal mixture of one-to-one or small group conversations with larger group activities in both formal and informal settings. They could be passive spectators or active participants according to their inclinations. The comprehensive information marketplace provided opportunities for seeking solitude or company in many frameworks.

What is especially striking about the universe of leisure activities in which these four men dwelled is the extent to which word-centered activities dominated. Was this because, as one scholar has argued "Mid-Victorians taught that words liberated the nature of a self by bringing it to consciousness?"[106] For Mickle, Weaver, Carpenter, and Fletcher it appears that information-related activities possessed just such a power for self-realization, for self-culture. Perhaps this was why, as Tocqueville observed, the white American, even the pioneer, "wears the clothes and talks the language of the town." Maybe this was the reason that when an American, a Calvin Fletcher, "a very civilized man prepared for a time to face life in the forest," he brought "his Bible, ax, and newspapers."[107] The "power of utterance" and literacy were not merely necessary technical skills, they were crucial to the identity of a free man. They revoked "the great law of subordination," and permitted the fulfillment of liberty. For many women of the era, one scholar maintains, "cultivation of the mind [w]as the great key to freedom."[108] So it was also for northern white men, who not only believed that the welfare of the republic depended on their exertions, but that their own self-worth required being informed. By the 1840s choosing when and how to acquire information was essential for free Americans.

Chapter 10

The Dynamics of Contagious Diffusion: The Battles of Lexington and Concord, George Washington's Death, and the Assassination of President Lincoln, 1775–1865

In early America information usually passed along well-worn paths. Routine relationships of neighborhood and family, of occupation and social circle, both defined what information was worthy of attention and also provided its conduits. Whether the subject concerned politics, commerce, or salvation, for Samuel Sewall and William Byrd in the early 18th century as well as for people like Sarah and Calvin Fletcher, Isaac Mickle, and Lucy Breckinridge in the mid-19th century, the acquisition and further dissemination of information was predictable, tied as it was not only to one's geographic location but to one's social milieu and aspirations. Although direct observation permitted everyone to be informed about the weather no matter their age, gender, or social rank, most other kinds of information were less available and usually possessed only limited audiences. Even the homilies delivered from the pulpit, although aimed at people of all conditions, could touch only those who were pious enough to attend and sufficiently alert to listen. Information did not radiate uniformly across the flat surface of a still pond. Rather, it moved slowly or swiftly in streams that could be broad or narrow, straight or crooked, marked out as they were according to the prevailing cultural values and institutions of the social order, which reflected its economy, politics, and technology.

But if information ordinarily moved within customary channels limited by the pace of commerce and printing, there were exceptional circumstances

' Stop Major ! I'll give you a ride.' —
' Cant stop ; got an express for the Gineral.'

Express Election

Here the close connections between several communication means are fancifully pre-
sented as an express rider, whose horse is injured, runs off to deliver a specially printed
newspaper with election results. A U.S. mail coach, following its appointed schedule
and route, is too slow for the messenger. All parties are shouting to each other. The
woodcut comes from Seba Smith's The Life and Writings of Major Jack Downing
(Boston, 1833).
Courtesy of the American Antiquarian Society

when it overflowed such channels, racing from person-to-person and place-
to-place and touching people of every description. News of war and peace,
of epidemic diseases, of disastrous fires and sensational crimes provoked
such general concern that this information spread like a contagion from
person-to-person, almost irrespective of social roles and relationships. In
any given locality months or even years might pass between such events, but
they were frequent enough to touch every adult life. Whether it was news of
the great fire, the smallpox epidemic or word of French and Indian attacks in
Samuel Sewall's Boston, or the shocking Purinton murders that brought
hundreds to witness the grisly aftermath in Martha Ballard's Hallowell, or
General Lee's surrender at Appomattox in Lucy Breckinridge's Virginia,
sooner or later information of such an event reached everyone.

In most cases the spatial limits of contagious diffusion were set by perceptions of relevance that often depended on one's proximity to an event. A fire
in Boston or a murder in Maine was a matter of general concern to anyone
within a day's journey of the scene, but interest and hence diffusion of the

information was attenuated by distance, so that west and south of the Hudson River these events might disappear from general attention. Even more than proximity, however, the extent of contagious diffusion depended on perceived relevance. In the 1790s there was keen general interest in New York City when word arrived that yellow fever had broken out in Philadelphia not simply because it was nearby and New Yorkers were closely linked to Philadelphians, but owing to the recognition that New York City was almost equally vulnerable to the epidemic disease and was subject to infection from the Pennsylvania capital.[1]

In the cases we will be examining here—the Battles of Lexington and Concord in 1775, the death of George Washington in 1799, and the assassination of President Lincoln in 1865—the territorial reach of the contagious diffusion of information was national precisely because information on these events was widely understood to be pertinent to public life, while also possessing a powerful human dimension that gave each event personal as well as public importance. Proximity played a role, especially in disseminating information on the Battles of Lexington and Concord, but it was the national relevance of these events that made them so distinctive and so illuminating for understanding the ways in which the diffusion of information were changing in the century beginning with the American Revolution. In 1775 word-of-mouth transmission together with signed, handwritten messages furnished the primary means of spreading information, with print—newspapers and broadsides—playing only a secondary role.[2] But by 1865 changes in society, coupled with the development of the telegraph, had made print so swift, authoritative, and ubiquitous, that it assumed a primary role. The age of impersonal mass communication had arrived.

I

The diffusion of information regarding the Battles of Lexington and Concord was at once contagious, spreading spontaneously from person-to-person and place-to-place, and prearranged and channeled through patriot networks. As a result word of the bloody conflict moved with a rapidity, social penetration, and territorial reach never before witnessed in colonial America. Indeed for white people from Maine to Georgia no event was more interesting to more people in the 18th century than the beginning of active hostilities with Britain. The diffusion of this news prefigured the thrust of key 19th-century developments, when speed, penetration, and reach would become hallmarks of American information diffusion.

The backbone of diffusion in this case was the patriot network of minutemen and Committees of Correspondence, and it began on April 18 with Paul Revere's famous "one, if by land, and two, if by sea" signal lanterns in the belfry high above Boston's Old North Church.[3] That evening, an hour after the typical nine o'clock New England curfew bell, Dr. Joseph Warren, a leading patriot and member of the province's revolutionary Committee of Safety, asked Revere and William Dawes to ride by different routes to Lexington in order to warn Samuel Adams and John Hancock that the British would soon be marching to capture them and the patriot military stores at Concord. Revere rowed across the harbor to Charlestown where, after learning that the signal telling the army's path was two lanterns indicating the shorter northern route, he mounted a fast horse and sped off with the message. His first destination was Medford, some eight miles to the northwest, and when he arrived there after midnight he roused the captain of the minutemen. Then he set off for Lexington, eight miles further west, stopping to alert nearly every family along the way until he reached Parson Jonas Clarke's house where he awakened Adams and Hancock and handed them Warren's written message. He was soon joined by his fellow express-rider, Dawes, who had taken the southern route. After a rest, they set out to alarm Concord, which Dawes and a local physician, Samuel Prescott, succeeded in doing after Revere was intercepted by a British patrol, manhandled, and turned back.[4] By this time it was daylight and information on the march and supposed objectives of the redcoats was spreading both contagiously and by design as guns and church bells rang out and drums and volunteer messengers called minutemen to arms. By noon the people of every household within twenty miles knew that a confrontation was at hand.

What happened next—the skirmish between British troops and the Lexington minutemen, the march to Concord and the haphazard destruction of supplies, followed by an engagement with the Concord militia that ended in a torturous, bloody British withdrawal back to Boston—became known as the Battles of Lexington and Concord. By nightfall on April 19, 1775, word of these battles, elaborated with casualty statistics and accounts of atrocities, was moving across the landscape both spontaneously and by design. The information was carried mostly by word of mouth, though also in private letters and official patriot reports that were being carried south, both to the Continental Congress sitting at Philadelphia, and beyond to Maryland, Virginia, and the Carolinas. Within a day or two, rival loyalist and patriot versions were dispatched to London in a race to achieve maximum political influence.

The pace at which news of the battle spread from town to town and colony to colony was unprecedented.[5] On April 20, people in Maine and Connecticut began to learn of the event; the news reached New York City on April 23, and Philadelphia the next day, only five days after the battle. It took another five days to reach the Virginia capital at Williamsburg and ten days more to arrive in Charleston, South Carolina, about 1000 miles south of Boston. Since patriots sent no express to Savannah, Georgia, and contact with Charleston was relatively infrequent though it was only one hundred miles further south, its people learned of the event almost three weeks after that by a report arriving by ship from New York City. Still, by the end of May, all of the colonies' thirty-seven newspapers had printed accounts of the battle.[6] By contemporary standards the speed and extent of the diffusion was remarkable.

Yet the three-week lag between the arrival of the news in Charleston and in Savannah, the former an integral part of the patriot network, the latter a loyalist stronghold, reveals two central reasons why the information moved so rapidly through most of the colonies—patriot alarm systems and partisan sympathies. The first sped the news across long distances, and the second spread it through the population. The sense that everyone must respond actively to the event accelerated the contagious diffusion of information and misinformation about the battle.

First of all, reports of the battle were passed to the insurgent leaders in each colony by patriot express riders in order to mobilize political support. Beginning with Committee of Safety member Joseph Palmer's message composed at ten o'clock in the morning on April 19 at Watertown just west of Cambridge, in which the encounter at Lexington was reported, a series of accounts inviting assistance were sent by chains of express riders. Tradition has it that Israel Bissel covered the distance to Worcester, thirty-six miles west of Watertown, in just two hours and that when he reached the meeting house his horse dropped dead from exhaustion.[7] Subsequently the pace, while rapid, was less frenzied and riders stopped long enough so that copies of the report could be endorsed by members of local Committees of Correspondence or other officials so as to assure their colleagues in the next town that the message was authentic. In addition transcriptions were made for further distribution before a fresh horse, and sometimes a fresh rider, resumed the express journey. The copy of Palmer's alarm that reached Elizabeth Town, New Jersey, on the evening of April 23 had been forwarded through eleven communities before the Committee there sent it on. The rider from New York to Philadelphia traveled all night, stopping at New Brunswick, Princeton, and Trenton before making his final push.[8] As there was nothing at all secret in the report, thousands of people learned its contents along the way, well before it arrived in Philadelphia, for express riders shared the news at each tavern and stable where they stopped, and local patriots immediately rushed it into print—as early as April 21 in Portsmouth, New Hampshire, the next day in Providence, Rhode Island, and the day after that in New York City.[9] Knowledge that the battle had occurred was "melancholy" news, but it did relieve the tension of waiting for a resolution of the imperial crisis, and it was greeted with a certain expectancy by patriots, just as people with loyalist leanings responded with gloomy foreboding.[10]

These responses—energetic action on the one hand, distress and depression on the other—seem to have influenced the spontaneity of the diffusion significantly. For the loyalist-leaning Ashley Bowen in Marblehead, some thirty miles from the scene of the action, word arrived on the day of the battle, but he was inclined to dismiss it. "A hubbub as no truth goes. A hubbub about soldiers. News from afar talks of war," he noted, but he did not drop his tools and hurry off to tell others or to march to battle; he went on repairing the "schooner *Patty*'s blocks."[11]

The reactions of patriots were radically different. On April 20 a school teacher, Paul Litchfield, in Scituate, Massachusetts, was roused before daylight to hear the news and "ordered to appear in arms immediately."[12] Isaac Hasey, a parson in Lebanon, Maine, was awakened at four o'clock the same morning to learn "news of ye Regulars fighting." To his mind this was "good news" and he busied himself to assist in mustering "ye Minute Men" to march the next day.[13] Already men who lived nearby had entered the fray. A characteristic report came from James Stevens, an Andover, Massachusetts, carpenter, who said that on April 19 "a bout seven aclok we had alarum that the Reegelers was gon to Conkord[;] we gathered to the meting hous & then started for Concord."[14] His experience was repeated by thousands of tradesmen and farmers who, like James Parker of Shirley, were armed and marching by afternoon.[15] Such patriots made the British march back to Boston an almost continual ambush.

Farther away, where it took longer for word of the fighting to penetrate, the news was gradually confirmed as more and more information became available. The experiences of James Jeffrey, a traveler from Albany to Salem, reveal the mixture of system and spontaneity that was characteristic of this episode in contagious diffusion. Word of the battle caught up with Jeffrey on April 22 at Young's tavern in Great Barrington, about 140 miles west of Boston, where he "heard that an express came up yesterday which brot in account of a scurmish between some of the regular troops and some of the country people."[16] That evening when he stopped some fifteen miles further east at Spring's tavern in Greenwood he had "a confirmation of the skirmish, with this addition, that the Regulars were drove back from Lexington to Boston and that they went out to stop Handcock & Adams from going to the Congress at Philadelphia & to destroy magazines that were form-[in]g."[17] The next morning as Jeffrey set out for Springfield he was joined by "two men who were going to Roxberry or Cambridge to hear particulars of the engagement," and along the way they heard "various reports." At Springfield on April 24 Jeffrey breakfasted with "Adams the postman" who was coming north from Hartford and who filled in everyone on activities at the Connecticut capital. By the time Jeffrey set off again he was part of a company of five men, "three from Connecticut & one Docr. Bennet from Birkshire county all after news." As they traveled they met many returning minutemen, indeed they found "the roads very full of travellers."[18] The next morning when they stopped to refresh themselves at Worcester they ran into John Hancock and Samuel Adams who were on their way to Philadelphia and whose passage through the countryside as Revolutionary celebrities lent further immediacy and sense of connection to the unfolding story.

People who lived in hamlets and farms isolated from the principal roads learned of events more slowly, but the circulation of soldiers, officials, and persons engaging in ordinary farming, commercial, and family errands would spread information about the great events to virtually everyone, male and female, young and old. Typically it was husbands who brought the information into the family, either because they were notified as part of the minutemen's alarm, or because it was they who most often left the farm premises on routine business. In the Connecticut River Valley at Hadley, one hundred miles west of Boston, Mrs. Elizabeth Phelps noted on Sunday, April 23, that her husband was setting off "for Brookfield as a post, to hear what News, for last Wednesday the Troops and our men had a Battle, numbers lost on both sides, but it seems as if we were most favored."[19] By this time, Sunday, it appears that everyone in New England had heard something about the battle. Indeed it was because Hadley officials knew the bare facts and wanted to know more, that after church meeting they had asked Charles Phelps to make the twenty-five-mile ride to Brookfield on the Worcester-Springfield road to pick up the latest news. His wife, kept at home by her domestic role and responsibilities, responded to the call for action by issuing a prayer that expressed characteristic female concerns: "O most gracious Lord, save from the spilling of human Blood, pray save Thy people."[20] A few days earlier the genteel Cambridge spinster Dorothy Dudley expressed the same kind of humane concern when she noted that "several of our brave Cambridge men are killed. Mrs. Hicks sent her eldest boy to look for his father as night came on. He found him lying dead by the roadside, and near him Mr. Moses Richardson and Mr. William Marcy."[21] To her the battle was no exciting abstraction; it was painfully concrete. A concentration on the same kind of particular, personal information—"Who do I know that suffered?"—was manifested by Mrs. Experience Wright Richardson, a Sudbury grandmother who like Dudley lived near the battle site and was, in addition, the mother of one of the participants: "not only Minnetmen but almost all our men took up their armes & marched there & a dreadful fight they had . . . & some of our men wear killed it is said about forty in all & two that belong to this part of our town." For the moment she could only pray that her son Josiah was not one of them.[22] Such displays of piety and concern for the suffering that the battle created were not, of course, exclusively female; but as with accidents and other calamities, they were more characteristic of women than men. Ultimately the information most relevant to women's experience was not battlefield action but the caring for the wounded, the orphans, and the widows while simultaneously managing household affairs. In cases like this, as with any other kind of information, people paid special attention to news they found pertinent to their own concerns as they passed messages to others.

As distance separated people from the immediacy of the event the intensity of their responses did not necessarily subside. New Haven, Connecticut, was a patriot community, so although no minutemen dropped what they were doing to rush off to battle, the information was sufficiently upsetting on Friday, April 21, the day it arrived. A Yale student, Ebenezer Fitch, noted it was "impossible to pursue our studies to any profit."[23] The following week in the politically divided city of New York a recent Moravian immigrant, the Reverend Evald Gustav Schaukirk who was himself aloof from politics, observed there was "commotion and confusion." Word-of-mouth reports coupled with newspaper stories had brought "trade and public business" to a standstill and "fear and panic seized many of the people, who were prepared to move to the country."[24] If there was fighting around Boston, they reasoned, New York might be next.

Reactions in the Virginia interior the following week were more muted, perhaps because the British presence was more remote and no local consequences were immediately apparent. A Scots immigrant physician, Robert Honeyman, was traveling from Dumfries to Falmouth, Virginia, when he stopped at a tavern where "at Dinner heard the dreadful news . . . by express."[25] The next day near Fredricksburg just down the road, another recent Scots immigrant, the plantation tutor John Harrower, picked up "by an express from Boston" an early, incomplete report of the battle.[26] Though neither of these Scotsmen, the one a passerby and the other a servant, had any business with the news—they were not local landowners and voters—the express rider's message came to them as public news accessible to all, just as James Jeffrey had found out at Young's tavern in Great Barrington, Massachusetts. When the same news reached the capital at Williamsburg the next evening it generated a great stir, and on the following day William Purdie published an extra of his *Virginia Gazette* which, it was said, was excitedly read on the streets. Its closing words were: "The sword is now drawn, and God knows when it will be sheathed."[27] News of such a sensational event moved more swiftly by word of mouth than print, but sketchy oral reports also aroused a hunger for the fuller accounts that newspapers could provide, and supplied copy for the press while stimulating a wider audience for newspapers' narrow columns.

Purdie's final invocation—"the sword is now drawn"—points to a further characteristic often shared by word-of-mouth and written reports; they expressed an interpretive position. For although the message composed by Joseph Palmer on April 19 at Watertown to be carried south by expresses was a brief statement of fact, the message that was circulated became increasingly partisan. "The Regular Troops began the Quarrel by firing on our Men," a New Englander noted in words that were much the same as many other Patriots' accounts of what "they" did to "our" people.[28] Atrocity stories, though often founded on verifiable facts, took on a life of their own. Shots fired at the British soldiers from residential houses "so enraged" them, one of their officers admitted, "that they forced open many of the houses from which the fire proceeded, and put to death all those found in them."[29] Not surprisingly, as news of these actions circulated, it became impossible to convey the information without interpretive embellishment. Before a week had gone by, a Salem deacon was publicly lamenting in the *Essex Gazette* that "the savage Barbarity exercisd upon the Bodies of our unfortunate Brethren who fell, is almost incredible. Not content with shooting down the unarmed[,] aged and infirm[,] they disregarded the Cries of the wounded, killing them without mercy and mangling their Bodies in the most shocking manner."[30] Having heard no reports of patriot atrocities—these were circulating among loyalists in Boston—he concluded that "our victorious Militia . . . breathed higher Sentiments of Humanity" because, unlike the British, they were "listening to the Merciful Dictates of the Christian Religion."[31] Here, as was often the case, the messenger expressed his own sentiments in shaping the message that he passed on to others.

It was inevitable, of course, that in extended chains of communication where much of the information flow relied on word-of-mouth exchanges, some partisan distortion should occur. Indeed it was an appreciation of the fallibility of oral messages the led to the use of expresses who bore written accounts whose relative objectivity and consistency across hundreds of miles supplied a framework of solid information on which to act. It was this concern for accuracy, not mere curiosity, that led many communities, such as Hadley to send riders like Charles Phelps out to bring back information. Indeed at Concord on the very morning of the battle when, at Revere's direction, Dr. Samuel Prescott rode into town with the alarm, even though town leaders knew and trusted Prescott they immediately dispatched "several posts . . . that returning confirmed ye Account of ye Regulars arrived at Lexington, & that they were on their way to Concord."[32] After the false alarm of September 1774, when thousands of Massachusetts and Connecticut minutemen had marched for Boston in response to an erroneous report of a British attack on the Massachusetts capital, local officials were keenly aware of the need to verify information that called for an instant military response. On that earlier occasion, because the alarm had not been confirmed at its source, the false news had spread via "authenticated," written reports all the way to the Congress at Philadelphia.[33] Now, in April 1775, having lived through a fall and winter of exaggerated rumors, such a mistake would not be repeated. Though anxiety and partisanship would lead people to embroider accounts of the battle, because of its military and political implications accuracy was joined to speed in spreading news of the Lexington-Concord story.

II

Word of the peaceful death of George Washington, while arresting and dismaying to vast numbers of Americans throughout the new republic, possessed no such urgency or momentous consequences as the Battles of Lexington and Concord, and so generated much less excitement. Washington was, after all, in his sixty-eighth year and living in retirement, so the primary significance of his passing was sentimental. At the same time, because of his uniquely heroic stature in every region of the United States, the event was more than a matter of sentimental human interest. The death of Washington became the occasion for a grand expression of national consciousness. Indeed it became an episode of hitherto unmatched didactic proportions that churchmen, public officials, and Washington's fellow Freemasons employed to advance their own visions of America. Considering the hundreds of civic processions it generated and the vast body of prose and verse eulogies that swiftly made their way into print, not to mention the barrels of souvenir crockery and handkerchiefs that English trinket-makers hastily imprinted with suitable memorials and shipped to the United States, it appears that in important respects Washington's death on December 14, 1799, was the new nation's first great media event.

The conjunction between the actual event—the reality of an old man's passing—and what was made of it rhetorically offers a revealing comparison to the Lexington-Concord story of a quarter-century before. In contrast to the 1775 battle, Washington's death had no concrete, practical consequences for the vast majority of Americans who had no personal knowledge of the great Revolutionary War leader and first President. Unlike news of smallpox or yellow fever, of Indian raids or war with Britain, the peaceful departure of the retired hero could only touch them psychologically, and then only in proportion to their own national, patriotic sense. Moreover since it was no one's particular responsibility to inform Americans of this event, the speed, territorial reach, and social penetration of this information explains much about the market-driven workings of America's information system at the opening of the 19th century. For the great man's death supplied rich opportunities, not only for printers whose presses worked overtime to satisfy the demand for information concerning Washington, but also for those groups and individuals who sought to promote a political or religious message, or simply to advance their own public reputation.

The principal networks that carried this melancholy news to the far corners of the union were commercial and political. Letters written by merchants, and emanating from Alexandria, Virginia, the commercial center nearest to Washington's home at Mount Vernon, were the primary means whereby the information of Washington's sudden illness and death was communicated to Williamsburg, Baltimore, Philadelphia, and beyond. The contents of these letters, sent variously to other merchants, members of Congress, and to several newspaper editors, immediately entered word-of-mouth networks and were soon printed in regular editions of newspapers. Because the early information was so terse, and the facts would never be much elaborated even in newspaper accounts two weeks later, there was no need for hurried broadsides. In urban centers local officials at once directed that church bells be tolled in Washington's honor and so, hours or even days before the first locally printed newspaper accounts appeared, the inhabitants of Charlestown, Richmond, Philadelphia, New York, and Boston, as well as lesser towns like Norwich, Connecticut, and Salem, Massachusetts, were informed that Washington was dead. As had always been true in the past, word-of-mouth messages from known, reliable people were the fastest medium for transmitting information and fully adequate for a short, simple fact like this one.

Yet in the case of Washington's death newspaper reports were much more important than they had been in 1775, chiefly because here there was no mechanism of Committees of Correspondence, express riders, and militia officials concerned with this news. As a result, for many communities it was the "early" Philadelphia or New York newspaper accounts of December 18 and 19—not letters or express riders—that confirmed word-of-mouth stories and so enabled officials to act publicly to notify inhabitants. At Norwich, Connecticut, a minor port ten miles up river from New London, on the morning of December 23 a local gentleman returning from New York City brought "the melancholy tidings" in a New York paper dated December 19. The newspaper report was conclusive because it printed copies of a Virginia congressman's letter dated at Philadelphia and two letters from Alexandria merchants.[34] Evidently the same or a similar report served to inform the inhabitants of Hartford, where the publisher of the *American Mercury* also reprinted a letter from Alexandria. Even Salem, a major port whose merchants traded with Philadelphia and Baltimore, received word in the same way on December 23, when "Capt. Odell, who arrived here last night from Newyork per stage" supplied local leaders with an "extract from Mr. Snowden's Newyork paper of the 19th inst."[35] For New England it is evident that clippings traveled just as fast or faster than personal letters and served to authenticate oral reports. Indeed the *Columbian Centinel and Massachusetts Federalist* of Boston, which had access to an original Alexandria letter, only published the news on the day after the *Salem Gazette* printed the conclusive New York report.[36] In the South the pattern of reporting from Richmond to Charleston to Savannah was much the same, with newspaper clippings overtaking personal reports. North and south in communities that did not lie along the main stage and postal routes—where most Americans lived—it was word-of-mouth reports, ultimately confirmed by news accounts, that informed the general population of the news.

Perhaps because Washington was a private citizen and his death was not at first a public event, technically speaking, merchants as often as public officials took the lead in organizing the memorial ceremonies that people all over America craved to honor the hero, signalize his virtues, and to assuage their sense of loss. Linked as merchants were to newspapers as subscribers, advertisers, and frequent suppliers of extra-local information, they exercised a central role in the dissemination of public information and commonly acted as self-appointed community leaders in areas that lay outside the pre-

scribed duties of public officials. Although in Salem it was the town selectmen that took the lead on the evening that news arrived, ordering that the
next day church bells toll from sunrise through sunset and that shops close
from three to four in the afternoon while guns were fired on the town
common at one minute intervals during that hour of reflection, in Baltimore
and Hartford it was local merchants who called meetings to arrange tributes.
As the new year of 1800 began, crepe stocks all over America were depleted
so as to festoon public and private buildings and, in some towns, to supply
men and women with black ribbons to wear for the thirty-day mourning
period recommended by Congress.[37] Private emotional responses merged
with the culture of civic virtue to generate an unprecedented memorial
festival across the nation.

Information touching on Washington, his career, his virtues, and his admonitions to present and future generations, lay at the heart of this outpouring of memorials, and the chief consequence of his passing was a torrent of
exhortations to civic commitment united with appeals for public and private
morality. The preferred media were the eulogies of clergymen and politicians, public processions in which men of all occupations participated, and
print—newspapers, pamphlets and, to a lesser extent, books. During the
first eight weeks of the new century, from January 1, 1800, through Washington's birthday on February 22, the day Congress and President Adams recommended for memorial observances, reminders of the fallen leader's courage, sagacity, and virtue were everywhere.

In hundreds of communities memorial or funeral processions were staged
together with public eulogies, often the first public oratory other than sermons ever witnessed in the locale.[38] Since such elaborate rites were not held
everywhere, interested people traveled to attend the ceremonies in neighboring communities. Sally Ripley, the fifteen-year-old daughter of a prominent
Greenfield, Massachusetts, merchant and official, accompanied her father
when he journeyed to the adjoining town of Deerfield to witness the memorial
procession held in that small agricultural and commercial center.[39] In rural
Pennsylvania people traveled to combined English and German ceremonies,
so broad was the interest in participating in commemorative occasions.[40]

In towns where there were Masonic lodges—virtually all port towns and
many inland commercial and political centers—costumed members of Washington's rapidly expanding fraternity marched displaying the symbols of their
ostentatiously secret, quasi-religious "craft."[41] Accounts of these processions, as well as those in which Masons were merely one group among many,
were subsequently published in black-bordered newspaper columns that also
supplied their readers with detailed accounts of Washington's actual funeral,
and a generous listing of participants in each rite. Synopses of eulogies were
often included in press accounts, while more than 230 separate editions of
these orations were published in pamphlet form.[42] The market for printed
memorials of the late hero—uplifting, consoling, didactic—was unprece-

dented and made such items the best-selling ephemera of 1800. Collections of Washington's own few writings, with titles like *Washington's Legacies* or *A Nation in Tears: Memory of Washington,* were published in book form and, as with many newspapers, included his farewell address, his letter to John Adams accepting command of the army in 1798 at the time of the XYZ affair, and his last will and testament. In addition, numerous collections of dirges, hymns, and anthems suitable for Washington memorials were rushed into the marketplace.[43]

Information was complemented by images to satisfy the appetite for memorabilia. While much of this material was imported, American-made bas-reliefs of Washington "in imitation of White Marble, framed and glazed," were sold. Among the other commercial offerings that appeared within weeks of Washington's passing were Washington lockets "for the Ladies," Washington medals in gold, silver, and "composition," the latter intended "to imprint on the Minds of All, especially of Youth, the Memory and important Services of him who bought our Freedom" and suitable for "Children of all Classes."[44] By February 1800 Washington's death was no longer news, but people were reluctant to let go of it, and printers catered to this demand by selling Washington-related publications and images until several weeks after Washington's birthday, when attention to the departed leader finally subsided.

Yet several months later, when all the eulogies were past, there was a remarkable echo of the Washington mourning festival in the abortive slave revolt led by Gabriel Prosser at Richmond, Virginia. In his oft-published last will and testament Washington had implicitly repudiated slavery by providing for the manumission of all his slaves.[45] Whether the stalwart and literate rebel Prosser had read any of these Washington memorials may only be guessed; but his declaration to the court that condemned him suggests that he had, for he echoed the sentiments of the nation's hero:

> I have nothing more to offer [in my defense] than what General Washington would have had to offer, had he been taken by the British and put to trial by them. I have adventured my life in endeavouring to obtain the liberty of my country-men, and am a willing sacrifice to their cause.[46]

Though one cannot be certain of the link, it appears that in Virginia the social penetration of the memorial effusions was so complete that even the slave population—which was never an intended audience—was affected. Reaching from the highest strata of American society to the lowest, knowledge of George Washington's life and death coupled to interpretations of its significance, had captured the American imagination. Sustained on a hitherto unparalleled scale by communication media—a multitude of processions, orations, publications, and visual icons—Americans pressed his memory into patriotic service immediately and massively.

III

Sixty-five years later the spread of information concerning the death of Abraham Lincoln bore obvious similarities to the occasion of Washington's demise. This news also reached everyone in America though, as with the Lexington-Concord story and Washington's death, at an uneven pace; and reactions varied from anger and grief on the one hand to a certain jubilation on the other. In contrast to Washington, Lincoln was a controversial states- man, the active commander-in-chief of the Union army, felled not by the ravages of age in the serenity of retirement, but by a single bullet fired into his brain by a vengeful assassin. In much of the nation Lincoln would swiftly be elevated to the pantheon of American heroes of which Washington was hitherto the sole member. But in Southern and border states public mourn- ing was often perfunctory and news and information concerning Lincoln died out only a little after his corpse was laid to rest.

Because Lincoln was the first president to be murdered in office, his death created the most sensational news story of the century. Bulletins on the attack, on Lincoln's condition, and on the assassins were immediately tele- graphed across thousands of miles so that within just twelve hours of the event, the daily papers of every city from Boston to San Francisco, from Chicago to Saint Louis, featured the story. Raw human interest combined with immediate political consequences to make this a compelling story for whites and blacks, north and south. For the mass media of oratory and print, now highly developed, honed by wartime experience, and organized on a national scale, the Lincoln assassination provided a spectacular occasion for demonstrating the extent and speed of their reach and penetration. To- gether, advanced technology, commercial organization, and social values made Lincoln's death a modern media event, particularly in the Northern states.

It was the telegraph, in conjunction with the newspapers that employed this electronic marvel, that exercised the central, dominant role in conveying the calamitous news to the public.[47] The sole exception was in parts of the collapsing Confederacy, where for over a week the information moved slowly and irregularly, conveyed both as public news and secretly as military intelligence by an occasional express rider.[48] Everywhere else, in Union and border states which were integrated into national communication networks, the early news of the attack on Lincoln on the night of April 14 was followed by word of his death the following morning.

The telegraph carried this news across space, and newspapers placed detailed reports in American homes and stores, hotels and taverns, work- shops and markets, everywhere the printed message could enter the multi- farious networks of face-to-face diffusion. As had always been true, nothing could match the speed of face-to-face transmission within a locality; but unlike spoken reports, newspapers now bore the badge of authoritative

"War News from Mexico," an 1848 painting by the Baltimore native Richard Caton Woodville, illustrates the close connection between the diffusion of information by printed and oral means. The intensity of interest depicted here suggests that the contents of this "Extra" edition will also spread contagiously. Here the news is being read aloud at the entrance of the post office which is located in a hotel. That this political news concerns white men chiefly is suggested by the cluster of eight white men of all ages in the center of the picture. It is also noteworthy that at the periphery a black man and a child are also taking in the information, as is a woman, in shadow, at the open window to the right (only partially visible).

From an engraving, courtesy of the American Antiquarian Society, Worcester, Mass.

confirmation because of their known reliance on telegraph dispatches. Indeed because the first reports of the attack on Lincoln were so confused, the
early editions of some newspapers simply printed the dispatches from Washington verbatim, allowing readers to draw their own conclusions.[49] But unlike the letters from Alexandria, Virginia, merchants that confirmed George
Washington's death and the certified reports of the Battles of Lexington and
Concord that were carried to Congress and beyond, the telegraph bulletins
of 1865 crossed distances more swiftly than word-of-mouth news could possibly travel, carrying their own confirmation of authenticity. And although
within communities most people first heard of the event contagiously by
word of mouth, they then rushed to buy papers and thronged public places
where newspapers were read aloud, seeking to confirm their knowledge and
to acquire additional information.

In cities the combination of the old and new forms of diffusion—tolling
bells and telegraphy—could be so complementary as to intensify the speed
and social penetration of the news. At Worcester, Massachusetts, ninety
years after the express rider Israel Bissel rushed the news of Lexington-
Concord into the village on his dying horse, the city fathers responded with
like urgency when the telegraph clerk informed them of the shocking events
in Washington. As they would have done in the past in the case of fire or
Indian attack, they ordered that church bells be tolled immediately; so at
three o'clock in the morning the predominantly Republican city of 25,000
people was awakened to learn the national news and invited to pray for the
stricken president.[50] Although city leaders in most communities did not see
fit to waken their neighbors so precipitately, by sunrise the news was circulating in every city with a telegraph office.

In Indianapolis, the prominent Republican lawyer Calvin Fletcher was
just "sitting down to breakfast" at six-thirty when one of his adult sons came
in from outdoors "pale & in trouble of countenance & announced the assassination of President Lincoln & Secretary of state, Seward, last night." Later
that day, after Fletcher had read the newspaper reports he noted that "the
scene in W[ashington] cant be described nor the shock on our city & the
whole community in our land as the wires flashes the intelligence over the
land."[51] The precise time at which people learned the news varied according
to household routines, but the circumstances were much the same, with
newspapers confirming and substantiating word-of-mouth reports.

At Germantown, near Philadelphia, the patrician Sidney Fisher was in his
dressing room at eight o'clock when his nine-year-old son knocked at the door
to report "Father, Lincoln is shot." "Nonsense," Fisher rejoined, "how did
you hear that?" "It is true," the boy replied, the servant "Cornelius heard it at
the village. He [Lincoln] was shot because he tried to shoot Seward." This
garbled, oral version was incredible on its face, since Lincoln could not possibly have tried to kill Seward; but a few moments later Fisher's wife came to the
door, asserting from the same source, Cornelius, "that the President had been

"Newsboy Selling New York Herald" is an 1857 work of the New York City painter James Henry Cafferty. This scene of a newsboy, who hawks his papers before a backdrop of over a dozen printed advertisements for the sale of books, dry goods, furs, shoes, and wine, as well as notices for political and theatrical performances, a restaurant, and a lost dog, exemplifies the wide availability of cheap print. The intensity with which the public was being bombarded with printed messages by the 1850s, especially in urban areas, made it imperative for people of all classes to become more selective participants in the information marketplace than ever before.
Courtesy of Lucille and Walter Rubin Collection

killed," and that "she thought the story probable enough." Nevertheless she had immediately sent a servant out for the paper, and so soon after, Fisher recorded, "when I was half dressed, she brought the paper and read to me, half crying & in a tremulous voice, the sad & terrible story."[52] At New York City the gentlemen-politician George Templeton Strong had also been informed of the astonishing news by his early-rising wife who was up supervising the household.[53] In Boston, where the boardinghouse-keeper Susan Forbes learned "the sad tidings" from one of her lodgers, as in other major cities it was the people who were up and out earliest who brought the public news into private dwellings.[54]

But the early reports of Lincoln's shooting and then his death from the wound—two separate stories at first—provoked more public curiosity than they satisfied. Because the news seemed so momentous emotionally and politically—Fisher remarked, "I felt as tho I had lost a personal friend, for indeed I have & so has every honest man in the country," and his wife "said she was as much agitated as if she had lost a relation"—there was an urgent demand for information as well as succor.[55] Who had plotted the crime and with what object, whether they could be captured, and the consequences for the nation were matters of keen public concern. Newspaper publishers, ever eager to satisfy public desires, responded with extra editions, filling their columns with late bulletins, speculation, and commentary on the assassination, the conspiracy, and within a day or so, on the "martyred" Lincoln.

As at Philadelphia, where "the newsboy's cry awoke the people to a knowledge of the tragedy," so were Bostonians, New Yorkers, and Chicagoans informed when "they rose from their beds and read the full details in the morning papers. . . . Businessmen who always take their paper with their coffee, were startled by the news, and hundreds of breakfasts were forgotten." In all the major Union cities the pattern was the same; reports and rumors moved swiftly and contagiously through the population, producing a kind of frenzy for news, so that virtually all business and labor stopped. Incredulous, people went out to seek further information: "The streets [of Chicago] were early filled with anxious faces, the newspaper offices were besieged with inquiries."[56] An "immense crowd" gathered at Wall Street in New York City and in Philadelphia "the crowd on Chestnut Street grew larger minute after minute, until by ten o'clock the thoroughfare was almost impassable." All were eager to get the latest reports as they came from the telegraph, so similar scenes were acted out again and again as "bulletins and extras followed each other in quick, contradictory succession" both fed and fueled public interest.[57]

In New York, as elsewhere, "first emotions were so overpowering that little else could be uttered than . . . exclamations of horror and anguish." Then, wishfully, there "followed a momentary flash of doubt. It might not be true, it might be a hoax, or it might not be so bad as represented. But no, the details were too minute and the confirmations too numerous to admit of any doubt."[58] With each passing hour the conviction spread that the portentous story was true.

In this calamity, face-to-face exchanges assumed an importance reminiscent of the previous century. At Philadelphia it was reported that "two gentlemen conversing together were sure to attract notice, and collect a crowd of listeners eager to learn the sentiments of the speakers or perhaps to gather a crumb of comfort." So intense were people's emotions that they needed to share their thoughts and feelings. In a smaller city, Buffalo, New York, the news had "passed from mouth to mouth until within a space of time almost incredibly short it was diffused over the entire city . . . [and] men stood in knots and conversed about the sad event." Here, as in the great cities, signs of mourning, on persons and on buildings, were everywhere— "from the dwelling of the humblest colored family to the mansion of the most opulent citizen, fluttered the half-mast flag."[59] As acutely stratified and as generally anonymous as American cities had become by 1865 with their tens and hundreds of thousands of inhabitants, the assassination of President Lincoln struck a common chord. It was a sensation of consequence to ragpickers, street urchins, and the penny press crowd no less than for genteel literati and men of leisure like Fisher or merchant princes like Strong.

In the Northern countryside the pattern of diffusion was much the same as in the cities, although the pace was slower, word of mouth played a larger role, and the impact of the telegraph was less immediate. Whereas most everyone in the great cities from Boston to San Francisco knew the basic facts long before noon on Saturday, at Chambersburg, Pennsylvania, less than one hundred miles northwest of Washington, Rachel Cormany, whose husband was off in the army, did not learn the news until the afternoon when "a neighbor came in & told us a dispatch had come" telling of Lincoln's death.[60] Much farther away at Westfield, Vermont, the farmer Don Avery Winslow heard about the assassination the same day, but the word-of-mouth report was not from an authoritative dispatch so, he noted, "I cannot hardly believe it." The next day, Easter Sunday, when he arrived at services he found "the church dressed in mourning." and the president's death was positively "confirmed."[61] Though word had circulated earlier in many rural areas it appears that, as at Westfield, Vermont, and Tioga County, New York, it was only at Sunday church meetings, that positive, verified information was disseminated.[62]

The impact of the news and the appetite for more was much the same in rural as in urban locales. Just as Elizabeth Fisher, the Philadelphia lady, had suffered real grief from the death of this public figure, so too did the Chambersburg housewife who confessed she felt "like weeping over the nation's loss."[63] And at Pittsfield, Vermont, two village stores—the rural equivalent of New York's Wall Street—were filled all day with "the conversation of the village loafers and customers about the martyred President."[64] Here there were no telegraph dispatches and no extra editions, but the same eagerness

to assimilate the news and to comprehend its implications was characteristic
of Northerners everywhere.

The near uniformity and speed of the contagious diffusion process in the
Northern states is dramatized by the contrast with the ways in which the
news penetrated regions in the South that had so recently been at war with
the Union. Indeed word of Lincoln's murder moved so slowly in much of the
arc from Virginia to Georgia, Louisiana, and Texas, that its spread cannot
be considered uniformly contagious. The universal sense of relevance that
gripped Northerners was understandably absent in localities where immediate military events and information on the collapsing Confederate government commanded public emotional engagement. More to the point, the
Confederate telegraph systems and news organizations were not integrated
with those of the Union and, never as extensive as those of the north to
begin with, like Confederate commercial and transportation links they had
been seriously damaged by the war. Urban centers in particular were crucial
for the rapid diffusion of information, and the destruction in key Southern
cities such as Atlanta, Charleston, Richmond, and Savannah, was devastat-
ing for rapid information diffusion. Consequently cultural, political, and
technical circumstances combined to retard, if not to interrupt, the diffusion
of what was in all sections and among all sorts of people an intrinsically
compelling story. With long-distance communications disrupted and with
the demise of their armies and government taking center stage from courthouse to great house, it was the private tragedies resulting from public
defeat that were crowding in upon white families. The death of the Yankee
president, while keenly interesting, was not truly urgent news, so it did not
always spread contagiously.

The assassination story penetrated the upper South first. At Richmond,
Virginia, the *Whig* announced Lincoln's death, but without particulars, on
Monday, April 17, the same day that the story was carried in the Memphis,
Tennessee, *Bulletin,* and that a central Kentucky farmer, George Richard
Browder heard "the startling news!"[65] The next day, the Raleigh, North
Carolina, *Daily Progress,* carried "the mournful intelligence," but in a brief
item that misstated the date of the murder. Two days later, on April 20, the
story was corrected and a fuller account given in an issue which, in contrast to
Northern papers, did not carry the black borders of mourning.[66] By now, five
days after the news had circulated in places like Cincinnati, Ohio, Madison,
Wisconsin, and Sacramento, California, it was just being communicated to
the people of Charleston, South Carolina, and New Orleans, Louisiana.[67] At
more remote locations it took even longer for news of the enemy president's
death to arrive. In Chester, South Carolina, word was brought on April 22,
and then not as a public report printed in a newspaper or passing by word of
mouth, but as a sealed military dispatch directed to a Confederate general, as
if Lincoln's fate was strategic intelligence of the highest significance. At inland
locations still farther south at Augusta and Macon in Georgia, and at Green-

ville in south central Alabama, and at Houston, Texas, near the Gulf of Mexico, Lincoln's death was not yet current information as late as April 25, a full ten days after inhabitants of the great cities and most of the Northern countryside learned of the event. Within the next several days, however, Lincoln's assassination became common knowledge, interpreted in some Confederate circles as a "foul murder" that would "bring down worse miseries on us," and in others as "righteous retribution," and "one sweet drop among so much that is painful."[68] But whether it was cause for anxiety or solace, news of the assassination lacked the emotional impact it possessed for Yankees, who at some level had a personal identification with their president. To Confederates, Lincoln was an alien, the "black Republican" who had brought misery upon them; and so since they possessed much less emotional stake in his life or death than in the well-being of Confederate troops and of their homeland, even though the assassination news was sensational, it lacked the urgency it possessed for the Union and so moved more slowly through the Confederacy's war-torn communication networks.

In contrast, bells had tolled everywhere in 1800 and word of Washington's passing had spread contagiously because George Washington "belonged" to nearly everyone, even, it seems, to some slaves. In 1865 in the North the division of the nation made Lincoln's murder an even more spectacular occasion for contagious diffusion because of the mutual reinforcement of political sentiments and circumstances with the well-oiled wartime mechanisms for transmitting information. But in the Confederacy there was no such appetite for this information, and so the story never attained the urgency and life-of-its-own characteristic of other national contagious diffusion episodes.

IV

Today, as in the past, every adult in America has had some experience with the contagious diffusion of news—the death of President Franklin Roosevelt near the close of the Second World War; the assassination of President John Kennedy, his brother Senator Robert Kennedy, and the Nobel Laureate the Reverend Martin Luther King, Jr., in the 1960s; the attempted assassinations of President Ronald Reagan and Pope John Paul II, and the explosion of the spaceship *Challenger* in the 1980s, all come to mind. And these experiences have all been fundamentally similar to the diffusion of the Lincoln assassination story, wherein information has been passed by impersonal electronic media—telegraph, radio, television—into print and word-of-mouth networks almost instantaneously. Now as then the speed and extent of penetration has never been uniform owing to differences in outlook and interest among people, but all of these episodes testify to both a widespread confidence in the reliability of impersonal sources of information and to a measure of cosmopolitan or at least supra-local consciousness that makes information about these events of interest to nearly everyone.

In the 18th century as we have seen, most clearly in the case of the Battles of Lexington and Concord and in a slightly altered way at the time of George Washington's death, a slower diffusion technology joined with a more localistic, face-to-face social milieu to make contagious diffusion of information a more intricate transaction than it would become later. Far less dependent on impersonal mass media—newspapers were still too slow to be dominant sources—the contagious passage of information worked through existing social relationships instead of bypassing them. As with the ordinary diffusion of information, husbands often brought news to their wives, and clergymen certified the accuracy of reports to their parishioners. Indeed so far as minutemen were concerned, the importance of hierarchy was reinforced in that officers sent word to their men.

But whether or not information flowed with or against the grain of hierarchy, proximity of event and audience played a central role. Diffusion was most rapid and complete near the scene of the action, radiating out along the most heavily traveled routes where casual encounters along the road, in taverns, and in shops and dwellings by the way supplied opportunities for face-to-face exchanges. In such settings individual judgments as to the credibility of the information were required, and personal distortion was always a possibility. Under such circumstances the everyday criteria for assessing reliability came into play so that the social stature of informants and the degree to which they were known heightened or diminished their credibility. Information regarding the events at Lexington and Concord, sketchy, various, and colored by word-of-mouth retelling, was not the readily verified, uniform commodity that such momentous news would become by the time the newspapers published reports of Lincoln's assassination. In 1775, in New England particularly, where further military action might be imminent, people went out canvassing information centers, officially and on their own, to find out what was happening. By the time of Washington's death circumstances had already changed; although in the case of a life-and-death event such as a battle on their own turf the diffusion pattern in 1800 most likely would have been similar to 1775. It was because there was no essential urgency to reports of Washington's demise that newspapers, still outpaced by word of mouth, could play a more important role. Admittedly the circumstances were different from 1775, but it is nonetheless significant that newspapers were now the authorities to which people turned to confirm word-of-mouth reports. Newspaper publishers' long-standing practice of printing documents verbatim, whether letters from Alexandria merchants, presidential proclamations, or congressional resolutions, had established their credibility in spite of their tendency also to publish hyperinflated partisan rhetoric, so that nothing more than a news clipping—impersonal and mass produced—was needed to send community after community into mourning.

Impersonal scraps of printed paper replaced well-known acquaintances and respectable citizens as reliable sources of information.

By the era of the Civil War the telegraph, news correspondents, and more frequent publication of newspapers would propel this pattern of reliance on mass media to a climax. At war's end when Lincoln was assassinated, an information system was already in place that had been tested repeatedly by battle news, from Fort Sumter in 1861, to Gettysburg in 1863, to the fall of Richmond shortly before Lincoln's death. Even in cases like these where contagious diffusion remained most active and inclusive of all sorts of people, newspapers served as conduits of telegraph bulletins and became decisive agents for swift, widespread, and authoritative information. Telegraphy had erased the importance of distance except within the actual locale of an event. And in great cities such as Washington, though virtually everyone first learned of the assassination contagiously through word-of-mouth reports, the rapid production and dissemination of newspapers during the day meant that by Saturday evening, April 15, people in the District of Columbia—like their counterparts in Indianapolis, Indiana—were relying more on the press for information than on any other source. Flashing with almost lightning speed across hundreds or thousands of miles, proximity to telegraph stations and newspapers, rather than to events themselves, became the decisive factor for information about those special events which possessed the drama and importance to excite contagious diffusion.

Although, as in the past, urban development and rural transportation routes made some rural localities more accessible to outside information than others, by the 1860s such distinctions mattered less than heretofore, especially in the North, since differences were now measured in hours or at most a day, rather than in the days or weeks of 1775 and 1800. What mattered most, indeed, as the record of assassination diffusion in the Confederacy reveals, were the regular channels of mass communication—the telegraph, newspapers, transportation, and commercial networks—which brought the news swiftly to all parts of the Union, but only haphazardly to the Confederacy. For while it is true that in many respects the rise of the mass media—the newspaper in particular—supplemented rather than transformed existing ways of transmitting information through society, where contagious diffusion was concerned the impact of the press was sharper, more revolutionary. As the diffusion of the Lincoln assassination story demonstrates, within the span of a lifetime like Calvin Fletcher's, Americans had developed a new reliance on the impersonal mass medium of the newspaper.

Conclusion

United States society in 1865 bore little resemblance to the society of early 18th-century British America. It was, obviously, organized on a totally different scale, with some 36 million people occupying some 3 million square miles in 1865, where there had been about 250,000 people scattered across an area not one-tenth that size around the year 1700.[1] Indeed such quantitative differences are so vast that it is appropriate to ask whether this was in any meaningful sense the same society. Certainly the colonies of 1700 or even 1750 were scarcely recognizable in the United States of the middle decades of the following century. The scale of economic activity, the speed and extent of the transportation systems, the democratic ethos of the system of representative government and electoral politics—the sheer heterogeneity of America's people and institutions—point to the conclusion that the country had been transformed so fundamentally as to become utterly distinct from the colonial era.

Political history and civic culture have reinforced, even exaggerated, such perceptions by treating the date of independence, 1776, as the beginning of the new society, the *novus ordo seclorum,* as Congress proclaimed officially in 1782. In reality, however, such assertions have expressed aspirations more than they have described behavior, because the social continuities that bridged the entire revolutionary era were numerous and profound. Benjamin Franklin, the nation's first diplomat and a prominent signer and supporter of the Constitution, had been nurtured on the teachings of Cotton Mather. George Washington, John Adams and Thomas Jefferson, men whose roots ran deep into the colonial past, lived on to shape the first twenty years of the new national government, and Abraham Lincoln himself was born during the last weeks of Jefferson's presidency. Notwithstanding political turning points, social and cultural experience did not break cleanly at any one date nor for any one generation, not in 1763, 1776, or 1789, nor in any of the decades that followed.

The transformation of society was a cumulative phenomenon, where patterns of belief and behavior shifted unevenly and irregularly—sometimes quite abruptly and publicly, as in the Revolutionary era, and other times

"The Progess of the Century," a popular Currier and Ives print of the centennial era
*(1876), places the telegraph at the forefront of the communication and transportation
revolution of the 19th century. The steam press (which dramatically accelerated large-
scale printing), the railroad, and the steam boat underscore the importance placed on
extensive and rapid communication. The telegraph message itself, which joins Daniel
Webster's 1830 unionist epigram with the universal message of Luke in the Bible,
suggests that progress in communications promotes national union, piety, and peace.*
The Library of Congress

much more gradually and inconspicuously, as with the expansion of commercial activities into rural regions and the related enlargement of local consciousness. Because society took its character from an endless, variegated
stream of activities, there could be no distinct boundary between the colonial society of Sewall's, Byrd's, and Hempstead's contemporaries and American society in Abraham Lincoln's day. Though changed radically by 1865, in
its origins and descent as well as some of its ruling principles, it remained the
same society.

As Samuel Johnson observed in the 1770s, "society is held together by
communication and information;" and what was true of American society in
general was also true of the diffusion of information within it. Changes in the
American social order were linked with the means by which information was

defined and disseminated.[2] Consequently, by now looking more broadly at changes and continuities in the diffusion of information in America, spanning the century-and-a-half between Samuel Sewall and Abraham Lincoln, we can better understand America's social transformation. Though ultimate causation is beyond the reach of this study, describing what happened and when—to class and generational relationships, to gender roles, to experience in various stages of the life cycle and in specific kinds of settings—is feasible in many cases. Description, it is true, is only the beginning of explanation. But there can be no inquiry into why events happened until just what occurred has been established. To do that in any comprehensive way is not now possible; but a preliminary overview, drawn chiefly from the experience recounted in the preceding chapters, can supply a useful if sometimes inexact map of the terrain. Because only some points on the landscape are established with certainty and precision, as with most exploratory maps, much will also have to be inferred and extrapolated from sparse data. At present no more will be attempted than a sketch of the outlines of this vast social continent, locating the mouths of its rivers, supplying a few glimpses upstream, and identifying a handful of the most conspicuous mountain ranges.

From Scarcity to Abundance

The most obvious feature of the American information environment at the beginning of the 18th century was the relative scarcity of information, its limited topical range, and the crucial importance of social stature and social role in determining who possessed access to the full range of information that was available. Samuel Sewall in Boston and William Byrd living by the James River enjoyed access to a wide spectrum of information, a fact which set them apart from all but a few of their neighbors. Their wealth and public offices placed them within the prestigious circle of colonial cosmopolitans, almost exclusively men, who not only maintained numerous contacts with people who dwelled beyond their immediate vicinity but who also corresponded across the Atlantic and conversed routinely with people who moved between England and America.[3] Their wide range of contacts up and down the social ladder meant that virtually any information of communal or public concern came to them by word of mouth, while their genteel learning, wealth, and personal inclination towards knowledge enabled them to read extensively. Byrd, who sedulously amassed a great gentleman's library, and Sewall, whose taste ran more to theology and devotional works, personally handled many hundreds of imported books in the course of their lives. Indeed, for size and comprehensiveness, Byrd's personal library rivaled the largest American college collection of the day, at Harvard.[4]

The extensive information that Sewall and Byrd commanded, while not unique, certainly marked them off as possessors of exceptional abundance in societies of scarcity. Printed matter was generally an imported luxury available, with certain exceptions such as the Bible and devotional books, only to the wealthy few. Cosmopolitan contacts were similarly unusual because most settlers in New England and the Chesapeake region, like common people everywhere, spent most of their time at labor, where they conversed with household members and neighbors within their own locale. If they deferred to their betters in a broad range of social, religious, and public activities, it was not only because they were imbued with the custom and doctrine of deference, but because they rarely possessed information of more than personal significance independently of their social superiors. The Sewalls and the Byrds of early 18th-century America possessed greater information about what was going on, as well as the political assurance that came from knowing that they knew and others didn't. Cultivating knowledge in an economy of scarcity, where literacy was not universal, and sharing it with the general populace only to sustain order and authority, or for didactic purposes that promoted their own values, Sewall's and Byrd's experiences reflected and reinforced the status quo.

That people who were highly placed like Sewall and Byrd did share important elements of high culture with the common people surrounding them gave colonial society much of its cohesiveness and stability in an otherwise unstable economic and social setting. Virtually everyone, high or low, listened to the same sermons and, within a particular community, followed much the same sorts of religious practices on a weekly basis and in the life-cycle rituals of christening, marriage, and death.[5] Nor was any effort made to conceal political and economic theory and natural philosophy, which, by a trickle-down process, seem to have influenced common beliefs.[6] Except for the knowledge of Christ, common people were seen to have no more need for information than for periwigs, and so the system which joined information and privilege was secure.

Indeed, the constricted pattern of information diffusion characteristic of the early 18th-century colonial world, in which distinctions of rank, wealth, and gender were both socially prescribed and functional, possessed an inertia and staying power that in some settings permitted its survival for generations. By the mid-19th century, however, it had vanished for most white Americans. Now printed works in a variety of genres were widely available; public speech emanated from a multitude of secular and religious platforms; and associational activities had become so well-established in the Northeast that even the old boundaries of common people's word-of-mouth networks, their family and neighborhood, were being breached. Where gaining access to information had once been a notable achievement for ambitious climbers like Benjamin Franklin and John Adams, the challenge of the 19th century was to achieve a sense of mastery and control of information in an economy of abundance.[7]

In a society where printing and public speech were ubiquitous—as they were throughout the northern states and in the urban South of the mid-19th century—the relationship of information to social stature became far more complicated. If during Philip Fithian's Virginia sojourn in the 1770s a college degree could be compared to a £10,000 estate in the marriage market of the Tidewater aristocracy, then by Lucy Breckinridge's day its value had fallen sharply. Not only were college degrees more plentiful, but their significance was altered because there was scant distance between a formal college education and the level of self-education that men like Isaac Mickle and Calvin Fletcher could attain. Debating societies and political clubs supplied exercise in public speaking; visiting different churches and reading religious treatises furnished the rudiments of theology; while history and natural science or philosophy were available in lyceum-style lectures, in books, periodicals, and even newspaper features. There was no longer any need to sequester oneself for years at a college—paying tuition and foregoing earnings—in order to pass for a gentleman or, indeed, to become one. The abundance of information that was literally circulating through society enabled poor but talented men like Calvin Fletcher to pursue the crucial badges of gentility, money and cosmopolitan knowledge, simultaneously.

Selecting what information to acquire replaced access itself so as to emerge as a central challenge for people in varied social circumstances. Their decisions, both unconscious and deliberate, divided them in new ways. The common culture that the gentry and clergy had shared with their neighbors and coparishioners, and which had transcended class, gender, and generational boundaries, was undermined by new possibilities.[8] Until the 19th century, that common culture of Trinitarian Christianity, of deference within a social hierarchy, and of mutual obligations, wherein corporate identities of family and community took precedence over individual aspirations, had been secure. In fact the few voices that were raised to challenge the common culture could scarcely be heard. The channels for information flow had been so much controlled by men who expressed the ruling conventions, and so unified within particular colonies that, lacking institutional bases of support, there was meager sustenance for alternative notions. Indeed, so long as gentlemen and clergy did not go to war with each other, the status quo seemed secure. Even on the periodic occasions when they did embroil themselves in controversy, the system remained untouched because their arguments were confined indoors—to courtrooms and assembly halls. When they entered print via newspapers and pamphlets, their readers were usually numbered in the hundreds, not the thousands. Because such controversy was not the business of common folk in the ordinary course of things, the constricted information system based on scarcity passed through numerous such contentious episodes intact. But the Great Awakening, an extended controversy of remarkable dimensions, one that engaged people at all levels, shook the system to its foundations. So profound was the challenge, some would argue, that it cracked the status quo. The Awakening's affront to the hierarchical and deferential customs on which the system rested so weakened it that it later would crumble under the stresses of the Revolutionary era.[9]

There is, of course, reason to doubt whether a single movement, even one so profound and so extensive as the Great Awakening, could shatter the common culture and the information system that sustained it, since both were closely attached to the actual circumstances and customary social functions of so many people. Nevertheless it must be recognized that in the Awakening the notion of individual choice was forcefully asserted, together with the exercise of personal preference by ordinary people who announced that they would henceforth decide what religious information they would choose to hear. And a further consequence of the Awakening was the formation of separate churches that created the institutional foundation for a competition for the attention and allegiance of people in all walks of life, men, women, and youth. Though as yet the competition was confined to issues of salvation, which large numbers of people ignored for long periods of time, the information system could never again be quite so unitary and deferential as before. Still, the common culture and its restricted information system survived; and, if in many communities common people could exercise individual choice in selecting their preacher, they remained within an economy of scarcity where the range of choices was narrow and confined to this single aspect of social life. Compared to the array of possibilities among which the men and women of the 1840s and 1850s exercised their preferences, the Great Awakening, which might seem to have changed so much theoretically, made little practical difference.

The selections 19th-century people made for acquiring information mixed deliberation and impulse. In contrast to Fletcher and Mickle, most people were not keenly aware of the fact that they were making choices. Indeed, they were more like the cabinetmaker's apprentice, Edward Jenner Carpenter, and the plantation daughter, Lucy Breckinridge; they conversed, read, and attended public gatherings chiefly to satisfy personal needs and to express their sociable nature. Moreover in this environment of abundance the distinction between accumulating information and consuming it that had once affected only a small fraction of the gentry became a central feature of general experience. The old practice of collecting newspapers and binding them for future reference, as Samuel Sewall had done at the beginning of the 18th century and as Martha Moore Ballard was still doing at the century's close, faded out as newspapers became items of ephemeral mass consumption.[10] Some responded by clipping newspapers and magazines in order to compile scrapbooks which enabled them to retain and accumulate a fraction of the emphemeral print that passed before them. Though there were no clear boundaries between accumulation and consumption, since the information one person chose to accumulate another might merely consume, much of what people attended—lectures, sermons, orations—as well as much of what they read, was chiefly for diversion. Information had became so plentiful that it could be consumed in momentary entertainments rather than being hoarded up for permanent possession.

As always it was generally understood that, whether for momentary consumption or long-term accumulation, information activities reflected social class. What abundance promoted was "the democratization of gentility," whereby knowledge of classical and modern history, world geography, and natural science—all badges of genteel rank in colonial society—was broadcast to a vast, amorphous middle class through printing and public lectures.[11] The seemingly inexhaustible market for this sort of personal improvement information, as well as dozens of editions of Lord Chesterfield's and other guides to respectable conversation and deportment, demonstrates conclusively that much of the expansion of access to information in the 19th century—an expansion of historic dimensions—was driven by a popular desire to enjoy such material and psychological benefits as gentility afforded.

There were, however, other motives of comparable power that also fed the burgeoning information industry. One was the hunger for religious knowledge, which, though certainly tilted toward middle-class respectability, often differentiated people who labored with their hands from those who didn't. The multitudes of men, women, and youths who attended camp meetings and outdoor revivals in rural areas and the great evangelical assemblies held in urban auditoriums were participating to satisfy emotional and spiritual needs and aspirations, not to enhance their social rank. Much the same might be said of the tens of thousands of subscribers to sectarian monthlies and the even more numerous purchasers of popular religious treatises and sermons. The moral and spiritual self-improvement that pointed to salvation was compelling to people of every social rank.[12]

Religious information, like secular information, had various uses. Some was hoarded up for long-term retention, but much was swiftly consumed to satisfy momentary appetites. The several genres of print and public speech served both purposes. To young religious dilettantes like Isaac Mickle in Philadelphia and Edward Carpenter in Greenfield, attending the services of various sects might provide some information that would add to their store of knowledge, but their primary reason for attendance was amusement. Conversely, popular novels were intended chiefly to entertain, and though their didactic lessons could be instructive for readers like Mary Guion and Candace Roberts, and could even satisfy serious emotional needs, they were more often read for amusement, as when Edward Carpenter spent his Sundays alone in the shop reading adventure stories. There were also forms of information that deliberately combined information and entertainment. Carpenter's knowledge of Attila the Hun came from just such popular publications; and lectures on subjects like human anatomy and phrenology were similarly designed to amuse and inform simultaneously, and that was why he paid to attend them.

Indeed the distinction between the two, like the distinction between information that was consumed and accumulated, was always subjective, whether in the colonial era of scarcity or the republican era of abundance. But the information abundance of the 19th century certainly allowed for more specialized choices than had ever before been available to ordinary people. When few choices were at hand, as with Abner Sanger and his neighbors in Keene, New Hampshire, readers of print and auditors of oratory made no such specialized distinctions; they gleaned such information and amusement as they could. But when there was a wide array of choices available, as there often was by the 1840s, one could specialize and seek instruction in one setting or genre, and amusement in another. Such an array of choices reinforced distinctions based on occupation and class.[13] For if, as with farming and most trades, one's work and social milieu chiefly required information drawn from experience— and if one had no concern for rising in social esteem—then the most frequent reason to turn to print or public speech might be to fulfill religious or recreational desires. In contrast, people whose occupations were professional, commercial, or involved some branch of the information business, as well as the thousands of farmers and tradesmen who held some public office, repeatedly had occasion to seek information in printed matter and other public forums that they could employ directly in their work. They might also seek information to achieve or maintain a cosmopolitan appearance. A further complication of the distinction between information as knowledge and as entertainment, in a period when knowledge in all its forms was respected and socially approved, was the fact that for some people mastering a body of specialized knowledge was itself a recreation.

Nevertheless, broadly speaking, it seems clear that abundance enabled— indeed, required—a broad segment of Americans to specialize when it came to the acquisition of information. Within this context, and notwithstanding the subjective character of the categories of accumulation and consumption, the most basic forms of specialization involved accumulation for the sake of knowledge, and consumption for the sake of recreation. Accumulating knowledge was understood to provide long-term advantages—for career, for social stature, for religious well-being. Consumption for recreation, on the other hand, satisfied current desires for diversion, for sociability, for freedom from the required duties and dimensions of daily experience, and if such recreational consumption promoted career, or personal stature, or religious condition, that was an incidental benefit.

This pattern of specialization led to the development of two distinct information marketplaces. For even though all print and public speech, whether religious or secular, was operating in a competitive environment that tended to blur distinctions between knowledge-oriented and entertaining informa-

Mercantile Library

Here the male world of commercial information is depicted at mid-morning. Newspapers from all over the United States are being consulted at the right. Elsewhere, information is being exchanged mostly through conversation. At the rear there are stacks of books. A mercantile library such as this fulfilled the information functions of the 18th-century coffeehouse in a more complete and highly specialized way. This view appeared in Ballou's Pictorial, *March 8, 1856.*
Courtesy of the Boston Atheneum

tion, their markets were shaped by different people and values. Where knowledge was the focus, the primary objective was either some didactic goal or else information itself. Such forms of information were guided and shaped by the expert, prestigious, educated few; whereas recreational information was propelled by the demands of the many and tailored to popular fashions, tastes, and capacities. The former maintained continuity with the days of scarcity, when there had been essentially one information marketplace dominated by gentlemen, merchants, and clergymen whose preferences were in turn powerfully influenced by genteel English standards. The popular entertainment market, however, was something new, many-sided, and intricate which, as time went on, came to shape American culture decisively.[14] This dynamic marketplace, catering to the preferences of apprentices, clerks, farmers—and their sisters, daughters, and wives who worked in homes, common schools, and factories—was beyond anyone's direction or control.

It was not the specialized consumption of information that was new—that was an elite prerogative of long standing—rather, it was the fact that virtually everyone was now engaged in making such choices, with the result that a popular market of entertaining information was challenging the received standards of the past. Already by 1803 a clergyman complained that "the *spirit of trade . . .* leads men to write . . . in accommodation to the *public taste,* however depraved, and with a view to the most *advantageous sale.*"[15] Indeed, he asserted that "*Booksellers*" had replaced aristocrats as "the *great patrons of literature,*" with the result that now a flood of books was appearing—"thousands of worthless volumes . . . which could never have found their way to the press in a different state of society."[16] Books, however, were only the beginning. Periodicals and newspapers were even more popular forms of print, and by 1837 Ralph Waldo Emerson, who was trained as a minister and traced his descent to a long line of New England clergymen who were used to directing the reading and controlling and public speech of their parishes, exclaimed in frustration that "the only aristocracy in this country is—the editors of newspapers," a disparate, non-college educated breed of self-made men whose information judgments were dictated by political and pecuniary advantage.[17] Nearly a decade earlier, President John Quincy Adams had remarked on a similar shift toward popular taste in public speech when he noted in 1828 that "one of the most remarkable peculiarities of the present time is that the principal leaders of the political parties are travelling about the country from State to State, and holding forth, like Methodist preachers, hour after hour, to assembled multitudes, under the broad canopy of heaven."[18] As stump-speaking, slogans, and torchlight parades came to typify American elections, it was evident that political entertainment rather than the imparting of information was campaigning's paramount function.

There had, of course, always been distinctions between high culture and popular culture, but in the past the canons prescribed by the few both for themselves and for the many had dominated print and public speech and thereby monopolized the major arteries for the diffusion of information of general concern. And even with the emergence of a vast, popular information marketplace, insofar as learning and information for the sake of knowledge was concerned, an enlarged social elite, together with merchants and professionals, retained critical influence by writing the texts that dominated all branches of education and by dictating standards of respectable knowledge. But in the other great sphere of information diffusion, wherein entertainment was the chief end, the preferences of common people ruled. The rule of social hierarchy in American culture, which had always been supported by the information diffusion system, came to be undermined by it in the 19th-century economy of abundance.

A second key change in the diffusion of information that was tied to abundance was a shift in the function and importance of face-to-face exchanges for the dissemination of public news. In the era of scarcity, public and political information normally passed through society by word of mouth. For a few people, chiefly office-holding notables, letters also provided such news, but in either case, face-to-face or via letter, the process was interpersonal, whether it was private or not. The ramifications of this personal connection for the transmission and reception of information were numerous and significant. Many indeed, can only be dimly perceived, but they all began with the persona and credibility possessed by the information-giver and with the level of urgency that person assigned to the news.

As we have seen repeatedly in cases drawn from the 18th and 19th centuries, the subject matter, the social rank and present relationship of the parties, as well as the particular circumstances of the information exchange, were all crucial for establishing credibility and urgency. Where these were conveyed successfully, the information was not only assimilated instantly, it was understood to command a response, either some direct, personal action, or else a further transmission to other people in other households. Sometimes consciously, though often not, people acted with the understanding that information moved from person to person and so, if it was important, they ought to pass it along to others who would not only expect them to do so, but who had done the same for them in the past as they would also in the future. The reciprocal passing of appropriate information was crucial to the social order and a source of community vitality.

It was just such exchanges as we are considering here—face-to-face transmission among people dwelling in relationships anchored by their knowledge of each other and their social roles—that were much the most common means of conveying public information in a world of scarcity. Politics, church doings, word of sickness and death, like news of accidental calamities, were all authenticated and assigned importance within such a framework. Here no news was unbiased or uninflected. First, the fact that word was passed along was a statement of its importance. Second, it was inevitably colored by a tone of pleasure or dismay, certainty or doubt, expectancy or resignation, or any combination of these or a hundred other unspoken comments. There was, consequently, an invitation to the recipient to share the news-bearer's view of the information that was imparted. The influence of face-to-face communication might be brutally straightforward, as when a clergyman joined his own admonitions to reports on the transgressions of his parishioners, or it could be more subtle, as when a comment on a Napoleonic battle indirectly urged the hearer toward cosmopolitanism. In all cases, however, decorum required that attention be paid to the speaker; and though the listener might actively or passively resist the speaker's words, a listener could seldom be oblivious to what was spoken. Indeed since most conversations were entered mutually, people normally spoke and listened attentively, simultaneously seeking information and opinion from a familiar face.

Obviously this kind of information exchange has never disappeared, and remains crucial in everyday experience. However, the shift from a world where information was scarce to one where it was so abundant and swiftly delivered that printing could supplant personal networks as the paramount mechanism for the dissemination of public news exerted profound consequences on overall patterns of information diffusion. When the diffusion of public information moved from face-to-face networks to the newspaper page, public life and the society in which politics operated shifted from a communal discipline to a market-oriented, competitive regimen in which the foundations of influence changed. This did not happen everywhere all at once, or for every type of public information, but by the middle decades of the 19th century so much of public affairs were being conducted through the press that where extra-local public information was concerned, word-of-mouth networks had been largely relegated to a subordinate role. Indeed in Philadelphia, New York, and other great cities where daily newspapers flourished, printing was even encroaching on the face-to-face dissemination of local news.

Information conveyed face-to-face was always governed by the relationship of speaker and listener, and because it was passed in a communal setting, both speaker and listener were constrained to conform to their social roles and under constant pressure to agree so as to interact harmoniously. In contrast, information conveyed through the impersonal medium of print required no such inhibitions. Although the speaker was subject to some restraints as a writer, the listener-reader could react privately and therefore freely. Instead of attending politely, a reader could frown, object out loud, or simply ignore a printed piece entirely—all at a moment of personal convenience. As a result, acquiring public information no longer required sociable exchanges in a communal setting, so social boundaries and collective restraints were undermined. When printing became abundant, people were free to exercise privately their individual preferences for public information. As a result the measure of indoctrination, influence, and communal cohesion that accompanied face-to-face diffusion of information vanished.[19]

Moreover now it was the task of print, not word of mouth, to impart public information. Face-to-face exchanges were understood to serve personal and private information needs in a more specialized way than before. The result was that individualism and privatism were reinforced from two directions. Face-to-face conversation became more purely personal, while printing reinforced individuality rather than conformity, and encouraged personal choice instead of communal values.

Although as agents of public information newspaper publishers moved in two contrary directions in the century from 1765 to 1865, everything they did reinforced the importance of individual preference. One strategy they adopted was a neutral, non-partisan stance in which they printed whatever opinions came to hand. The advantage of this approach, they hoped, was that they could befriend all parties by opening access to their columns while their inclusive journalism would appeal to subscribers of all opinions. The other method was to pursue a frankly partisan line which guaranteed a like-minded body of advertisers and readers. It was this approach which ultimately became dominant in the wake of the intensely partisan rivalry between Federalists and Jeffersonians in the 1790s. Hereafter most newspapers adopted party identifications, and to subscribe became a statement of political preference.[20] In either case, however, whether papers were neutral or partisan, once they became cheap and abundant, people expressed their own individuality by choosing to read or ignore the information they contained.

The aspect of the partisan journalism of the 1790s and succeeding decades that underscores the contrast with the passage of public information through word-of-mouth networks was the flowering of unbridled invective. Articles, often published over pseudonyms—another revealing contrast to face-to-face expression where there was no anonymity—employed inflated rhetoric that was often harshly divisive. Raw, competitive advocacy led to verbal attacks that, if delivered face-to-face, would have led to slander suits if not personal combat.[21] Open competition, always difficult to conduct in a communal setting because of its challenge to order and harmony as well as its perils for ongoing relationships, was facilitated by the impersonal medium of print. In a newspaper column a speaker could escape the familiar faces of his listeners and could display rhetorical virtuosity without violating the canons of social behavior. The fact that such controversies attracted readers and engaged their loyalties helped make journalism a paying proposition.

Such a change in the roles of print and face-to-face diffusion was emblematic of the underlying shift from a society of scarcity, where public information and learning generally flowed from the upper reaches of the social order downward to common people—a hierarchical diffusion pattern—to a society of information abundance, where popular and hierarchic elements were combined in a diffusion marketplace animated by a multitude of preferences and constituencies. What this meant in practical terms was that in the North nearly everyone could gain access to whatever information they craved. For the traditional elite of wealthy, cultivated gentlemen who continued to demand the high culture of Britain, the ease of access steadily improved, so libraries of more than 1000 volumes, once exceedingly rare, could now be found in a scattering of town houses and mansions all over the United States. Public and quasi-public libraries of various types, almost unknown in the colonial era, were now commonplace through much of the North, and apprentices, artisans, and clerks, as well as mill girls and domestic servants, were afforded the opportunity to read extensively.[22] Professionals and quasi-professionals, always eager to control technical information, also enjoyed unprecedented access to books and periodicals treating religious, legal, and medical topics. For every occupation, whether manufacturers and tradesmen or bankers and mariners, there were practical manuals intended to

"The Young Traders," by William Page, appeared in The Gift: A Christmas and New Year's Present *(Philadelphia, 1844) to illustrate a moralistic story of the same title set in New York City by Seba Smith. In the story, the newsboy works to overcome the handicaps of a family broken by his father's drinking and improvidence. The girl who sells raspberries is also from a respectable but sinking family. The image is striking not only for the would-be respectability of the newsboy who wears a waistcoat and necktie but also for its presentation of a girl absorbed in reading a newspaper. By the 1840s, newspapers were so widely available and so broadly appealing in their content that even those most removed from the world of politics and commerce found them interesting.*

augment and refine information gained from actual experience. Reformers and evangelists, men and women of almost every occupation who eagerly promoted a hundred different causes, created and consumed a host of publications, from weekly newspapers and monthly magazines to polemics, treatises, textbooks, didactic fiction, and reference works. They were, in addition, the sponsors and patrons of a multitude of platform lecturers whose diverse origins—college-bred to slave-bred, male and female—betrayed how thoroughly the market-oriented diffusion process was established alongside the older hierarchical one.

In addition to all these avenues of knowledge-oriented information there were comparable opportunities to acquire entertaining, recreational information. The old hierarchical diffusion pattern may be said to have influenced some portion of recreational high culture, but only slightly because of the extensive competition from the popular marketplace. For if a sheltered young woman of wealth and breeding like Lucy Breckinridge mixed the reading of popular novels with works by such heroes of general culture as Charles Dickens, together with more general 18th- and 19th-century books, then it is evident that choice rather than prescription ruled in a competitive setting. Breckinridge's older contemporary, the lawyer's clerk Isaac Mickle, confined his recreational reading to a more consistently elevated plane and rejected popular literature entirely, but he did so as a matter of choice, not because of a lack of alternatives or anyone's prescription. When Mickle studied law, he read the treatises his mentors prescribed, exemplifying hierarchic diffusion. But once he closed the black-lettered law books and ranged into French and Latin classics, he was making his own choices. By the mid-19th century it is evident that information was so abundant and available that it was acquired and consumed amidst a host of alternatives in which the expression of individual preference was legitimate, even for a deferential young woman like Lucy Breckinridge, for apprentices like Edward Carpenter and Mathias Weaver, and for a law student such as Mickle.

Under circumstances such as these, the diffusion of all kinds of information became a strenuous competition, among authors and publishers, lecturers and promoters, not so much for physical access to the public as for the attention of a suitable, responsive audience. The most common solution to this challenge was the creation of specialized messages packaged to appeal to known audiences or markets. Perhaps this technique had begun with party newspapers, where the loyalties of partisans had been crucial to the survival of struggling printers. But whether its origins were with public information or with the publication of common schoolbooks, specialized identities and products came to dominate the information marketplace. Every religious denomination, every reform committee, every political group, every taste found expression as the decades passed. The pattern was so pronounced that there was even a specialized type of publication—the digest and encyclopedia—aimed at overcoming the problems created by the multiplication of specialities. Indeed supplying a general overview and guide for acquiring knowledge in this confusing marketplace was one of the major functions of touring lecturers.[23] Their fame and their eloquence, rather than social or political rank, made their prescriptions authoritative.

Abundance and the availability of individual choice were broadly characteristic of mid-19th-century American society. But it is also true that in both the 18th and 19th centuries wealth, gender, and slave status influenced the range of possibilities. As the escaped slave Frederick Douglass explained, nearly all slaves were kept illiterate so that they could never acquire access to information beyond word-of-mouth networks. And if they lived in rural areas, as some 90 percent did, those networks were sharply restricted by local circumstances. While certain kinds of information could move effectively within such limits—one South Carolina slave recalled that on "Hiring-day . . . the slave is sure to know who is the most humane, or cruel master, within forty miles of him,"—a broad range of communication was impossible. Urban slaves, and those who worked in taverns and stores, like slave teamsters, riverboatmen and stevedores, might all possess enlarged access to information, as could domestic servants who overheard their masters' conversation, but, compared to literate free people, they exercised few choices. Similarly, the rural poor, white or black, literate or not, had little time or occasion for reading, and except for the Bible and almanacs, there is not much evidence of access either. For them conditions remained much like the 18th century, except that now their word-of-mouth networks were influenced not just by preachers and magistrates but by competitive electoral politics and by the larger society's general abundance of information. The urban poor, who evidently read the lurid human interest stories in the penny press, listened to outdoor oratory, and possessed a more varied range of word-of-mouth networks than their rural counterparts, could exercise some choice; but the fact that they had so little discretionary income meant that, even when they were hungry for information, their opportunities were restricted.[24]

It is not until one rises to the level of clerks, artisans, mill women, and yeoman farmers—what might be loosely described as the lower-middle and middle classes—that the multiplication of choices becomes readily apparent. Yet here gender was an important boundary. For the most part women were closed out of colleges and the learned professions, excluded from public office, and made to feel unwelcome at political gatherings. They were free to listen to public lectures and sermons—though not to deliver them—and they might, of course, read widely. The most important factors limiting their choices, however, were not social prescriptions, but the actual circumstances of their lives. While the saying, "man's work is from sun to sun, but women's work is never done," was not literally true, it does appear that, once women in the middle ranks of society reached maturity and bore the responsibilities of supervising a home and family, they did not enjoy much leisure time. Where they did have options, the choices they made reveal that the information they sought related to their own lives; so they seldom regarded their exclusion from large categories of "male" information as troublesome. Moreover as family-oriented newspapers and periodicals came to flourish in the 1830s and thereafter, much of the male sphere of knowledge was popularized so as to become accessible to all. What mattered most was not prescription itself but women's own perceptions of what was important.

Here it is not surprising to find that women's choices were influenced

significantly by their stage in the life cycle. Before marriage it is evident that novels, which mixed recreational rewards with instruction in sentiment and morality, joined devotional literature as their preferred reading. After marriage, with less time available for reading, they cut back, perhaps more on novels than religion. While devotional reading was prescribed culturally and enjoyed a more favorable reputation than novels, it is also reasonable to conclude that women continued to read such works in adulthood because they reinforced their role as family religious caretaker and were also emotionally rewarding. Because of women's comprehensive engagement in caregiving within their families as well as attending to neighbors in childbirth, illness, and death, Christian messages of resignation in the face of suffering, and of faith and hope in eternal life, seem to have possessed extraordinary meaning and power for women as compared with men. It was women, after all, who brought forth life from the womb, who fed and nurtured people from infancy onward, and who, at the end, washed and dressed their corpses for the grave. And if they enjoyed only a few hours of leisure in a week, mostly on the Sabbath, worship services and devotional reading were appealing. History, politics, natural philosophy, and a host of other subjects interested particular women, but it was the world of sentiment that religion and the novel both expressed, which held priority.[25]

Underlining the different emphasis of men's and women's information activities was the propensity of women for visiting and non-business letter-writing.[26] Men were also interested in news of friends and family, but often their interest had a practical, business dimension. With women, however, news of the health and feelings of relatives and friends was frequently the principal motive for visits and letters, not a by-product. Information concerning the personal, the private, and interior, possessed greater relative importance for women than most public information. This was the sphere where they were most active and effective, in contrast to the business and public world where men were the central actors.[27]

When women worked together with neighbors indoors, as at sewing tasks, their conversation and reading choices were the same. At a New England charitable society meeting in the 1830s, where the product would be linens

---

"Moses, the Baltimore News Vendor," by Thomas Waterman Wood, dates from 1858. Because selling newspapers was low-status work traditionally done by boys, it was also suitable for a black. Hawking their papers by calling attention to the stories they contained, "newsboys" were generally literate. That Moses, presumably a free black in a slave city, was a fixture in the distribution of newspapers indicates that, at least in urban settings, public information networks which mixed print and face-to-face exchanges could include blacks. Moses' friendly smile and deferential doffing of his hat were no doubt reassuring to white customers who might otherwise be concerned at his part in the diffusion of public information.
Courtesy of the Fine Arts Museums of San Francisco, Mildred Anna Williams Collection

for a poor woman's family, the texts chosen for reading aloud were religious essays and, for a treat, a novel. In such a setting the mutually reinforcing influences of prescription and affinity were apparent.[28]

The fact that women made most of their information choices within a more confined spectrum than did men should not, however, suggest that they had so few choices that their situation in the mid-19th century resembled that of their male counterparts in the era of scarcity a century earlier. Publishers in Britain and the United States issued a multitude of sermons and religious essays as well as thousands of popular novels. Even when they were reading exactly the same novels as their neighbors, they made decisions individually. Though levels of wealth mattered, among people of middling ranks, women as well as men, fashion dictated their choices far more often than scarcity.

Though the individualism that this competitive information marketplace seemed to encourage was sometimes more apparent than real, its cumulative impact on social relations was significant. America had gone from a society where public information had been scarce, and chiefly under the control of the learned and wealthy few, to a society in which it was abundant and under no control other than the interests and appetites of a vast, popular public of consumers. In place of a society where nearly all public information was acquired via word-of-mouth sources and disciplined by a community where consciousness of rank was ever present, American society was now characterized by the movement of public information from distant, impersonal sources direct to individuals—independent of family, neighborhood, or any face-to-face connections. A competitive marketplace in which public information was shaped to the tastes of the audience had supplanted a system in which public information was disseminated within a communal order. And because society was so large and diverse in its tastes, specialized printing and public speech, perhaps also specialized conversation, became far more prominent than ever before. A comprehensive common culture had never been fully realized as everyday experience—not even in Samuel Sewall's Boston; but now it became ever more remote, no longer even an ideal. The distribution of information favored individual realization, whether independently or as part of like-minded groups that collected around competing religious doctrines, political agendas and among others, occupational interests. Patterns of information diffusion that had once reinforced social cohesion had now become foundations of social diversity.

Sources of Change

Explanations for these changes are embedded in the economic, social, and political history of early America and cannot be disentangled simply from the general history of the society. As mentioned at the outset, the most palpable change in American society between the era of scarcity and that of abundance was growth both in the territorial spread of settlement and the geometric increase in the number of people. Theoretically such growth could have occurred without much affecting the diffusion of information—through a process whereby more people in more places simply reproduced earlier patterns—but in reality the growth of American society and its dynamic features were interconnected at many levels.

In the case of information diffusion, the most critical connections were with transportation and commercial development. In order to facilitate commercial exchange, American settlers had always been interested in both overland and waterborne transport. But in the colonial era, with settlement concentrated within 100 miles of the coast, in the bays and river valleys that drained into the Atlantic—and with a government in London intent on maintaining the status quo—improvements in transportation were a minor concern, and they came about slowly. The only substantial overland project was the post road which ran from Portsmouth, New Hampshire, to Philadelphia; and it was an irregularly-constructed and maintained horse path that could accommodate wagons only along portions of its route.[29] Since inland agriculture remained close to subsistence levels, there was little demand for better transportation. The British victory in the French and Indian War in 1763, however, followed by the Revolution, opened up interior settlement and stimulated the pace of population growth and commercial development. With national and state governments friendly to trade and encouraging the construction of roads and bridges, and canals, and later railroads, the revolution in production and consumption that was transforming Britain, America's chief trading partner, thoroughly permeated the society of the new republic as well.[30]

The consequences for the diffusion of information were magnified and multiplied because Americans were broadly committed to an ethos that prescribed the diffusion of knowledge as essential to the well-being of society. Everyman and everywoman, farmers, mechanics, even republican mothers—not just the wealthy few—had to be informed cosmopolitans in order to fulfill their social responsibilities in the "new" society. "Despots keep their subjects ignorant," "liberty and knowledge are inseparable"— these were the shibboleths of the early republic, and they were reflected widely both in public policy and private behavior.[31] The national government under the auspices first of the Federalists and then the Jeffersonian Republicans, created a vast, comprehensive postal system whose offices reached directly into 4500 communities by 1820.[32] Animated by the same ideology, the national government subsidized newspaper publishers with reduced rates for delivering their issues to subscribers, and by enabling publishers to exchange copies free of charge.[33] The national policy of setting aside a portion of every township in the Northwest Territory to support a public school, like the statutory commitments to common schools in the

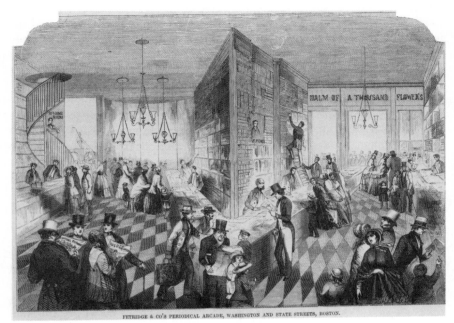

FETRIDGE & CO'S PERIODICAL ARCADE, WASHINGTON AND STATE STREETS, BOSTON.

Periodical Arcade

The specialized reading marketplace of the mid-century is exemplified by the scene in this periodical store where a vast array of titles satisfies the preferences of many different customers, men, women, and children. The store also included a reading room at the left rear. This view appeared in Gleason's Pictorial, *July 31, 1852.*
Courtesy of the Boston Atheneum

northern states, flowed not from commercial exigencies but from this same ideology of liberty tied to the diffusion of knowledge.

Politicians repeatedly backed their advocacy of an informed citizenry with money from the public treasury, but overall private expenditures on information diffusion dwarfed those in the public sector. The production and distribution of newspapers, periodicals, and books—a small-scale enterprise in the colonial era which relied chiefly on imports and never involved the full-time labors of more than one hundred people at any one time—became a big business, so that by 1850, 22,000 men (and a lesser number of women and children) were not only printing and binding billions of items annually, but producing the river of ink, the mountain of paper, and the type required for all this printing.[34] Sales and distribution of printed goods, while not usually a full-time, specialized occupation, and the production of printing machinery and the textiles and leathers used for bindings, involved thousands more people who were scattered through virtually every county in the United

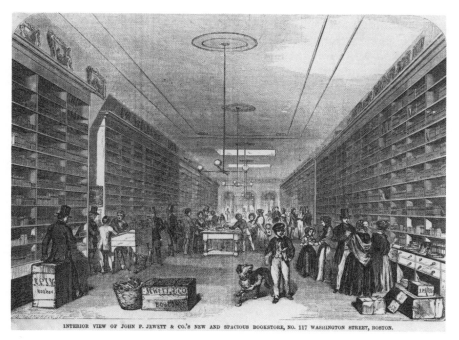

INTERIOR VIEW OF JOHN P. JEWETT & CO.'S NEW AND SPACIOUS BOOKSTORE, NO. 117 WASHINGTON STREET, BOSTON.

Jewett's Bookstore

This view graphically illustrates the vast scope of the mid-19th-century book market. Here thousands of volumes were on display in a gas-lit interior. Women as well as men and children are among the patrons. This picture appeared in Gleason's Pictorial, *December 2, 1854. A generation earlier, no American bookstore would have maintained such a large inventory.*
Courtesy of the Boston Atheneum

States. The total dollars laid out on intinerant lecturers and preachers, on the lyceum movement, on debating clubs, and on partisan electoral activities were probably less, but, when the tens of thousands of activists who staged and presented these performances are considered, the expenditure of man-hours was substantial. Diffusing information was a great national enterprise.

Both cultural and economic factors made it possible for Americans to devote such quantities of money and time to producing and consuming all this information. Commercial development and the consumer revolution that was bound up with the industrial revolution generated increases in both discretionary income and time. When, for example, all of the time-consuming tasks required for turning raw wool into cloth were removed from the home, women could turn to the production of butter and cheese, or such handicrafts as sewing shoes and weaving straw hats, which brought them cash or credit at the local store. Though most of that money went to purchase the cloth they no longer produced at home, there was an increment of time and money that could be spent on cultural enrichment that usually included the acquisition of information. Moreover, as commercial development made it possible for men, women, and children to make all their waking hours productive, more attention was given to using time efficiently. Casual socializing and the exchange of local gossip were downgraded in favor of more purposeful activity, both in work and recreation. "Time is money," Benjamin Franklin's observation in the highly commercial Philadelphia of the 18th century, became a literal reality for 19th-century Americans who were increasingly engaged in the web of commerce.[35]

Reading, the meetings of voluntary associations, and lecture- and sermon-going were all highly respected alternatives to using discretionary time simply to produce more goods. These uses of time were elevating, and enabled people with genteel and middle-class aspirations to become more polished and cosmopolitan and to approach mastery of a general body of knowledge that embraced religion, history, geography, and natural sciences in addition to public affairs. The drinking clubs of genteel city dwellers and the tavern-going of country people lost respectability. Instead, purposeful activity, either producing goods or building a more culturally elevated society, were prescribed by clergymen, educators, journalists, and politicians as the proper uses of one's leisure time.

The foundations of these changes lay in the expanding economy and in the cultural dynamics of Anglo-America—after all, trends in Britain were similar. Everywhere the old ways of information diffusion had acted as a bottleneck that retarded economic development. But the American Revolution broke the bottleneck by accelerating and intensifying the cult of information diffusion, and not only by creating the republican ideology of an informed citizenry. In numerous concrete, practical ways the Revolution promoted widespread participation in public affairs, in office-holding of all sorts, in committee activity and, by 1800, in electioneering. All of the post-1776 governments—local, state, and national—required public attention if the idea of government by the consent of the governed was to operate. As a result men—but not yet women—were suddenly expected to have opinions on public men and measures, and these opinions were said to matter, as was often the fact. Beginning with the ratification of constitutions—that of Massachusetts in 1778 and 1780 and that of the United States in 1787–1788—highly complicated public affairs became subjects that newspapers and conversation must bring to every man. Issues like currency and finance, once safely left to colonial elites to figure out, were now the province of ordinary citizens. And when people remained partially or wholly ignorant, as they had been in the past, they were said to be deficient. Parochial ignorance was no longer legitimate.

Legitimate or not, where political elites were united and electoral competition rare, old ways lingered and the new ideology ran counter to actual behavior.[36] But when elites divided and competition was intense, they appealed to people through the most popular diffusion methods—the impersonal media of newspapers and public address, the thoroughly personal techniques of party organization, and the mixed method of public ceremonies and demonstrations. Party organization, a new creation of the early republican era that grew directly out of electioneering needs, worked through acquaintance networks from the state, county, and town committees, down to precinct captains and their assistants, who made personal calls on their neighbors so as to reinforce local loyalties and to explain how to vote. By combining impersonal messages in the mass media with popular processions and demonstrations of loyalty as well as the face-to-face networks of party organizations, Americans created political mobilization on an unprecedented scale. By 1810 some state contests generated 80 percent turnouts of an electorate in which almost all men were eligible to vote. And by 1840, when these techniques were effectively coordinated on a national scale, even an office so remote from local concerns as the national presidency could draw 70 percent of adult white men to the polls. All these men were certainly not well-informed—but they did know when and where the election was being held, and enough about the parties, candidates, and personal loyalties to make their choice. Owing to the creation of popular republican government in the Revolutionary era, an institutional framework for promoting information diffusion—the state and national electoral systems—had been erected at the center of public life.[37]

The fact that the electoral system, like the world of production and trade, was shaped by competition reinforced the belief that it was legitimate for information diffusion to lead toward diversity rather than uniformity and orthodoxy. It was not that advocates of any cause—Democrat, Whig, Anti-Mason, Temperance, Anti-Slavery, and the others—wanted competition and division; they all sought the triumph of their own political orthodoxy. At the same time, however, they generally recognized the merits of open competition and in most cases lacked the power to extinguish it. Though restrictions were placed on the diffusion of abolition literature in the southern states and other widely accepted abridgements of free speech and free religious practice were exercised locally, there was also a general recognition of the merits of open competition, and only infrequently, at certain times in certain places, a consensus in favor of curtailing it. The same outlook that ruled the marketplace for goods and services—competition—informed religion and politics. As a result, the diversity within American society was reinforced and intensified by a diffusion system which, while it might hold the potential for promoting mass uniformity, taken as a whole supplied a platform for every opinion and catered to every taste.

Individual Choice, Competition, and Pluralism

It is, perhaps, a truism that the manner of circulating information within stable societies normally conforms to the character of that society. A uniform, homogeneous society will exhibit an information diffusion system that is suitably monolithic, while a pluralistic society such as the United States, will be marked by an appropriately pluralistic mode of diffusing information. Such an ideal is plausible, at least. Yet particular examination of information diffusion over time in the United States reveals that the reality was far more complicated. Moreover, when one considers the transition from the era when learning and public information were scarce, exclusive commodities primarily accessible to the few, to the decades after 1790, when they became abundant and available to the many, it is evident that information diffusion was more than a dependent variable. That is, the modes of conveying information in the society—by word of mouth, public ceremony and address, and the several forms of printing—were in themselves so inextricably bound up with each other and historical processes that they became forces shaping the character of society. Individualism and pluralism, competition and mobility, became hallmarks of American society partly because its people developed both an ideology and practice of information diffusion that was not just consistent with such values and behavior but that actually released and promoted them.[38]

Individualism was not, obviously, a creation of 19th-century society, for it had been embedded in colonial experience from the era of settlement onward. Whether it was individual Puritans who sought salvation through conversion, or enterprising farmers, planters, and merchants who worked to squeeze profits from agriculture, land speculation, and trade, early American circumstances had always encouraged a generous measure of individualism. Yet colonial society, with its ethos of hierarchy and the subordination of individuals to family and community well-being, had also curbed individual liberty and expression.[39] Colonial patterns of diffusing information reinforced order, hierarchy, and tradition by limiting access to the full range of information—extensive knowledge—to the few. The information system allowed a William Byrd or a Samuel Sewall the full realization of his personal values and preferences; but for most men and women, the Joshua Hempsteads and Martha Ballards, circumstances supplied neither the desire, wealth, nor discretionary time to indulge the impulse toward self-realization in any singular way. The information system fulfilled all their actual requirements, and allowed unusual farmers' sons like James Parker, the farmer become gentleman, and John Adams, the lawyer and farmer, to acquire the books and education that supplied extensive knowledge. But the system did not promote such behavior.

It was only in the Revolutionary era that the pattern changed. Now the ideology of an informed citizenry, joined with the republican belief in a social hierarchy based on achievement rather than heredity, acted to propel information diffusion toward the many. The acquisition of extensive knowledge was prescribed for republican citizens in all walks of life, and the widespread aspirations for gentility released by the Revolution made it increasingly attractive from a commercial standpoint to bring books, periodicals, newspapers, and public speech to a vast audience of common people. Just as a consumer revolution was supplying the other accoutrements of gentility—printed textiles and ceramic crockery for example—so too it was bringing a wealth of information to the general public.[40]

For information, as with other consumer goods, there was a complicated interaction between individual choices and collective goals. Styles in information as well as fashions in dress and the decorative arts promoted a certain competition to conform with approved tastes so that individual aspirations became collective. In 18th-century Virginia, as we have seen, gentry clamored for the latest novels as well as newspapers and magazines from England, owing not only to intrinsic interest but also because the information these printed goods supplied enabled them to be as stylish in word and thought as they were in their dress, furnishings, and manners. Like the common people of the northern colonies, they continued to consume steady sellers—the staple, mostly religious works of authors like Isaac Watts—but, in addition, they often sought out works that were all but inaccessible to the general public. What changed in the first decades of the 19th century was that now such aspirations could be expressed by the many, and for them, as for the 18th-century gentry, information diffusion offered opportunities for social conformity as well as individual expression.

That the two motives were fully compatible and were both reinforced by the system of information diffusion is evident in the activities of voluntary associations and in the profusion of special interest publications and oratory that flourished in the wake of America's political revolution and the ensuing social and commercial developments of the early republic. For women there were at first charitable and missionary societies of various sorts, and then the mixed-gender educational lyceums and even political engagement as members of temperance and antislavery societies. For men there were numerous civic, political, educational, and profit-seeking and occupational associations.[41] Nearly all of these generated periodical publications and platform oratory extending their specialized information beyond the networks that formed in their face-to-face meetings. By joining clubs and societies, men and women could simultaneously express their individuality in relation to family and community, while also associating themselves voluntarily with a group that reinforced their chosen identity as a particular friend of Christian missions, or Jefferson, or Methodism, or temperance. People developed methods of diffusing information to satisfy these objectives, and, as a kind of system took shape, it created not only an abundance of available information and the requirement that every free person make choices, but also occasional efforts to censor unpopular views. Extra-local public information and information activities became so ubiquitous that opponents had to organize; and even ignoring information activity and staying aloof required an active kind of negative choice—such as Ashley Bowen, the loyalist sympathizer, had exercised regarding the news from Lexington and Concord in 1775.

Choices, the multiplicity of groups and individuals generating information, the widespread diversity of religious and political opinion that circulated through commercially developed regions—these realities made pluralism a central feature of American society. Information diffusion did not, of course, create the foundations of this phenomenon; but the many ways in which information was effectively spread through the social order encouraged the pluralistic pattern. However diverse colonial America had been overall, within rural communities scarcity had all but required conformity of perceptions since nearly everyone shared access to the same information and to the same interpretive commentaries on it. And although abundance is commonly associated with mass communication and conformity, in America mass communication encouraged individualism among the many. Public opinion was acknowledged to be powerful, but there were numerous competing public opinions. So, although there was not an absolutely pure individualism, when compared with the familial and communal boundaries of women's and men's information in the colonial past, adults were now liberated to listen to or to read whatever information appealed to them from among a welter of competing alternatives.

Individual choice in a competitive, pluralistic society—this was what the development of information diffusion yielded for much of America in the 19th century. A polity that rejected orthodoxy and monopoly in politics, religion, and economic affairs made competition one of the ruling principles of institutional and personal life, and so sustained a multi-layered information diffusion system. For alongside the old, face-to-face networks of families and localities, new modes of distributing information flourished. As a result, the functions of the old ways became narrower and more specialized. Family, friends, neighbors, and business associates were no longer responsible for disseminating public information, and so the functions that they did retain—the dissemination of news regarding their own set—became more exclusive and specialized than before. Impersonal media gained the dominant role in conveying public information. As a result, the importance of social hierarchy and the power of the elite in defining and interpreting public information and general cultural information declined. The professional, merchant, and landed elites still retained superior access to extensive information as a result of their greater wealth, leisure, and more cosmopolitan experience, but they were no longer the information gatekeepers for their neighbors. Moreover to the extent that popular tastes came to dominate the mass information marketplace, the situation as to prescription was reversed, so it was the elite that was pressed to consume the information favored by common men and women. The information marketplace and the diffusion system became vehicles for two-way influences, with common people consuming the genteel information that elevated them socially, while genteel men and women were drawn into popular culture as with electoral politics and popular novels. With extensive information on all kinds of subjects circulating widely in a marketplace where every taste could be served, both specialized types of information such as the *Collections of the American Statistical Association* (1847), and general information found in popular periodicals like *Leslie's Illustrated Weekly* (1855) were available to almost anyone who wanted them.[42] What kinds of information would prevail were beyond any clergyman's or gentleman's, any public leader's, or any group's prescription.

Underlying these developments was a rapidly urbanizing social order built on geographic and social mobility. To move from one farm to another, from farm to city, or from one city to another, was at some stage in free people's lives a real, frequently exercised option. More often than not, the objective was to better oneself economically and socially. For these activities access to information was critical; and the fact that the post office and the press made it feasible for massive numbers of people to relocate, while retaining familiar ties and remaining within the same public information circle, eased the social and cultural consequences of geographical movement. At the same time the fact of general rather than exclusive access to the information that sustained the gentrification of millions of families made it an acceptable process in republican, rather than aristocratic, terms. The character of the information diffusion system was so closely attuned to American social and economic development as to seem inevitable.

Whether inevitable or not, however, the history of the diffusion of information in American society points to changes that were affected less by technology and specific actors, and more by cultural and economic events that were spread across several generations.[43] The speed at which information traveled across space was ultimately less important than the question of whom it touched as it moved through society. The shift from an England-oriented elite and a deferential populace to a United States–centered general population, in which elites played subtle and circumscribed roles, shaped the character of the information system decisively, while at the same time information diffusion practices were influential in sustaining both colonial and republican social arrangements. What mattered most were social roles and their prescriptions concerning appropriate levels of learning, knowledge, and information for men and women, for farmers and clergymen, for merchants, lawyers, and everyone else. These roles and prescriptions shaped behavior substantially, so that, when republicanism redefined citizenship and commercial expansion launched the consumer revolution, they transformed the information marketplace and the information activities of most Americans. No new printing or transportation technology exerted any influence until the 1820s, and by then the changeover from scarcity to abundance was well underway.

All the implications of these changes are beyond the scope of this study, but one, at least, jumps out from the evidence assembled here. Colonial society, for all its diversity, had been essentially a collection of local societies in which both a patina and much of the substance of a common, coherent Christian culture was maintained. Reading and oratory were dominated by religious messages, and the themes of order and stability expressed by church and state were mutually reinforcing.[44] Competition, while real, was subordinate to cooperation in community and even, in many instances, in commercial life. But as the 19th-century republic developed, coherence was supplanted and competition ruled. Clergymen like Henry Ward Beecher, politicians like Daniel Webster who could win the largest followings, lyceum speakers who could sell the most tickets, authors whose works sold widely became influential not because of any office they held or any prescribed public role, but because of their engaging popular performances. In a competitive environment of regional or national dimensions, where purveyors of each type of information had to compete with others conveying similar information as well as with a multitude of entirely different sorts of information, each individual was invited to discover his or her own coherent culture from within the galaxy of religious sects, political parties, and reform societies that were thriving in the new republic. The new patterns for the diffusion of information were not in themselves responsible for these developments, but they would have been inconceivable without the new configuration of information diffusion that offered many choices to many people.

Appendix

The data on the distribution of clergymen by college affiliation for 1740 and 1770 tabulated below was compiled from Frederick L. Weis, *The Colonial Clergy and the Colonial Churches of New England* (Baltimore, 1936).

Connecticut		Harvard	Yale	Non-Degree	Other Degrees
Fairfield Co.	1740	2	16	0	0
	1770	1	29	0	1
Hartford Co.	1740	17	19	1	1
	1770	6	45	5	2
Litchfield Co.	1740	1	9	0	0
	1770	0	23	0	1
New Haven Co.	1740	5	24	1	1
	1770	2	37	2	2
New London Co.	1740	12	9	3	2
	1770	6	14	13	1
Windham Co.	1740	11	4	0	0
	1770	7	14	7	1
Massachusetts					
Barnstable Co.	1740	10	1	3	0
	1770	13	1	2	0
Berkshire Co.	1740	0	2	0	0
	1770	1	11	0	0
Bristol Co.	1740	11	1	3	0
	1770	10	2	9	1
Cumberland Co.	1740	2	1	1	1
	1770	10	0	3	1
Dukes Co.	1740	2	0	0	1
	1770	3	0	1	0
Essex Co.	1740	39	0	2	1
	1770	51	4	1	3
Hampshire Co.	1740	10	8	1	0
	1770	13	23	2	2

Massachusetts (continued)		Harvard	Yale	Non-Degree	Other Degrees
Lincoln Co.	1740	0	0	0	0
	1770	4	0	1	2
Middlesex Co.	1740	26	2	0	0
	1770	35	3	2	0
Nantucket Co.	1740	1	0	0	0
	1770	1	0	0	0
Plymouth Co.	1740	22	0	0	0
	1770	21	3	0	2
Suffolk Co.	1740	43	0	0	3
	1770	38	3	1	4
Worcester Co.	1740	16	1	2	1
	1770	40	8	7	2
York Co.	1740	5	0	0	0
	1770	10	3	0	0
New Hampshire					
Cheshire Co.	1740	1	1	0	0
	1770	6	2	1	0
Grafton Co.	1740	0	0	0	0
	1770	1	1	0	1
Hillsborough Co.	1740	3	0	0	0
	1770	9	1	0	4
Rockingham Co.	1740	18	0	0	4
	1770	26	0	2	8
Strafford Co.	1740	3	0	0	0
	1770	4	1	1	0
Rhode Island					
Bristol Co.	1740	3	1	0	0
	1770	1	0	0	2
Kent Co.	1740	0	0	3	0
	1770	0	0	5	0
Newport Co.	1740	4	2	2	0
	1770	5	1	6	1
Providence Co.	1740	1	0	5	1
	1770	1	0	10	0
South Co.	1740	2	0	5	1
	1770	3	0	3	0

Summary		Harvard	Yale	Non-Degree	Other Degrees	Total
Connecticut	1740	48	81	5	4	138
	1770	22	162	27	8	219
Massachusetts	1740	187	16	12	7	222
	1770	240	61	28	17	346
New Hampshire	1740	25	1	0	4	30
	1770	46	5	4	13	68
Rhode Island	1740	10	3	15	2	30
	1770	10	1	24	3	38

New England	1740	270	101	32	17	420
	1770	318	229	83	41	671

The data on the distribution of clerical authorship in Massachusetts, 1740–1799, is tabulated below by town.

Town	No. of Clerical Publications
Abington	—
Amesbury	5
Andover	17
Arlington	5
Ashburnham	2
Ashby	5
Attleborough	1
Barnstable	11
Barre	3
Berkeley	3
Beverly	11
Billerica	—
Boston	193
Boxborough	6
Boxford	2
Boylston	1
Braintree	14
Brewster	2
Bridgewater	7
Brighton	1
Brimfield	1
Brockton	4
Brookfield	9
Brookline	2
Cambridge	33
Canton	6
Carver	—
Charlestown	14
Charlton	1
Chatham	—
Chelmsford	8
Chester	1
Chesterfield	9
Chilmark	1
Cohasset	2
Concord	8
Danvers	18
Dedham	9
Deerfield	7
Dighton	1

Town (continued)	No. of Clerical Publications
Dorchester	14
Dover	1
Dracut	2
Dunstable	1
East Bridgewater	1
Eastham	1
Edgartown	1
Essex	9
Fitchburg	2
Framingham	2
Franklin	18
Georgetown	7
Gloucester	13
Grafton	9
Great Barrington	13
Greenfield	3
Greenwich	2
Groveland	11
Halifax	8
Hamilton	6
Hanover	1
Hanson	7
Harvard	6
Harwich	1
Hatfield	16
Haverhill	14
Hingham	20
Holden	4
Hull	17
Ipswich	13
Jamaica Plain	5
Kingston	5
Lancaster	3
Leominster	5
Lexington	9
Lincoln	5
Littleton	2
Longmeadow	2
Lunenburg	11
Lynn	2
Lynnfield Center	1
Malden	4
Mansfield	4

Marblehead	5
Marlborough	2
Marshfield	3
Mattapoisett	4
Medfield	9
Medford	12
Mendon	9
Methuen	3
Middleborough	7
Milford	1
Millbury	6
Millis	4
Milton	4
Montague	2
Natick	4
Needham	14
New Bedford	6
New Braintree	3
Newbury	14
Newburyport	20
New Marlborough	5
New Salem	3
Newton	7
Northampton	53
North Andover	4
North Attleborough	2
Northborough	3
North Brookfield	11
Northfield	2
North Reading	4
Norwell	6
Norwood	5
Orleans	1
Oxford	—
Palmer	4
Peabody	1
Pelham	1
Pembroke	3
Pepperell	4
Plymouth	21
Plympton	4
Princeton	1
Quincy	3
Randolph	2
Reading	1
Revere	1

Town (continued)	No. of Clerical Publications
Rockport	1
Rowley	15
Roxbury	19
Royalston	4
Rutland	4
Salem	25
Sandwich	3
Scituate	1
Sheffield	3
Sherborn	3
Shirley	—
Shrewsbury	1
Southhampton	2
South Hadley	1
Spencer	2
Springfield	9
Sterling	12
Stockbridge	13
Stoneham	7
Sudbury	2
Taunton	1
Templeton	1
Topsfield	—
Upton	11
Uxbridge	1
Wakefield	9
Waltham	7
Ware	1
Warwick	1
Wayland	3
Westborough	1
West Bridgewater	2
West Brookfield	—
Westfield	2
Westhampton	1
West Newbury	9
Weston	10
West Roxbury	4
West Springfield	25
Westwood	5
Williamsburg	2
Wilmington	2
Windsor	5
Woburn	7
Worcester	18
Worthington	1

Notes

INTRODUCTION

1. The Biblical passage is from Prov. 24:5; the Shakespeare quotation is from his 1590 play, *2 Henry VI* iv.7.79, quoted in *The Oxford Dictionary of English Proverbs,* comp. by William George Smith (Oxford, 1936), p. 254. The Bacon quotation is from his 1597 religious meditation, *De Haeresibus (Of Heresies),* X, quoted in J.A. Simpson, ed., *The Concise Oxford Dictionary of Proverbs* (Oxford, 1982), pp. 126–27. The English proverb "knowledge is power" is identified in H. L. Mencken, ed., *A New Dictionary of Quotations on Historical Principles* (New York, 1952, first pub. 1942), p. 638.

2. My perspective on the role of printing has been influenced by Elizabeth Eisenstein, *The Printing Press as an Agent of Change: Communications and Cultural Transformations in Early Modern Europe,* 2 vols. (Cambridge, 1979) and Lucien Febvre and Henri-Jean Martin, *The Coming of the Book: The Impact of Printing 1450–1800* (London, 1976).

3. William Charvat, *Literary Publishing in America, 1790–1850* (Philadelphia, 1959); Lewis A. Coser, Charles Kadushin, and Walter W. Powell, *Books: The Culture and Commerce of Publishing* (New York, 1982); Charles E. Clark, " 'Metropolis' and 'Province' in Eighteenth-Century Press Relations: The Case of Boston," *Journal of Newspaper and Periodical History* (London, forthcoming 1989) and with Charles Wetherell, "The Measure of Maturity: The Pennsylvania Gazette, 1728–1765," forthcoming in *William and Mary Quarterly,* 3d ser. 51 (1989); Eisenstein, *Printing Press as an Agent of Change;* James Gilreath, "American Book Distribution," *Proceedings of the American Antiquarian Society,* 95 pt. 2 (1986), pp. 501–83; Milton Hamilton, *The Country Printer, New York State, 1785–1830* (New York, 1936); William Joyce, David D. Hall, Richard D. Brown, and John Hench, eds., *Printing and Society in Early America* (Worcester, Mass., 1983); Sidney Kobre, *Development of the Colonial Newspaper* (Pittsburgh, 1944); Hellmut Lehmann-Haupt et al., eds., *The Book in America: A History of the Making, the Selling, and the Collecting of Books in the United States,* rev. ed. (New York, 1951); Frank Luther Mott, *American Journalism: A History, 1690–1960,* 3d ed. (New York, 1962); Frank Luther Mott, *A History of American Magazines,* 5 vols. (Cambridge, Mass., 1930–68); Douglas C. McMurtrie, *A History of Printing in the United States* (New York, 1936); Dan Schiller, *Objectivity and the News: The Public and the Rise of Commercial Journalism* (Philadelphia, 1981); Michael Schudson, *Discovering the News: A Social History of American Newspapers* (New York, 1978); Mitchell Stephens, *A History of News: From the Drum to the Satellite* (New York, 1988); John Tebbel, *A History of Book Publishing in the United States* (New York, 1972–81); Robert M. Weir, "The Role of the Newspaper Press in the Southern Colonies on the Eve of the Revolution: An Interpretation," in Bernard Bailyn and John B. Hench, eds., *The Press & the American Revolution* (Worcester, Mass., 1980), pp. 99–150.

4. Richard D. Altick, *The English Common Reader: A Social History of the Mass Reading*

Public, 1800–1900 (Chicago, 1957); Nina Baym, *Novels, Readers, and Reviewers: Responses to Fiction in Antebellum America* (Ithaca, N.Y., 1984); Kenneth E. Carpenter, ed., *Books and Society in History* (New York, 1983); Miriam Usher Chrisman, *Lay Culture, Learned Culture: Books and Social Change in Strasbourg, 1480–1599* (New Haven, 1982); David Cressy, *Literacy and the Social Order: Reading and Writing in Tudor and Stuart England* (Cambridge, 1980); Robert Darnton, *The Business of the Enlightenment: A Publishing History of the Encyclopédie* (Cambridge, Mass., 1979), *The Literary Underground of the Old Regime* (Cambridge, Mass., 1982), and "What Is the History of Books?" *Daedalus,* 111 (1982): 65–83; Cathy N. Davidson, *Revolution and the Word: The Rise of the Novel in America* (New York, 1986); Febvre and Martin, *Coming of the Book;* Norman Fiering, "The Transatlantic Republic of Letters: A Note on the Circulation of Learned Periodicals," *William and Mary Quarterly,* 3d ser., 33 (1976): 642–60; William J. Gilmore, "Elementary Literacy on the Eve of the Industrial Revolution: Trends in Rural New England, 1760–1830," *Proceedings of the American Antiquarian Society,* 92, pt. 1 (1982): 87–178, and *Reading Becomes a 'Necessity of Life': Material and Cultural Life in Rural New England 1780–1830* (Knoxville, 1988); Harvey J. Graff, *The Literacy Myth: Literacy and Social Structure in the Nineteenth-Century City* (New York, 1979); Robert A. Gross, "Much Instruction from Little Reading: Books and Libraries in Thoreau's Concord," *Proceedings of the American Antiquarian Society,* 97, pt. 1 (1987): 129–88; David D. Hall, "The Uses of Literacy in New England, 1600–1850," in Joyce et al., eds., *Printing and Society in Early America* (Worcester, Mass., 1983), pp. 1–47; Joseph F. Kett and Patricia A. McClung, "Book Culture in Post-Revolutionary Virginia," *Proceedings of the America Antiquarian Society* 94, pt. 1 (1984): 97–147; Kenneth Lockridge, *Literacy in Colonial New England: An Enquiry into the Social Context of Literacy in the Early Modern West* (New York, 1974); David Lundberg and Henry May, "The Enlightened Reader in America," *American Quarterly,* 28 (1976): 262–93; Isabel Rivers, ed., *Books and their Readers in Eighteenth-Century England* (New York, 1982); Jesse H. Shera, *Foundations of the Public Library: The Origins of the Public Library Movement in New England, 1629–1855* (Chicago, 1949); Margaret Spufford, *Small Books and Pleasant Histories: Popular Fiction and Its Readership in Seventeenth-Century England* (Athens, Ga., 1982); Roy McKeen Wiles, "The Relish for Reading in Provincial England Two Centuries Ago," in *The Widening Circle: Essays on the Circulation of Literature in Eighteenth-Century Europe,* ed. by Paul Korshin (Philadelphia, 1976), pp. 85–115.

5. Richard R. John, Jr., "Managing the Mails: The U.S. Postal System in National Politics, 1823–1836," Ph.D. diss., Harvard Univ., 1989; Richard B. Kielbowicz, "News in the Mails, 1690–1863: The Technology, Policy, and Politics of a Communication Channel," Ph.D. diss., Univ. of Minnesota, 1984. Among the works I have found informative are: James M. Banner, Jr., *To the Hartford Convention: The Federalists and the Origins of Party Politics in Massachusetts, 1789–1815* (New York, 1970); James H. Broussard, *The Southern Federalists, 1800–1816* (Baton Rouge, 1978); Donald B. Cole, *Jacksonian Democracy in New Hampshire* (Cambridge, Mass., 1970); William Nisbet Chambers and Walter Dean Burnham, eds., *The American Party Systems: Stages of Political Development,* 2d ed. (New York, 1975); David Hackett Fischer, *The Revolution of American Conservatism: The Federalist Party in the Era of Jeffersonian Democracy* (New York, 1965); Ronald P. Formisano, *The Birth of Mass Political Parties: Michigan, 1827–1861* (Princeton, 1971), and *The Transformation of Political Culture: Massachusetts Parties, 1790s–1840s* (New York, 1983); Paul Goodman, *The Democratic-Republicans of Massachusetts: Politics in a Young Republic* (Cambridge, Mass., 1964); Daniel Walker Howe, *The Political Culture of the American Whigs* (Chicago, 1979); Linda K. Kerber, *Federalists in Dissent: Imagery and Ideology in Jeffersonian America* (Ithaca, 1970); Paul Kleppner et al., *The Evolution of American Electoral Systems* (Westport, Ct., 1981); Richard P. McCormick, *The Second American Party System: Party Formation in the Jacksonian Era* (Chapel Hill, 1966); Edward Pessen, *Jacksonian America: Society, Personality, and Politics;* rev. ed. (Homewood, Ill., 1978); Joel H. Silbey, Allan G. Bogue, and William Flanigan, eds., *The History of American*

Electoral Behavior (Princeton, N.J., 1978); Alfred F. Young, *The Democratic Republicans of New York: The Origins. 1763–1797* (Chapel Hill, 1967).

6. Altick, *The English Common Reader;* Baym, *Novels, Readers, and Reviewers* and *Women's Fiction: A Guide to Novels by and about Women in America, 1820–1870* (Ithaca, 1978); Paul S. Boyer, *Urban Masses and the Moral Order in America, 1820–1870* (Cambridge, Mass., 1978); Richard D. Brown, "The Emergence of Urban Society in Rural Massachusetts, 1760–1820," *Journal of American History,* 61 (1974): 29–51; Mary Kupiec Cayton, "The Making of an American Prophet: Emerson, His Audiences, and the Rise of the Culture Industry in Nineteenth-Century America," *American Historical Review,* 92 (June 1987): 597–620; Lawrence A. Cremin, *American Education: The National Experience, 1783–1876* (New York, 1980); Gross, "Much Instruction from Little Reading;" Neil Harris, *Humbug: The Art of P. T. Barnum* (Boston, 1973); Carl F. Kaestle, *The Evolution of an Urban School System: New York City, 1750–1850* (Cambridge, Mass., 1973) and *Pillars of the Republic: Common Schools and American Society, 1780–1860* (New York, 1983); Carl F. Kaestle and Maris A. Vinovskis, *Educational and Social Change in Nineteenth-Century Massachusetts* (Cambridge, Mass., 1980); Michael B. Katz, *The Irony of Early School Reform: Educational Innovation in Mid-Nineteenth Century Massachusetts* (Cambridge, Mass., 1968); Stanley Schultz, *The Culture Factory: Boston Public Schools, 1789–1860* (New York, 1973); Donald M. Scott, "The Popular Lecture and the Creation of a Public in Mid-Nineteenth Century America," *Journal of American History,* 66 (Mar. 1980), 791–809, and "Print and the Public Lecture System, 1840–1860," in Joyce et al., eds., *Printing and Society,* pp. 278–99; Shera, *Foundations of the Public Library;* Theodore Sizer, ed., *The Age of the Academies* (New York, 1964); Lee Soltow and Edward Stevens, *The Rise of Literacy and the Common Schools in the United States: A Socioeconomic Analysis to 1870* (Chicago, 1981).

7. Among the influential exceptions are: Joy Day Buel and Richard Buel, Jr., *The Way of Duty: A Woman and Her Family in Revolutionary America* (New York, 1984); John Putnam Demos, *Entertaining Satan: Witchcraft and the Culture of Early New England* (New York, 1982); Robert A. Gross, *The Minutemen and Their World* (New York, 1976); Christopher M. Jedrey, *The World of John Cleaveland: Family and Community in Eighteenth-Century New England* (New York, 1979).

8. The key bibliographies are Harriette Merrifield Forbes, comp., *New England Diaries, 1602– 1800: A Descriptive Catalogue of Diaries, Orderly Books and Sea Journals* (New York, 1923, reprinted, 1967); William Matthews, *American Diaries: An Annotated Bibliography of Published American Diaries and Journals* (to 1861). Expanded and revised by Laura Arksey, Nancy Preis, and Marcia Reed. First pub. 1945 (Detroit, 1983), and his *American Diaries in Manuscript, 1580–1954: A Descriptive Bibliography* (Athens, Ga., 1974).

9. Here I am following Richard L. Bushman's approach in "American High-Style and Vernacular Cultures," in *Colonial British America: Essays in the New History of the Early Modern Era,* ed by Jack P. Greene and J. R. Pole (Baltimore, 1984), pp. 345–83.

10. The interplay of latent and manifest events is discussed in Bernard Bailyn, "The Challenge of Modern Historiography," *American Historical Review,* 87 (Feb. 1982): 1–24.

11. A remarkable example of how a full 17th-century diary may be analyzed exhaustively is Alan Macfarlane's penetrating *The Family Life of Ralph Josselin, a Seventeenth-Century Clergyman: An Essay in Historical Anthropology* (Cambridge, England, 1970).

12. Until now the key work on American literacy has been Kenneth A. Lockridge, *Literacy in Colonial New England: An Enquiry into the Social Context of Literacy in the Early Modern West* (New York, 1974). See also Linda Auwers, "The Social Meaning of Female Literacy: Windsor, Connecticut, 1660–1775," Newberry Library Papers in Family and Community History, No. 77–4A, Newberry Library, Chicago; Ross W. Beales, Jr., "Studying Literacy at the Community

Level: A Research Note," *Journal of Interdisciplinary History,* 9 (Summer 1978): 93–102; Harvey J. Graff, *The Legacies of Literacy: Continuities and Contradictions in Western Culture and Society* (Bloomington, Ind., 1987); Carl F. Kaestle, "The History of Literacy and the History of Readers," *Review of Research in Education,* 12 (1985): 11–53; Linda K. Kerber, *Women of the Republic: Intellect and Ideology in Revolutionary America* (New York, 1986), pp. 164–65, 191–93; Gloria L. Main, "Female Literacy in Early New England: Signatures, Books, and Schooling," paper given at American Antiquarian Society seminar in American social and political history, May 1988. The general comments here are derived chiefly from these sources.

13. E. Jennifer Monaghan, "Literacy Instruction and Gender in Colonial New England." *American Quarterly,* 40 (1988): 18–41.

14. Richard D. Brown, "From Cohesion to Competition," in Joyce et al., eds., *Printing and Society,* 300–309; David D. Hall, "The Uses of Literacy in New England, 1600–1850," in Joyce et al., eds., *Printing and Society,* pp. 1–47.

15. Donald M. Scott, "The Popular Lecture and the Creation of a Public in Mid-Nineteenth Century America," *Journal of American History,* 66 (Mar. 1980): 791–809, and "Print and the Public Lecture System, 1840–1860," in Joyce et al., eds., *Printing and Society, pp. 278–99.*

16. Richard John, "Managing the Mails: The U.S. Postal System in National Politics, 1823–1836," unpublished Ph.D. diss., Harvard Univ., 1989, "Introduction," pp. 14, 40–41, n. 53.

17. Richard D. Brown, *Modernization: The Transformation of American Life, 1600–1865* (New York, 1976), p. 166.

18. Alexander Anderson to Julia Anderson Halsey, New York City, May 1865, New-York Historical Society, Manuscript Dept. Anderson wrote: "There are iron boxes put up in different parts of the city to accommodate people at a distance from the Post-office, in one of these I have often dropt my letters." Also see: Richard R. John, Jr., "Private Mail Delivery in the United States during the Nineteenth Century: A Sketch," *Business and Economic History,* 2d ser., 15 (1986):135–47.

19. Brown, *Modernization,* p. 143.

20. Brown, *Modernization,* p. 165. The information was collected by Allen R. Pred, *Urban Growth and the Circulation of Information: The United States System of Cities, 1790–1840* (Cambridge, Mass., 1973), pp. 37, 53.

CHAPTER 1. INFORMATION AND AUTHORITY IN SAMUEL SEWALL'S BOSTON, 1676–1729

1. This and succeeding Boston population estimates are from G. B. Warden, *Boston, 1689–1776* (Boston, 1970), pp. 3, 67, 81, 103, 104. An insightful, perceptive examination of Sewall's Boston is sketched in David D. Hall, "The Mental World of Samuel Sewall," *Proceedings of the Massachusetts Historical Society,* 92 (1980): 21–44.

2. Warden, *Boston,* ch. 1. Carl Bridenbaugh, *Cities in the Wilderness: The First Century of Urban Life in America, 1625–1742* (New York, 1938). Quotation from Mather is in Warden, *Boston,* p. 16.

3. Warden, *Boston,* p. 102.

4. Ian K. Steele, *The English Atlantic, 1675–1740: An Exploration of Communication and Community* (New York, 1986), pt. 3; G. A. Cranfield, *The Development of the Provincial Newspaper, 1700–1760* (Oxford, 1962), ch. 1. See also Charles E. Clark on early American journalism.

5. Samuel Sewall to Ezekiel Cheever, Nathaniel Williams, Boston, Apr. 1, 1708, *Letter-Book of Samuel Sewall,* Massachusetts Historical Society, *Collections,* 6th ser., 1 (Boston, 1886): 365–66.

6. David Weir Conroy, "The Culture and Politics of Drink in Colonial and Revolutionary Massachusetts, 1681–1790." Unpub. Ph.D. diss. Univ. of Connecticut, 1987, chs. 2 and 3.

7. *The Diary of Samuel Sewall, 1674–1729,* ed. by M. Halsey Thomas (New York 1973), 1: 32n.; *Letter-Book,* 1:411–12, Aug. 9, 1711; Aug. 4, 1712, to Mr. Love. Thomas provides a chronology of Sewall's life, 1:xxiii–xxviii, and a list of Boston churches and clergy in Sewall's era (2:1113–15). The best biography of Sewall is T. B. Strandness, *Samuel Sewall: A Puritan Portrait* (East Lansing, Mich., 1967). For the commercial context see Bernard Bailyn, *The New England Merchants in the Seventeenth Century* (Cambridge, Mass., 1955), chs. 5–7.

8. Francis J. Bremer, "Increase Mather's Friends: The Trans-Atlantic Congregational Network of the Seventeenth Century," *Proceedings of the American Antiquarian Society,* 94, pt. 1 (Apr. 1984):59–96; David Cressy, *Coming Over: Migration and Communication between England and New England in the Seventeenth Century* (Cambridge, 1987).

9. Sewall to Israel Chauncy, n.p., Jan. 9, 1697, *Letter-Book,* 1:181; *Diary* 1:363–64.

10. *Diary,* 1:366–67. Soon after this confession of repentance Sewall enjoyed dreams of salvation.

11. *Diary,* 1:350, May 18, 1696; 1:576, Nov. 18, 1707. The close, dense network of family relationships is comparable to that described by Alan Macfarlane, *The Family Life of Ralph Josselin: An Essay in Historical Anthropology* (Cambridge, Eng., 1970), and which was based on the text published in *The Diary of Ralph Josselin, 1616–1683,* Alan Macfarlane, ed. (London, 1976).

12. *Diary,* 1:30, Dec. 21, 1676; *Letter-Book,* 1:88–89, Sewall to Edward Hull, n.p., Oct. 8, 1688; *Letter-Book,* 1:136–37, Sewall to Edward Hull, n.p., Oct. 24, 1693.

13. *Diary,* 1:9, Nov. 5, 1674; *Letter-book,* 1:23–25, Mar. 1, 1686; for the general context see Cressy, *Coming Over,* ch. 9 (" 'A constant intercourse of letters': the transatlantic flow of information").

14. *Diary,* 1:284, Dec. 2, 1691.

15. *Diary,* 1:348–349, Feb. 22, 1696; Feb. 26, 1696; May 3, 1696.

16. John Demos, *A Little Commonwealth: Family Life in Plymouth Colony* (New York, 1970), pp. 46–48. Neither the cottages of the poor nor the mansions of the rich placed much emphasis on creating private spaces in the 17th century.

17. *Diary,* 1:256, Apr. 15, 1690.

18. The "tribalism" idea was employed in Edmund S. Morgan, *The Puritan Family* (Boston, 1944), ch. 6. Steele, *The English Atlantic,* chs. 8–11, emphasizes influence of more newspapers and commercial activity.

19. All references to frequency are based on a compilation of entries in the Sewall diary. The top ten, all with more than 200 separate entries, were: Joseph Dudley (Harvard College, 1665, major, colonel, governor, and in-law), Joseph Sewall (son, Harvard College 1707, minister of Old South Church), Cotton Mather (Harvard College 1678, minister of North Church), Isaac Addington (Secretary of Massachusetts, Chief Justice), Samuel Willard (Harvard College 1659, minister of Old South Church, vice-president of Harvard College), Increase Mather (Harvard College 1656, minister of North Church, president of Harvard College), Samuel Sewall, Jr. (son, merchant), Ebenezer Pemberton (Harvard College 1691, minister of Old South Church), Hannah Hull Sewall (wife), Wait Still Winthrop (Harvard College 1662, major, colonel, Chief Justice).

20. *Diary,* 2:863–64, Oct. 19, 1717.

21. *Diary,* 1:454, 454n.; Sewall to Cotton Mather, n.p., Oct. 21, 1701, *Letter-Book,* 1:263.

22. *Diary,* 1:474–75, Sept. 15, 1702.

23. *Diary,* 2:705–6n.

24. Warden, *Boston,* pp. 91–97, ch. 5 passim.

25. *Diary,* 1:29–30, Dec. 18, 1676.

26. *Diary,* 1:32, Jan. 6, 1677.

27. Steele, *The English Atlantic,* ch. 6.

28. *Letter-Book,* Massachusetts Historical Society, *Collections,* 6th ser., 2 (Boston, 1888): 183–84, June 4, 1725.

29. *Diary,* 2:1040, Dec. 13, 1725; 2:1063, Oct. 28, 1728.

30. *Diary,* 2:1052–53, May 14, 1727.

31. *Diary,* 2:1061–62, June 23, 1728.

32. *Diary,* 2:1065, Feb. 5, 1729.

33. *Diary,* 2:1066, Mar. 31, 1729; Apr. 2, 1729. Sewall's distribution of sermons complemented a larger pattern whereby clergymen, especially, distributed religious pamphlets and books. See George Selement, *Keepers of the Vineyard: The Puritan Ministry and Collective Culture in Colonial New England* (Lanham, Md., 1984), ch. 4.

34. As late as 1748 the privacy of legislative debates was still being defended in the Boston press on the ground that it permitted legislators to speak freely. (Robert Zemsky, *Merchants, Farmers, and River Gods: An Essay on Eighteenth-Century America Politics* (Boston, 1971), p. 18.)

35. *Diary,* 2:632, Feb. 3, 1710.

36. *Diary,* 2:631, Jan. 2, 1710.

37. *Diary,* 2:631–32, Jan. 28, 1710.

38. *Diary,* 1:505–6, Jun. 9, 1704. Account in *Boston News-Letter* of June 12–19, 1704, is reprinted in *Diary,* 1:506–8.

39. *Diary,* 1:4, Apr. 15, 1674; 1:48, Feb. 3, 1681; 1:165, Apr. 18, 1688.

40. *Diary* 1:391, Apr. 12, 1698.

41. *Diary,* 1:329, Mar. 29, 1695.

42. *Diary,* 2:1016, May 3, 1724.

43. *Diary,* 1:155, Dec. 25, 1687; 2:1015, May 1, 1724.

44. On funeral practices see David Stannard, *The Puritan Way of Death: A Study in Religion, Culture, and Social Change* (New York, 1977), ch. 5. In 1683 a critic of English Puritan funerals commented that "to look at those who accompany the body, to see them so immodest and laughing all along the way, it would appear as though they were going to a comedy rather than to a funeral." (Stannard, *Puritan Way of Death,* 106.) There is no reason to suppose that levity characterized Boston funeral processions, but secular conversations did occur.

45. *Diary,* 1:600–601, Aug. 26, 1708.

46. *Diary,* 1:103, Apr. 1, 1686.

47. *Diary,* 2:646–47, Nov. 28, 1710.

48. Ibid.

49. *Diary,* 2:640, July 15 and 17, 1710.

50. Cressy, *Coming Over*, 259, notes that "information was a kind of wealth, but one that could easily be shared."

51. *Diary*, 1:276, Mar. 28, 1691; Cressy, *Coming Over*, explains that letters often abbreviated the news, referring recipients to word-of-mouth sources.

52. There was some disagreement regarding the desirability of publishing current prices of goods in *Boston Gazette* in 1719. See text below, p. 38–39.

53. Benjamin W. Labaree, *Colonial Massachusetts: A History* (Millwood, N.Y., 1979), p. 132; Zemsky, *Merchants, Farmers, and River Gods*, pp. 17–18.

54. Harry S. Stout, *The New England Soul: Preaching and Religious Culture in Colonial New England* (New York, 1986), chs. 4–9 treat the sermon during Sewall's lifetime.

55. *Diary* 2:785, Feb. 4, 1715; Barbara Lambert and M. Sue Ladr, "Civic Announcements: The Role of Drums, Criers and Bells in the Colonies," in Barbara Lambert, ed., *Music in Colonial Massachusetts, 1630–1820*, 2:871–933. (Colonial Society of Massachusetts, *Collections*, vol. 54 (Boston, 1985).)

56. *Diary*, 1:409, Apr. 27, 1699.

57. *Diary*, 2:613, Jan. 16, 1709.

58. *Diary*, 1:415, Oct. 23, 1699.

59. *Diary*, 1:78, Sept. 22, 1685.

60. *Diary*, 1:78, Sept. 23, 1685.

61. *Diary* 1:79, Oct. 1, 1685. Steele, *The English Atlantic*, p. 94ff. deals with the problem of misinformation during the Glorious Revolution.

62. *Diary*, 1:492, Sept. 6, 1703.

63. *Diary*, 1:492, Sept. 19, 1703.

64. *Diary*, 2:801, Oct. 4, 1715. William Byrd, the Chesapeake planter, reported on May 11, 1712 "we went to church where I saw a man who told us he had read in a gazette that the King of France was dead." (William Byrd, *Secret Diary, 1709–1712*, ed. by L. B. Wright and M. Tinling (Richmond, Va., 1941), p. 528.)

65. *Diary*, 2:1065, 1065n., Feb. 14, 1729. Account of funeral in *New-England Weekly Journal*, Feb. 24, 1729.

66. *Diary*, 2:697, Aug. 25, 1712.

67. *Diary*, 1:50, Jul. 24, 1681.

68. *Diary*, 2:668, Sept. 17, 1711.

69. *Diary*, 1:552, Sept. 21, 1706.

70. Frank Luther Mott, *American Journalism, A History: 1690–1960*, 3d ed. (New York, 1962), p. 13. There is no way of ascertaining the exact population of the Boston region at this time; however, in 1716 the entire population of the colony was reported at 94,000 whites, 2000 slaves, and 1200 Christian Indians. (John Stetson Barry, *The History of Massachusetts. The Provincial Period*, 4th ed. (Boston, 1856), 2:106n.)

71. *Diary*, 1:501, Apr. 24, 1704.

72. Sewall's file of 86 Boston *News-Letters* from number 1 to 192 is at the New-York Historical Society and carries a heading "Book 1st Memorandums." His 4-page calendar, begun in 1704, is interleaved in the volume which was rebound in the present century. A later volume, without index or calendar, but including some broadsides, is at the Boston Atheneum. See *Diary*, 1:501–2n. On the general interpretation see Steele, *The English Atlantic*, 151.

73. *Letter-Book*, 2:105, Feb. 16, 17, 1720; *Diary*, 2:1004, Jan. 12, 1723. Steele, *The English Atlantic*, ch. 8 ("The Papers"), analyzes the role of the press in reinforcing intercolonial and transatlantic consciousness.

74. For example, *Diary*, 2:895, 959, 962, 965, 966, 992, 999.

75. *Diary*, 2:853, Apr. 26. 1717.

76. *Boston Gazette*, Dec. 21, 1719.

77. *Boston Gazette*, Jan. 4, 1720.

78. Mott, *American Journalism*, pp. 15, 16.

79. *Public Occurrences*, Sept. 25, 1690; Mott, *American Journalism*, p. 10; Steele, *The English Atlantic*, pp. 146–47.

80. *Diary*, 2:599, Aug. 18, 1708. Although he does not touch on the case of Edward Holyoke's almanac, the fullest analysis of press censorship is in Clyde Augustus Duniway, *The Development of Freedom of the Press in Massachusetts* (Cambridge, Mass., 1906), chs. 5–7 treat 1686–1763.

81. *Diary*, 2:680, Feb. 23, 1712; E. Savage to Cotton Mather, Boston, Feb. 28, 1717, *Letter-Book*, 2:2–3.

82. Duniway, *Development of Freedom of the Press*, p. 107, notes that on Dec. 16, 1729, the Massachusetts Governor's Council ordered that newspaper printers "be directed not to presume hence forward to insert in any part of their Prints that the same is published by Authority," since such a claim constituted false advertising.

CHAPTER 2. WILLIAM BYRD II AND THE CHALLENGE OF RUSTICITY AMONG THE TIDEWATER GENTRY

1. *The New England Mind: From Colony to Province*, 2:6. Quoted in John Clive and Bernard Bailyn, "England's Cultural Provinces: Scotland and America," *William and Mary Quarterly*, 3d ser., 11 (1954): 209.

2. Ian K. Steele argues plausibly that improving communications fed a sense of community, a view which, I believe, is compatible with the idea of an increased *perception* of distance owing to a lively sense of the full meaning of inclusion. (Steele, *The English Atlantic, 1675–1740: An Exploration of Communication and Community* (New York, 1986). "Creole" and "hermit" were used by William Byrd II from time to time in his letters, e.g., February 12, 1728, and February 17, 1741, in Marion Tinling, ed., *The Correspondence of the Three William Byrds of Westover, Virginia, 1684–1776* (Charlottesville, 1977), 1:372; 2:582.

3. Richard Beale Davis, "Chesapeake Pattern and Polestar: William Fitzhugh in His Plantation World, 1676–1701," in Davis' *Literature and Society in Early Virginia, 1608–1840* (Baton Rouge, 1973), p. 67. For the general context see Martin H. Quitt, "Immigrant Origins of the Virginia Gentry: A Study of Cultural Transmission and Innovation," *William and Mary Quarterly*, 3d ser., 45 (1988): 629–55; Carole Shammas, "English-Born and Creole Elites in Turn-of-the-Century Virginia," in Thad W. Tate and David L. Ammerman, eds., *The Chesapeake in the Seventeenth Century: Essays on Anglo-American Society* (Chapel Hill and New York, 1979), pp. 274–96.

4. Letter of January 30, 1687, quoted in R. B. Davis, *Literature and Society*, p. 68.

5. Ibid.

6. Ibid., pp. 68–70.

7. In *William Byrd of Virginia: The London Diary (1717–1721) and Other Writings*, ed. by

Louis B. Wright and Marion Tinling (New York, 1958), pp. 4, 8. Hereafter, because William Byrd II is the only William Byrd mentioned, the number II is to be understood, and will be dropped from the text. A searching analysis of Byrd's personality is offered in Kenneth A. Lockridge, *The Diary, and Life, of William Byrd II of Virginia, 1674–1744* (Chapel Hill, 1987). Another insightful reading of Byrd's diary is presented in Michael Zuckerman, "William Byrd's Family," *Perspectives in American History,* 12 (1979): 253–311.

8. Steele, *The English Atlantic;* David Cressy, *Coming Over: Migration and Communication Between England and New England in the Seventeenth Century* (Cambridge, 1987).

9. Steele, *The English Atlantic,* ch. 11; Byrd to Lynde, February 20, 1736, *Three William Byrds,* 2:437–74. On long-distance British networks see Susan O'Brien, "A Transatlantic Community of Saints: The Great Awakening and the First Evangelical Network, 1735–1755," *American Historical Review,* 91 (Oct. 1986): 811–32.

10. Evident from entries of 1774–1775 in *Journal & Letters of Philip Vickers Fithian. 1773–1774: A Plantation Tutor of the Old Dominion,* ed. with an intro. by Hunter Dickinson Farish (Williamsburg, 1943), and *The Journal of John Harrower, An Indentured Servant in the Colony of Virginia, 1773–1776,* ed. with an intro. by Edward Miles Riley (Williamsburg, 1963).

11. Though New England shipping was not common in the Chesapeake, it was common enough to reinforce prejudices against New Englanders similar to those against Scots, who were associated with sharp dealing and pious cant. David C. Klingaman, "The Development of the Coastwise Trade of Virginia in the late Colonial Period," *Virginia Magazine of History and Biography,* 77 (1969): 26–45.

12. Carl Bridenbaugh, "The Chesapeake Society" in *Myths & Realities: Societies of the Colonial South* (New York, 1963), first pub. 1952.

13. Byrd to John Pratt, June 24, 1736, *Three William Byrds,* 2:481.

14. *The Secret Diary of William Byrd of Westover, 1709–1712,* ed. by Louis B. Wright and Marion Tinling (Richmond, 1941), June 13, 1709, p. 47.

15. William Byrd to Anne Taylor Otway, Virginia, June 30, 1736, *Three William Byrds,* 2:481–83.

16. *Secret Diary of Wm. Byrd,* June 16, 1709, p. 49.

17. Ibid., Oct. 28, 1709, p. 98.

18. This estimate represents a conservative guess. Most of Byrd's letters have not survived. The estimate is based on his diary entries, where he often says he wrote letters, without noting how many. If one includes the letters he wrote to Virginia destinations, to overseers, neighbors, relatives, and political associates, the estimate will seem low. The largest batch of surviving letters, 30, from 1740, includes only a half-dozen items to persons in Virginia and no commercial correspondence. An estimate of 200 per year would not be unreasonable.

19. T. H. Breen, *Tobacco Culture: The Mentality of the Great Tidewater Planters on the Eve of the Revolution* (Princeton, 1985) analyzes the profound cultural significance of commercial correspondence. On p. 62 he quotes a 1762 letter of Robert Beverly ordering china. Louis Morton, *Robert Carter of Nomini Hall: Virginia Tobacco Planter of the Eighteenth Century* (Williamsburg, 1941), provides details of orders sent to London for flatware and plate (p. 209). On shipping books, Byrd to Mr. Spencer, Virginia, May 28, 1729, *Three William Byrds,* 1:399–400. Cressy reports that in New England, too, letters often mixed personal and political news with business transactions (*Coming Over,* p. 215). For an analysis of the financial side of the transatlantic connection see Jacob M. Price, *Capital and Credit in British Overseas Trade: The View from the Chesapeake, 1700–1776* (Cambridge, Mass., 1980).

20. *Secret Diary of Wm. Byrd,* Sept. 16, 1709, p. 84.

21. The usages employed in Byrd's diary and letters suggest that the term "friend" is used to

describe family members, in-laws, and unrelated persons of high rank with whom Byrd has a positive relationship. Cf. Cressy, *Coming Over,* ch. 9.

22. Byrd to Anne Taylor Otway, Virginia, June 30, 1736, *Three William Byrds,* 2:481–83.

23. Byrd to Charles Boyle, Earl of Orrery, Virginia, May 27, 1728, *Three William Byrds,* 1:375.

24. *Secret Diary of Wm. Byrd,* Jan. 26, 1711, p. 292.

25. Byrd to John Boyle, Baron of Broghill, Virginia, Feb. 12, 1728, *Three William Byrds,* 1:371–73. Cressy notes that saving and rereading letters was a common practice (*Coming over,* p. 214).

26. William Fitzhugh to Nicholas Hayward, Virginia, Jan. 3, 1687, quoted in Davis, *Literature and Society,* p. 75.

27. Steele, *The English Atlantic,* ch. 13.

28. *Secret Diary of Wm. Byrd,* Sept. 1 and 3, 1710, and October 2, 1710, pp. 225 n.2, 226, 238. Dr. Henry Sacheverell attacked the Whigs from the pulpit; and his trial became a contest over the Whig settlement of the Glorious Revolution.

29. Richard B. Davis, "William Byrd II: Taste and Tolerance," in *Literature and Society,* pp. 97–132, and *Three William Byrds,* 1:311–13, 354–59, 370–71, 375, 413, 429; 2:580–83, and passim.

30. Byrd to Charles Boyle, Earl of Orrery, Virginia, July 5, 1726, *Three William Byrds,* 1:354–56.

31. Byrd to Mrs. Armiger, June 25, 1729, *Three William Byrds,* 1:413.

32. Byrd to John Boyle, Baron of Broghill, Virginia, Feb. 12, 1728, *Three William Byrds,* 1:372; Byrd to Charles Boyle, Earl of Orrery, Virginia, May 27, 1728; 1:375; Edwin Wolf, "The Dispersal of the Library of William Byrd of Westover," *Proceedings of the American Antiquarian Society,* 68 (Apr. 1958): 21–22; the article includes a description of the library collection. According to Maude H. Woodfin, ed., *Another Secret Diary of William Byrd of Westover, 1739–1741. With Letters & Literary Exercises, 1696–1726,* ed. by Maude H. Woodfin, translated and collated by Marion Tinling (Richmond, Va., 1942), p. xlii, the library included "some four thousand volumes." She cites J. S. Bassett, *The Writings of "Colonel William Byrd of Westover in Virginia, Esqr."* (New York, 1901), pp. 413–43. That Byrd shared these aspirations with other colonial gentlemen beyond the Chesapeake is evident. See Norman S. Fiering, "The Transatlantic Republic of Letters: A Note on the Circulation of Learned Periodicals to Early Eighteenth-Century America," *William and Mary Quarterly,* 3d ser., 33 (1976): 642–60.

33. George K. Smart, "Private Libraries in Colonial Virginia," *American Literature,* 10 (1938): 24–52.

34. Parke Rouse, Jr., *James Blair of Virginia* (Chapel Hill, 1971), p. 193

35. Davis, *Literature and Society,* p. 68.

36. *Secret Diary of Wm. Byrd,* March 28, 1711, p. 320.

37. Ibid., Sept. 24, 1710, p. 235.

38. When the Royal Navy mounted its great marine expedition to the Arctic under Sir John Franklin in the 1840s, the officers equipped themselves with porcelain dinner services, sterling flatware, and a library of 2900 titles. Extensive, civilized reading and conversation over a refined dining table were understood as essentials. During a long, isolated voyage the symbolic importance of these accoutrements was vital for maintaining morale and self-respect. (Owen Beattie and John Geiger, *Frozen in Time: The Fate of the Franklin Expedition* (London, 1987), pp. 13–14; Francis Leopold M'Clintock, *In the Arctic Seas. A Narrative of the Discovery of the Fate of Sir John Franklin and his Companions* (Philadelphia, n.d. (1860)), pp. 334–39; Paul

Nanton, *Arctic Breakthrough: Franklin's Expedition, 1819–1847* (Toronto, Vancouver, 1970), p. 229n.)

39. *Secret Diary of Wm. Byrd,* Aug. 31, 1709, p. 77.

40. Fithian, *Journal & Letters,* June 18, 1774, pp. 160–61.

41. Ibid., Feb. 19, 1774, p. 88.

42. *The National Union Catalog of Pre-1956 Imprints* lists scores of editions of the 4th Earl of Chesterfield's advice letters. The greatest concentration lies in the period 1770–1900, when well over 100 editions appeared under titles such as: *The Accomplished gentleman; The Beauties of Chesterfield; Elements of a Polite Education; Letters written by Lord Chesterfield to his son; Practical morality; or A guide to men and manners, Lord Chesterfield's Maxims; Principles of Politeness, And of Knowing the World.* John E. Mason, *Gentlefolk in the Making: Studies in the History of English Courtesy Literature and Related Topics from 1531 to 1774* (Phila., 1935), pp. 105–12 on Chesterfield. Advice books for gentlemen had been influential for generations. William Byrd II modeled himself on such works according to Kenneth Lockridge, *The Diary and Life of William Byrd* (Chapel Hill, 1987), pp. 20–25.

43. *Another Secret Diary of William Byrd of Westover, 1739–1741. With Letters & Literary Exercises, 1696–1726,* ed. by Maude H. Woodfin, translated and collated by Marion Tinling (Richmond, 1942), Feb. 21, 1723, p. 280.

44. The term "servant" was generally used without differentiating white indentures and black slaves; however for purposes of analysis it seems useful to differentiate whenever the evidence permits.

45. *Another Secret Diary of Wm. Byrd,* March 9, 15, 1740, pp. 46, 47.

46. *The Diaries of George Washington,* ed. by Donald Jackson and Dorothy Twohig (Charlottesville, 1976) 1:1748–65, April 8, 1760; 1:264. During his presidency, Washington used detailed letters to direct the management of his Mount Vernon estate.

47. Byrd records an incident of subordinate concealment prompted by a guest's (Mrs. Mary Jeffreys Dunn) countermanding Byrd's orders to his servants or slaves, and then threatening them with punishment if they told. Byrd therefore "brandisht a good cudgel over the weavers head protesting I wou'd break his bones, if he did not discover what disturb'd him. When he found himself in this jeopardy he fell down upon his knees, and told me how he had been us'd for obeying my orders." "Dunella," ca. 1711–1715?, *Three William Byrds,* 1:278.

48. Evidence of these tensions is scattered in nearly all the plantation diaries I have consulted; for selected examples see: *Secret Diary of Wm. Byrd,* Feb. 20, 1709, p. 6; *Diaries of George Washington,* May 7, 1760, 1:276; *Journal of John Harrower,* Feb. 14, 1775, p. 84; July 22, 1775, p. 104; April 6, 1776, p. 144; April 11, 1776, p. 146.

49. Daniel Blake Smith, *Inside the Great House: Planter Family Life in Eighteenth-Century Chesapeake Society* (Ithaca, N.Y., 1980), ch. 5, "Kin, Friends, and Neighbors: The Social World Beyond the Family," pp. 175–230, systematically analyzes the extent and intensity of relationships beyond the conjugal unit. The operation of stratified social circles in 18th-century Virginia is analyzed in Darrett B. and Anita H. Rutman, *A Place in Time: Middlesex County, Virginia: 1650–1750* (New York, 1984), ch. 8, "Circles," pp. 234–49.

50. Allan Kulikoff, *Tobacco and Slaves: The Development of Southern Cultures in the Chesapeake, 1680–1800* (Chapel Hill, 1986), pp. 240–60; Rutman and Rutman, *A Place in Time,* pp. 199–230; and Byrd diaries.

51. *Secret Diary of Wm. Byrd,* Jan 9, 1712, p. 467.

52. Ibid., Jan. 15, 1712, p. 470.

53. Ibid., Jan. 21, 1712, p. 473.

54. Ibid., Jan. 24, 1712, p. 474.

55. Ibid., Apr. 22, 1712, pp. 518–19.

56. This proverb can be traced back to James I in 1616 if not earlier (G. L. Apperson, *English Proverbs and Proverbial Phrases: A Historical Dictionary* (London, 1929, repub., 1969), p. 450).

57. Davis, *Literature and Society*, p. 68, Jan. 30, 1687. Yet it is noteworthy that as late as 1762 a great planter such as Robert Beverly was comforting himself in his self-conscious Virginia isolation by importing a set of "china of the most fashionable sort." Reported by Breen, *Tobacco Culture*, p. 130.

58. "Journal of Col. James Gordon of Lancaster County, Va.," *William and Mary Quarterly,* 1st ser., 11 (1902–3): 105, June 17, 1759.

59. Smart, "Private Libraries," pp. 45–46. Puritans placed special emphasis on public, communal worship because of their conviction that the sermon was the centerpiece of worship. Anglicans, who relied on the *Book of Common Prayer* and church liturgy, were more accepting of private worship as a substitute for attendance at church. See Horton Davies, *Worship and Theology in England: From Watts and Wesley to Maurice, 1690–1850* (Princeton, 1961), pp. 31, 218–20.

60. Fithian, *Journal & Letters,* Dec. 12, 1773, p. 38.

61. Fithian to John Peck, *Journal & Letters,* Aug. 12, 1774, p. 220.

62. Ibid., Dec. 12, 1773, p. 38. I am grateful to Professor Harry S. Stout for suggesting the comparison between New England and Virginia churchgoing.

63. Rhys Isaac, *The Transformation of Virginia, 1740–1790* (Chapel Hill, 1982), ch. 5; A. G. Roeber, *Faithful Magistrates and Republican Lawyers: Creators of Virginia Legal Culture, 1680–1810* (Chapel Hill, 1981), chs. 3 and 4.

64. Hugh Jones, quoted in Rouse, *James Blair,* p. 221.

65. Hugh Jones, quoted in Rouse, *James Blair,* p. 189; anonymous visitor quoted in Breen, *Tobacco Culture*, p. 37.

66. Biographical information from Stephen Saunders Webb, "The Strange Career of Francis Nicholson," *William and Mary Quarterly,* 3d ser., 23 (1966): 513–48, and Leonard Woods Labaree, "Nicholson, Francis," in *Dictionary of American Biography* (New York, 1934), 13:499–502. Webb notes that Nicholson was known for his "insane temper" (p. 526).

67. Quoted in Rouse, *James Blair,* p. 157.

68. Ibid., p. 156.

69. *Secret Diary of Wm. Byrd,* June 23, 1710, p. 195; Oct. 26, 1710, p. 248.

70. These themes are prominent in the secondary literature. See T. H. Breen, "Horses and Gentlemen: The Cultural Significance of Gambling among the Gentry of Virginia," *William and Mary Quarterly,* 3d ser., 34 (1977): 239–57; Jane Carson, *Virginians at Play* (Charlottesville, Va., 1965); Elliott J. Gorn, " 'Gouge and Bite, Pull Hair and Scratch': The Cultural Significance of Fighting in the Southern Backcountry," *American Historical Review,* 90 (Feb. 1985): 18–43; Kulikoff, *Tobacco and Slaves,* ch. 7.

71. Bailyn and Clive, "England's Cultural Provinces," p. 209.

72. Various authors have used the term, for example Hunter D. Farish in *Journal & Letters of Philip Vickers Fithian,* p. xvii, and Richard Beale Davis, *Literature and Society,* p. 149.

73. Fithian, *Journal & Letters,* Aug. 12, 1774, p. 212.

74. Ibid., Aug. 25, 1774, p. 233.

75. Ibid., Aug. 12, 1774, pp. 210–11.

76. Quoted in Isaac, *Transformation of Virginia,* p. 43.

77. *Secret Diary of Wm. Byrd,* Feb. 19, 1711, p. 304.

78. Entries scattered in Byrd, Fithian, and Landon Carter diaries attest to this expectation.

79. *Another Secret Diary of Wm. Byrd,* Feb. 21, 1723, p. 281.

80. *Secret Diary of Wm. Byrd,* Dec. 5, 1709, p. 114.

81. Ibid., Nov. 11, 1709, p. 105.

82. Ibid., Nov. 10, 1709, p. 105.

83. Ibid., Nov. 23, 1709, p. 109; Apr. 5, 1709, p. 17; July 30, 1710, pp. 210–11.

84. Ibid., Jan. 23, 1712, p. 474.

85. Ibid., May 1, 1709, p. 29.

86. Kulikoff, *Tobacco and Slaves,* ch. 5.

87. Smith, *Inside the Great House,* p. 63; Kulikoff, *Tobacco and Slaves,* pp. 197–99, 218, treats differences in expectations of male and female literacy.

88. Quoted in Smith, *Inside the Great House,* p. 93.

89. Fithian to John Peck, *Journal & Letters,* Aug. 12, 1774, p. 212.

90. Fithian, *Journal & Letters,* intimates that Mrs. Carter is seeking to find him a spouse among the Carter circle. Jenny Washington is particularly mentioned. Fithian's successor, John Peck, also an impecunious Princeton graduate, married one of the Carter daughters, Anne Tasker Carter. (Louis Morton, *Robert Carter of Nomini Hall* (Williamsburg, 1941) p. 228.)

91. Newspaper publication began at Annapolis (*Maryland Gazette*) in 1727 and continued with a hiatus from 1735–1745. In Virginia the first newspaper, the *Virginia Gazette,* started in 1736 and continued almost without interruption through the Revolution. No papers were published outside Annapolis and Williamsburg until the revolutionary era, the 1770s and 1780s. See Robert M. Myers, "The Old Dominion Looks to London: A Study of English Literary Influences Upon *The Virginia Gazette* (1736–1766)," *Virginia Magazine of History and Biography,* 54 (1946): 195–217.

92. Davis, in "The Intellectual Golden Age in the Colonial Chesapeake Bay Country," *Literature and Society,* pp. 149–67, extols the intellectual achievements of the region which, he asserts, equal or excel those of northern colonies. Regardless of their merit, the wide array of intellectual endeavors Davis cites testify to the extent and seriousness of intellectual pretensions. See also Kulikoff, *Tobacco and Slaves,* ch. 7.

93. As an intimate of his mentors Dr. William Small, a William and Mary professor, and the lawyer George Wythe, young Jefferson became a regular dinner companion of Governor Francis Fauquier, and in the "habitual conversations" of this cultivated company he gained "much instruction." (*Autobiography of Thomas Jefferson,* with an intro. by Dumas Malone (New York, n.d. (1959), p. 20.)

94. Thomas Jefferson to Ralph Izard, Paris, July 17, 1788, *The Papers of Thomas Jefferson,* ed. by Julian P. Boyd (Princeton, 1956) 13:372; William Fitzhugh remark on necessity of English education, Jan. 30, 1687, cited in Davis, *Literature and Society,* p. 68. Jefferson's attack on education in England is in his letter to John Banister, Jr., Paris, Oct. 15, 1785, *Papers of Thomas Jefferson* (Princeton, 1953) 8:635–37. The popularity in America of the bucolic idea is suggested by the republication of John Pomfret's bucolic ideal poem *The Choice* (1700), which appeared in four American editions between 1751 and 1792 and which was imitated by American authors. (Carl F. Kaestle, "The Public Reaction to John Dickinson's Farmer's Letters," *Proceedings of the American Antiquarian Society,* 79, pt. 2 (1969): 335–36.)

95. Isaac, *Transformation of Virginia,* chs. 11 and 12.

96. His "Bill for the More General Diffusion of Knowledge" is in *Papers of Thomas Jefferson* (Princeton, 1950) 2:526–35. His explanation of it is in *Notes on Virginia, Works of Thomas Jefferson,* collected and ed. by Paul Leicester Ford (New York, 1904), 4:60–64. A parallel, though somewhat different interpretation of this phenomenon, in which "Jefferson transformed radical country ideas into a new agrarian republicanism," is presented in Breen, *Tobacco Culture,* p. 210. Another distinct but not incompatible perspective is offered by Kulikoff (*Tobacco and Slaves,* pp. 312–13, 423–28). See also Emory Evans, "The Rise and Decline of the Virginia Aristocracy in the Eighteenth Century: The Nelsons," in Darrett B. Rutman, ed., *The Old Dominion: Essays for Thomas Perkins Abernathy* (Charlottesville, 1964), pp. 62–78, and Evans' *Thomas Nelson of Yorktown: Revolutionary Virginian* (Charlottesville, 1975); William D. Liddle, "Virtue and Liberty': An Inquiry into the Role of the Agrarian Myth in the Rhetoric of the American Revolutionary Era," *South Atlantic Quarterly,* 7 (1978): 15–38; Robert P. Sutton, "Nostalgia, Pessimism, and Malaise: The Doomed Aristocracy in Late-Jeffersonian Virginia," *Virginia Magazine of History and Biography,* 76 (1968): 41–55.

CHAPTER 3. RURAL CLERGYMEN AND THE COMMUNICATION NETWORKS OF 18TH-CENTURY NEW ENGLAND

1. Ebenezer Baldwin to Bethiah Baldwin, 8 May 1770, Baldwin Papers (Yale University manuscript collections).

2. Robert Redfield discusses the relationship between local culture and elite culture in *The Little Community, and Peasant Society and Culture* (Chicago, 1963).

3. Figures compiled from Harold Field Worthley, *An Inventory of the Records of the Particular (Congregational) Churches of Massachusetts Gathered 1620–1805,* Harvard Theological Studies, vol. 25 (Cambridge, Mass., 1970); also issued as *Proceedings of the Unitarian Historical Society,* vol. 16, pts. 1 and 2 (1966–69). The lowest vacancy rate, 3 percent, was shared by 9 parishes, all founded in the 17th century. The highest vacancy rate where a minister actually served was in Middlefield, a parish started in 1783, which was vacant 53 percent of the years from its founding to the end of the century. The quintile breakdown follows:
   vacant 3.0–4.3 percent, parishes founded 1630–1730
   vacant 4.4–7.0 percent, parishes founded 1630–1753
   vacant 7.0–10.6 percent, parishes founded 1630–1768
   vacant 10.8–21.4 percent, parishes founded 1666–1771
   vacant 22.0–100 percent, parishes founded 1728–1797

4. Alice M. Baldwin, *The New England Clergy and the American Revolution* (New York, 1965 ed.; first pub. 1928). Baldwin cites Oliver on the clergy repeatedly, pp. 98, 113, 116, n.31, 122 n.1, 155ff. The quotation is from *Peter Oliver's Origin & Progress of the American Rebellion, A Tory View,* ed. Douglass Adair and John A. Schutz (Stanford, 1961), p. 41.

5. Bernard Bailyn, *The Ideological Origins of the American Revolution* (Cambridge, 1967); Alan Heimert, *Religion and the American Mind: From the Great Awakening to the Revolution* (Cambridge, 1966); Harry S. Stout, "Religion, Communications, and the Ideological Origins of the American Revolution," *William and Mary Quarterly,* 3d ser., 34 (1977): 519–41. For the 17th century see also George Selement, *Keepers of the Vineyard: The Puritan Ministry and Collective Culture in Colonial New England* (Lanham, Md. 1984), ch. 4.

6. Charles W. Akers, *The Divine Politician: Samuel Cooper and the American Revolution in Boston* (Boston, 1982); Charles E. Clark, "Disestablishment at the Grass Roots: Curtis Coe and the Separation of Church and Town," *Historical New Hampshire,* 36 (Winter, 1981): 280–305; Edward M. Griffin, *Old Brick: Charles Chauncy of Boston, 1705–1787* (Minneapolis,

1980); Nathan O. Hatch, *The Sacred Cause of Liberty: Republican Thought and the Millenium in Revolutionary New England* (New Haven, 1977); Christopher M. Jedrey, *The World of John Cleaveland: Family and Community in Eighteenth-Century New England* (New York, 1979); Edmund S. Morgan, *The Gentle Puritan: A Life of Ezra Stiles, 1727–1795* (New Haven, 1962); Donald M. Scott, *From Office to Profession: The New England Ministry, 1750–1850* (Philadelphia, 1978); Patricia J. Tracy, *Jonathan Edwards, Pastor: Religion and Society in Eighteenth-Century Northampton* (New York, 1980); Louis Leonard Tucker, *Puritan Protagonist: President Thomas Clap of Yale College* (Chapel Hill, 1962); Laurel T. Ulrich, "Psalm-tunes, Periwigs, and Bastards: Ministerial Authority in Early Eighteenth Century Durham," *Historical New Hampshire,* 36 (Winter 1981), 255–79; Robert J. Wilson III, *The Benevolent Deity: Ebenezer Gay and the Rise of Rational Religion in New England, 1696–1787* (Philadelphia, 1984); J. William T. Youngs, Jr., *God's Messengers: Religious Leadership in Colonial New England, 1700–1750* (Baltimore, 1976).

7. Oliver, *Origin & Progress,* p. 145.

8. The data on clergymen and clerical families that follow was compiled from Frederick Lewis Weis, *The Colonial Clergy and the Colonial Churches of New England* (Lancaster, Mass., 1936). It is notable that most clerical families were purely Harvard or purely Yale graduates. The distribution (including fathers, fathers-in-law, sons, sons-in-law, brothers, brothers-in-law, uncles, nephews) of clerical relatives living simultaneously was:

1740 no. of relatives	0	1	2	3	4	5	6	7	8	9	10	
no. of clerics	249	95	57	11	14	4	5	3	2	0	1	441

1770 no. of relatives	0	1	2	3	4	5	6	7	8	9	10	
no. of clerics	431	157	53	11	17	3	7	4	1	0	0	684

9. Edmund S. Morgan, *The Gentle Puritan: A Life of Ezra Stiles, 1727–1795* (New Haven, 1962), pp. 133, 276. The isolation of rural Rhode Island is vividly portrayed in Daniel P. Jones, "From Radical Yeomen to Evangelical Farmers: The Transformation of Northwestern Rhode Island, 1780–1850." Ph.D. diss., Brown Univ., 1987.

10. It is important to note that a larger number of clerics possessed kinship ties to deceased clergymen. Genealogies of New England clergymen frequently intersect in several generations. Perhaps the most remarkable tribe of 18th-century New England clergy is chronicled in Kevin Michael Sweeney, "River Gods and Related Minor Deities: The Williams Family and the Connecticut River Valley, 1637–1790," Ph.D. diss., Yale Univ., 1986.

11. The expression "in the wilderness" is a translation of the Rev. John Cleaveland's pseudonym, "Johannes in Eremo," Jedrey, *World of John Cleaveland,* p. 131.

12. *The Diary of Ebenezer Parkman, 1703–1782,* ed. by Francis G. Walett (Worcester, 1974), p. 18 (entry for Nov. 1726).

13. Clifford K. Shipton, *Biographical Sketches of Those Who Attended Harvard College in the Classes 1713–1721, Sibley's Harvard Graduates* (Boston, 1942), 6:514.

14. Oliver, *Origin & Progress,* p. 145.

15. Ibid., p. 148.

16. This judgment is based on a perusal of the period 1765–74 in John Ballantine, Journal, 1737–1774, transcribed and annotated in the Joseph D. Bartlett Notebooks, nos. 2 and 7, 1886; copied in 1938 as a project of the National Youth Administration (American Antiquarian Society).

17. Oliver, *Origin & Progress,* pp. 41, 53, 63, 106.

18. Baldwin, *New England Clergy,* p. 14.

19. Compiled from Worthley, *An Inventory of the Records of the Particular (Congregational) Churches of Massachusetts Gathered 1620–1805*. These estimates do not include surviving manuscript sermons which would doubtless increase the number of political performances significantly. In the 17th century, George Selement found that 69 percent of clerical publications were popular homilies and that another 10 percent were devotional and instructional treatises. (*Keepers of the Vineyard*, p. 61.) Though these percentages would vary in the 18th century, religious, not political, sermons remained overwhelmingly preponderant.

20. Maris A. Vinovskis, " 'Aged Servants of the Lord': Changes in the Status and Treatment of Elderly Ministers in Colonial America," paper prepared for AAAS symposium on "Aging from Birth to Death: Socio-Temporal Perspectives," Toronto, Jan. 1981; James W. Schmotter, "Ministerial Careers in Eighteenth-Century New England: The Social Context, 1720–1760," *Journal of Social History* (Winter 1975), 9:249–67.

21. Nathaniel Bouton, *The History of Concord from its First Grant in 1725 to the Organization of the City Government in 1853* (Concord, 1856), pp. 556–63; Joseph B. Walker, "The House of the First Minister," *Granite Monthly*, (1899), 27:172; Shipton, *Biographical Sketches . . . 1722–1725, Sibley's Harvard Graduates* (Boston, 1945), 7:612–13.

22. Oliver, *Origin & Progress*, p. 104.

23. Bouton, *Concord*, p. 562.

24. Heman Packard DeForest, *The History of Westborough, Massachusetts* (Westborough, 1891), p. 187.

25. Ibid., pp. 134–35.

26. Ibid., pp. 177–79.

27. Ibid., p. 181.

28. Baldwin, *New England Clergy*, p. 95.

29. Lyman Abbott, *Reminiscences* (Boston, 1915), p. 17.

30. See note 1, above.

36. Quoted in Franklin B. Dexter, *Biographical Sketches of the Graduates of Yale College* (New York, 1896), 2:330.

32. Justus Forward, Diary, 28 Jan. 1762 (American Antiquarian Society (AAS) manuscript collections).

33. Justus Forward, Diary, 1 Aug. 1759, Justus Forward Papers (Yale University manuscript collections).

34. Forward, Diary, Sept. 1762 (AAS).

35. Forward, Diary, 27 Sept. 1759 (Yale).

36. Samuel Dunbar, *Brotherly Love, The Duty and Mark of Christians: A Sermon Preached at Medfield November the 6th, 1748* (Boston, 1749), p. 27.

37. Forward, Diary, 24 July 1766 (AAS).

38. Forward, Diary, 31 May 1778 (Yale).

39. Forward, Diary, 22, 23, 24 Aug. 1786 and end of month notes (AAS).

40. Forward, Diary, 2, 3 Nov. 1786 (AAS).

41. Forward, Diary, 7, 14, 18 Dec. 1786 (AAS).

42. Forward, Diary, 7 Nov. 1802 (Yale).

43. Forward, Diary, 20 Aug. 1812 (Yale).

44. Forward Diary, 16 Mar. 1797 (AAS); DeForest, *History of Westborough*, pp. 177–79.

45. Scott, *From Office to Profession*, pp. 3–4, 74; Daniel H. Calhoun, *Professional Lives in America: Structure and Aspiration, 1750–1850* (Cambridge, Mass., 1965), ch. 4; Gerard W. Gawalt, *The Promise of Power: The Emergence of the Legal Profession in Massachusetts, 1760–1840* (Westport, Conn., 1979), pp. 200–201, furnishes statistics that point in the same direction, though not drawn from the whole careers of the clergy.

46. Compiled from data in Gawalt, *Promise of Power*, pp. 14, 200, and Worthley, *An Inventory*. Professor Bruce Steiner, Ohio University, reported a comparable pattern in Connecticut in a paper given at the American Antiquarian Society Seminar in Social and Political History on Nov. 19, 1982, "Lawyers, Dissenting Churches, and Connecticut's Republican Party, 1790–1820."

47. Lyman Beecher, quoted in Scott, *From Office to Profession*, p. 5. See also Donald Weber, *Rhetoric and History in Revolutionary New England* (New York, 1988), pp. 148–49, 152.

48. Timothy Walker, *Diaries of Rev. Timothy Walker, The First and Only Minister of Concord, N.H., from his ordination November 18, 1730, to September 1, 1782*, ed. Joseph B. Walker (Concord, 1889), p. 58 (entries for 1 Apr. and 30 June 1780); Jacob B. Moore, *Annals of the Town of Concord* (Concord, 1824), p. 111. Warfare increased newspaper readership. As early as King George's War in the 1740s, Kenneth Minkema reports, Jonathan Edwards "kept regular tallies from newspaper reports of the numbers of French ships captured or sunk, as well as soldiers killed or captured." ("The Edwardses: A Ministerial Family in Eighteenth-Century New England," Ph.D. diss., University of Connecticut, 1988, ch. 6, p. 15. Minkema cites Stephen Stein, ed., *Apocalyptic Writings* (of Jonathan Edwards) (New Haven, 1977), 365.) In nearly all of the clerical diaries I have seen there was a marked increase in references to newspaper reports during periods of war.

49. Richard D. Brown, "The Emergence of Urban Society in Rural Massachusetts, 1760–1820," *Journal of American History*, 61 (June 1974): 40–42, 43–44.

50. Hatch, *Sacred Cause of Liberty*, pp. 178–79; Massachusetts Society for Promoting Agriculture, "Reverend Sir, More than three years ago . . . ," Broadside circular letter, Boston, 1 Nov. 1796, copy addressed to the Rev. William Bentley (American Antiquarian Society). The Massachusetts Medical Society also invited communications from the clergy.

51. *An Oration, Pronounced in the Brick Meeting-House, in the City of New-Haven, on the Fourth of July, A.D. 1787* (New Haven, n.d.), p. 6.

52. Quoted in Scott, *From Office to Profession*, p. 72.

CHAPTER 4. LAWYERS, PUBLIC OFFICE, AND COMMUNICATION PATTERNS IN PROVINCIAL MASSACHUSETTS

1. Gerard W. Gawalt, *The Promise of Power: The Emergence of the Legal Profession in Massachusetts, 1760–1840* (Westport, Conn., 1979), pp. 84–85 supplies the data for these assertions.

2. Gerard W. Gawalt, "Sources of Anti-Lawyer Sentiment in Massachusetts, 1740–1840," *American Journal of Legal History*, 14 (1970): 283–307.

3. Ibid., p. 296.

4. John M. Murrin, "The Legal Transformation: The Bench and Bar of Eighteenth-Century Massachusetts," in Stanley N. Katz and John M. Murrin, eds., *Colonial America: Essays in Politics and Social Development*, 3d ed. (New York, 1983), pp. 540–72; Stephen Botein, "The Legal Profession in Colonial North America," in Wilfred Prest, ed., *Lawyers in Early Modern Europe and America* (New York, 1981), pp. 129–46, esp. 131–36.

5. Gawalt, *Promise of Power,* pp. 37–38; Murrin, "The Legal Transformation;" Charles R. McKirdy, "Massachusetts Lawyers on the Eve of the American Revolution: The State of the Profession," in *Law in Colonial Massachusetts,* ed. with an intro. by Daniel R. Coquillette, Publications of the Colonial Society of Massachusetts, *Collections,* 62 (1984): 313–58.

6. Murrin, "Legal Transformation," pp. 565–66.

7. Alexis de Tocqueville, *Democracy in America,* translated by Henry Reeve, ed. with an essay by Phillips Bradley (New York, n.d.), 1:286–90, esp. pp. 288–89; Murrin, "Legal Transformation;" Gawalt, *Promise of Power.* In Virginia a comparable rise in the role of attorneys occurred. Sec A. G. Roeber, *Faithful Magistrates and Republican Lawyers: Creators of Virginia Legal Culture. 1680–1810* (Chapel Hill, 1981).

8. The Sutton, Mass., delegate Amos Singletary, attacked lawyers particularly, *Debates, Resolutions and Other Proceedings of the Convention of the Commonwealth of Massachusetts. Convened at Boston, on the 9th of January, 1788 . . .* (Boston, 1808), pp. 136–37. On the persistent anti-lawyer tradition see Maxwell H. Bloomfield, *American Lawyers in a Changing Society, 1776–1876* (Cambridge, Mass., 1976).

9. Lawyers were especially prominent in the Federalist party, which dominated Massachusetts for most of the period ca. 1794–1820. The first Democratic-Republican governor, James Sullivan, elected in 1807 and 1808, was also a lawyer.

10. This ethos is explained in Michael Zuckerman, *Peaceable Kingdoms: New England Towns in the Eighteenth Century* (New York, 1970).

11. It is notable that the "attorneyship" concept of representation, where the representative served as the agent of his constituents rather than a wiser protector of theirs and the general interest, arose during this era. Bernard Bailyn, *The Ideological Origins of the American Revolution* (Cambridge, Mass., 1967), pp. 171–75; Gordon S. Wood, *The Creation of the American Republic, 1776–1787* (Chapel Hill, 1969), pp. 371, 598. A different but related explanation for the rise of lawyers is presented by Robert A. Ferguson, *Law and Letters in American Culture* (Cambridge, Mass., 1984), pp. 11–12.

12. Sketch of Paine's early career is based on Clifford K. Shipton, "Robert Treat Paine," in his *Sibley's Harvard Graduates* (classes of 1746–1750) (Boston, 1962), 12:462–82; Ralph Davol, *Two Men of Taunton* (Taunton, 1912); Stephen Thomas Riley, "Robert Treat Paine and His Papers," Ph.D. diss., Clark Univ., 1953; Stephen T. Riley, "Robert Treat Paine and John Adams: A Colonial Rivalry," in *Sibley's Heir: A Volume in Memory of Clifford Kenyon Shipton,* Publications of the Colonial Society of Massachusetts, *Collections,* 59 (Boston, 1982), pp. 415–29.

13. Robert Treat Paine to Abigail Paine, Lunenburgh, Sept. 23, 1749, Robert Treat Paine Papers, Massachusetts Historical Society. Hereafter abbreviated as RTP papers, MHS.

14. Richard Cranch to Robert Treat Paine, Boston, Oct. 9, 1749 (RTP papers, MHS).

15. Robert Treat Paine to Eunice Paine, Lunenburg, Feb. 16, 1750 (RTP papers, MHS).

16. Robert Treat Paine to Thomas Paine, Boston, Dec. 10, 1754 (RTP papers, MHS). Paine's father, at Halifax, Nova Scotia, was also deciding at this time to make himself a lawyer so as to retrieve his fortunes (Abigail Paine Greenleaf to Robert Treat Paine, Boston, July 1, 1755 (RTP papers, MHS)). On the county courts see Hendrik Hartog, "The Public Law of a County Court: Judicial Government in Eighteenth-Century Massachusetts," *American Journal of Legal History,* 20 (Oct. 1976): 282–329.

17. Robert Treat Paine to Eunice Paine, Lancaster, Feb. 12, 1755, Feb. 17, 1755, Mar. 24, 1755 (RTP papers, MHS).

18. Robert Treat Paine to Eunice Paine, Lancaster, May 9, 1755 (RTP papers, MHS).

19. There are numerous biographies of Adams. For basic family background and chronology I

have relied on L. H. Butterfield's "Introduction" in *Diary and Autobiography of John Adams,* ed. by L. H. Butterfield et al. (Cambridge, Mass., 1962), 1:xiii–lxxiv; Clifford K. Shipton, "John Adams," in his *Sibley's Harvard Graduates* (classes of 1751–1755) (Boston, 1965), 13:513–20. An insightful analysis of Adams' personality is in Peter Shaw, *The Character of John Adams* (Chapel Hill, 1976).

20. John Adams, "Autobiography," in *Diary and Autobiography of John Adams,* 3:256–57.

21. Ibid., p. 256. Though John Adams, Senior, possessed modest means on a provincial scale, he was among the most prosperous farmers of Braintree, and certainly in the top quintile province-wide. When he died in 1761 his entire estate was valued at £1330, mostly in the real estate he provided for his three sons. He possessed a clock valued at £2, "Sundrey Books & Pamphlets" worth £2.10s, and ample tools, furniture, and linens. The only silver in the household was three spoons valued at 16s. The inventory is in *Papers of John Adams,* ed. by Robert J. Taylor et al. (Cambridge, Mass., 1977), 1:51–53.

22. Adams, *Diary,* 3:263.

23. Ibid.

24. Ibid., p. 262.

25. Ibid., p. 256.

26. Ibid., p. 264.

27. Ibid.

28. John Adams to Charles Cushing, Worcester, Apr. 1, 1756, *Papers of John Adams,* 1:13.

29. Ibid.

30. Ibid., pp. 12–13.

31. Ibid., p. 13.

32. Aug. 22, 1756, Adams, *Diary,* 1:42–43.

33. Ibid., p. 43. The challenge that legal practice posed for one who would be virtuous was by no means special for John Adams. James Allen, a young Philadelphia lawyer noted in his diary, "The further I engage in law matters, I find it necessary to put a guard on my Virtue. . . . I have just written in the first blank leave in my Coke on Littleton a Lawyers prayer as a memento to myself." ("Diary of James Allen, Esq., of Philadelphia, Counsellor-at-Law, 1770–1778," *Pennsylvania Magazine of History and Biography,* 9 (1885): 181.)

34. Gawalt, *Promise of Power,* pp. 140–45.

35. Ibid., pp. 170–76. As time went on after the Revolution, it appears that the proportion of lawyers whose fathers were clergymen declined, while the proportion drawn from the families of lawyers and judges continued to rise. Gawalt reports an increasingly integrated professional class of clergy, lawyers, and physicians. See also Ferguson, *Law and Letters in American Culture,* ch. 1, esp. p. 6.

36. See Murrin, "The Legal Transformation;" Mary Beth Norton, *The British Americans: The Loyalist Exiles in England, 1774–1789* (Boston, 1972), ch. 5.

37. Young lawyers commonly addressed each other as "brother" in their letters in the 1750s and 1760s.

38. Stephen Botein, "Cicero as a Role Model for Early American Lawyers: A Case Study in Classical 'Influence,' " *Classical Journal,* 73 (1977–78): 313–21; James McLachlan, "Classical Names, American Identities: Some Notes on College Students and the Classical Tradition in the 1770s," in *Classical Traditions in Early America,* ed. by John W. Eadie (Ann Arbor, Mich., 1976), pp. 81–98.

39. The experiences of Jacob Bailey, a charity scholar who ranked last socially in John Adams'

class of twenty-five at Harvard, exemplifies this phenomenon. As Shipton puts it, "the doors of all the mansions were open to him as a scholar, and even Sir William Pepperrell [was] glad to be his host and to listen to his conversation." ("Jacob Bailey," in Shipton, *Sibley's Harvard Graduates,* 13:523.)

40. Murrin, "The Legal Transformation," pp. 548–56; Carol Berkin, *Jonathan Sewall: Odyssey of an American Loyalist* (New York, 1974), chs. 1–3 and passim.

41. John Adams to Robert Treat Paine, Braintree, Dec. 6, 1759, Adams, *Papers,* 1:31–32. On Dec. 5, 1758 Adams wrote a character sketch of Paine in his *Diary,* 1:59–60.

42. John Adams to Jonathan Sewall, Braintree, Feb. 1760, Adams, *Papers,* 1:42.

43. John Adams to Robert Treat Paine, Braintree, Dec. 6, 1759, Adams, *Papers,* 1:31.

44. Among the authors mentioned in their letters and diaries are Bolingbroke, Samuel Johnson, Catherine Macaulay, Pope, Tillotson, Trenchard and Gordon, and Voltaire. Their tastes included the most conventional literature as well as some lesser known British and continental authors.

45. Feb. 2, 1756, Adams, *Diary,* 1:4.

46. Feb. 22, 1756, Adams, *Diary,* 1:9.

47. John Adams to Nathan Webb, Worcester, Oct. 12, 1755, Adams, *Papers,* 1:5.

48. Dec. 5, 1758, Adams, *Diary,* 1:59–60.

49. July 25, 1756, Adams, *Diary,* 1:37.

50. Oct. 5, 1758, Adams, *Diary,* 1:44–45.

51. Oct. 25, 1758, Adams, *Diary,* 1:54–55.

52. Oct. 25, 1758, Adams *Diary,* 1:55. "The Bostoner amused her with religious cant," remarked the Annapolis physician Alexander Hamilton in August 1744. (Alexander Hamilton, *Gentleman's Progress: The Itinerarium of Dr. Alexander Hamilton, 1744,* ed. with an intro. by Carl Bridenbaugh (Chapel Hill, 1948) p. 160.)

53. Nov. 6, 1758, Adams, *Diary,* 1:58.

54. Nov. 6, 1758, Adams, *Diary,* 1:59.

55. Gawalt, *Promise of Power,* p. 25. One of their friends and peers who enjoyed superior connections was Jonathan Sewall, who remained in Boston and made a career in government service; subsequently Sewall became a loyalist and refugee. (Carol Berkin, *Jonathan Sewall: Odyssey of an American Loyalist.*)

56. Adams, *Diary,* 3:270. Adams declined his mentor James Putnam's invitation to practice in Worcester.

57. Mar. 14, 1759, Adams, *Diary,* 1:78.

58. Apr. 8, 1759, Adams, *Diary,* 1:81.

59. Spring 1759, Adams, *Diary,* 1:100.

60. Ibid.

61. Spring 1759, Adams *Diary,* 1:96, 97. Adams' viewpoint is similar to that expressed in Benjamin Franklin's autobiography, where a like concern for reputation as a key to success is expressed. (Benjamin Franklin, *The Autobiography of Benjamin Franklin & Selections from his other Writings,* with an intro. by Henry Steele Commager (New York, 1950), pp. 69–70, 75.)

62. Spring 1759, Adams, *Diary,* 1:98.

63. Dec. 29, 1758, Adams, *Diary,* 1:64–65.

64. Spring 1759, Adams, *Diary,* 1:96.

65. Spring 1759, Adams, *Diary,* 1:98.

66. Spring 1759, Adams, *Diary,* 1:100.

67. June 23, 1760, Adams, *Diary,* 1:140.

68. June 24, 1760, Adams, *Diary,* 1:140.

69. Jan. 1761, Adams, *Diary,* 1:193.

70. June 19, 1760, Adams, *Diary,* 1:136–37.

71. Robert Treat Paine, Diary, July 12, 1765 (RTP papers, MHS).

72. John Adams, *Legal Papers of John Adams,* ed. by L. Kinvin Wroth and Hiller B. Zobel (Cambridge, Mass., 1965), 1:lxxviii–lxxix; Gawalt, *Promise of Power,* pp. 18–22.

73. July 28, 1766, Adams, *Diary,* 1:316.

74. Robert Treat Paine repeatedly noted dining with province notables in his diary. Over thirty-five years later Adams described details of a weekend visit to Jeremiah Gridley's home in Brookline (Adams, *Diary,* 3:286.)

75. "Catalogue of Books belonging to Robert Treate Paine January 1768" (RTP papers, MHS). Because this list was reworked in 1805 and includes some obvious additions later than 1768, like Adam Smith's *Wealth of Nations,* one must be cautious in generalizing from it. There were 83 law titles, 73 poetry and belles lettres, theology, physiology and philology, and 50 history. The categories are Paine's, and he places Voltaire and Trenchard and Gordon in the "poetry and belles-lettres" group. There is a total of 448 titles, less than 10 percent by American authors. The list of loans includes twenty-one men and five women.

76. Robert Treat Paine to Gawen Brown, Boston, Aug. 14, 1758 (RTP papers, MHS).

77. Benjamin Church to Robert Treat Paine, London, Dec. 3, 1758 (RTP papers, MHS). The reference is to Sir George Croke's *Reports of Select Cases in the Courts of King's Bench and Common Pleas.* . . . At this time there were three editions: London, 1657–1661; London, 1669; London, 1683–1685.

78. Jeremy Condy to Robert Treat Paine, London, Dec. 11, 1760 (RTP papers, MHS); Robert Treat Paine to Samuel Eliot, Boston, Jan. 12, 1770 (RTP papers, MHS).

79. Robert Treat Paine to Eliphalet Dyer, Boston, August 28, 1758 and April 10, 1759; Elipha-let Dyer to Robert Treat Paine, Windham, Conn., May 8, 1759 (RTP papers, MHS).

80. Robert Treat Paine to Eliphalet Dyer, Boston, Dec. 24. 1760 (RTP papers, MHS).

81. Oxenbridge Thacher to Robert Treat Paine, Boston, Dec. 9, 1763 (RTP papers, MHS). Reference is made to Benjamin Pratt's library.

82. In a letter to Eliphalet Dyer at Windham, Conn., Aug. 28, 1758, Paine reported that the Boston bookseller had a copy of Sir John Strange's *Reports of Adjudged Cases in the Courts of Chancery, King's Bench, Common Pleas, and Exchequer* (London, 1755). Paine explained that the London price was £3.3, and that Condy offered it for $20, adding it "would not be unsold long as they are scarce." Boston, Aug. 28, 1758 (RTP papers, MHS).

83. Adams, *Diary,* 1:274.

84. Adams, *Diary,* 1:286.

85. Jan. 30, 1768, Adams, *Diary,* 1:337–38.

86. L. H. Butterfield, "The American Interests of the Firm of E. and C. Dilly, with Their Letters to Benjamin Rush, 1770–1795," Bibliographical Society of America, *Papers,* 45 (1951): 283–332.

87. Adams to Isaac Smith, Jr., Boston, April 11, 1771, *Adams Family Correspondence,* ed. by L. H. Butterfield et al. (Cambridge, Mass., 1963), 1:75.

88. Adams to Isaac Smith, Jr., Boston, Apr. 11, 1771, *Correspondence*, 1:74–75.

89. Adams, *Diary*, 1:274.

90. Jan. 30, 1768, Adams, *Diary*, 1:337.

91. According to Clifford K. Shipton ("Thomas Hutchinson," *Sibley's Harvard Graduates* (1726–1730) (Boston, 1951), 8:174–76) the attack on the library was motivated by private hostility, perhaps in order to destroy particular land records.

92. Jan. 30, 1768, Adams, *Diary*, 1:337.

93. July 29, 1766, Adams, *Diary*, 1:317. Auchmuty was the son of one of the founders of the legal profession in Boston, a Scots immigrant trained at the London Inns of Court.

94. Spring 1759, Adams, *Diary*, 1:90. Otis's decision was much like Joseph Greenleaf's (Paine's brother-in-law) ridicule of the Reverend Samuel Checkley, who "after an hours Tryal of his skill [did] prove that Snow was White." (Joseph Greenleaf to R. T. P., Boston, Apr. 30, 1755 (RTP papers, MHS).

95. June 8, 1762, Adams, *Diary*, 1:227. On the Otises see: John J. Waters, Jr., *The Otis Family in Provincial and Revolutionary Massachusetts* (Chapel Hill, 1968).

96. Dec. 21, 1758 and Jan. 24, 1765, Adams, *Diary*, 1:63, 251–53.

97. Samuel Fayerweather to Robert Treat Paine., Dec. 8, 1770. Quoted in Stephen T. Riley, "Robert Treat Paine and his Papers," p. xxxii.

98. July 5, 1771, Adams, *Diary*, 2:44–45.

99. The politicization of court meetings intensified in the 1770s when the administration attempted to use the judges' charges to the grand juries to educate or indoctrinate the public. (Richard D. Brown, *Revolutionary Politics in Massachusetts: The Boston Committee of Correspondence and the Towns, 1772–1774*, Cambridge, Mass., 1970, pp. 84–85; John D. Cushing, "The Judiciary and Public Opinion in Revolutionary Massachusetts," in *Law and Authority in Colonial America*, ed. by George A. Billias (Barre, Mass., 1965), pp. 168–86.) On Otis's famous performance see: John J. Waters, Jr. and John A. Schutz, "Patterns of Colonial Politics: The Writs of Assistance Case and the Rivalry between the Otis and Hutchinson Families," *William and Mary Quarterly*, 3d ser., 24 (1967): 543–67.

100. June 8, 1762, Adams, *Diary*, 1:227.

101. Mar. 12, 14, 1767, Robert Treat Paine, Diary (RTP papers, MHS).

102. Jan. 30, 1768, Adams, *Diary*, 1:337–38.

103. Jan. 31, 1767, Abigail Adams to Mary Smith Cranch, Braintree, *Adams Family Correspondence*, 1:58. Adams' letters to his wife are in *Correspondence*, vol 1, passim.

104. Jan. 30, 1768, Adams, *Diary*, 1:338.

105. May 30, 1771, Adams, *Diary*, 2:17. Jonathan Carver, *Travels through the Interior Parts of North America in the years 1766, 1767, and 1768* was published in London, 1778. This book, whose text was probably drafted by its publisher, John Coakley Lettson, later become popular and was printed in twenty-three editions, including French and German translations. Its descriptions of Indians were particularly good. Adams must have seen a manuscript or newspaper version. Carver (1710–1780) was a Canterbury, Connecticut shoemaker. (Edward G. Bourne, "The Travels of Jonathan Carver," *American Historical Review*, 11 (Jan. 1906): 287–302.

106. Nov. 8, 1766 and July 1, 1770, Adams, *Diary*, 1:323, 355–56.

107. Aug. 19, 1760, quoted in Adams, *Diary*, 1:152–53. Adams reported this to be a verbatim quotation of Pratt's exact words.

108. Apr. 22, 1761, John Adams to Samuel Quincy, *Papers of John Adams*, 1:50.

109. Aug. 1, 1761, Adams, *Diary*, 1:220.

110. Adams, *Papers*, 1:58–66, 90–94. Adams' "Humphrey Ploughjogger" essays were aimed in part at recognizing the good sense of common men.

111. June 7, 1771, Adams, *Diary*, 2:27. Adams was at Somers, Conn.

112. May 25, 1773, Adams, *Diary*, 2:82–83.

113. Brown, *Revolutionary Politics in Massachusetts*, pp. 24–25.

114. Mar. 3, 1766 and Mar. 10, 1766, Adams, *Diary*, 1:302–5. The incumbent, Ebenezer Thayer, was part of a large, long-established tribe. Over 20 percent of the people in Braintree were named Thayer, and many more were related.

115. Richard D. Brown, "The Massachusetts Convention of Towns, 1768," *William and Mary Quarterly*. 3d ser., 26 (1969): 94–104. Paine made the only known list of delegates to the convention.

116. Sept. 20, 1773 (RTP papers, MHS). Some of the legal issues that drew communities into controversy during the colonial era are treated in Bruce Hartling Mann, "Parishes, Law, and Community in Connecticut, 1700–1760," Ph.D. diss., Yale Univ., 1977.

117. The first lawyer to become governor was Increase Sumner, elected in 1797, 1798, and 1799 after Samuel Adams declined to stand for re-election owing to infirmity. Thereafter lawyers were regularly elected in succession: Caleb Strong, 1800–1806, James Sullivan, 1807, 1808, Christopher Gore, 1809–1811.

118. As Donald Weber puts it in *Rhetoric and History in Revolutionary New England* (New York, 1988), "in the post-Revolutionary era a rising generation of intellectuals embraced law above theology, a vocational shift that displaced the ministerial fathers to the cultural margins" (pp. 148–49). "By the end of the 18th century," Weber asserts, "the once-powerful cohort of ministers was displaced by the new class of lawyers, whose rhetorical eloquence and political vision enabled the emergent nation to evolve from traditional to modern society" (p. 152).

CHAPTER 5. COMMUNICATIONS AND COMMERCE

1. Carl Bridenbaugh, *Cities in Revolt: Urban Life in America, 1743–1776* (New York, 1955), ch. 9 and passim; Ian K. Steele, *The English Atlantic, 1675–1740: An Exploration of Communication and Community* (New York, 1986); Allen R. Pred, *Urban Growth and the Circulation of Information: The United States System of Cities, 1790–1840* (Cambridge, Mass., 1973); see also his "Urban Systems Development and Long-Distance Flow of Information through Pre-electronic U. S. Newspapers," *Economic Geography*, 47 (1971): 498–524, and "Large City Interdependence and Preelectronic Diffusion and Innovations in the U. S.," *Geographical Analysis*, 3 (1971): 165–81.

2. Harry B. Weiss, "A Graphic Summary of the Growth of Newspapers in New York and Other States, 1704–1820," *Bulletin of the New York Public Library*, 52 (1948): 182–96; G. Thomas Tanselle, "Some Statistics on American Printing, 1764–1783," *The Press & the American Revolution*, ed. by Bernard Bailyn and John B. Hench (Worcester, Mass., 1980), pp. 315–63.

3. The number of surviving urban diaries for the 18th century is surprisingly small. Other than those of Samuel Sewall (Boston) and the Reverend William Bentley (Salem), used elsewhere in this study, I have been able to locate only a handful of substantial diaries. When clergymen are omitted the number is small indeed. The sources used here, apart from their obvious limitations as to race, class, and gender, also leave obscure the role of transient people of all ranks. Transients, who were not knit into the established local communication networks, may have

exercised a significant impact on the information flow of port towns, but how, and when, and why remains to be evaluated. In wartime their reports of events seem to have been especially important.

4. The principal sources referred to are *Letters and Diary of John Rowe, Boston Merchant, 1759–1762, 1764–1779,* ed. by Annie Rowe Cunningham (Boston, 1903); George Nelson Diary, 1780–1781, 1790–1792, manuscript department, Historical Society of Pennsylvania; *The Diary of William Pynchon of Salem* (1776–1789), ed. by Fitch Edward Oliver (Boston, 1890); John Anderson, Jr., Diary, 1794–1798, and the papers of John Anderson, Sarah Anderson, Alexander Anderson, 1775–1869, manuscript department, New-York Historical Society; *The Journals of Ashley Bowen (1728–1813) of Marblehead,* 2 vols., ed. by Philip Chadwick Foster Smith, Publications of the Colonial Society of Massachusetts, vols. 44 and 45 of *Collections* (Boston, 1973). Two of the relevant ports are analyzed in Thomas M. Doerflinger, *A Vigorous Spirit of Enterprise: Merchants and Economic Development in Revolutionary Philadelphia* (Chapel Hill, 1986); and Christine Leigh Heyrman, *Commerce and Culture: The Maritime Communities of Colonial Massachusetts, 1690–1750* (New York, 1984), pt. 2 treats Marblehead. A functional analytic overview is offered in Jacob M. Price, "Economic Function and the Growth of American Port Towns in the Eighteenth Century," *Perspectives in American History,* 8 (1974): 123–86.

5. A sketch of Rowe is provided by Edward Lillie Pierce in the *Letters and Diary of John Rowe.* John W. Tyler, *Smugglers & Patriots: Boston Merchants and the Advent of the American Revolution* (Boston, 1985) presents evidence that among other activities Rowe was a smuggler.

6. Perhaps the most spectacular of this truism was the rise of the house of Rothschild, whose private communication system during the Napoleonic Wars catapulted the family to preeminence.

7. Bridenbaugh, *Cities in Revolt,* pp. 161–63, 363–64, and passim.

8. Rowe, *Diary of John Rowe,* Oct. 2, 3, 4, 1764, p. 65; Oct. 12 and 23, 1764, p. 66; Nov. 2, 1764, p. 67; Dec. 9, 1764, p. 70.

9. Ibid., Sept. 11, 1764, pp. 61–62.

10. Ibid., Jan. 15, 1765, p. 74.

11. Ibid., Jan. 19, 1765, p. 74.

12. Ibid., Jan. 20, 1765, p. 74; Jan. 21, 1765, p. 75.

13. Ibid., Feb. 11, 1768, pp. 150–51.

14. Ibid., Jan. 10, 1769, p. 182.

15. Ibid., Apr. 11, 13, 1766, pp. 89–90; Sept 21, 1766, p. 111; May 25, 1768, p. 163.

16. The sole exception to this pattern evident in the diary is a comment on John Green (1706?–1779), "Improvement of the Mind," a sermon or treatise by the Bishop of Lincoln, which Rowe compared to a sermon of Reverend William Walter. (*Diary of John Rowe,* Mar. 13, 1774, p. 266.)

17. *Diary of John Rowe,* Dec. 2, 1766, pp. 116–17; Mar. 17, 18, 1767, p. 125.

18. Harbottle Dorr, a Boston merchant whose collection of newspapers from the Revolutionary era survives at the Massachusetts Historical Society, annotated his newspapers heavily, responding vigorously in the margins. The "high society" in which Rowe often moved was not always so genteel as one might suppose. Admiral James Montague, with whom Rowe often dined and went fishing, was described by John Adams as one whose "continual language is cursing and damning and God damning, 'my wifes d——d A——se is so broad that she and I cant sit in a Chariot together'—this is the Nature of the Beast and the common Language of the Man." (*Diary and Autobiography of John Adams,* ed. by L. H. Butterfield et al. (Cambridge,

Mass., 1962), Dec. 28, 1772, 2:73.) The comment on Mather is from *The Diary of William Bentley* (Salem, Mass., 1914), 4:199, Sept. 19, 1813.

19. George Nelson, Diary, Oct. 6, 1790 and June 23, 1781.

20. Ibid., May 25, 1780 and May 25, 1781.

21. *Diary of John Rowe,* July 4, 1760, p. 361; Aug. 11, 1765, p. 88; Apr. 24, 1770, p. 201; George Nelson, Diary, Apr. 22, 1780, June 6 and 9, 1780.

22. George Nelson, Diary, Mar. 26, 1781.

23. *Diary of John Rowe,* Mar. 25, 1775, p. 291.

24. Newspapers were advertised by coffeehouse and chocolatehouse proprietors routinely: Steele, *The English Atlantic, 1675–1740,* p. 158; John Rowe to Capt. Edward Cahill, Jan. 6, 1761, *Diary of John Rowe,* p. 385; also letter to Philip Cuyler, Sept. 24, 1759, *Diary of John Rowe,* p. 337.

25. To Peter Hubbert, Mar. 24, 1760, *Diary of John Rowe,* p. 346; to Jacob Rowe, Apr. 21, 1760, *Diary of John Rowe,* p. 347.

26. To Jacob Rowe, Sept. 20, 1759, *Diary of John Rowe,* pp. 335–36.

27. George Nelson, Diary, Oct. 3 and Nov. 15, 1780; Aug. 11, 1790.

28. Ibid., Feb. 6, 1781.

29. Ibid., Feb. 8, 1781.

30. Ibid. See also Feb. 23, 1780.

31. Transients of varied social rank were most likely to join in local information networks at places of public entertainment, where convention encouraged inquiries and "public" conversation.

32. "William Pynchon," in *Sibley's Harvard Graduates* (1741–1745), by Clifford K. Shipton (Boston, 1960), 11:295–301. Pynchon's family stature is reflected in his high class rank—fourth in a class of thirty-nine students.

33. The papers of the Andersons at the New-York Historical Society reveal the powerful emotional attachments of parents and children. Both John, Jr., and his brother Alexander, a physician who turned to a career as an engraver, kept detailed diaries that furnish rich information on family bonds. The entire body of papers reveals an unusually sensitive and affectionate family.

34. *Diary of William Pynchon,* Dec. 8, 1780, pp. 80–81; Dec. 9, 1782, p. 138.

35. Bridenbaugh, *Cities in Revolt,* pp. 188–91, 393–98.

36. *Diary of William Pynchon,* Nov. 25, 1782, p. 137; Dec. 13, 1784, p. 202.

37. John Anderson, Diary, June 15, 1795; August 7, 1794; Jan. 29, 1794; Nov. 9, 1795; Jan. 19, 1796; Nov. 9, 1795; Bridenbaugh, *Cities in Revolt,* pp. 179–84, 380–88; David Paul Nord, "A Republican Literature: A Study of Magazine Reading and Readers in Late Eighteenth-Century New York," *American Quarterly,* 40 (1988): 42–64.

38. That people of more humble status, including artisans, shared such aspirations of enlightenment is evident from the Junto, a mutual self-improvement club that the printer Benjamin Franklin and his friends formed in Philadelphia in the 1720s. At weekly meetings they discussed "morals, politics, or natural philosophy . . . in the sincere spirit of inquiry after truth." (Benjamin Franklin, *The Autobiography and Other Writings,* ed. by L. Jesse Lemisch (New York, 1961) p. 72.) Nord, "A Republican Literature," p. 48, reports that a substantial number of magazine subscribers were artisans and shopkeepers in New York City in the 1790s.

39. John Adams was so hungry for "philosophical" conversation when he was at Worcester that he clubbed with the unconventional deists Ephraim Doolittle (a petty merchant), Nathan

Baldwin (register of deeds), and Joseph Dyer (shopkeeper and pettifogger). "All the Nonsense of these last twenty Years, were as familiar to them as they were to Condorcet or Brissot," Adams recalled in 1804, and "I spent the more Evenings with these Men, as they were readers and thinking Men, though I differed with them all in Religion and Government, because there were no others in Town who were possessed of so much literature, [the Reverend] Mr. Maccarty and Mr. Putnam excepted." (Adams, *Diary,* 3:265–66.)

40. *Diary of William Pynchon,* Feb. 13, 1786, p. 231.

41. *Diary of John Quincy Adams,* ed. by David Grayson Allen et al. (Cambridge, Mass., 1981), 2:326 (Dec. 6, 1787); 2:416 (June 12, 1788).

42. John Anderson, Diary, Jan. 22, 1794; Feb. 7, 1794; Sept. 4, 1795; Aug. 7, 1794; May 12, 1797; June 12, 1798; June 14, 1798; Bridenbaugh, *Cities in Revolt,* pp. 162–63, 288, 363–64.

43. Richard D. Brown, "The Emergence of Urban Society in Rural Massachusetts, 1760–1820," *Journal of American History,* 61 (June, 1974): 29–51.

44. "Pursue the Study of the Law rather than the Gain of it," Gridley told Adams. (Adams, *Diary,* Oct. 25, 1758, 1:55.)

45. For an analysis of the Marblehead of Bowen's youth see Heyrman, *Commerce and Culture,* pt. 2. Bowen's father, Nathan, she explains, played a significant role in Marblehead religious divisions, and actively opposed the New Lights.

46. *Bowen,* June 18, 1775, 2:445; Sept. 9, 1768, 1:186; May 13, 1774, 2:394; Sept. 5, 1770, 1:253; Dec. 6, 1775, 2:466.

47. *Bowen,* 1:253.

48. *Bowen,* May 13, 1774, 2:394. Bowen was correct. (*Diary of John Rowe,* p. 269.)

49. *Bowen,* May 25, 31, 1774, 2:395–96.

50. *Bowen,* Sept. 4, 1774, 2:408.

51. *Bowen,* June 16, 17, 18, 1775, 2:445.

52. *Bowen,* Apr. 19, 1775, 2:435.

53. Bowen's journal supplies an all but complete record of Marblehead entries and departures during the years when his rigging business was active.

54. By 1778 Bowen was forced to leave home as a mariner, and for the next few years he was gone from Marblehead much of the time. (*Bowen,* 2:530ff.)

55. *Bowen,* 2:508 (1777).

56. The theme of Marblehead insularity is in Samuel Roads, Jr., *History and Traditions of Marblehead* (1880).

57. For example, *Bowen,* Apr. 7, 1773, 2:339; May 14, 1773, 2:341–42; Oct. 23, 1773, 2:363.

58. *Bowen,* Oct. 17, 1769, 1:224; June 3, 1771, 1:274.

59. *Bowen,* Nov. 11, 1771, 1:288.

60. *Bowen,* Oct. 19, 1773, 2:361–62; Nov. 9, 1773, 2:368.

61. *Bowen,* Aug. 1 and 2, 1788, 2:563.

62. *Bowen,* Dec. 14, 16, 17, 1788, 2:570.

63. *Bowen,* Feb. 19, 1793, 2:593. This is the only mention of French politics in Bowen's surviving journals. Since Bowen spent most of his formative years at sea, cut off from ready access to news beyond his ship and fleet, Bowen might have had two reactions: either a great hunger for news or, as seems likely, a habit of unconcern.

64. William Bentley, Diary, Nov. 30, 1804; Jan. 13, 1806; Dec. 4, 1807; Feb. 15, 1809, quoted in *Bowen,* 2:609–10, 611, 617, 620. Part of Bentley's fascination with Bowen stemmed from the

fact that Bowen had served as a mariner in the same fleet that Bentley's father served in as a carpenter. Bentley had long been alienated from his father and so through Bowen he could learn something of his father's adventures in the days around the time of his own birth.

65. William Bentley, Diary, Feb. 4, 1813, in *Bowen,* 2:624.

66. *Bowen,* May 11, 1813, 2:626, and obituary of Bowen in *Salem Register,* Feb. 6, 1813, by Bentley in *Bowen,* 2:626.

67. *Diary of John Rowe,* June 15, 1776, p. 311. The rumor was spread by a woman and may have concerned Rowe's business practices.

68. George Nelson, Diary, Mar. 19, 1780.

69. *Diary of William Pynchon,* Oct. 9, 1784, p. 196; Oct. 30, 1784, p. 199.

70. Bridenbaugh, *Cities in Revolt,* pp. 179–84, 380–88. Other than personal collections of books, libraries were almost unknown in the countryside. The few that were founded from the 1730s onward had only a limited array of titles and usually a short term of existence. See Jesse H. Shera, *Foundations of the Public Library: The Origins of the Public Library Movement in New England. 1629–1855* (Chicago, 1949), pp. 50–53, and ch. 4.

71. Elizabeth Carroll Reilly, "The Wages of Piety: The Boston Book Trade of Jeremy Condy," in *Printing and Society in Early America,* ed. by William L. Joyce et al. (Worcester, Mass., 1983), pp. 83–131, esp. 111.

72. Bridenbaugh, *Cities in Revolt,* pp. 388–89.

73. See Carl F. Kaestle, "The Public Reaction to John Dickinson's *Farmer's Letters,*" *Proceedings of the American Antiquarian Society,* 78 (1968): 323–59.

74. The quotation is from Newport, R.I., 1774. (Bridenbaugh, *Cities in Revolt,* p. 275.)

75. John Anderson, Jr., Diary, July 5, 11, 14, 25, Aug. 16, 1795. Anderson borrowed Winchester's *A Course of Lectures on the Prophesies . . .,* vol. I (Norwich, Conn., 1794), and also read in his *Ten Letters Addressed to Mr. Paine* (Boston, 1794, and New York, 1795), an answer to Paine's *Age of Reason.*

76. George Nelson, Diary, Aug. 13, 1790; Sept. 6, 8, 1790; Nov. 17, 18, 1790.

77. John Anderson, Jr., Diary, July 4, 1794.

CHAPTER 6. INFORMATION AND INSULARITY

1. *Diary of Joshua Hempstead of New London, Connecticut, 1711–1858,* Collections of the New London Country Historical Society (Providence, 1901), 1:485, July 30 and 31, 1747.

2. The literature on New England farming in the 18th and 19th centuries is extensive. Some of the works which I have used for a general understanding are Howard S. Russell, *A Long, Deep Furrow: Three Centuries of Farming in New England* (Hanover, N.H., 1976); and Michael Bellesiles, "The World of the Account Book: The Frontier Economy of the Upper Connecticut Valley, 1760–1800," paper given at Organization of American Historians, Apr. 1986; Michael A. Bernstein and Sean Wilentz, "Marketing, Commerce, and Capitalism in Rural Massachusetts," *Journal of Economic History,* 44 (1984): 171–73; Percy W. Bidwell, "Rural Economy in New England at the Beginning of the Nineteenth Century," *Transactions of the Connecticut Academy of Arts and Sciences,* 20 (1916): 241–399; Christopher Clark, "The Household Economy, Market Exchange and the Rise of Capitalism in the Connecticut Valley, 1800–1860," *Journal of Social History,* 13 (1979): 169–89; Susan Geib, " 'Changing Works': Agriculture and Society in Brookfield, Massachusetts, 1785–1820," Ph.D. diss., Boston Univ., 1981; James A. Henretta, "Families and Farms: *Mentalité* in Pre-Industrial America," *William and Mary Quar-*

terly, 3d ser., 35 (1978): 3–32; Gregory Nobles, "The Making of a Rural Merchant Class: Regional Networks of Commercial Connection in Eighteenth-Century New England," paper given at Organization of American Historians, New York, Apr. 1986; Winifred B. Rothenberg, "The Market and Massachusetts Farmers, 1750–1855," *Journal of Economic History,* 41 (1981): 283–314; Kevin Sweeney, "Gentleman Farmers and Inland Merchants," in his 1986 Yale University Ph.D. diss., "River Gods and Related Minor Deities: The Williams Family and the Connecticut River, 1637–1790"; *The Farm,* ed. by Peter Benes, The Dublin Seminar for New England Folklife, Annual Proceedings, 1986 (Boston, 1988).

3. Thomas Gray, "Elegy Written in a Country Churchyard." *The Poetical Works of Thomas Gray* (Philadelphia, 1861), pp. 53–54. Even a century after Gray's poem was written a young New Jersey gentleman who observed farmers at work would note that they were "singing as they wrought, some rustic ditty that showed their hearts light and their lots happy." (Isaac Mickle, *A Gentleman of Much Promise: The Diary of Isaac Mickle, 1837–1845,* ed. with an intro. by Philip English Mackey (Philadelphia, 1977), 1:117.)

4. That date was June 12, 1750, according to *The Dictionary of National Biography* (London, 1921–1922), 8 (Glover-Harriett): 467. For Hempstead see *Hempstead,* June 12, 1750, p. 551.

5. *Hempstead,* Dec. 26, 1726, p. 178.

6. Frances Manwaring Caulkins, *History of New London, Connecticut . . . 1612 to 1852* (New London, 1852), p. 273; Hempstead's work on gravestones is explained in Ernest Caulfield, "Connecticut Gravestones XII: John Hartshorn (1650–c.1738) *vs.* Joshua Hempstead (1678–1758)," *Bulletin of the Connecticut Historical Society,* 32, no. 3 (July 1967): 65–79, and Ernest Caulfield and James H. Slater, "The Gravestone Carvings of John Hartshorn," *Puritan Gravestone Art II,* ed. by Peter Benes, The Dublin Seminar for New England Folklife, Annual Proceedings (3d) (Boston, 1978).

7. Hempstead referred to a book he owned called "Ye Seven Wonders of the World" on Sept. 6, 1756 (p. 674), which he loaned to a young woman. I have not identified this work. Cotton Mather published *The Wonders of the Invisible World, being an account of the Trials of the several Witches . . .* (Boston, 1693), and Robert Calef published *More Wonders of the Invisible World* (London, 1700). After 1810 a number of books using "The Seven Wonders of the World" in the title were published, all dealing with architectural achievements.

8. "An Inventory of the Estate of Joshua Hempstead, Esqr. Late of New London deceased . . . ," Jan. 5, 1759, Connecticut Archives, Hartford, Conn.

9. Caulkins, *New London,* pp. 668–69. No one with the surname Hempstead graduated from Harvard or Yale before 1800.

10. *Hempstead,* p. 711.

11. Ibid., Sept. 17, 1711, p. 1; and Aug. 8, 1757, p. 689.

12. Ibid., Jan. 13, 1712, p. 6.

13. Ibid., July 6, 1749, p. 526.

14. Ibid., July 28, 1749, p. 533.

15. Ibid., June 5, 1741, p. 377. See Harry S. Stout and Peter Onuf, "James Davenport and the Great Awakening in New London," *Journal of American History,* 70 (Dec. 1983): 556–78; Peter Onuf, "New Lights in New London: A Group Portrait of the Separatists," *William and Mary Quarterly,* 3d ser., 37 (Oct. 1980): 627–43.

16. *Hempstead,* March 27, 1743, pp. 406–7.

17. Ibid., Oct. 7, 1741, pp. 382–83; Feb. 26, 1742, p. 389; Aug. 8–12, 1745, pp. 446–47.

18. Ibid., March 31, 1743, p. 407.

19. Nathan Cole quoted in Leonard W. Labaree, "George Whitefield Comes to Middletown," *William and Mary Quarterly,* 3d ser., 7 (1950): 590–91.

20. *Hempstead,* Dec. 26, 27, 1726, p. 178.

21. Ibid., Oct. 2, 1711, p. 2.

22. Ibid., Oct. 19, 1711, p. 3.

23. *A Journal for the years 1739–1803, by Samuel Lane of Stratham, New Hampshire,* ed. by Charles Lane Hanson (Concord, N.H. 1937) includes a brief biographical introduction. In 1775 the population of Stratham was 1137 people according to Stella H. Sutherland, *Population Distribution in Colonial America* (New York, 1936), p. 11.

24. Lane, *Journal,* iii.

25. Ibid., p. 14.

26. (New York, 1794), p. 179, pt. 6, line 567.

27. Jesse H. Shera, *Foundations of the Public Library: The Origins of the Public Library Movement in New England, 1629–1855* (Chicago, 1949), p. 51.

28. Lane, *Journal,* p. 8. On *Robinson Crusoe's* popularity see Robert B. Winans, "Bibliography and the Cultural Historian: Notes on the Eighteenth-Century Novel," in *Printing and Society in Early America,* ed. by William L. Joyce, David D. Hall, Richard D. Brown, and John B. Hench (Worcester, Mass., 1983), 178–79. Among the twenty-seven novels most frequently listed in American catalogs of books (1750–1800), *Crusoe* ranked twelfth. It led all others in abridged versions with a total of thirty-nine.

29. Lane, *Journal,* May 9, 1760, p. 38; Feb. 11, 1764, p. 39.

30. Lane, *Journal,* 1748, pp. 32–33; Lane, *Journal,* p. 9.

31. Lane, *Journal,* July 4, 1765, and Apr. 11, 1766, p. 40.

32. Among Lane's accoutrements was a tall clock of the post-Revolutionary era and a pocketbook with the words "Liberty" and "Unity" elaborately tooled into the leather (Lane, *Journal,* facing p. 23 and 62, 63). For an analysis of farmers' possessions see Abbot L. Cummings, ed., *Rural Household Inventories, 1675–1775* (Boston, 1964).

33. Lane, *Journal,* Apr. 16, 1790, p. 56; spring and summer 1800, pp. 60–61.

34. Ibid., March 7, 1794, p. 58.

35. Ibid., p. 69, 1752; pp. 101–2, hay (1799). Others, p. 62; Feb. 20. 1788; p. 57, Aug. 1793.

36. Page 179, pt. 1, line 567.

37. *The Diary of Matthew Patten of Bedford, N.H.* (Concord, N.H., 1903) and Kenneth Scott, "Matthew Patten of Bedford, New Hampshire," *Journal of the Presbyterian Historical Society,* 28 (Sept. 1950): 129–45. The population of Bedford in 1775 was 495 people (Sutherland, *Population Distribution,* p. 13.)

38. Patten, *Diary,* p. 26, March 31, 1756.

39. Ibid., p. 19, Aug 23, 1755; p. 29, Aug. 2, 1756.

40. Ibid., p. 174.

41. Ibid., p. 149, March 27, 1765.

42. Ibid., p. 77, March 19, 1760.

43. Ibid., p. 83.

44. Ibid., p. 74, Jan. 18, 1760 (almanac); p. 352, Dec. 8, 1775 (almanac).

45. Ibid., p. 83, July 22, 1760.

46. Ibid., p. 325, July 14, 1774.

47. Ibid., p. 342, Apr. 22, 1775.

48. Ibid., p. 361, July 20, 1776. Patten erroneously entered this as May 1776.

49. Ibid., p. 361, July 21, 1776.

50. Ibid., p. 362, Aug. 6–16, 1776.

51. The population estimate is from Lynn Warren Turner, *The Ninth State: New Hampshire's Formative Years* (Chapel Hill, 1983), p. 363. Though Patten lived until 1795, his diary exists only to 1788, so whether Patten became a newspaper reader in the 1790s, when Lane did, remains unknown.

52. Sanger's journal for Oct. 1, 1774 through Dec. 6, 1782, and a memorandum and journal book for Dec. 3, 1791 through Dec. 11, 1794, survive at the Library of Congress. They have been printed, together with Sanger's few surviving letters, in an annotated edition with spelling and punctuation modernized and abbreviations spelled out by Lois K. Stabler, *Very Poor and of a Lo Make: The Journal of Abner Sanger* (Portsmouth, N.H., 1986). Stabler supplies a biographical sketch of Sanger, his genealogy, biographical notes on persons mentioned by Sanger, and a glossary of obscure and obsolete words and phrases. All citations below are to Stabler's edition of the journal. The population of Keene in 1775 was 756 people. (Sutherland, *Population Distribution*, p. 13.)

53. Sanger, *Journal*, 224, Dec. 30, 1778; pp. 193–94, Apr. 22, 1778.

54. Ibid., p. 424, July 15, 1782.

55. Ibid., p. 422.

56. Ibid., pp. 422–23, July 5, 1782.

57. Ibid., p. 424, July 10, 1782.

58. Ibid., p. 425, July 16, 1782.

59. Ibid., p. 433, Aug. 26 and 27, 1782. For a discusion of gender relations and Sanger in particular see Laurel Thatcher Ulrich and Lois K. Stabler, " 'Girling of it' in Eighteenth-Century New Hampshire," *Families and Children*, Peter Benes, ed., The Dublin Seminar for New England Folklife, Annual Proceedings, 1985 (10th) (Boston, 1987), pp. 24–36.

60. Sanger, *Journal*, p. 428, Aug. 3, 1782.

61. Ibid., p. 426, July 26, 1782.

62. Ibid., p. 112, Sept. 9, 1776.

63. Ibid., p. 172, Dec. 20, 1777.

64. Ibid., p. 311, Sept. 1, 1780.

65. Ibid., p. 401, Feb. 7, 1782; p. 402, Feb. 15, 1782.

66. Ibid., p. 212, Sept. 25, 1778; p. 185, Feb. 9, 1778; p. 431, Aug. 20, 1782.

67. Ibid., pp. 270–71, Nov. 26. 1779.

68. Ibid., p. 165, Nov. 3, 1777.

69. Ibid., pp. 432–33, Aug. 24, 1782.

70. Ibid., p. 449, Oct. 22, 1782.

71. Ibid., p. 514, July 5, 1794.

72. Ibid., p. 450, Oct. 25, 1782.

73. Ibid., pp. 453–54, Nov. 6, 1782.

74. Ibid., p. 458, Nov. 21, 1782.

75. Every mention Sanger makes of a book is in relation to its shared use. On Dec. 1, 1782, the particular work was two volumes of Dr. Isaac Watts "Christianity Morality Sermons." (Sanger, *Journal,* p. 460.) Also, Ulrich and Stabler, " 'Girling of it' in Eighteenth-Century New Hampshire," p. 32.

76. Sanger, *Journal,* p. 441, Sept. 29, 1782: p. 444, Oct. 3, 1782.

77. Ibid., p. 455, Nov. 10, 1782; p. 371, July 31, 1781. The reference is to Joseph Butler (d. 1752), the Bishop of Durham, whose *The Analogy of Religion* was published at London in 1736. (Sanger, *Journal,* p. 66, n.2.)

78. Sanger, *Journal,* p. 441, Sept. 29, 1782.

79. Ibid., p. 518, July 27, 1794.

80. Ibid., p. 521, Aug. 6, 1794.

81. Information on Parker is drawn from Ethel Stanwood Bolton's "Extracts from the Diary of James Parker of Shirley, Mass.," *New England Historic and Genealogical Register (NEHGR),* 69 (1915): 8–17, 117–27, 211–24, 294–308; and 70 (1916): 9–24, 137–46, 210–20, 294–308, her *Shirley Uplands and Intervales* (Boston, 1914), and Seth Chandler, *History of the Town of Shirley, Massachusetts, from its early settlement to A.D. 1882* (Shirley, Mass., 1883). See also Barbara Russell Karsky, "Profiles of Protest: Regulators and their Families in Shays' Rebellion," paper given at conference on Shays's Rebellion, Deerfield, Mass., Nov. 1986, and her "Sociability in Rural New England," in Barbara Karsky and Elise Marienstras, eds., *Time and Work in Pre-Industrial America/Travail et Loisir dans l'Amérique pré-industrielle* (Nancy, France, 1989).

82. Parker, *NEHGR* 69:223, March 18, 1782; p. 300, May 16, 1786.

83. Chandler, *History of the Town of Shirley,* p. 123.

84. Sutherland, *Population Distribution,* p. 17, reports population of Shirley at 704 people according to Massachusetts census of 1776.

85. Parker, *NEHGR* 69:119, Sept. 7, 1773; he read a sermon.

86. Parker, *NEHGR* 69:214, June 5, 1778.

87. Parker, *NEHGR* 69:213, Sept. 30, 1777.

88. Parker, *NEHGR* 69:121, April and May, 1774.

89. Parker, *NEHGR* 69:121, Feb. 5, 1774.

90. Parker, *NEHGR* 69:126, Oct. 12, 1776; p. 224, Dec. 20, 1782; p. 299, June 1785; p. 304, Feb. 10, 1789.

91. Parker, *NEHGR* 70:11, Dec. 30, 1791; p. 13, Dec. 19, 24, 1792; p. 11, Dec. 21, 1791; p. 9, Jan. 22, 1791.

92. Parker, *NEHGR* 70:11, Feb. 29, 1792; p. 12, May 23 and June 4, 1792; p. 13, Nov. 2, 1792; p. 15, June 24, 1793; p. 17, July 15, 1795. As early as June 24, 1778 (*NEHGR* 69:214) Parker mentioned a Masonic meeting at Lancaster, so his membership may have originated earlier.

93. Parker, *NEHGR* 70:20, March 25, 1797; p. 139, Dec. 3, 1799.

94. Parker, *NEHGR* 70:23, Apr. 25, 1798.

95. Parker, *NEHGR* 69:122, Jan. 2, 1775; p. 123, Feb. 21 and March 28, 1775.

96. Parker, *NEHGR* 69:222, Oct. 15, 1781.

97. Parker, *NEHGR* 69:302, Jan. 1, 1787. This claim must be tentative. Gubernatorial proclamations had been publicly read in many towns during the colonial era, and in 1772 and 1773 the Boston Commmittee of Correspondence pamphlet stating the rights of the colonists was read publicly in some towns. See Richard D. Brown, *Revolutionary Politics in Massachusetts: The*

Boston Committee of Correspondence and the Towns, 1772–1774 (Cambridge, Mass., 1970), ch. 5, "The Emergence of Local Opinion."

98. Parker, *NEHGR* 70:11, Feb. 29, 1792; p. 12, May 23, 1792.

99. Parker, *NEHGR* 70:15, June 24, 1793.

100. Parker, *NEHGR* 70:15, July 17, 1793.

101. Peter Thacher gave the sermon at the Brattle Street Church, Parker, *NEHGR* 70:15, Oct. 14, 1793.

102. Parker, *NEHGR 70:140, Feb. 23, 1800.*

103. Parker, *NEHGR* 70:211, Apr. 24, 1803.

104. Parker, *NEHGR* 70:300, July 31 and Oct. 31 and Nov. 7, 1814.

105. Parker, *NEHGR* 70:307, Nov. 3, 1828.

106. *Nailer Tom's Diary. Otherwise The Journal of Thomas B. Hazard of Kingstown, Rhode Island, 1778 to 1840.* Intro. by Caroline Hazard (Boston, 1930). The village of Little Rest, now called Kingston, lies within the township of Kingstown, later South Kingstown, in King's, later Washington County—also called South County by Rhode Islanders. Caroline Hazard supplies biographical data on Thomas B. Hazard, some of which seems erroneous. She reports that Thomas B. Hazard was the grandson of "College Tom" Hazard on his father's side and, on his mother's side, "Abram Redwood for whom the Redwood library in Newport is named," (p. vii). Yet according to *Sibley's Harvard Graduates* and Dexter's *Biographical Sketches of the Graduates of Yale College,* no one named Hazard, Hasard, or Haszard attended either Harvard or Yale before 1756. So what does "College" signify in Grandfather Hazard's name? More crucial, the identity of T. B. Hazard's mother is uncertain. If his mother was Mehitable Redwood, as Caroline Hazard claims, then her report of the deaths of both parents during T. B. Hazard's childhood is doubtful. Clifford K. Shipton, in *Sibley's Harvard Graduates,* 12:132–33, notes in his sketch of Benjamin Ellery of the class of 1747, that Ellery married Mehitable Redwood, the only daughter of Abraham Redwood of Newport in 1769 and, quoting the *Massachusetts Gazette* of Feb. 2, 1769, adds that she brought with her a fortune of £5000 sterling. She lived until 1794 and her father, the wealthy Abraham, lived to 1788. Thus the fact that Thomas B. Hazard was an orphan apprenticed to a blacksmith in the 1770s and subsequently dwelling in near-poverty makes it unlikely that he was the son and grandson of these rich people. According to evidence in T. B. H.'s diary he did have Redwood relatives in Newport, but the nature of the connection is not clear. He never called on either of these two Redwoods when he visited Newport, nor did he take note of their deaths. There are so many Hazards in Rhode Island, many sharing common first names, that it is easy to imagine tracking errors in T. B. H.'s genealogy.

107. *Nailer Tom's Diary,* p. 28, Jan. 12, 1782.

108. Ibid., pp. 16–21, Sept. 5, 6, 16, 18, Oct. 7, 8, Dec. 20, 1780, Jan. 20, Apr. 15, May 7, 1781.

109. Ibid., p. 18, Dec. 20, 1780.

110. Ibid., p. 153, July 31, 1793. When he went fishing on May 5, 1782 (p. 33) he notes that he "keacht afew."

111. The persistence of intense localism into the 19th century is delineated in an analysis of the Sturbridge, Massachusetts, farmer Philemon Shepard (b. 1790), whose "most distant trading partner lived less than three miles away." (Andrew H. Baker and Holly Izard Paterson, "Farmers' Adaptation to Markets in Early Nineteenth-Century Massachusetts," *The Farm,* ed. by Peter Benes, p. 10.)

112. *Nailer Tom's Diary,* p. 140, Aug. 20, 1792; p. 145, Dec. 20, 21, 1792; p. 160, March 25, 1794.

113. Ibid., p. 140, Aug. 20, 1792; p. 160, March 24, 1794.

114. Ibid., p. 139, July 14, 1792; p. 158, Feb. 4, 1794.

115. Ibid., p. 143, Nov. 3, 1792.

116. Ibid., pp. 168–69, Dec. 14 and 21, 1794.

117. Ibid., p. 151, June 9, 1793; p. 162, June 12, 1794; p. 163, June 20, 1794; p. 173, April 17, 1795.

118. Ibid., p. 271, March 17, 1806.

119. Ibid., p. 274, June 4, 1806; p. 275, June 17, 1806.

120. Ibid., p. 293, Aug. 24, 1807.

121. Ibid., p. 272, April 19, 1806.

122. Ibid., p. 272, April 14, 1806.

123. Ibid., p. 277, Aug. 12 and 13, 1806.

124. My understanding of Rhode Island politics during this era is drawn from Patrick T. Conley, *Democracy in Decline: Rhode Island's Constitutional Development, 1776–1841* (Providence, 1977). For this particular election see pp. 175–76.

125. *Nailer Tom's Diary,* p. 284, Jan. 22, 1807.

126. Ibid., p. 288, May 6, 1807. Conley, *Democracy in Decline,* 116, n. 19, associates Hazard with the "country party." In 1807 he ran on a printed ballot as part of a statewide slate of fifteen candidates, including ten assistants (members of the upper house) of which he was one, the governor, and four other general state officers. The property requirement, $134 worth of assets, included most Rhode Island farmers. Hazard's selection was evidently based partly on his own wide acquaintance as a blacksmith and farmer, and partly on his connection with the great tribe of Hazards who were prominent in Rhode Island affairs for several decades.

127. Conley, *Democracy in Decline,* pp. 155, 159; *Nailer Tom's Diary,* p. 322, May 3, 1809.

128. *Nailer Tom's Diary,* p. 302, Feb. 27, 1808; p. 300, Jan. 10, 1808; p. 305, May 4–7, 1808.

129. Ibid., p. 286, March 21, 1807; p. 320, Mar. 21, 1809.

130. Ibid., p. 320, March 28, 1809. The newspaper, *The Rhode-Island Republican* was first published by William Simons, March 22, 1809.

131. Ibid., p. 140, August 20, 1792; p. 175, June 15, 1795; p. 603, Sept. 11, 1823; p. 607, Nov. 26, 1823.

132. Ibid., p. 546, Aug. 29, 1820.

133. Ibid., p. 549, Oct. 27, 1820; p. 604, Sept. 21, 1823.

134. Ibid., p. 673, July 19, 1827; p. 799, April 19, 1839.

135. Ibid., p. 765, Nov. 10 and Dec. 11, 1834; p. 769, May 28, 1835; p. 806, May 16, 1840.

136. On almanacs see George L. Kittredge, *The Old Farmer and His Almanac* (Boston, 1904) and Marion Barber Stowell, *Early American Almanacs: The Colonial Weekday Bible* (New York, 1977). The quotations are from the *Christian Almanack . . . 1828* (Rochester, N.Y., (1827), II, no. 1, p. 19.

137. (Boston, 1835).

138. *Williams' Calendar, or the Utica Almanac . . . 1834* (Utica, N.Y. (1833).

139. *Farmer's Almanack . . . 1839* (Boston, 1838), no. 47, October, 1839.

CHAPTER 7. DAUGHTERS, WIVES, MOTHERS

1. *Journal & Letters of Philip Vickers Fithian, 1773–1774: A Plantation Tutor of the Old Dominion,* ed. with an intro. by Hunter Dickinson Farish (Williamsburg, Va., 1943), pp. 160–61.

2. Ibid., p. 88, Feb. 19, 1774.

3. Quoted in Linda K. Kerber, *Women of the Republic: Intellect and Ideology in Revolutionary America* (Chapel Hill, 1980), p. 226.

4. William Bentley, *The Diary of William Bentley, D.D., Pastor of the East Church, Salem Massachusetts* (Salem, 1911, reprinted Gloucester, 1962), 3:47, Sept. 25, 1803. Italics added. The newspaper material was in *The Salem Register,* Sept. 26, 1803, p. 3. The deceased couple was memorialized by Thomas Cushing Thacher, *A Sermon preached at Lynn, July 17, 1803, occasioned by the death of Mr. Miles Shory and wife . . .* (Salem, 1803).

5. Much of what follows relies on Laurel Thatcher Ulrich's *Good Wives: Image and Reality in the Lives of Women in Nothern New England, 1650–1750* (New York 1982) and Mary Beth Norton's *Liberty's Daughters: The Revolutionary Experience of American Women, 1750–1800* (Boston, 1980), for the colonial and revolutionary periods. For the early national period I have drawn on: Joy Day Buel and Richard Buel, Jr., *The Way of Duty: A Woman and Her Family in Revolutionary America* (New York, 1984), Nancy F. Cott, *The Bonds of Womanhood: "Woman's Sphere" in New England, 1780–1835* (New Haven, 1977), and Linda K. Kerber, *Women of the Republic.* For the decades stretching beyond the early national years, Catherine Clinton's, *The Plantation Mistress: Woman's World in the Old South* (New York, 1982), Elizabeth Fox-Genovese's *Within the Plantation Household: Black and White Women of the Old South* (Chapel Hill, 1988); and her "Households and the Political Economy of Southern Women," paper at Society for the History of the Early Republic meeting, Knoxville, Tn., July 1986, Joan M. Jensen's *Loosening the Bonds: Mid-Atlantic Farm Women, 1750–1850* (New Haven, 1986), Suzanne Lebsock's *The Free Women of Petersburg: Status and Culture in a Southern Town, 1784–1860* (New York, 1984), Anne Firor Scott's, *The Southern Lady: From Pedestal to Politics, 1830–1930* (Chicago, 1970), pt. 1, and Carroll Smith-Rosenberg's *Disorderly Conduct: Visions of Gender in Victorian America* (New York, 1985) have influenced my understanding.

6. John Mack Faragher, "History from the Inside-Out: Writing the History of Women in Rural America," *American Quarterly,* 33 (1981): 553–54.

7. John Mack Faragher, *Women and Men on the Overland Trail* (New Haven, 1979), discusses the passage of information among women by word of mouth in ch. 5, "The Separate Worlds of Men and Women," pp. 110–43, esp. pp. 122–27.

8. "The Woman's Bible" (1895), in *Up From the Pedestal: Selected Writings in the History of American Feminism,* ed. with an intro. by Aileen S. Kraditor (Chicago, 1968), p. 114. See also Faragher, "History from the Inside-Out," pp. 537–57.

9. E. Jennifer Monaghan, "Literacy Instruction and Gender in Colonial New England," *American Quarterly,* 40 (1988): 18–41; Gloria L. Main, "Female Literacy in Early New England: Signatures, Books, and Schooling," given at American Antiquarian Society seminar in early American social and political history, May 1988; Cott, *Bonds of Womanhood,* pp. 10, 15, 101–3; Kerber, *Women of the Republic,* pp. 283–87 and passim.

10. Kerber, *Women of the Republic,* pp. 191–93, 199.

11. John Trumbull, "The Progress of Dulness," quoted in Kerber, *Women of the Republic,* p. 185.

12. Kerber, *Women of the Republic,* p. 241; Cathy N. Davidson, *Revolution and the Word: The*

Rise of the Novel in America (New York, 1986), ch. 3, See also illustrations on pages 179 and 195 of this book.

13. See Ruth H. Bloch, "American Feminine Ideals in Transition: The Rise of the Moral Mother, 1785–1815," *Feminist Studies*, 4 (1978): 100–126.

14. Kerber, *Women of the Republic*, pp. 226–27, 235, 239, 241, 257–58; Davidson, *Revolution and the Word*, ch. 4.

15. Mary Beth Norton, *Liberty's Daughters*, pp. 121–22, 188–90.

16. Brooks Palmer, *The Book of American Clocks* (New York, 1956), p. 268. Plate 67 shows a clockface probably decorated by Candace Roberts.

17. Diary of Candace Roberts, typescript transcription (1936) at Bristol, Conn. Public Library. All citations are to dates. January 26, 1802.

18. Diary of Candace Roberts, May 15, 1801; Aug. 6, 1801; Sept. 18, 1801; Nov. 27, 1801.

19. The general social environment in which Roberts dwelled is described in Cott, *The Bonds of Womanhood*.

20. Diary of Candace Roberts, Apr. 16, 1804.

21. For people away from home reading was a ready source of emotional comfort. Pamela Brown, a Vermont school teacher, reported in 1837 that she was "very lonesome" when she was without reading. (Blanche Brown Bryant and Gertrude Baker, eds., *The Diaries of Sally and Pamela Brown, 1832–1838, and the Diary of Hyde Leslie, 1887, Plymouth Notch, Vermont* (Springfield, Vt., 1970), p. 78.) Quoted in Nicholas and Virginia Westbrook, " 'Read Some, and Sewed': Reading in the Daily Round, A Vermont Case Study," Strong Museum Conference, Rochester, N.Y., Nov. 21–22, 1986, p. 24. Candace Roberts used "entertaining" repeatedly. The word evidently implied "interesting" as well as "amusing." Linda K. Kerber notes that "reading fiction could play a very important part in a woman's private life and imagination." (*Women of the Republic*, p. 236.) The studies on novels and women's fiction I have found most informative are: Nina Baym, *Novels, Readers, and Reviewers: Responses to Fiction in Antebellum America, 1820–1870* (Ithaca, 1984) and her *Women's Fiction: A Guide to Novels by and about Women in America, 1820–1870* (Ithaca, 1978); Davidson, *Revolution and the Word;* Mary Kelley, *Private Woman, Public Stage: Literary Domesticity in Nineteenth-Century America* (New York, 1984); Robert B. Winans, "The Growth of a Novel-Reading Public in Late Eighteenth-Century America," *Early American Literature*, 9 (1975): 267–75.

22. Diary of Candace Roberts, Jan. 19, 1804. Mrs. Regina Maria (Dalton) Roche's novel *Children of the Abbey* was first published at London in 1796. Between then and 1912 it went through seventy-two British and American editions, making it one of the great "best-sellers" of the 19th century, especially the first half. Roche (1764–1848) was also the author of *The Vicar of Lansdowne* (1789) and a number of other romantic novels. According to a New York bookseller's advertisement of 1799, the book contained "the most exalted sentiments, favourable to religion, morality, and virtue." (Quoted in Herbert Ross Brown, *The Sentimental Novel in America, 1789–1860* (New York, 1959), p. 26.)

23. Diary of Candace Roberts, Mar. 3, 1804.

24. Ibid., Apr. 1, 1804.

25. Jack Larkin, "The Merriams of Brookfield: Printing in the Economy and Culture of Rural Massachusetts in the Early Nineteenth-Century," *Proceedings of the American Antiquarian Society*, 96, pt. 1 (1986): 39–73.

26. Diary of Candace Roberts, Nov. 16, 1804; June 1806; Mar. 29, 1804.

27. Ibid., Mar. 4, 1804.

28. The use of letters by women is brilliantly explored in Carroll Smith-Rosenberg's "The Female World of Love and Ritual: Relations between Women in Nineteenth-Century, America," *Disorderly Conduct,* pp. 53–76, 305–13 (first published in *Signs,* 1 (1975): 1–29). On the 18th-century British culture of letter-writing, see Ruth Perry, *Women, Letters, and the Novel* (New York, 1980), esp. ch. 3, "The Social Context of Letters."

29. Mary Guion Diary, New-York Historical Society, p. 79, Jan. 1803.

30. Ibid., p. 217, Aug. 1805. Guion's courtship is discussed within a broader context in Ellen K. Rothman's *Hands and Hearts: A History of Courtship in America* (New York, 1981), pp. 26, 34, 39, 49, 77, 79–80.

31. Guion Diary, p. 74, Nov. 3, 1802.

32. Ibid., p. 65. Date unclear; it is before July 30, 1801 or 1802.

33. Ibid., p. 71, Oct. 4, 1802.

34. Ibid., p. 154, 1805. Faragher, *Women and Men on the Overland Trail,* p. 133, briefly discusses different patterns of male and female speech, a subject not yet well understood. One form of conversation often associated with women, gossip, is considered in a literary study by Patricia Meyer Spacks, *Gossip* (New York, 1985).

35. Guion Diary, p. 76, Dec. 8, 1802. Her father butchered a hog that day. Also her younger brother Tommy read Mrs. Roche's *Vicar of Lansdowne* to his sisters as they worked.

36. Guion Diary, p. 66, 1801 or 1802.

37. Ibid., p. 85, 1803.

38. Ibid., p. 76, Dec. 7, 1802; Baym, *Novels, Readers, and Reviewers,* pp. 28–29, 31, 60, and *Woman's Fiction,* pp. 18, 31.

39. Guion Diary, p. 70, 1801[?].

40. Ibid., July 13, 1799, and July 31, 1801.

41. *Lucy Breckinridge of Grove Hill: The Journal of a Virginia Girl, 1862–1864,* ed. by Mary D. Robertson (Kent, Ohio, 1979), pp. 2–4.

42. *Lucy Breckinridge,* p. 17, Aug. 11, 1862. See Perry, *Women, Letters, and the Novel,* chs. 4–6.

43. *Lucy Breckinridge,* p. 37, Sept. 3, 1862, for example of reading aloud.

44. Ibid., p. 22, Aug. 12, 1862. According to Rothman "sex roles became a favorite topic of discussion among middle-class men and women" in the decades after 1830 (*Hands and Hearts,* p. 96).

45. *Lucy Breckinridge,* p. 19, Aug. 11, 1862.

46. Ibid., p. 25, Aug. 13, 1862. The pattern of men speaking and women listening was neither new in the Victorian era, nor was it southern. A century earlier, in October 1754, Esther Edwards Burr imagined a scene at the Reverend Thomas Prince's home where "*Father* has the *talk,* and Mr. Burr has the *laugh,* Mr. Prince gets room to stick in a word once in a while. The rest of you set and see, and hear, and make observations to yourselves, . . . and when you get upstairs you tell you think." (Carol Karlsen and Laurie Crumpacker, eds., *The Journal of Esther Edwards Burr, 1754–1757* (New Haven, 1984), p. 54.)

47. *Lucy Breckinridge,* p. 169, Feb. 11, 1864. Almost a century earlier Sally Wister had commented that "Nothing scarcely lowers a man, in my opinion, more than talking of eating, what they love, and what they hate." ("Journal of Miss Sally Wister, 1777–1778," *Pennsylvania Magazine of History and Biography,* 9 (1885): 332).

48. *Lucy Breckinridge,* p. 155, Nov. 9, 1863, Bassett conversed with a visitor about novels. Faragher, *Women and Men on the Overland Trail,* ch. 5 ("The Separate Worlds of Men and

Women"), argues that an absence of verbal communication between women and men was a fundamental characteristic of 19th-century midwestern experience.

49. *Lucy Breckinridge,* p. 35, Aug. 30, 1862.

50. Ibid., p. 20, Aug. 11, 1862; see Kelley, *Private Woman, Public Stage.*

51. Baym, *Woman's Fiction,* discusses some of these authors, as does Kelley, *Private Woman, Public Stage.*

52. *Lucy Breckinridge,* p. 169, Feb. 3, 1864.

53. Ibid., p. 25, Aug. 15, 1862.

54. Ibid., p. 112, Apr. 4, 1863; p. 37, Sept. 3, 1862; p. 153, Oct. 26, 1863; and passim.

55. Ibid., p. 42, Sept. 10, 1862; p. 122, July 2, 1863; p. 125, July 10, 1863. On these occasions Breckinridge read in *The Southern Illustrated News,* which in each case had been sent to her as a gift.

56. *Lucy Breckinridge,* p. 54, Oct. 1, 1862; p. 57, Oct. 6, 1862; p. 60, Oct. 9, 1862; p. 64, Oct. 13, 1862.

57. Ibid., p. 137, Aug. 29, 1863; p. 154, Nov. 9, 1863.

58. Ibid., p. 30, Aug. 25, 1862.

59. Ibid., p. 27, Aug. 23, 1862.

60. Buel and Buel, *The Way of Duty,* p. 45, gives an example from 1766.

61. *Diary of Anna Green Winslow. A Boston School Girl of 1771,* ed. by Alice Morse Earle (Boston, 1894); *A Gentleman of Much Promise: The Diary of Isaac Mickle, 1837–1845,* ed. with an intro. by Philip English Mackey (Philadelphia, 1977). Lucy Breckinridge speculated that one day a daughter would read her diary. (*Lucy Breckinridge,* p. 85, Dec. 22, 1862.)

62. Mary Guion Diary, July 31, 1801.

63. The fundamental exploration of this phenomenon is Smith-Rosenberg's "The Female World of Love and Ritual: Relations Between Women in Nineteenth Century America," *Disorderly Conduct,* pp. 53–76, 305–13.

64. Breckinridge read the deceased "Fan's" letters, *Lucy Breckinridge,* p. 62, Oct. 12, 1862, and the absent Bassett's, *Lucy Breckinridge,* p. 194, Aug. 2, 1864. The emotional intensity personal correspondence could generate was poignantly expressed by a missionary, Harriet Winslow, in a letter to her parents from Oodooville, Aug. 14, 1820: "To see the handwriting of my dear parents, after this long separation, filled me with too much emotion. I opened one letter after another, but could not read them. If I attempted it, I was obliged to lay them entirely aside, and take one from a more common friend, which would affect me less. I could scarcely believe, what I found to be the fact, that almost every other letter was read before I got through one page from my dear family." (Miron Winslow, *Memoir of Mrs. Harriet L. Winslow* (New York, 1840), p. 210.) Winslow's remarks are reminiscent of William Byrd II's comments about his wife's reaction to family letters a century earlier. (See above, p. 46.)

65. *Lucy Breckinridge,* p. 190, July 20, 1864.

66. Ibid., p. 147, Sept. 29, 1863; Joanna Bowen Gillespie, " 'The Clear Leadings of Providence': Pious Memoirs and the Problems of Self-Realization for Women in the Early Nineteenth Century," *Journal of the Early Republic,* 5 (Summer 1985): 197–221; Irene Quenzler Brown, "Death, Friendship, and Female Identity During New England's Second Great Awakening," *Journal of Family History,* 12 (1987): 367–87.

67. *Lucy Breckinridge,* p. 99, Jan. 19, 1863.

68. Ibid., p. 43, Sept. 11, 1862.

69. In 1775 several of John Adams' letters criticizing his colleague in the Continental Congress, John Dickinson, were captured and published—to the embarassment of both Adams and the Congress. (John Adams to James Warren, Phila., July 24, 1775, *Papers of John Adams,* ed. by Robert J. Taylor et al. (Cambridge, Mass., 1979), 3:89 and note 89–93; also John Adams to Abigail Adams, Phila., July 24, 1775, *Adams Family Correspondence,* ed. by Lyman Butterfield and Wendell D. Garrett (Cambridge, Mass., 1963), 1:255–56.) Adams' report of Samuel Adams' destruction of papers is in his letter to William Tudor, Quincy, June 5, 1817, in *The Works of John Adams,* ed by Charles Francis Adams (Boston, 1856), 10:264.

70. *Lucy Breckinridge,* p. 209, Dec. 3, 1864.

71. Ibid., p. 211, Dec. 16, 1864.

72. Despite its novelistic form, *Uncle Tom's Cabin* was unquestionably a political statement of great scope and with radical implications. For recent discussion of both the popularity and the social and political significance of Harriet Beecher Stowe's novel see Thomas F. Gossett, *Uncle Tom's Cabin and American Culture* (Dallas, 1985), esp. ch. 10, "The Reception of Uncle Tom's Cabin in the North" and ch. 11, "The Reaction to Uncle Tom's Cabin in the South"; Eric J. Sundquist, ed., *New Essays on Uncle Tom's Cabin* (Cambridge, 1986).

73. *Lucy Breckinridge,* p. 166, Jan. 9, 1864, reading *Les Misérables.*

74. Guion Diary, p. 76, Dec. 7, 1802.

75. Ulrich, *Good Wives,* carefully explains the role of "deputy husband," and Lebsock, *Free Women of Petersburg,* treats property rights.

76. Nancy Shippen Livingston's experience is sketched in *Nancy Shippen Her Journal Book,* comp. and ed. by Ethel Armes (Philadelphia, 1935). Fanny Kemble's quasi-bondage to her husband is discussed in John Anthony Scott in "Politics Outside the Party System: The Journal of Frances Anne Kemble's Residence on a Georgia Plantation," paper delivered at New England Historical Assn. meeting Apr. 26, 1986, Worcester, Mass. See also Scott's biographical introduction to his edition of Kemble's *Journal of a Residence on Georgia Plantation* (New York, 1961).

77. *Lucy Breckinridge,* p. 22, Aug. 12, 1862. For these same views expressed in novels see Kelley, *Private Woman, Public Stage,* p. 279. The common view that married women were not happy was also expressed by Angelina Grimké. (Rothman, *Hands and Hearts,* p. 61.)

78. Laurel Thatcher Ulrich, "Martha Ballard and Her Girls: Women's Work in Eighteenth-Century Maine," in *Work and Labor in Early America,* ed. by Stephen Innes (Chapel Hill, 1988), pp. 70–105.

79. Information on Ballard and her family is drawn from Charles Elventon Nash, *The History of Augusta, First Settlements and Early Days as a Town. Including the Diary of Mrs. Martha Moore Ballard (1785 to 1812)* (Augusta, 1904; reprinted 1961). Cited hereafter as Nash, *Diary of Martha Moore Ballard.* The Nash abridgement includes about one-third of the original diary and is biased toward genealogy; however Ulrich reports that it represents the range of material found in the complete document (Ulrich, "Martha Ballard and Her Girls," 70, n. 1).

80. Ballard noted with surprise a trip made from Boston to Hallowell in two days on November 12, 1786, Nash, *Diary of Martha Moore Ballard,* p. 254.

81. Nash, *Diary of Martha Moore Ballard,* p. 293, July 4, 1790.

82. Ibid, p. 246, Feb. 27 and Mar. 1, 1786.

83. Ibid., p. 246, Mar. 5, 1786.

84. Ibid., p. 431, July 9, 1806. I have inverted Ballard's phrase for the sake of clear prose. The meaning is unchanged.

85. Ibid., p. 431, July 10, 1806.

86. The story was printed in the Boston *Columbian Centinel* on July 16, 1806, page 2, from a letter received from Hallowell dated July 11, 1806.

87. Nash, *Diary of Martha Moore Ballard,* p. 379, Jan. 26, 1799.

88. Ibid., p. 256, Jan. 25, 1787.

89. Ibid., p. 274, Oct. 30, 1788.

90. Ibid., p. 275, Nov. 21, 1788.

91. Ibid., p. 276, Dec. 18, 1788.

92. Ibid., p. 314, May 19, 1792; p. 299, Feb. 13, 1791.

93. Ibid., p. 377, Dec. 5, 1798.

94. Ibid., p. 362, Mar. 29, 1797.

95. Ibid., p. 398, Feb. 4, 1801.

96. Ibid., p. 349, sums for the years 1794 through 1797 are entered here.

97. Ibid., p. 306, Sept. 14, 1791.

98. Ibid., p. 299, Feb. 28, 1791.

99. For example, Nash, *Diary of Martha Moore Ballard,* p. 392, July 4, 1800; p. 408, July 5, 1802; p. 420, July 4, 1804; p. 424, July 4, 1805; p. 430, July 4, 1806.

100. Ibid., p. 444, July 20, 1808; p. 459, Feb. 4, 1811.

101. Ibid., p. 457, Aug. 5, 1810; p. 463, Feb. 26, 1812.

102. Ibid., p. 439, Aug. 3, 1807.

103. Ibid., p. 462, Jan. 17, 1812; p. 441, Nov. 7, 1807; p. 454, Jan. 6, 1810 and Feb. 13, 1810.

104. Ibid., p. 455, Mar. 20, 1810.

105. Ibid., p. 424, Apr. 14, 1805.

106. Ibid., p. 459, Dec. 19, 1810; p. 385, Sept. 11, 1799.

107. Ibid., p. 457, Aug. 20 and Sept. 30, 1810.

108. *The Holyoke Diaries, 1709–1856,* with an introduction and annotations by George Francis Dow (Salem, Ma. 1911), p. xvi. The diaries of Mary (Vial) Holyoke, Salem, 1760–1800, and two of her daughters, Margaret Holyoke, Salem, 1801–1823, and Mrs. Susanna (Holyoke) Ward, Salem, 1793–1856, are included, together with diaries of three Holyoke men. Hereafter this will be cited as *Holyoke Diaries* for entries on Mary (Vial) Holyoke.

109. As of 1760, Salem (4469) was behind Newport (6500) and Marblehead (4954) as well as Boston. By 1790 its population had grown to 7917 and Newport's had fallen to 6744 from a prewar high of 9209, so that Salem became New England's second largest port. (Lester B. Cappon et al., eds., *Atlas of Early American History: The Revolutionary Years, 1760–1790* (Princeton, 1976), p. 97.)

110. *Holyoke Diaries,* p. 50, May 22, 1761; p. 54, Dec. 10, 1761.

111. Ibid., p. 137, Oct. 19, 1798.

112. Ibid., p. 71, Aug. 11 and Oct. 10, 1769; p. 72, Mar. 8, 1770; p. 75, Jan. 2, 1771.

113. Ibid., p. 56, Sept. 15, 1762; p. 65, May 21, 1766; p. 118, June 23, 1787.

114. Ibid., pp. 93–94, July and August 1776, includes many social notes.

115. Samuel Adams to Elizabeth Adams, Feb. 1, 1781, *Writing of Samuel Adams,* ed. by Harry

Alonzo Cushing (New York, 1908, reprinted 1968), 4:248, quoted in Norton, *Liberty's Daughters,* p. 171.

116. *Holyoke Diaries,* pp. 48–49, Jan.–Feb. 1761; p. 60, Jan. 1764; p. 61, Mar. 9, 1764; p. 96, June 18, 1777.

117. For example, *Holyoke Diaries,* p. 134, Jan. 14, 1796; p. 135, Mar. 5, 1797.

118. Ibid., p. 80, June 17, 1773; p. 84, Oct. 6, 1774.

119. Nathaniel Southgate Shaler, *Kentucky, a pioneer commonwealth* (Boston, 1885; reprinted New York, 1973), p. 108.

120. Information on Sarah Hill Fletcher and her husband is found in *The Diary of Calvin Fletcher,* ed. by Gayle Thornbrough et al., 9 vols. (Indianapolis, 1972–1983). The Sarah Hill Fletcher diary (1821–1824) and letters (1821–1829) are in vol. 1, hereafter cited as *Fletcher Diary.*

121. *Fletcher Diary,* 1:86, Dec. 31, 1821.

122. Ibid., 1:87, letter to brother Michael Fletcher, Indianapolis, Feb. 23, 1823.

123. *Fletcher Diary,* 1:50, Jan. 13, 1822; 1:62, May 17, 1822. Already in 1780 Abigail Adams and Mercy Otis Warren were criticizing Chesterfield's disparaging estimate of female vanity, and Warren's comments were printed in 1781 and reprinted in 1784 and 1790 (Norton, *Liberty's Daughters,* pp. 115–16). Nonetheless Chesterfield remained the most common guide to gentility and conversation in the early republic and went through dozens of British and American editions.

124. *Fletcher Diary,* 1:43, Nov. 14, 1821; 1:70, Nov. 23 and 24, 1822; 1:82, Nov. 9, 1821. He was reading Jane Austen's *Emma.*

125. Jesse H. Shera, *Foundations of The Public Library: The Origins of the Public Library Movement in New England, 1629–1855* (Chicago, 1949), chs. 3 and 4 treat social libraries. See also Joseph F. Kett and Patricia A. McClung, "Book Culture in Post-Revolutionary Virginia," *Proceedings of the American Antiquarian Society,* 94, pt. 1 (1984): 97–147.

126. *Fletcher Diary,* 1:74, Jan. 25, 1824, and n. 78. On magazines see Bertha M. Stearns, "Early Western Magazines for Ladies," *Mississippi Valley Historical Review,* 18 (1931): 319–30.

127. *Fletcher Diary,* 1:69, Nov. 2, 1822.

128. Ibid., 1:69, Nov. 5, 1822.

129. Ibid., 1:66, July 4, 1822.

130. Ibid., 1:50, Jan. 8, 1822.

131. Ibid., 1:51, Jan. 29, 1822. The role of visiting among women is beginning to be studied. See Nancy Tomes, "The Quaker Connection: Visiting Patterns among Women in an Eighteenth-Century Pennsylvania Town, 1750–1800," in *Friends and Neighbors: Group Life in America's First Plural Society,* ed. by Michael Zuckerman (Philadelphia, 1982), pp. 174–95.

132. *Fletcher Diary,* 1:50, Jan. 16, 1822.

133. Ibid., 1:73, Dec. 12, 1823.

134. Ibid., 1:51, Jan. 26, 1822. This was a debating club, *Fletcher Diary,* 1:100, Dec. 13, 1823.

135. Ibid., 1:73, Dec. 12, 1823.

136. Ibid., 1:86, Dec. 31, 1821; 1:98, Nov. 30, 1823.

137. Throughout the Calvin Fletcher diary, vols. 1 through 5, there are sporadic references to Sarah Hill Fletcher's activities.

138. *Fletcher Diary,* 1:74, Jan. 1, 1824; 1:102, Jan. 1, 1824.

139. "The Minister's Wooing," *Atlantic Monthly,* 2 (Dec. 1858): 885.

140. *Diary of Joshua Hempstead of New London, Connecticut,* Collections of the New London County Historical Society, 1 (New London, 1904): 496, Feb. 21, 1748.

141. Linda K. Kerber, "Daughters of Columbia: Educating Women for the Republic 1787–1805," in Stanley Elkins and Eric McKitrick, eds., *The Hofstadter Aegis* (New York, 1974), pp. 36–59, and her *Women of the Republic,* esp. chs. 7–9; also Janet Wilson James, *Changing Ideas About Women in the United States, 1776–1825* (New York, 1981).

142. *Farmers Almanack for the year 1838,* no. 46 (Boston, 1837), May 1838.

143. Print by Tompkins H. Matteson in N. Parker Willis, ed., *The Winter Wreath* (New York, 1853), follows p. 49. Parker includes an exegesis of the image. See page 195 in this book for image and explanation.

144. Guion, Diary, p. 76, Dec. 7, 1802.

145. *Philadelphia Album and Ladies Literary Portfolio,* Aug 22, 1827. (Quoted in Stearns, "Early Western Magazines for Ladies," *Mississippi Valley Historical Review,* 18 (1931): 321.) Cott, *The Bonds of Womanhood,* Alan Dawley, *Class and Community: The Industrial Revolution in Lynn* (Cambridge, Mass., 1976), Thomas Dublin, *Women at Work: The Transformation of Work and Community in Lowell, Massachusetts, 1826–1860* (New York, 1979); Anne Firor Scott, "On Seeing and Not Seeing: A Case of Historical Invisibility," *Journal of American History,* 71 (June 1984): 8–12. In Mrs. Caroline Gilman's first novel, *Reflections of a Housekeeper* (1834), an attorney's wife expresses jealousy toward her husband's books. (Kelley, *Private Woman, Public Stage,* pp. 70–71.)

CHAPTER 8. WILLIAM BENTLEY AND THE IDEAL OF UNIVERSAL INFORMATION IN THE ENLIGHTENED REPUBLIC

1. Quoted in Joseph G. Waters, "A Biographical Sketch of Rev. William Bentley," in William Bentley, *The Diary of William Bentley, D.D.* (Salem, Mass., 1905–1914), 1:xviii.

2. On Sept. 2, 1803, Bentley brought his student Benjamin Crowninshield to Harvard for an entrance examination and the tutors, "before unknown to me," rejected Crowninshield. Bentley was upset, the moreso because he believed Crowninshield was more capable than the tutors who judged him. None of his students had previously been rejected. Bentley concluded, "My connections with Cambridge cease." (Bentley, *Diary,* 3:40.)

3. William A. Robinson, "William Bentley," *Dictionary of American Biography* (New York: 1928–1937), 2:207–08.

4. Benjamin F. Browne, quoted in Bentley, *Diary,* 4:638.

5. Bentley's journalistic prowess was emphasized in Joseph T. Buckingham, *Specimens of Newspaper Literature* (Boston, 1850), 2:120–26, 341–50, and recognized in Frank Luther Mott's classic textbook *American Journalism: A History: 1690–1960,* 3d ed. (New York, 1960), pp. 153–54. The key article on the subject is Louise Chipley's "William Bentley, Journalist of the Early Republic," *Essex Institute Historical Collections,* 123 (1987):331–47.

6. See Anne Farnam, "A Society of Societies: Associations and Voluntarism in Early Nineteenth-Century Salem," *Essex Institute Historical Collections,* 113 (1977): 181–90, and entire number of *Collections* devoted to Bentley's Salem, pp. 145–232.

7. William T. Whitney, Jr., "The Crowninshields of Salem, 1800–1808: A Study in the Politics of Commercial Growth," *Essex Institute Historical Collections,* 94 (1958): 1–36, 79–118.

8. In this he was similar to another "forgotten" notable clergyman, Ezra Stiles. See Edmund S. Morgan, *The Gentle Puritan: A Life of Ezra Stiles, 1727–1795* (New Haven, 1962).

9. In addition to the 1868 sketch of Bentley by Joseph G. Waters in the published *Diary,* there is also an 1897 account by Marguerite Dalrymple filled with anecdotes and Bentley lore from her childhood. Bentley, *Diary,* 1:xxiii–xxxvi.

10. Waters, "Sketch of William Bentley," Bentley, *Diary,* 1:xviii.

11. Quoted in obituary in *Essex Register,* Jan. 5, 1820, p. 2.

12. Richard John "Managing the Mails: The United States Postal System and the Communications Revolution," Ph.D. diss., Harvard Univ., 1989; Richard Burket Kielbowicz, "News in the Mails, 1690–1863: The Technology, Policy, and Politics of a Communication Channel," Ph.D. diss., Univ. of Minnesota, 1984.

13. Bentley, *Diary,* 3:54–55, Oct. 19, 1803; 4:370, Jan. 15, 1816.

14. Bentley learned about the terror in Revolutionary France from Salem mariners, (Bentley, *Diary,* 2:108, Oct. 2, 1794), about Salem archaeology from a mason and a laborer (Bentley, *Diary,* 3:110, Sept. 13, 1804), and ship construction from a shipwright (Bentley, *Diary,* 4:202, Sept. 28, 1813). He was the friend of the mulatto Benjamin Chase of Beverly and Danvers (Bentley, *Diary,* 4:227–28, Jan. 13, 1814), a guest by invitation at the wedding of a black servant (Bentley, *Diary,* 1:186, July 15, 1790), and he conversed with a black New Light when he went fishing on September 3, 1791 (Bentley, *Diary,* 1:294–95). The only hesitancy he ever displayed in conversing, and it was warranted, was with young women in situations where his own and their reputations might be subject to gossip.

15. Bentley, *Diary,* 1:51, Feb. 5, 1787.

16. For example, on May 30, 1789 Bentley translated French funeral papers for Captain J. Chever (Bentley, *Diary,* 1:124).

17. Bentley supplied a traveling library for Captain Benjamin Hodges that included Joseph Priestley's short tracts on "the simple doctrines of Christianity," Busching's geography of Europe, Bolingbroke on history, politics, study, and exile, in addition to essays by Hume and Dr. Richard Price, Alexander Pope's poetry, and Campbell's account of contemporary Europe. (Bentley, *Diary,* 1:111, Dec. 11, 1788).

18. Bentley's relations with nearby clergy were correct, but distant. When he proposed a town-wide fast on account of the Yellow Fever epidemic in Philadelphia, the suggestion was first rebuffed, only to be adopted subsequently without consulting Bentley (Bentley, *Diary,* 2:63–64, Sept. 26, 1793 and Oct. 4, 1793). Bentley did not make an issue of it, but inwardly he was resentful. Similar episodes regarding church ceremonies, ministerial councils, and pulpit exchanges occurred with sufficient frequency to inhibit much intimacy between Bentley and his Essex peers. Bentley's disdain for the printed attacks that the aging New Light minister John Cleaveland of Chebacco (Ipswich) made on the Universalists led him, writing as "Civis," to give Cleaveland a lashing in the *Salem Gazette.* A few days later Bentley noted that his criticisms were generally regarded as "too severe," a judgment rendered by his fellow clergy. (Bentley, *Diary,* 1:231, Jan. 19 and 22, 1791). He refers to the absence of "literary men" in the East Parish in Bentley, *Diary,* 1:37, May 9, 1786.

19. Bentley, *Diary,* 2:27–28, May 30, 1793.

20. Same, 1:278–79, July 23, 1791.

21. Same, 1:100, May 28, 1788. The embarrassed clergyman was evidently Oliver Everett (Harvard, 1779) who served the New South Church in Boston and who was later the father of Edward Everett, the Harvard Professor of Greek who delivered the sermon at Bentley's funeral and, many years and careers later, gave the principal address at Gettysburg in 1863.

22. Gibaut, Bentley, *Diary,* 2:88, May 2, 1794; Crowninshield, 1:231, Jan. 20, 1791.

23. Bentley, *Diary,* 1:72, Aug. 11, 1787; 1, 274–75, July 12, 1791; 2:74, Nov. 18, 1793.

24. William Bentley, *A Sermon Preached at the Stone Chapel in Boston, September 12, 1790* (Boston, 1790), p. 21.

25. Bentley, *Diary,* 1:165–66, May 5–7, 1790; see "John Thayer" in *Dictionary of American Biography* (New York, 1928–1937), 18:406–7.

26. Bentley, *Diary,* 3:23, May 14, 1803.

27. Ibid., 3:55, Oct. 22, 1803.

28. Massachusetts Historical Society, *Collections,* 6 (1799): 212–88; reprinted by Little and Brown, Boston, 1846.

29. Buckingham, *Specimens of Newspaper Literature,* 2:346.

30. Bentley, *Diary,* 4:257, May 27, 1814.

31. Massachusetts Historical Society, *Proceedings,* 1 (1798): 116; 1 (1801): 138.

32. Louise Chipley, "The Enlightened Library of William Bentley," *Essex Institute Historical Collections,* 122 (1986): 2–29, provides a thoughtful analysis of Bentley's reading choices, a part of which is derived from the distribution analysis of Bentley's library that forms the basis of the next five paragraphs.

33. Bentley, *Diary,* 1:59, Apr. 11, 1787, he counted 605 bound and 62 sewed books. The discussion of the library which follows is based primarily on a quantitative analysis of the manuscript inventory of the library in William Bentley Papers, Octavo vol. 12, at the American Antiquarian Society. According to Buckingham, *Specimens of Newspaper Literature,* 2:344, it was "the largest and best *private* library in the nation, except that of Mr. Jefferson," however Chipley notes that John Adams' library had 4800 volumes at his death in 1826 ("Enlightened Library of William Bentley," unpublished seminar paper, University of Connecticut, June 1984, p. 25, n. 4.), so Bentley's library may actually have ranked third. As of 1790 the largest American college library, Harvard's, had 9296 titles. In 1791 Yale had 1582 titles and in 1793 Rhode Island College (Brown) had 1214 titles. (Joe W. Kraus, "The Book Collections of Early American College Libraries," *The Library Quarterly,* 43 (Apr. 1973): 152, 155, 156.)

34. Bentley's correspondence with Ebeling lasted from 1795 until Ebeling's death in 1817: "Letters of Christoph Daniel Ebeling to Rev. William Bentley of Salem, Mass., and to Other American Correspondents," William Coolidge Lane, ed., *Proceedings of the American Antiquarian Society,* new ser., 35 (1925): 272–451. Most of the correspondence deals with exchanges of books, though there was some commentary on their substance and on liberal religious and political affairs. Bentley conveyed his view of Jedidiah Morse as a narrow, bigoted opportunist, and charged him with plagiarizing from Thomas Jefferson's *Notes on the State of Virginia.*

35. Bentley reported a scandal from an incident where a copy of Allen's work was rumored to belong to him. (Bentley, *Diary,* 1:82, Nov. 24?, 1787.) Bentley referred to Paine's *Age of Reason* as a "scandalous insult . . . upon all the institutions of religion" (Bentley, *Diary,* 2:107, Sept. 19, 1794), yet he remarked that "he is thought a dunce in politics who has not read Paine." (Bentley, *Diary,* 3:42, Sept. 10, 1803.)

36. See Bentley papers at American Antiquarian Society.

37. Bentley, *Diary,* 2:59–60, Aug. 19, 1793. He described Isaiah Thomas' bookstore as stocked with common books.

38. Bentley, *Diary,* 3:87, May 23, 1804.

39. Ibid., 4:168, 170–71, May 9 and 21, 1813.

40. Ibid., 4:151, Feb. 14, 1813.

41. Ibid., 1:415, Dec. 7, 1792.

42. Ibid. On the Salem book trade after Bentley's death see C. Deidre Phelps, "Printing, Publish-

ing, and Bookselling in Salem, Massachusetts, 1825–1900," *Essex Institute Historical Collections,* 124 (1988):227–64. A directory of the Salem book trade is included at pages 265–98.

43. For example, *Bentley, Diary,* 1:62–63, May 20, 1787; 1:78, Oct. 23, 1787; 1:88, Mar. 7, 1788; 1:103, Aug. 15, 1788. Examples like these could be multiplied many times over.

44. In the chief collection of his letters at the American Antiquarian Society there are items received from 392 correspondents. Bentley letters to several other persons have been published, but no record has been compiled of all Bentley's outgoing mail. I believe the numbers given here, while conservative estimates only, represent the right order of magnitude.

45. Ashley Bowen to Rev. William Bentley, Marblehead, May 14, 1807, in William Bentley Corres., box 2, folder 8, at American Antiquarian Society (AAS), and Bentley, *Diary,* 3:368–70, July 1, 1808.

46. Thomas Jefferson to Rev. William Bentley, Monticello, July 9, 1819, and John Adams to Rev. William Bentley, Quincy, July 15, 1819, in William Bentley Corres., box 3, folder 6, at AAS.

47. William Mason, a Salem agent who settled for a time in Charleston, South Carolina, sent Bentley a series of lengthy descriptions, and scattered among his letters, and in his diary, are many such items.

48. For example, William Bentley to Benjamin Hodges, Salem, Feb. 19, 1789, Bentley, *Diary,* 1:115.

49. Buckingham, *Specimens of Newspaper Literature,* 2:343.

50. For example, Bentley, *Diary,* 1:40–41, Aug. 27, 1786; 1:113, Jan. 16, 1789; 1:39, July 1, 1786; 1:48, Dec. 18, 1786; 1:150, Mar. 1, 1790.

51. For example, Bentley, *Diary,* 1:113, Jan. 1, 1789; 1:115, Feb. 11, 1789; 1:123, May 25, 1789; 1:124, May 30, 1789; 1:165, May 4, 1790; 1:184, July 12, 1790. In 1797 Thomas C. Cushing asked Bentley to make an English summary of a treaty between France and the Holy Roman Emperor to publish in his newspaper, Bentley Corres., box 1, folder 6, at AAS.

52. Buckingham, *Specimens of Newspaper Literature,* 2:344. When Albert Gallatin came to the United States as a nineteen-year old Genevan immigrant, Bentley befriended him and successfully recommended him for a post at Harvard as a French instructor. (Bentley, *Diary,* 2:12, Mar. 23, 1793.)

53. Buckingham, *Specimens of Newspaper Literature,* 2:342.

54. *Impartial Register,* May 26, 1800.

55. *Salem Gazette,* June 3 and 10, 1796.

56. Mott, *American Journalism,* p. 153.

57. *Salem Gazette,* June 3, 1796, page 3.

58. Ibid.

59. Ibid.

60. Bentley, *Diary,* 3:54–55, Oct. 19, 1803.

61. Ibid., 4:370, Jan. 15, 1816.

62. Henry F. May, *The Enlightenment in America* (New York, 1976).

63. Joseph Story, Bentley's republican associate, and a whole generation of Harvard graduates in the early years of the republic shared high ambitions for public service and fame. (R. Kent Newmyer, *Supreme Court Justice Joseph Story: Statesman of the Old Republic* (Chapel Hill, 1985), pp. 23, 30–36.)

64. *Salem Gazette,* June 3, 1796, page 3.

CHAPTER 9. CHOOSING ONE'S FARE

1. Numbers of newspapers for 1760 and 1820 were compiled by the author from Edward Connery Lathem, comp., *Chronological Tables of American Newspapers. 1690–1820* (Barre, Mass., 1972). Because copies of all 518 listed newspaper titles for 1820 are not extant, there is reason to doubt the accuracy of this figure. It is presented here to provide a general index of the incidence of newspapers. As of 1840 there were 1403 newspapers, and by 1860 there were 4051, according to S.N.D. North, *History and Present Conditions of the Newspaper and Periodical Press of the United States* (Tenth U.S. Census Report (1880), 8:47, 187. Numbers of post offices are found in United States, Bureau of the Census, *Historical Statistics of the United States: Colonial Times to 1970* (Washington, D.C., 1975), pt. 2, p. 805. See also Richard B. Kielbowicz, "News in the Mails, 1690–1863: The Technology, Policy, and Politics of a Communication Channel," Ph.D. diss., Univ. of Minnesota, 1984; Richard R. John, Jr., "Managing the Mails: The U.S. Postal System in National Politics, 1823–1836," Ph.D. diss., Harvard Univ., 1989. Data on the spatial diffusion of information is presented in Allan R. Pred, *Urban Growth and the Circulation of Information: The United States System of Cities, 1790–1840* (Cambridge, Mass., 1973); see esp. maps 2.12, 2.14, and 2.18, pp. 64, 69, 74.

2. While no systematic, national study of voluntary associations exists, the phenomenon is well-known and has been treated in a variety of contexts. See Ann Firor Scott, "On Seeing and Not Seeing: A Case of Historical Invisibility," *Journal of American History,* 71 (June 1984): 8–12; Don H. Doyle, *The Social Order of a Frontier Community: Jacksonville, Illinois, 1825–70* (Urbana, Ill., 1978); Anne Farnam, "A Society of Societies: Associations and Voluntarism in Early Nineteenth-Century Salem," *Essex Institute Historical Collections,* 113 (July 1977): 181–90; Richard D. Brown, "The Emergence of Voluntary Associations in Massachusetts, 1760–1830," *Journal of Voluntary Action Research,* 2 (1973): 64–73, and "The Emergence of Urban Society in Rural Massachusetts, 1760–1820," *Journal of American History,* 61 (June 1974): 29–51.

3. During the last two generations hundreds of articles and books have appeared which treat these subjects. A handful of those which have most directly and immediately influenced and informed this chapter are Richard D. Altick, *The English Common Reader: A Social History of the Mass Reading Public, 1800–1900* (Chicago, 1957); Nina Baym, *Novels, Readers, and Reviewers: Responses to Fiction in Antebellum America* (Ithaca, 1984) and *Women's Fiction: A Guide to Novels by and about Women in America, 1820–1870* (Ithaca, 1978); Paul Boyer, *Urban Masses and the Moral Order in America; 1820–1920* (Cambridge, Mass., 1978); Burton J. Bledstein, *The Culture of Professionalism: The Middle Class and the Development of Higher Education in America* (New York, 1976); James W. Carey, "Technology and Ideology: The Case of the Telegraph," *Prospects,* 8 (1983): 303–25; John G. Cawelti, *Apostles of the Self-Made Man* (Chicago, 1965); Mary Kupiec Cayton, "The Making of an American Prophet: Emerson, His Audiences, and the Rise of the Culture Industry in Nineteenth-Century America," *American Historical Review,* 92 (June 1987): 597–620; James Curran, "The Press as an Agency of Social Control: an Historical Perspective," *Newspaper History from the Seventeenth Century to the Present Day* (London, 1978), pp. 51–75; Lennard J. Davis, *Factual Fictions: The Origins of the English Novel* (New York, 1983); William J. Gilmore, "Elementary Literacy on the Eve of the Industrial Revolution: Trends in Rural New England, 1760–1830," *Proceedings of the American Antiquarian Society,* 92 (1982): 87–178; James Gilreath, "American Book Distribution," *Proceedings of the American Antiquarian Society,* 95 (1985): 501–83; David Grimsted, "Books and Culture: Canned, Canonized, and Neglected," and "A Comment on Mr. Grimsted's Paper" by Robert Chartier, *Proceedings of the American Antiquarian Society,* 94 (1984): 197–343; David D. Hall, "On Native Ground: From the History of Printing to the History of the Book," *Proceedings of the American Antiquarian Society,* 93 (1983): 313–36; Neil Harris, *Humbug: The Art of P. T. Barnum* (Boston, 1973); Oliver W. Holmes and Peter T. Rohrbach, *Stagecoach Days in the East from the Colonial Period to the Civil War* (Washington,

D.C., 1983); Joseph F. Kett, *Rites of Passage: Adolescence in America, 1790 to the Present* (New York, 1977); Joseph F. Kett and Patricia A. McClung, "Book Culture in Post-Revolutionary Virginia." *Proceedings of the American Antiquarian Society,* 94 (1984): 97–147; Richard B. Kielbowicz, "News in the Mails, 1690–1863," cited above; Jack Larkin, "The Merriams of Brookfield: Printing in the Economy and Culture of Rural Massachusetts in the Early Nineteenth Century," *Proceedings of the American Antiquarian Society,* 96 (1986): 39–73; Leonard L. Richards, *"Gentlemen of Property and Standing:" Anti-Abolition Mobs in Jacksonian America* (New York, 1970); Donald M. Scott, "The Popular Lecture and the Creation of a Public in Mid-Nineteenth Century America," *Journal of American History,* 66 (Mar. 1980): 791–809, and "Print and the Public Lecture System, 1840–1860," in William L. Joyce, David D. Hall, Richard D. Brown, and John B. Hench, eds., *Printing and Society in Early America* (Worcester, Mass., 1983), 278–99; J. A. Sutherland, *Victorian Novelists and Publishers* (Chicago, 1976); Alan Trachtenberg, *The Incorporation of America: Culture and Society in the Gilded Age* (New York, 1982); Anthony F. C. Wallace, *Rockdale: The growth of an American Village in the Early Industrial Revolution* (New York, 1978); Irwin G. Wyllie, *The Self-Made Man in America: The Myth of Rags to Riches* (New Brunswick, N.J., 1954); Ronald J. Zboray, "Antebellum Reading and the Ironies of Technological Innovation," *American Quarterly,* 40 (1988): 65–82.

4. The chief source for Mickle is *A Gentleman of Much Promise: The Diary of Isaac Mickle, 1837–1845,* ed. with an intro. by Philip English Mackey, 2 vols. (Philadelphia, 1977). Additional material comes from the Isaac Mickle Journals, the Isaac Mickle Letter-Books, and miscellaneous Mickle papers and memorabilia at the Camden (N.J.) Historical Society. Background information on Camden is drawn from Jeffery M. Dorwart and Philip English Mackey, *Camden County, New Jersey 1616–1976: A Narrative History* (Camden, N.J., 1976).

5. Isaac Mickle to J. W. Mickle, Burlington (N.J.), May 30, 1839. Isaac Mickle Papers, Camden Historical Society.

6. Isaac Mickle, Journal, 1:67 (ca. Nov. 1840). Ms. 235–6. At this time Mickle prepared an address to the young men of Camden in which he advocated learning and public speaking.

7. *The National Union Catalog of Pre-1956 Imprints* lists scores of editions of the 4th Earl of Chesterfield's advice letters. The greatest concentration lies in the period 1770–1900, when well over 100 editions appeared under titles such as *The Accomplished gentleman; The Beauties of Chesterfield; Elements of a Polite Education: Letters written by Lord Chesterfield to his son; Practical morality; or A guide to men and manners, Lord Chesterfield's Maxims; Principles of Politeness, And of Knowing the World.* John E. Mason, *Gentlefolk in the Making: Studies in the History of English Courtesy Literature and Related Topics from 1531 to 1774* (Philadelphia, 1935), pp. 105–12 on Chesterfield. Advice books for gentlemen had been influential for generations. William Byrd II modeled himself on such works according to Kenneth Lockridge, *The Diary and Life of William Byrd* (Chapel Hill, 1987), pp. 20–25.

8. Steven Greenblatt, *Renaissance Self-Fashioning: From More to Shakespeare* (Chicago, 1980); John Trusler, *Principles of Politeness, and of Knowing the World; by the Late Lord Chesterfield. Methodified and digested under distinct Heads, With Additions, by the Reverend Dr. John Trusler: Containing Every Instruction necessary to complete the Gentleman and Man of Fashion, to teach him a Knowledge of Life, and make him well received in all Companies* (Phila., 1778).

9. *Diary of Isaac Mickle,* 1:30, Feb. 17, 1838; 1:151, Apr. 17, 1841.

10. William Ellery Channing, *Self-Culture. An Address Introductory to the Franklin Lectures, Delivered at Boston, September, 1838* (Boston, 1838), p. 11.

11. Ibid., pp. 40, 50.

12. Ibid., p. 27.

13. Ibid., p. 28. Bledstein, *The Culture of Professionalism,* develops the same themes, esp. ch. 2, pp. 70, 73, 75.

14. *Isaac Mickle Diary,* 2:508, Mar. 23, 1845.

15. Ibid., 1:64, July 31, 1840.

16. Mickle to Sarah M. Haines (n.d. (1845)), Mickle Papers, Letter-Book, Ms. 235–14.

17. *Isaac Mickle Diary,* 1:50, Jan. 29, 1839.

18. Isaac Mickle Journal, Jan. 1841, Ms. 235–6, page 91. Mickle listed the 32 members and their occupations: 18 artisans, 7 merchants and/or storekeepers, 3 students, and in addition a laborer, an apprentice, a gentleman, and a "loafer."

19. *Isaac Mickle Diary,* 1:114–15, Jan. 18, 1841.

20. Ibid., 1:155, Apr. 26, 1841.

21. Ibid., 1:127, Mar. 5, 1841; 1:129, Mar. 8, 1841.

22. Ibid., 1:111, Jan. 1, 1841.

23. Ibid., 1:116, Jan. 21, 1841.

24. Ibid., 1:123, Feb. 25, 1841.

25. Ibid., 1:116, Jan. 21, 1841. In urban areas members of some humble occupations were expected to be so fully informed as to serve as talking directories and guide books. One recalled that "the New York cartman should be an encyclopedia and an intelligence office combined." (Isaac S. Lyon, *Recollections of an Old Cartman,* intro. by Graham Hodges (New York, 1984), p. 5. First published in 1872.)

26. *Isaac Mickle Diary* 1:218, Aug. 20, 1841.

27. Ibid., 1:220–21, Aug. 27, 1841; 2:323, Aug. 31, 1842; 2:345–46, Dec. 30, 1842.

28. Trusler, (Chesterfield's) *Principles of Politeness,* p. 39.

29. *The Laws of Etiquette; or Short Rules and Reflections for Conduct in Society. By a Gentleman* (Philadelphia, 1836), p. 172; *The Canons of Good Breeding; or the Handbook of the Man of Fashion. By the author of "The Laws of Etiquette."* (Philadelphia, 1839), p. 119.

30. *Canons of Good Breeding,* p. 154.

31. Donald M. Scott, "The Popular Lecture," and "Print and the Public Lecture;" Thomas Wentworth Higginson, "The American Lecture-System," *Every Saturday,* 5 (Apr. 18, 1868): 489–94.

32. *Isaac Mickle Diary,* 2:252, Jan. 1, 1842.

33. Ibid., 1:239, Nov. 12, 1841; 2:266, Feb. 23, 1842.

34. Ibid., 2:344, Dec. 24, 1842; 2:260, Jan. 24, 1842.

35. Ibid., 2:393–94, Aug. 12, 1843; 2:465–66, Aug. 13, 1844. Van Buren was acquainted with Mickle's uncle, John Mickle.

36. *Isaac Mickle Diary,* 1:167, May 15, 1841.

37. Ibid., 2:441, May 2, 1844.

38. Ibid., 2:252, Jan. 1, 1842.

39. *Canons of Good Breeding,* pp. 96–97; *Isaac Mickle Diary,* 2:252, Jan. 1, 1842.

40. *Isaac Mickle Diary,* 1:169, May 16, 1841.

41. Ibid., 2:252, Jan. 1, 1842.

42. Information on Weaver is drawn primarily from the Matthias Shirk Weaver Diaries, 1840–1843, at the Ohio Historical Society, Columbus, Ohio. Collection numbers: vols. 751, 752, 753,

754. These materials are on Microfilm 135, and include biographical information compiled by an unidentified author. Weaver's diaries are inexpensive pocket volumes, e.g., *Diary for 1840; or Daily Register, for the use of Private Families and Persons of Business: containing a blank for every day in the year, for the record of events that may be interesting, either past or future* (Samuel M. Stewart, Philadelphia.)

43. Weaver, Diary, Jan. 12, 1842. On July 7, 1841 he had praised the Bible but regretfully noted that he did not read it.

44. The paths of Mickle and Weaver crossed, but never apparently at the same time. Weaver visited Niagara Falls in Oct. 1840 and again in late Sept. 1842; Mickle traveled there in Aug. 1844. Mickle met Senator James Buchanan at the Page law office on Nov. 1, 1842; Weaver had traveled with him in the same stagecoach on Sept. 1, 1840. On at least one occasion they listened to the same lecturer, Joseph R. Chandler, "Influence of the Christian Religion upon the Character & Condition of women," but Weaver heard the talk in Philadelphia on Mar. 15, 1842, while Mickle heard it in Camden three weeks later on Apr. 6, 1842. Both Weaver and Mickle heard the same violinist, John Nagel in Philadelphia three days apart (Apr. 29 and May 2, 1843) and on June 13, 1843, both were among the crowds who witnessed the launching of the ship *Raritan*. On the class-oriented character of some public spectacles see Susan G. Davis, *Parades and Power: Street Theatre in Nineteenth-Century Philadelphia* (Philadelphia, 1986).

45. Weaver, Diary, Mar. 10, 1841; Sept. 28, 1841. Later that year (Dec. 15, 1841) he referred to his Ohio correspondence as "one of my greatest comforts."

46. Weaver, Diary, Aug. 30, 1842.

47. Ibid., Mar. 1, 1840.

48. Ibid., May 26, 1841.

49. Ibid., 1842.

50. Ibid., June 6, 9, 1840 (ice cream); June 18, 1840.

51. Ibid., Aug. 18, 1841; Apr. 4, 1841.

52. Hiram N. Peck Diary, New-York Historical Society, Nov. 5, 30, 1830. Peck, born in Fairfield County, Conn. (either Brookfield or Newtown), on Oct. 29, 1806, was seeking to make a career as a merchant.

53. E. D. Hirsch, Jr., *Cultural Literacy: What Every American Needs to Know,* with an appendix "What Literate Americans Know," by E. D. Hirsch, Jr., Joseph Kett, James Trefil (Boston, 1987).

54. Weaver, Diary, Mar. 25, 1840.

55. Ibid., June 8, 1841; Apr. 6, 1840; May 27, 1842.

56. Ibid., Dec. 20, 1840.

57. Ibid., Jan. 6, 1841.

58. Ibid., Jan. 23, 1841.

59. *Isaac Mickle Diary,* 2:395, Aug. 14, 1843.

60. John, "Managing the Mails: The U.S. Postal System in National Politics, 1823–36," and "Private Mail Delivery in the United States during the Nineteenth Century: A Sketch," *Business and Economic History,* 2d ser., 15 (1986): 135–47; Kielbowicz, "News in the Mails, 1690–1863," pp. 87, 188, 190. All of the men treated in this chapter engaged in this common practice of newspaper exchange. Women also exchanged papers. See Nicholas and Virginia Westbrook, "Read Some and Sewed': Reading in the Daily Round, A Vermont Case Study," paper delivered at conference on "A Century of Reading in America," Strong Museum, Rochester, N.Y., Nov. 1986, p. 25.

61. As with most generalizations, examples of contrary behavior may be found, especially in cases where the letter-writer was an eyewitness to events that were also covered by the newspapers. In such cases, when the letter-writer disagreed with the newspaper accounts, a letter might indeed supply information on public events. For example, Henry Ware, Jr.'s letter to Harriet Ware, Boston, June 16, 1825, contains a critical account of the disorders accompanying the dedication of the Bunker Hill Monument in Charlestown, Mass. Newspaper reports were much more positive. (John Ware, *Memoir of the Life of Henry Ware, Jr.* (Boston, 1846), p. 168.)

62. Information concerning Edward Jenner Carpenter has been drawn from his Journal, 1844–1845, at the American Antiquarian Society, Worcester, Mass. Additional sources include Winfred C. Gates, "Journal of a Cabinet Maker's Apprentice," *The Chronicle of the Early American Industries Association,* 15 (June and Sept., 1962): 23, 24, 35, 36; obituary in Brattleboro, Vt., *Sunday Reporter,* May 22, 1892; letter of J. K., Moore to E. Jenner Carpenter, 21 May 1848, Misc. Mss. "M" Boxes at AAS.; and Lucy C. Kellogg, *History of the Town of Bernardston, Franklin County, Massachusetts. With Genealogies,* 2 vols. (Greenfield, Mass., 1902). In April 1989, the Edward J. Carpenter journal was published with an introduction and annotation by Christopher Clark, with the assistance of Donald M. Scott, "The Diary of an Apprentice Cabinetmaker: Edward Jenner Carpenter's 'Journal' 1844–45," *Proceedings of the American Antiquarian Society,* 98, pt. 2 (1989): 303–94.

63. *Isaac Mickle Diary,* 1:156–57, Apr. 30, 1841.

64. Carpenter, Journal, Mar. 1, 1844; June 6, 1844. Delivery of newspapers cost 1¢ within 100 miles, 1.5¢ for longer distances until the reform act of March 3, 1845, eliminated all charges for delivery of newspapers within 30 miles, and maintained the 1794 schedule for delivery up to 100 miles and in state (1¢), and 1.5¢ for longer distances: Kielbowicz, "News in the Mails, 1690–1863," pp. 188, 190.

65. Throughout the period 1792–1863 newspapers were delivered at no cost to other newspapers on an exchange basis. As a result every newspaper office possessed an ample supply of out-of-town papers. See Kielbowicz, "News in the Mails, 1690–1863," p. 337.

66. Carpenter, Journal, Mar. 10 and 13, 1844.

67. *The Lowell Offering: Writings by New England Mill Women (1840–1845),* ed. with an intro. and commentary by Benita Eisler (New York, 1980), supplies evidence of the popularity of novels among women at the Lowell mills. In one story, for example, one worker criticizes another's expenditures on dress and confections, asserting: "She had better do as I do—spend her money for books, and her leisure time in reading them. I buy three novels every month, and when that is not enough I take some from the circulating library, I think it our duty to improve our minds as much as possible" (p. 99.) See also Baym, *Novels, Readers, and Reviewers.*

68. Carpenter, Journal, Mar. 14, 1844.

69. Ibid., Mar. 5 and 6, 1845.

70. *Putnam's Magazine,* Oct. 1854, quoted in Baym, *Novels, Readers, and Reviewers,* p. 31.

71. John Donald Carrick, *Life of Wallace* (London, 1840); George Wilkins Kendall, *Narrative of the Texan Santa Fe Expedition* (New York, 1844). Whether Carpenter read these editions or others is conjecture. Both existed in several editions at the time Carpenter mentioned them in his journal, Aug. 18, 1844; Feb. 5 and 9 and Mar. 2, 1845.

72. Weaver, Diary, Apr. 3 and 4, 1840. Weaver's keen Negrophobia was evident in entries such as Nov. 9 and 13, 1840: "Working at the Masonic Diploma alias Nigger rigmarole;" "Finished darned Nigger concern."

73. "Mr. Wilson" visited the shop twice in fifteen months.

74. Carpenter, Journal, Mar. 22, 1844.

75. Ibid., May 21, 1844.

76. Ibid., June 2 and 4, 1844.

77. Traveling lecturers also sold books, pamphlets, and newspaper subscriptions concerned with their cause or topic. The abolitionist Abigail Kelley Foster reported in a letter to E. D. Hudson, Bozrahville, Conn., Apr. 13, 1841: "I have obtained 26 subscriptions for the *Monthly Offering,* 2 for the *Standard,* and 2 for the *Liberator.*" (Abigail Kelley Foster Papers, American Antiquarian Society.)

78. Carpenter, Journal, Aug. 20, 1844; July 17, 1844. "Big bugs" meant social elite in the slang of the 1840s. (Lyon, *Recollections of an Old Cartman,* p. 3.)

79. Carpenter, Journal, April 2, 1844.

80. All information on Calvin Fletcher is drawn from the superb Indiana Historical Society edition: *The Diary of Calvin Fletcher, 1817–1866,* 9 vols., ed. with intro. to each volume by Gayle Thornbrough, Dorothy L. Riker, and Paula Corpuz (Indianapolis, Ind., 1972–1983). This work is heavily annotated, thoroughly indexed, and includes correspondence, the diary of Sarah Hill Fletcher, numerous pictures, chronologies, and genealogies.

81. *Diary of Calvin Fletcher,* 3:35, Apr. 29, 1844.

82. Ibid., 3:54, July 3, 1844; 3:80, Oct. 21, 1844; 3:71, Aug. 24, 1844. The outcome of the 1844 election was in doubt for days, even in New York City. Word of mouth from Albany first brought the erroneous information that Henry Clay had won. (Lyon, *Recollections of an Old Cartman,* pp. 50–51.)

83. *Diary of Calvin Fletcher,* 3:64, July 29, 1844.

84. Ibid., 3:81, Oct. 24, 1844.

85. Ibid., 3:79, Oct. 17, 1844.

86. Ibid., 3:60, July 17, 1844.

87. Ibid., 3:65, July 31, 1844.

88. Ibid., 3:16, Feb. 4, 1844.

89. Ibid., 2:100, June 16, 1839; 2:390, Feb. 13 and 15, 1842.

90. Ibid., 3:17, Feb. 4, 1844.

91. Comment based on Fletcher's readings in vol. 3 of his diary, 1844–1847. Prior to this time he had already read widely.

92. *Diary of Calvin Fletcher,* 3:67, Aug. 3 and 4, 1844.

93. Ibid., 3:39, May 12, 1844.

94. Ibid., 3:25, Mar. 10, 1844. Fletcher read Biblical commentaries from time to time.

95. Ibid., 3:70–71, Aug. 24, 1844. On the occasion of Cass's speech Fletcher was prevented from attending by illness, though he did receive an oral account.

96. Calvin Fletcher to Michael Fletcher in Staatsburg, N.Y., Feb. 23, 1823, *The Diary of Calvin Fletcher,* 1:89.

97. Bledstein, *Culture of Professionalism,* pp. 70, 73.

98. Channing, *Self-Culture,* p. 11.

99. Letter to Edward Carrington, Paris, Jan. 16, 1787, in *Papers of Thomas Jefferson,* ed. by Julian P. Boyd, 19 vols. (Princeton, 1950–1977), 11:49, cited in Richard D. Brown, "From Cohesion to Competition," in William L. Joyce et al., eds., *Printing and Society in Early America,* p. 305.

100. Altick, *English Common Reader,* pp. 31–32.

101. The phrase "democratization of gentility" is Gordon S. Wood's.

102. This theme is treated in Richard L. Bushman, "American High-Style and Vernacular Cultures," in Jack P. Greene and J. R. Pole, *Colonial British America: Essays in the New History of the Early Modern Era* (Baltimore, 1984), pp. 345–83. That contemporaries thought in these terms is evident from the lyceum lecturer Charles Caldwell's "Thoughts Regarding the Moral and Other Indirect Influences of Rail-Roads," *New England Magazine*, 2 (Apr. 1832): 290; observers quoted in John Mack Faragher, *Women and Men on the Overland Trail* (New Haven, 1979), make the same point.

103. Charles Dickens, *American Notes for General Circulation,* ed. with an intro. by John S. Whitley and Arnold Goldman (Harmondsworth, England, 1985), p. 112. First published in 1842.

104. David D. Hall, "The Uses of Literacy in New England, 1600–1850," in William L. Joyce et al., eds., *Printing and Society in Early America,* pp. 1–47.

105. Mary Kupiec Cayton, "The Making of an American Prophet," p. 615, refers to the "culture industry," a term used by Max Horkheimer and Theodor Adorno in *The Dialectic of Enlightenment* (New York, 1969), pp. 120–67; Baym, *Women's Fiction: A Guide to Novels,* p. 27.

106. Bledstein, *Culture of Professionalism,* p. 75.

107. Quoted in John Mayfield, *The New Nation, 1800–1845* (New York, 1982), p. 54.

108. Baym, *Woman's Fiction: A Guide to Novels,* p. 31.

CHAPTER 10. THE DYNAMICS OF CONTAGIOUS DIFFUSION

1. John Anderson Diary, 1794, 1798, passim; Alexander Anderson Diary, 1794, 1798, passim, New-York Historical Society.

2. Frank Luther Mott, "The Newspaper Coverage of Lexington and Concord," *New England Quarterly,* 17 (1944): 489–505.

3. John H. Scheide, "The Lexington Alarm," *Proceedings of the American Antiquarian Society,* 50 (1940): 49–79.

4. The fullest account of the preliminaries of the battle and the engagement itself is Arthur Bernon Tourtellot, *Lexington and Concord: The Beginning of the War of the American Revolution* (New York, 1963). This was originally published as *William Diamond's Drum* (New York, 1959).

5. Peter Force, comp., *American Archives,* 4th ser., 6 vols. (Washington, D.C., 1837–1846), 2:363–69; Scheide, "The Lexington Alarm;" Lester B, Cappon et al., eds., *Atlas of Early American History: The Revolutionary Era. 1760–1790* (Princeton, 1976), pp. 42, 121. Cappon noted that as recently as 1972 more information on the spread of news regarding the Stamp Act was still turning up. That this remains true in 1989 regarding the Lexington and Concord battles is evident from the travel journal of Dr. Robert Honeyman which shows that the news reached Dumfries, Virginia as early as April 27, three days earlier than Cappon reports and one day before Cappon lists the information coming to Annapolis, Maryland and Alexandria, Virginia (Philip Padelford, ed., *Colonial Panorama, 1775* (San Marino, Calif., 1939), p. 77). According to John Harrower the news was at Fredericksburg, Virginia on April 28, two days sooner than Cappon reports (*The Journal of John Harrower: An Indentured Servant in the Colony of Virginia, 1773–1776,* ed. with and intro. by Edward Miles Riley (Williamsburg, Va., 1963), p. 94). The discrepancy between Cappon's dates and those noted here may result from Cappon's reporting the date of arrival of "express" riders, because it is certainly conceivable that by this time, over a week after the event, contagious word-of-mouth reports may have been moving

even faster than the expresses. The fact that Cappon notes a newspaper report published in Williamsburg, Virginia, on April 29, three days before he reports the arrival of an express rider, seems to supply conclusive evidence that the contagious movement of information through word of mouth was faster even than expresses.

6. Mott, "Newspaper Coverage," *New England Quarterly,* 17 (1944): 490, 504. A general discussion of "The Time-Lag in News," is offered by Clarence Brigham, *Journals and Journeymen: A Contribution to the History of Early American Newspapers* (Westport, Conn., 1971; first pub. 1950), pp. 55–59. In some cases, authors disagree as to the date news of the battles arrived. For example, word may have reached Savannah on May 10, 1775. (Harold E. Davis, *The Fledgling Province: Social and Cultural Life in Colonial Georgia, 1733–1776* (Chapel Hill, 1976), p. 255, n. 8.)

7. Scheide, "The Lexington Alarm," p. 63. Scheide, noting the discrepancy between the average pace of transmission and the speed reported here, doubts this account. My own guess is that the "legend," if it is that, is founded on fact. A reliable historian who spoke with survivors of 1775 confirmed the report, noting the arrival of the messenger "made vivid impression on memory." (William Lincoln, *History of Worcester,* Worcester, 1837, p. 108.)

8. Ibid., pp. 66–68.

9. Cappon, ed., *Atlas of Early American History,* p. 42; Mott, "Newspaper Coverage," pp. 494–95.

10. The patriot Matthew Patten called it "Melancholy," *The Diary of Matthew Patten of Bedford, N.H.* (Concord, N.H., 1903), p. 342.

11. *The Journals of Ashley Bowen (1728–1813) of Marblehead,* ed. by Philip Chadwick Foster Smith, publications of the Colonial Society of Massachusetts, vols. 44 and 45 of *Collections* (Boston, 1973), 45:435, Apr. 19, 1775.

12. "Diary of Paul Litchfield," Proceedings of the *Massachusetts Historical Society,* 1st ser., 19 (1881–1882): 377.

13. Reverend Isaac Hasey, diary, Apr. 20, 1775, in *Maine Historical Society Collections and Proceedings,* 2d ser., 9 (1898): 132.

14. "Journal of James Stevens." *Essex Institute Historical Collections,* 48 (1912): 41, Apr. 19, 1775.

15. "Extracts from the Diary of James Parker of Shirley, Mass.," *New England Historical and Genealogical Register,* 69 (1915): 123.

16. James Jeffrey, "Journal Kept in Quebec in 1775," *Essex Institute Historical Collections,* 50 (1914): 109.

17. Ibid., p. 110.

18. Ibid., p. 110.

19. Quoted in Arria S. Huntington, *Under a Colonial Roof-tree* (New York, 1891), p. 50.

20. Ibid. This concern over bloodshed calls to mind the present-day observations of the psychologist Carol Gilligan, that "women not only define themselves in a context of human relationship but also judge themselves in terms of that ability to care. Women's place in man's life cycle has been that of nurturer, caretaker, and helpmate." Values like these influenced the kinds of information women sought and the ways in which they participated in information diffusion. (*In a Different Voice: Psychological Theory and Women's Development* (Cambridge, Mass., 1982), pp. 17, 48, 100, 104–5, and passim.)

21. Arthur Gilman, ed., *Theatrum Majorum. The Cambridge of 1776* (Cambridge, Mass., 1876), p. 19.

22. Experience Wright Richardson, Diary, April 19, 24, 27, 1775. Manuscript collection, Massachusetts Historical Society.

23. Diary quoted in Reverend Calvin Durfee, *Sketch of the Late Reverend Ebenezer Fitch, D.D.* (Boston, 1865), p. 24.

24. "Occupation of New York City by the British," *Pennsylvania Magazine of History and Biography,* 10 (1886): 418.

25. Dr. Robert Honeyman journal quoted in Padelford, ed., *Colonial Panorama, 1775,* p. 77, Apr. 27, 1775.

26. *Journal of John Harrower,* p. 94, Apr. 28, 1775.

27. "Williamsburg—The Old Colonial Capital," *William & Mary College Quarterly Historical Magazine,* 16, no. 1 (July, 1907): 45.

28. "Extracts from Interleaved Almanacs kept by John White of Salem," *Essex Institute Historical Collections,* 49 (1913): 92.

29. Frederick Mackenzie, journal, in Allen French, ed., *A British Fusilier in Revolutionary Boston* (Cambridge, Mass., 1926), p. 56.

30. "Extracts from 'Text Books' of Deacon Joseph Seccombe," *Essex Institute Historical Collections,* 34 (1898), p. 36.

31. Ibid., p. 36. Seccombe's account was also published in *Massachusetts Spy,* at Worcester, on May 3, 1775.

32. *Diaries and Letters of William Emerson, 1743–1776, Minister of the Church in Concord, Chaplain in the Revolutionary Army* (Boston, 1972), p. 71.

33. The false "Powder Alarm" of September 1, 1774, was carefully studied at the time by the Newport clergyman and later Yale president, Ezra Stiles, *The Literary Diary of Ezra Stiles,* ed. by Franklin Bowditch Dexter, 3 vols. (New York, 1901), 1:476–85; it warrants scholarly investigation.

34. Norwich *Courier,* Dec. 25, 1799, page 3.

35. *Salem Gazette,* Dec. 24, 1799, page 3.

36. *Columbian Centinel and Massachusetts Federalist,* Dec. 25, 1799, page 3; *Salem Gazette,* Dec. 24, 1799, page 3.

37. *Salem Gazette,* Dec. 24, 1799, page 3; *American Mercury* (Hartford), Dec. 26, 1799, page 3; *Providence Gazette,* Dec. 28, 1799, page 3.

38. Margaret B. Stillwell, "Checklist of Eulogies and Funeral Orations on the Death of George Washington, December 1799–February, 1800," *Bulletin of the New York Public Library,* 20 (May 1916): 403–41. She cites some 440 eulogies, the greatest number being from the northeast, especially New England. An interpretation of one theme in this literature is presented by Robert P. Hay, "George Washington: American Moses," *American Quarterly,* 21 (1969): 780–91.

39. Sally Ripley, diary, Greenfield, Mass., Jan. 9, 1800, manuscript collection, American Antiquarian Society. On Dec. 26, 1799, at Greenfield, Ripley learned of Washington's death.

40. Nathaniel R. Snowden, Diary, Jan. 9, 1800, manuscript collection, Historical Society of Pennsylvania.

41. Dorothy Ann Lipson, *Freemasonry in Federalist Connecticut* (Princeton, 1977); Richard D. Brown, "The Emergence of Urban Society in Rural Massachusetts, 1760–1820, *Journal of American History,* 61 (June 1974): 40–43.

42. Compiled from Clifford K. Shipton, *The American Bibliography of Charles Evans,* 13 (1799–1800) (Worcester, 1955).

43. For example, *Columbian Centinel and Massachusetts Federalist* (Boston), Jan. 18, 22, 29; *J. Russell's Gazette Commercial and Political* (Boston), Jan. 2, 9, 13, 16, 20, 1800; *Providence Gazette,* Feb. 8, 1800.

44. *Columbian Centinel* (Boston), Jan. 29, 1800; Feb. 3, 1800; *Providence Gazette,* Feb. 15, 1800.

45. For example, the Norwich (Conn.) *Courier,* Feb. 26, 1800, printed the will, as did most other papers within a month or so after it became available. Literacy was certainly a barrier for some slaves, however it was not unusual for newspapers to be read aloud in public spaces such as taverns so even non-literate people had some access to texts. The substance, of course, could be conveyed by word of mouth.

46. Prosser's remarks were recorded by a lawyer who heard them and passed them on to Robert Sutcliff, who wrote *Travels in Some Parts of North America in the Years 1804, 1805, & 1806* (York and London, 1811), p. 50, cited in Herbert Aptheker, *American Negro Slave Revolts* (New York, 1943 and 1963), p. 233.

47. See David Homer Bates, *Lincoln in the Telegraph Office: Recollections of the United States Military Telegraph Corps During the Civil War* (New York, 1907), pp. 371–72.

48. Mary Boykin Miller Chesnut, *Mary Chesnut's Civil War,* ed. by C. Vann Woodward (New Haven, 1981), p. 791, Apr. 22, 1865.

49. For example, *New York Tribune,* Apr. 15, 1865.

50. Frederick Sumner Pratt, diary, Worcester, Mass., Apr. 15, 1865, manuscript collection, American Antiquarian Society. According to the *Population of the United States in 1860, the Eighth Census* (Washington, D.C., 1864), 1:226, Worcester had 24,688 people in 1860.

51. *Diary of Calvin Fletcher,* ed. by Gayle Thornbrough and Paula Corpuz (Indianapolis, 1983), 9:68, Apr. 15, 1865.

52. *A Philadelphia Perspective: The Diary of Sidney George Fisher Covering the Years 1834–1871,* ed. by Nicholas B. Wainwright (Philadelphia, 1967), p. 492, Apr. 15, 1865.

53. *Diary of George T. Strong,* ed. by Allan Nevins and Milton Thomas (New York, 1952), 3:582, Apr. 15, 1865.

54. Susan E. Parsons Brown Forbes, diary, Boston, Apr. 15, 1865, manuscript collection, American Antiquarian Society.

55. *A Philadelphia Perspective,* p. 492, Apr. 15, 1865.

56. Philadelphia, *Public Ledger,* Apr. 17, 1865, page 1; *Chicago Tribune,* Apr. 17, 1865, page 4. The practice of reading the morning paper over breakfast goes back to the 18th century. Fisher Ames of Dedham, Mass., aspired to such urbanity through improvements in the post office. (Letter to Timothy Pickering, Dedham, Feb. 1, 1806, in *Works of Fisher Ames,* ed. by Seth Ames, 2d. ed., (Boston, 1854), 1:357.)

57. George T. Strong, *Diary,* 3:583, Apr. 15, 1865; Philadelphia, *Public Ledger,* Apr. 17, 1865, page 1.

58. *New York Herald,* Apr. 16, 1865, page 5.

59. Philadelphia, *Public Ledger,* Apr. 17, 1865, page 1; *Buffalo Commercial Advertiser,* Apr. 17, 1865, page 3.

60. *The Cormany Diaries: A Northern Family in the Civil War,* ed. by James C. Mohr et al. (Pittsburgh, Pa., 1982), p. 543, Apr. 15, 1865.

61. Don Avery Winslow, diary, Westfield, Vermont, 1:213, Apr. 15 and 16, 1865, manuscript collection, American Antiquarian Society.

62. Sarah Woolsey Johnson (Mrs. C. F.), diary, Tioga County, N.Y., April 15, 1865, manuscript collection, New-York Historical Society.

63. Rachel Cormany, *The Cormany Diaries*, p. 543, Apr. 15, 1865.

64. Anson Smith Hopkins, *Reminiscences of an Octogenarian* (New Haven, Conn., 1937), p. 1; The key study of the aftermath of public sentiment regarding the assassination is Thomas Reed Turner, *Beware the People Weeping: Public Opinion and the Assassination of Abraham Lincoln* (Baton Rouge, 1982).

65. Richmond *Whig*, Apr. 17, 1865; *Memphis Bulletin*, Apr. 17, 1865; *The Heavens Are Weeping: The Civil War Diaries of George Richard Browder*, ed. by Richard L. Troutman (Grand Rapids, Mich., 1987), p. 193.

66. Raleigh *Daily Progress*, Apr. 18, 20, 1865.

67. *Cincinnati Daily Gazette*, Apr. 15, 1865; Apr. 17, 1865, page 2; Madison *Wisconsin State Journal*, Apr. 15, 1865; Sacramento *Daily Union*, Apr. 17, 1865; *Charleston Courier*, Apr. 20, 1865, page 1; New Orleans *Daily Picayune*, Apr. 20, 1865. The information had been published at New Orleans on April 19, 1865.

68. Chesnut, *Mary Chesnut's Civil War*, p. 791, Apr. 22, 1865; Mrs. Caroline S. Jones to Mrs. Mary Jones, Augusta, Georgia, Apr. 30, 1865, in Robert Manson Myers, ed., *The Children of Pride: A True Story of Georgia and the Civil War* (New Haven, 1972), p. 1268; Macon *Daily Evening News*, Apr. 26, 1865; Greenville *Weekly Observer*, Apr. 22, 1865, was carrying a report of Lee's surrender at Appomattox on Apr. 9, but had no word yet of the assassination; Houston *Tri-Weekly Observer*, Apr. 19, 1865, published reports from New Orleans papers of Apr. 12 and 13 reporting Confederate defeats in Virginia, although it cast doubt on these stories as probably being the result of Yankee "exaggeration."

CONCLUSION

1. Population estimates are drawn from United States Department of Commerce, Bureau of the Census, *Historical Statistics of the United States: Colonial Times to 1970* (Washington, D.C. 1975) pp. 8, 1168. The estimate for the land area of the United States for 1865 was calculated by substracting the area of Alaska and Hawaii from the present national area. The estimate for land area in 1700 was calculated as the sum of the land area of the 13 original states reduced by about 20 percent. For 1700 it would not be unreasonable to reduce the area much further since much of the larger colonies—Virginia, Georgia, North Carolina, Pennsylvania, New York, and Massachusetts—was settled only by Indians.

2. James Boswell, *The Life of Johnson*, Modern Library edition (New York, n.d.), p. 808, Apr. 16, 1778.

3. Francis J. Bremer, "Increase Mather's Friends: The Trans-Atlantic Congregational Network of the Seventeenth Century," *Proceedings of the American Antiquarian Society*, 94, pt. 1 (Apr. 1984): 59–96; David Cressy, *Coming over: Migration and Communication Between England and New England in the Seventeenth Century* (Cambridge, 1987); Ian K. Steele, *The English Atlantic: An Exploration of Communication and Community* (New York, 1986).

4. Joe W. Kraus, "The Book Collections of Early American College Libraries," *Library Quarterly*, 43 (1973): 144; Edwin Wolf, "The Dispersal of the Library of William Byrd of Westover," *Proceedings of the American Antiquarian Society*, 68 (Apr. 1958): 21–22.

5. David D. Hall, "Toward a History of Popular Religion in Early New England," *William and Mary Quarterly*, 3d ser., 41 (1984): 49–61.

6. An unremarkable example of this popularization can be found in almanac explanations of

the elements of astronomy in the 18th century. In the 1730s and 1740s, for example, Nathaniel Ames, the New England almanac-maker, routinely included one or two-page explanations of celestial phenomena.

7. Lewis P. Simpson, "The Printer as Man of Letters: Franklin and the Symbolism of the Third Realm," in *The Oldest Revolutionary: Essays on Benjamin Franklin,* ed. by J. A. Leo Lemay (Philadelphia, 1976), pp. 3–20.

8. This kind of an outcome has been associated with the shift from non-literate to literate societies by Ian Watt and Jack Goody in "The Consequences of Literacy," in Jack Goody, ed., *Literacy in Traditional Societies* (Cambridge, 1968), pp. 58–60. See also Jack Goody, *The Logic of Writing and the Organization of Society* (Cambridge, 1986) and his *The Interface Between the Written and the Oral* (Cambridge, 1987).

9. This argument is especially associated with Alan Heimert, *Religion and the American Mind: From the Great Awakening to The Revolution* (Cambridge, Mass., 1966) and with Harry S. Stout, "Religion, Communcations, and the Ideological Origins of the American Revolution," *William and Mary Quarterly,* 3d ser., 34 (1977): 519–41. Rhys Isaac has made a similar argument for the Chesapeake in "Evangelical Revolt: The Nature of the Baptists' Challenge to the Traditional Order in Virginia, 1765 to 1775," *William and Mary Quarterly,* 3d ser., 31 (1974): 345–68, and in his *Transformation of Virginia. 1740–1790* (Chapel Hill, 1982).

10. An indexed, bound volume of Samuel Sewall's newspapers, complete with marginal topic headings, survives in the New-York Historical Society. That Martha Moore Ballard used newspapers similarly is evident from her diary entry of January 26, 1799 (Charles Elventon Nash, *The History of Augusta, First Settlements and Early Days as a Town. Including the Diary of Mrs. Martha Moore Ballard (1785 to 1812)* (Augusta, 1904), p. 379.) It is evident from the large number of surviving 19th-century almanacs that the practice of stitching and retaining such nominally ephemeral works in a series over the years was a practice that persisted.

11. Richard D. Brown, "From Cohesion to Competition," in *Printing and Society in Early America,* ed. by William L. Joyce, David D. Hall, Richard D. Brown, and John B. Hench (Worcester, Mass., 1983), pp. 300–309; Donald M. Scott, "Print and the Public Lecture System, 1840–1860," in Joyce et al., *Printing and Society,* pp. 278–99.

12. Nathan O. Hatch, "Elias Smith and the Rise of Religious Journalism in the Early Republic," in *Printing and Society,* ed. by Joyce et al., pp. 250–77; David P. Nord, *The Evangelical Origins of Mass Media in America, 1815–1835,* in *Journalism Monographs,* no. 88 (Austin, Tx., 1984); Michael H. Harris " 'Spiritual Cakes Upon the Waters': The Church as a Disseminator of the Printed Word on the Ohio Valley Frontier to 1850," in *Getting the Books Out: Papers of the Chicago Conference on the Book in 19th-Century America,* ed. by Michael Hackenberg (Washington, D.C., 1987), pp. 98–120.

13. Watt and Goody, "The Consequences of Literacy," p. 58.

14. J. H. Plumb, "The Commercialization of Leisure," in Neil McKendrick, John Brewer, and J. H. Plumb, *The Birth of a Consumer Society: The Commercialization of Eighteenth-Century England* (Bloomington, Ind., 1982), pp. 265–85; Robert A. Gross, "Reconstructing Early American Libraries: Concord, Massachusetts, 1795–1850," *Proceedings of the American Antiquarian Society,* 97, pt. 2 (1987): 332.

15. Samuel Miller, *A Brief Retrospect of the Eighteenth Century* (New York, 1803, reprinted 1970), 2:422.

16. Ibid., 2:422, 423.

17. Ralph Waldo Emerson, quoted in Brown, "From Cohesion to Competition," p. 308.

18. Quoted in Richard D. Brown, "Where Have All the Great Men Gone?," *American Heritage,* 35 (Feb./Mar. 1984): 18.

19. Watt and Goody, "The Consequences of Literacy," pp. 58, 60; Jack Goody, "Evolution and Communication: The Domestication of the Savage Mind," *British Journal of Sociology*, 24 (1973): 11.

20. Stephen Botein, "Printers and the American Revolution," in *The Press and the American Revolution*, ed. by Bernard Bailyn and John B. Hench (Worcester, Mass., 1980), pp. 11–57; Frank Luther Mott, *American Journalism, A History: 1690–1960*, 3d ed. (New York, 1962), pp. 113–34, 243, 253.

21. An extreme case of partisan conflict that led to personal combat was the Selfridge-Austin affair in Boston in 1806. Here the newspaper was directly involved. See *The Trial of Thomas O. Selfridge, Attorney at Law, before the Hon. Isaac Parker, Esquire. For Killing Charles Austin, on the Public Exchange, in Boston, August 4th, 1806* (Boston, 1807); Thomas O. Selfridge, *A Correct Statement of the Whole Preliminary Controversy Between Tho. O. Selfridge and Benj. Austin* (Charlestown, Mass., 1807).

22. The higher incidence of books in the North and in urban areas where merchants and members of the learned professions most often dwelled has been a persistent aspect of American history. See James N. Green, "From Printer to Publisher: Matthew Carey and the Origins of Nineteenth-Century Book Publishing," in John Y. Cole, ed., *Books in Our Future: Perspectives and Proposals* (Washington, D.C., 1987), pp. 26–44; Robert A. Gross, "Much Instruction from Little Reading: Books and Libraries in Thoreau's Concord," *Proceedings of the American Antiquarian Society*, 97, pt. 1 (1987): 129–88 and "Reconstructing Early American Libraries: Concord, Massachusetts, 1795–1850," *Proceedings of the American Antiquarian Society.*, 97, pt. 2 (1987): 331–451; David Kaser, *A Book for a Sixpence: The Circulating Library in America* (Pittsburgh, 1980); Joseph F. Kett and Patricia A. McClung, "Book Culture in Post-Revolutionary Virginia," *Proceedings of the American Antiquarian Society*, 94, pt. 1 (1984): 97–147; Jesse H. Shera, *Foundations of the Public Library: The Origins of the Public Library Movement in New England, 1629–1855* (Chicago, 1949); Louis R. Wilson, *The Geography of Reading: A Study of the Distribution and Status of Libraries in the United States* (Chicago, 1938). Shera, *Foundations*, p. 260, shows a map locating public and quasi-public libraries in New England before 1851.

23. Donald M. Scott, "Print and the Public Lecture System, 1840–1860," in *Printing and Society in Early America*, pp. 278–99.

24. Harriet A. Jacobs, *Incidents in the Life of a Slave Girl, Written by Herself*, ed. by L. Maria Child. Ed. with an intro. by Jean Fagan Yellin (Cambridge, Mass., 1987), p. 15. Evidence of the impact of social and economic status on literacy is presented by Harvey J. Graff who argues that the urban poor were generally illiterate in *The Literacy Myth: Literacy and Social Structure in the Nineteenth-Century City* (New York, 1979).

25. Ann Douglas, *The Feminization of American Culture* (New York, 1977); Cathy N. Davidson, *Revolution and the Word: The Rise of the Novel in America* (New York, 1986), ch. 6.

26. For a comparison with present-day gender and socio-economic status reading preferences see Joseph F. Brinley, Jr., "The 1983 Consumer Research Study on Reading and Book Purchasing: A Summary," in John Y. Cole, ed., *Books in Our Future: Perspectives and Proposals* (Washington, D.C., 1987), pp. 92–105. Carroll Smith-Rosenberg, "The Female World of Love and Ritual: Relations Between Women in Nineteenth-Century America," *Signs*, 1 (1975): 1–29; Nancy Tomes, "The Quaker Connection: Visiting Patterns among Women in an Eighteenth-Century Pennsylvania Town," in *Friends and Neighbors: Group Life in America's First Plural Society*, ed. by Michael Zuckerman (Philadephia, 1982), pp. 174–95.

27. A particularly striking example may be found in the experience of Mary Fish as related by Joy Day Buel and Richard Buel, Jr., in *The Way of Duty: A Woman and her Family in Revolutionary America* (New York, 1984).

28. Jack Larkin, Old Sturbridge Village, Inc., unpublished paper on women's charitable society meeting in Shrewsbury, Mass., in the 1830s; Nancy Cott, *The Bonds of Womanhood: "Woman's Sphere" in New England, 1780–1835* (New Haven, 1977).

29. Isabel Mitchell, *Roads and Roadmaking in Connecticut* (Hartford, 1933), pp. 24–31, describes a part of the post road between Fairfield and New York City that was scarcely adequate for horsemen. See also Oliver W. Holmes and Peter T. Rohrbach, *Stagecoach East: Stagecoach Days in the East from the Colonial Period to the Civil War* (Washington, D.C., 1983).

30. Neil McKendrick, "Introduction. The Birth of a Consumer Society: The Commercialization of Eighteenth-Century England," and "Commercialization and the Economy," in McKendrick et al., *The Birth of a Consumer Society*, pp. 1–194; Robert W. Fogel and Stanley L. Engerman, eds., *The Reinterpretation of American Economic History* (New York, 1971), pt. 3; Thomas C. Cochran and Thomas B. Brewer, eds., *Views of American Economic Growth: The Agricultural Era* (New York, 1965), pts. 3 and 4; George Rogers Taylor, *The Transportation Revolution, 1815–1860* (New York, 1951); Ronald J. Zboray, "The Transportation Revolution and Antebellum Book Distribution Reconsidered," *American Quarterly*, 38 (1986): 53–71.

31. From John Adams, who included a section on the necessity of education in the Massachusetts Constitution of 1780, and Thomas Jefferson, who sponsored a "Bill for the More General Diffusion of Knowledge" in the Virginia legislature, onward, republican doctrine was bound up with the doctrine of an informed public. The role of women is discussed by Linda K. Kerber, "Daughters of Columbia: Educating Women for the Republic, 1787–1805," in *The Hofstadter Aegis: A Memorial*, ed. by Stanley Elkins and Eric McKitrick (New York, 1974), pp. 36–59 and in her *Women of the Republic: Intellect and Ideology in Revolutionary America* (Chapel Hill, 1980). One example that illustrates this common theme in public oratory and from which the quotations are drawn is James Humphrey Wilder, *An Oration delivered at the request of the young men of Hingham, on the fourth of July, 1832*, (Hingham, Mass., 1832), p. 30.

32. Richard D. Brown, "The Emergence of Urban Society in Rural Massachusetts, 1760–1820," *Journal of American History*, 61 (June 1974): 44, n. 30.

33. Richard Burket Kielbowicz, "News in the Mails, 1690–1863: The Technology, Policy, and Politics of a Communication Channel," Ph.D. diss., Univ. of Minnesota, 1984, pp. 191–210; Richard John, "Managing the Mails: The U. S. Postal System in National Politics, 1823–1836," Ph.D. diss. Harvard Univ., 1989.

34. According to the United States Census Office, 7th Census, 1850, *Statistical View of the United States*, by J. D. B. De Bow (Washington, D.C., 1854), pp. 126–28, there were the following numbers of males over age 15 employed: printers, 14,740; paper manufacturing, 2971; ink manufacturing, 348; bookbinding, 3414; typecutters and founders, 424. There were also some 1372 editors and 1720 booksellers and stationers. The growth and centralization of newspapers and printing were emphasized in Harold A. Innis, *Empire and Communications*, rev. by Mary Q. Innis, fwd. by Marshall McLuhan (Toronto, 1972), ch 7.

35. One use for discretionary income was improved lighting with glazed windows and lamps. See John E. Crowley, "Artificial Illumination in Early America and the Definition of Domestic Space and Time," in Barbara Karsky and Elise Marienstras, eds., *Time and Work in Pre-Industrial America/Travail et Loisir dans l' Amérique pré-industrielle* (Nancy, France, in press (1990). Robert A. Gross, "Culture and Cultivation: Agriculture and Society in Thoreau's Concord," *Journal of American History*, 69 (June 1982): 42–61.

36. This is the gist of Allan Kulikoff's conclusion on Virginia in the early republic. (*Tobacco and Slaves: The Development of Southern Cultures in the Chesapeake, 1680–1800* (Chapel Hill, 1986), pp. 425–28.)

37. James M. Banner, Jr., *To The Hartford Convention: The Federalists and the Origins of Party Politics in Massachusetts, 1789–1815* (New York, 1970); David Hackett Fischer, *The*

Revolution of American Conservation: The Federalist Party in the Era of Jeffersonian Democracy (New York, 1965); Ronald P. Formisano, *The Birth of Mass Political Parties: Michigan, 1827–1861* (Princeton, 1971) and *The Transformation of Political Culture: Massachusetts Parties, 1790s–1840s* (New York, 1983); Paul Goodman, *The Democratic-Republicans of Massachusetts: Politics in a Young Republic* (Cambridge, Mass., 1964); Paul Kleppner et al., *The Evolution of American Electoral Systems* (Westport, Conn., 1981); Richard P. McCormick, *The Second American Party System: Party Formation in the Jacksonian Era* (Chapel Hill, 1966); Edward Pessen, *Jacksonian America: Society, Personality, and Politics,* rev. ed. (Homewood, Ill., 1978); Joel H. Silbey, Allan G. Bogue, and William Flanigan, eds., *The History of American Electoral Behavior* (Princeton, 1978).

38. James Willard Hurst wrote a seminal essay on this theme: "The Release of Energy," in his *Law and the Conditions of Freedom* (Madison, Wisc., 1956), pp. 3–32.

39. James A. Henretta, "Families and Farms: *Mentalité* in Pre-Industrial America," *William and Mary Quarterly,* 3d ser., 35 (1978): 3–32.

40. McKendrick, Brewer, and Plumb, *The Birth of a Consumer Society.* Publishers self-servingly advocated these ideas early and late: David Paul Nord, "A Republican Literature: A Study of Magazine Readers and Reading in Late Eighteenth-Century New York," *American Quarterly,* 40 (1988): 57; Ronald J. Zboray, "Antebellum Reading and the Ironies of Technological Innovation," *American Quarterly,* 40 (1988): 65–82.

41. Barbara Epstein, *The Politics of Domesticity: Women, Evangelism, and Temperance in Nineteenth-Century America* (Middletown, Conn., 1981); Richard D. Brown, "The Emergence of Urban Society in Rural Massachusetts, 1760–1820."

42. In 1860 there were 4051 newspapers and periodicals being published in the United States, comprehending a total of 928 million copies annually. (United States Census Office, 8th Census, 1860, *Statistics of the United States . . . in 1860* (Washington, D.C., 1866).) On distribution see Kielbowicz, "News in the Mails, 1690–1863," pp. 188–270.

43. Zboray, "Antebelum Reading and the Ironies of Technological Innovation," challenges the view that the expansion of the book trade and reading was chiefly the result of technical innovation.

44. David D. Hall, "The Uses of Literacy in New England, 1600–1850," in Joyce et al., eds., *Printing and Society,* pp. 1–47; Richard D. Brown, "From Coherence to Competition," in *Printing and Society,* pp. 300–309.

Index

DATE DUE

Demco, Inc. 38-293